First World War

and Army of Occupation

War Diary

France, Belgium and Germany

41 DIVISION
123 Infantry Brigade
Queen's Own (Royal West Kent Regiment)
10th Battalion
25 April 1916 - 28 February 1919

WO95/2638/1

The Naval & Military Press Ltd
www.nmarchive.com
Published in association with The National Archives

Published by

The Naval & Military Press Ltd

Unit 10 Ridgewood Industrial Park,

Uckfield, East Sussex,

TN22 5QE England

Tel: +44 (0) 1825 749494

www.naval-military-press.com

www.nmarchive.com

This diary has been reprinted in facsimile from the original. Any imperfections are inevitably reproduced and the quality may fall short of modern type and cartographic standards.

Contents

Document type	Place/Title	Date From	Date To
Heading	10th Bn Roy. West Kents May 1916-Oct 1917. March 1918-1919 Feb.		
Heading	WO95/2638/1 10/Queen's Own (RW Kents) May'16-Oct'17		
War Diary	Aldershot	25/04/1916	03/05/1916
War Diary	Southampton	03/05/1916	03/05/1916
War Diary	Havre	04/05/1916	05/05/1916
War Diary	Moolenacker	06/05/1916	27/05/1916
War Diary	Bailleul	28/05/1916	28/05/1916
War Diary	Le Bizet	30/05/1916	30/05/1916
War Diary	H.Qr. Front. Line Despierre Farm. C.3.a.8.7.	31/05/1916	31/05/1916
Operation(al) Order(s)	Appendix I. 10th Bn. Royal West Kent Rgt. Operation Order No. I.		
Operation(al) Order(s)	Appendix 2. 10th Bn. R.W. Kent Regt. Special Battalion Order No. 2.	26/05/1916	26/05/1916
Miscellaneous	Daily Reports.		
Miscellaneous	Sheet No. 4. Time Table.		
Miscellaneous	March Table 10/Royal West Kent Regt.		
Operation(al) Order(s)	10th Bn. Royal West Kent Regt.-Operation Order No. 3. Appendix 3.		
Miscellaneous	10th Bn Royal West Kent Regt. Defence Scheme. Appendix 4.		
Miscellaneous	Addendum To Battalion Defence Scheme.		
Map			
War Diary	Bn. H. Qr. Despierre Fm. Ref. Map. 36. N.W. 2 1/10000. C.3.c.8.7. Front Line.	01/06/1916	05/06/1916
War Diary	Billets Le Bizet	06/06/1916	11/06/1916
War Diary	Despierre Fm	12/06/1916	17/06/1916
War Diary	Le Bizet	18/06/1916	24/06/1916
War Diary	Bn. H.Q. Despierre Fm.	24/06/1916	30/06/1916
Operation(al) Order(s)	10th Bn. Royal West Kent Regt.-Operation Order No. 4		
Miscellaneous	Table Of Reliefs.		
Operation(al) Order(s)	10th Bn. Royal West Kent Rgt. A Operation Order No. 5.	10/06/1916	10/06/1916
Miscellaneous	Sheet 3. Relief Table.		
Operation(al) Order(s)	10th Bn. Royal West Kent Regt.-Operation Order No. 6.	16/06/1916	16/06/1916
Miscellaneous	Table Of Reliefs.		
Operation(al) Order(s)	10th Bn. Royal West Kent Rgt. Operation Order No. 7.	23/06/1916	23/06/1916
War Diary	Bn. H.Q. Despierre Farm	01/07/1916	02/07/1916
War Diary	G.3.c	03/07/1916	04/07/1916
War Diary	Le-Bizet	05/07/1916	05/07/1916
War Diary	C.13.d	07/07/1916	07/07/1916
War Diary	Soyer Farm H. Qrs.	08/07/1916	08/07/1916
War Diary	B.6.d.	08/07/1916	08/07/1916
War Diary	Soyer Farm. H.Q.	09/07/1916	09/07/1916
War Diary	B.6.d.	10/07/1916	14/07/1916
War Diary	Despierre Farm. C.3.c	15/07/1916	15/07/1916
War Diary	Despierre Fm. H.Q. C.3.c.	15/07/1916	20/07/1916
War Diary	Despierre Fm C.3.c	21/07/1916	23/07/1916

War Diary	Soyer Fm. H.Qr.	24/07/1916	25/07/1916
War Diary	B.6.d	26/07/1916	26/07/1916
War Diary	Le Bizet, H. Qr. C.13.d.	27/07/1916	30/07/1916
Operation(al) Order(s)	10th Bn. Royal West Kent Regt.-Operation Order No. 8.	02/07/1916	02/07/1916
Operation(al) Order(s)	10th Bn. Royal West Kent Regt.-Operation Order No. 9	13/07/1916	13/07/1916
Miscellaneous	Table Of Reliefs, Routes, Etc. 10th Bn. Royal West Kent Regiment.		
Operation(al) Order(s)	10 Bn. Royal West Kent Regiment-Operation Order No. 10.	23/07/1916	23/07/1916
Operation(al) Order(s)	10th Bn. Royal West Kent Regiment-Operation Order No. 11	31/07/1916	31/07/1916
War Diary	Le Bizet	31/07/1916	01/08/1916
War Diary	H.Q. Despiere Farm	02/08/1916	07/08/1916
War Diary	H.2. Despierre Farm	08/08/1916	12/08/1916
War Diary	H.2. Le Bizet	13/08/1916	16/08/1916
War Diary	H.2. La Creche	17/08/1916	17/08/1916
War Diary	H.Q. Berthew	18/08/1916	18/08/1916
War Diary	Berthen	19/08/1916	23/08/1916
War Diary	H.Q. Bussus Bussuel	24/08/1916	31/08/1916
Operation(al) Order(s)	10th Bn. Royal West Kent Regiment-Operation Order No. 12.	11/08/1916	11/08/1916
Operation(al) Order(s)	10th (S) Bn. Royal West Kent Rgt.-Operation Order No. 13.	15/08/1916	15/08/1916
Miscellaneous	Movement Table.		
Operation(al) Order(s)	10th Bn. Royal West Kent Regt. Operation Order No. 14-Addendum.		
Operation(al) Order(s)	10th Battn. Royal West Kent Regt.-Operation Order No. 14.	21/08/1916	21/08/1916
War Diary	Bussus Bussuel H.Q.	01/09/1916	06/09/1916
War Diary	Becordel	07/09/1916	09/09/1916
War Diary	Fricourt Camp	10/09/1916	10/09/1916
War Diary	Montauban	11/09/1916	12/09/1916
War Diary	Delville Wood	13/09/1916	14/09/1916
War Diary	Pommieres Redoubt	15/09/1916	15/09/1916
War Diary	Switch Trench	16/09/1916	18/09/1916
War Diary	Becordel	19/09/1916	27/09/1916
War Diary	Pommieres Redoubt	28/09/1916	28/09/1916
War Diary	N.E. Of Flers	29/09/1916	30/09/1916
Operation(al) Order(s)	Quiet. Operation Order No. 21. App. 15	14/09/1916	14/09/1916
War Diary	N.E. Of Flers	01/10/1916	01/10/1916
War Diary	Muntauban	02/10/1916	03/10/1916
War Diary	S Of Mametz Wood	04/10/1916	07/10/1916
War Diary	Girdtrench	07/10/1916	10/10/1916
War Diary	Girdtrench De Maitetz Wood	11/10/1916	13/10/1916
War Diary	?	14/10/1916	19/10/1916
War Diary	Beishervelle	20/10/1916	22/10/1916
War Diary	Alberta Camp	23/10/1916	23/10/1916
War Diary	Dickebusch	24/10/1916	30/10/1916
War Diary	Chippewa Camp	31/10/1916	31/10/1916
Miscellaneous	Quiet-Warning Order.	06/10/1916	06/10/1916
Operation(al) Order(s)	10th Bn. Royal West Kent Rgt.-Operation Order No. 24.		
Operation(al) Order(s)	Battalion Order No. 27.	17/10/1916	17/10/1916
Operation(al) Order(s)	10th Bn. Royal West Kent Regt.-Order No. 28.	19/10/1916	19/10/1916
Operation(al) Order(s)	10th Bn. Royal West Kent Regt.-Order No. 29. App IV.	22/10/1916	22/10/1916

Operation(al) Order(s)	10th Bn. Royal West Kent Regt.-Order No. 30. App 5	22/10/1916	22/10/1916
Operation(al) Order(s)	Battalion Operation Orders No. 31		
War Diary	Chippewa Camp	01/11/1916	01/11/1916
War Diary	M.b.a.9.7	02/11/1916	03/11/1916
War Diary	Center Sub-Sect 123rd Brigade	04/11/1916	09/11/1916
War Diary	Chippewa Camp	10/11/1916	10/11/1916
War Diary	M.R. M6a 4.7.	12/11/1916	16/11/1916
War Diary	Dickebusch Belgium Maps. 28 H.28 A 7.1.	17/11/1916	23/11/1916
War Diary	Chippewa Camp	24/11/1916	28/11/1916
War Diary	Trenches Centre Lighten Sector	29/11/1916	30/11/1916
Operation(al) Order(s)	10th Bn. Royal West Kent Rgt.-Operation Order No. 32.	02/11/1916	02/11/1916
Miscellaneous	Battalion Order No. 33. Inter-Company Relief.	05/11/1916	05/11/1916
Miscellaneous	Addendum To Battalion Order No. 34. App IV	08/11/1916	08/11/1916
Operation(al) Order(s)	Battalion Operation Order No. 34.	08/11/1916	08/11/1916
Operation(al) Order(s)	10th Bn. Royal West Kent Regt.-Order No. 55.	15/11/1916	15/11/1916
Operation(al) Order(s)	10th Bn. Royal West Kent Regt.-Operation Order No. 56. App VI	22/11/1916	22/11/1916
Operation(al) Order(s)	Operation Order No. 37. App VII	27/11/1916	27/11/1916
War Diary	Centre Left Sub-Sector	01/12/1916	03/12/1916
War Diary	Chippewa Camp. M.6.a.4.7.	04/12/1916	09/12/1916
War Diary	Dickebusch B.H.2. Belgium Sheet 28 N.W. H.28.c.7.1	10/12/1916	15/12/1916
War Diary	Chippewa Camp M.6.a.4.7.	16/12/1916	22/12/1916
War Diary	Centre Left Sub-Sector	23/12/1916	29/12/1916
War Diary	Chippewa Camp M.6.a.4.7.	30/12/1916	31/12/1916
Operation(al) Order(s)	Battalion Order No. 38. App I	02/12/1916	02/12/1916
Operation(al) Order(s)	10th Bn Royal West Kent Regiment. Operation Order No. 39 Appx II	08/12/1916	08/12/1916
Operation(al) Order(s)	10th Bn Royal West Kent Regiment. Operation Order No. 40. Appx III	14/12/1916	14/12/1916
Operation(al) Order(s)	10th Bn. R.W. Kent Regt. Battalion Operation Order No. 45. Appx V		
Operation(al) Order(s)	10th Bn Royal West Kent Regt. Operation Order No. 41. App IV.	21/12/1916	21/12/1916
War Diary	Chippewa Camp M.6.a.4.7.	01/01/1917	03/01/1917
War Diary	Dickebusch Map. Ref. Belgium 25 NW H.25.0.7.1.	04/01/1917	08/01/1917
War Diary	Chippewa Camp M.6.a.4.7.	09/01/1917	15/01/1917
War Diary	Centre Left Sub-Sector	15/01/1917	22/01/1917
War Diary	Chippewa Camp M6.a.4.7	23/01/1917	28/01/1917
War Diary	Dickebusch M.R. Belgium 28 NW H.28.c.7.1.	29/01/1917	31/01/1917
Operation(al) Order(s)	10th Bn. Royal West Kent Regiment. Operation Order No. 46. Appx I	02/01/1917	02/01/1917
Operation(al) Order(s)	10th Royal West Kent Regiment. Operation Order No. 47. Appx II	07/01/1917	07/01/1917
Operation(al) Order(s)	10th Royal West Kent Regt. Battalion Order No. 46. Appx III	14/01/1917	14/01/1917
Operation(al) Order(s)	10th Bn. R.W. Kent Regt. Battalion Operation Order No. 52. Appx IV	21/01/1917	21/01/1917
Operation(al) Order(s)	10th Bn Royal West Kent Regiment. Battalion Operation Order. No. 53. Appx V	27/01/1917	27/01/1917
War Diary	Reserve Battn Dickebusch H28.c.7.1	01/02/1917	03/02/1917
War Diary	Chippewa Camp M6.a.4.7.	04/02/1917	10/02/1917
War Diary	Centre Left. Sub-Sector	11/02/1917	17/02/1917
War Diary	Chippewa Camp M.6.a.4.7.	18/02/1917	22/02/1917
War Diary	Centre Left Sub-Sector	23/02/1917	28/02/1917

Operation(al) Order(s)	10th Royal West Kent Regiment. Operation Order No. 54. Appx I	02/02/1917	02/02/1917
Operation(al) Order(s)	10th Royal West Kent Regiment. Operation Order No. 55. Appx II		
Operation(al) Order(s)	10th R.W. Kent Regt. Battalion Operation Order No. 58. Appx III	16/02/1917	16/02/1917
Operation(al) Order(s)	10th Royal West Kent Regiment. Operation Order No. 60. Appx IV	22/02/1917	22/02/1917
Operation(al) Order(s)	10th Bn. R.W. Kent Regt. Battalion Operation Order No. 63. Appx V	26/02/1917	26/02/1917
War Diary	Chippewa Camp M.6.a.4.7.	01/03/1917	05/03/1917
War Diary	Dickebusch H28.c.7.1.	06/03/1917	11/03/1917
War Diary	Chippewa Camp M6.a.4.7.	12/03/1917	17/03/1917
War Diary	Centre Left Sub-Sector	18/03/1917	23/03/1917
War Diary	Chippewa Camp M.6.a.4.7.	24/03/1917	31/03/1917
Operation(al) Order(s)	10th Bn Royal West Kent Regt. Battalion Operation Order No. 64. Appx I	04/03/1917	04/03/1917
Operation(al) Order(s)	Operation Order No. 65. Appx II	10/03/1917	10/03/1917
Operation(al) Order(s)	10th. Royal West Kent Regiment. Operation Order No. 66. Appx III	16/03/1917	16/03/1917
Operation(al) Order(s)	Battalion Operation Order No. 69. Appx. IV	22/03/1917	22/03/1917
Operation(al) Order(s)	Battalion Operation Order No 70. Appx V	29/03/1917	29/03/1917
War Diary	Dickebusch Belgium Sheet 28.N.W. H28.c.7.1.	01/04/1917	05/04/1917
War Diary	Chippewa Camp M6.a.4.7.	06/04/1917	06/04/1917
War Diary	Steenvoorde Sheet 28.B & France. G.4.c.2.6.	07/04/1917	07/04/1917
War Diary	Arneke Sheet 27.B & France H.12.a.9.36	08/04/1917	08/04/1917
War Diary	Moulle France S.E. Sheet 27.A. Q.11.c.8.6.	09/04/1917	23/04/1917
War Diary	Arneke Sheet 27. B. F. H 12.a. 9.3.	24/04/1917	24/04/1917
War Diary	Steenvoorde Sheet 27.b & F. Q. 4.c.2.6.	25/04/1917	25/04/1917
War Diary	Chippewa Camp M.6.a.4.7.	26/04/1917	30/04/1917
Operation(al) Order(s)	Operation Order No 71. Appx I	04/04/1917	04/04/1917
Operation(al) Order(s)	10th Royal West Kent Regiment. Operation Order No 72. Appx II		
Miscellaneous	Administrative Orders.		
Operation(al) Order(s)	10th Royal West Kent Regiment. Operation Order No. 73. Appx III	22/04/1917	22/04/1917
Miscellaneous	10th Royal West Kent Regiment. Administrative Orders.	22/04/1917	22/04/1917
War Diary	Chippewa Camp M.6.c.4.7.	01/05/1917	02/05/1917
War Diary	Left Battalion Sector	03/05/1917	12/05/1917
War Diary	Battn Support G.4.a. Lewis	13/05/1917	20/05/1917
War Diary	Chippewa Camp B. M6.a.4.7.	21/05/1917	26/05/1917
War Diary	Left Battalion Sector	27/05/1917	31/05/1917
Operation(al) Order(s)	10th Royal West Kent Regt. Operation Order No 74. Appx I	01/05/1917	01/05/1917
Operation(al) Order(s)	Battalion Operation Order 79. Appx II	12/05/1917	12/05/1917
Operation(al) Order(s)	Battalion Operation Order No 80. Appx III	18/05/1917	18/05/1917
Operation(al) Order(s)	Operation Order No. 82 Appx V	31/05/1917	31/05/1917
Operation(al) Order(s)	10th Royal West Kent Regiment. Operation Order No. 81. Appx IV	25/05/1917	25/05/1917
War Diary	Chippewa Camp M6a.4.7.	01/06/1917	05/06/1917
War Diary	Left Sub Sector	05/06/1917	07/06/1917
War Diary	Blue Line D 9 b 31 To 10.a.15.85	08/06/1917	11/06/1917
War Diary	Voormezeele Switch	12/06/1917	19/06/1917
War Diary	Left Sub Sector	23/06/1917	30/06/1917
Map	Div Boundaries		

Miscellaneous	Appx No 5		
Miscellaneous	Appdx. No 1		
Operation(al) Order(s)	10th Battn. Royal West Kent Regiment. Operation Order No. 83. Appdx 4	01/06/1917	01/06/1917
Miscellaneous	Appdx. No 2		
Miscellaneous		01/06/1917	01/06/1917
Operation(al) Order(s)	Battalion Operation Order No. 90. Appdx No. 6.	18/06/1917	18/06/1917
Operation(al) Order(s)	Battalion Operation Order No. 91. Appdx No 7	23/08/1917	23/08/1917
Miscellaneous	To M.O.	23/06/1917	23/06/1917
War Diary	Ontario Camp Rening Helst	01/07/1917	01/07/1917
War Diary	Fletre M.R. Sheet 27. S.E. W.12.d.5.9.	02/07/1917	21/07/1917
War Diary	Carnarvon Camp M.R. Harlebrouk 5.4. M10.b.6.5.	23/07/1917	31/07/1917
Operation(al) Order(s)	123rd Infantry Brigade Operation Order No. 102.	14/07/1917	14/07/1917
Miscellaneous	Further Administrative Instructions For Forthcoming Operations, Reference 123rd. Infantry Brigade Order No. 102 Of July 12th, 1917.	20/07/1917	20/07/1917
Miscellaneous	Advance Against Zandvoorde.	25/07/1917	25/07/1917
Operation(al) Order(s)	123rd Inf. Bde. Operation Order No. 102. Appendix II.		
Miscellaneous	Allotment Of Work For "Z" Day And "Z/A" Night.		
Operation(al) Order(s)	123rd Inf. Bde. Operation Order No. 102. Appendix IV.		
Miscellaneous		19/07/1917	19/07/1917
Miscellaneous	Plans Showing Waves And Lines On Tapes.		
Operation(al) Order(s)	123rd Inf. Bde. Operation Order No. 102. Appendix VII (a).		
Miscellaneous	123rd Inf. Bde. No. A. 56/711	22/07/1917	22/07/1917
Miscellaneous	Administrative Arrangements For Forthcoming Operations Reference 123rd Infantry Brigade Operation Order No. 102	16/07/1917	16/07/1917
Miscellaneous	Appendix "A"		
Miscellaneous	Appendix "B"		
Miscellaneous	Appendix "C"		
War Diary	Klein Zillebeke Red & Blue Line	01/08/1917	02/08/1917
War Diary	Ravine Wood	03/08/1917	03/08/1917
War Diary	Elzenwalle Chateau	04/08/1917	07/08/1917
War Diary	Front Line Kleinzillebeke	08/08/1917	10/08/1917
War Diary	Ridge Wood H.35.c.5.3.	11/08/1917	11/08/1917
War Diary	Meterin X.10.a.4.9.	12/08/1917	20/08/1917
War Diary	Stable O.29.b.0.8.	21/08/1917	21/08/1917
War Diary	Quelmes W.13.b.4.8.	22/08/1917	31/08/1917
Miscellaneous	Appendix "A"		
Operation(al) Order(s)	10th. Bn. Royal West Kent Regt. Operation Order No. 96.		
Operation(al) Order(s)	10th N.W. Kent Regt. Operation Order No. 103. Appx. II	15/09/1917	15/09/1917
Operation(al) Order(s)	No 104. Operation Order By Lt Col S.H. Beattie M.C. Appx III		
Operation(al) Order(s)	10th. Bn. R.W. Kent Regt. Operation Order No. 102. Appx I	13/09/1917	13/09/1917
Operation(al) Order(s)	Operation Orders No. 105. By. Lieut. Col. S.H. Beattie M.C. Commdg. 10th. Bn. R.W. Kent Regt Appx. IV	18/09/1917	18/09/1917
Operation(al) Order(s)	Order No. 106. 10th. Bn. R.W. Kent Regt. Appx 6		
War Diary	Ouelmes M.F. France 27 S.E. W.13.b.8.0.	01/09/1917	13/09/1917
War Diary	Quelmes W.13.b.8.0	14/09/1917	14/09/1917
War Diary	Staples U3.0.5.2. Sheet 27. Belgium	15/09/1917	15/09/1917
War Diary	Meterin X.15.e.15.r.	16/09/1917	16/09/1917
War Diary	Ontario Camp M.5.a.2.8.	17/09/1917	18/09/1917

War Diary	Ridge Wood	19/09/1917	19/09/1917
War Diary	Hedge St Tunnels	20/09/1917	20/09/1917
War Diary	Supports to 1222 174 Brigade	21/09/1917	21/09/1917
War Diary	1st Objective	22/09/1917	23/09/1917
War Diary	Caestre Area P.30.g.25.3.5.	24/09/1917	26/09/1917
War Diary	Teteghem Sheet 19 B & F I 15 Central	27/09/1917	27/09/1917
War Diary	Bray Dunes D9.b.9.9.	28/09/1917	30/09/1917
War Diary	Bray Dunes M.R. D.9.b.9.9.	01/10/1917	05/10/1917
War Diary	St Idesbalde M.R. W.11.c.4.6.	06/10/1917	06/10/1917
War Diary	Right Sub Sector	07/10/1917	11/10/1917
War Diary	Yorkshire Camp X.3.a.9.1. 11 S E	12/10/1917	15/10/1917
War Diary	Bray Dunes M.R. D.3.c.1.1	16/10/1917	30/10/1917
Heading	WO95/2638/2 10/Queen's Own (RW Kents) Mar'18-Feb'19		
Heading	10th Battn. The Queen's Own Royal West Kent Regiment. March 1918		
Miscellaneous	123 Infy. Bde.	05/03/1918	05/03/1918
Miscellaneous	123 Infy. Bde.	05/05/1918	05/05/1918
War Diary	S Georgio Della Pertiche	01/03/1918	07/03/1918
War Diary	Beaudricourt Map R4 Lens Sheet 11	08/03/1918	20/03/1918
War Diary	Achiet Le Grand Ref Map Lens II 1/100,000	21/03/1918	21/03/1918
War Diary	Fremicourt And Morchies	22/03/1918	23/03/1918
War Diary	Achiet Le Petit	23/03/1918	23/03/1918
War Diary	Bihucourt	24/03/1918	24/03/1918
War Diary	Gommcourt & Fonque Villers	25/03/1918	25/03/1918
War Diary	Gommcourt	26/03/1918	26/03/1918
War Diary	Ablainzevelle	29/03/1918	31/03/1918
Heading	Appendix No. 1. Report On Operations Near Beugny.		
Miscellaneous	10th Bn. Royal West Kent Regt. Report On Operations Near Beugny. Appendix No 1	05/04/1918	05/04/1918
Heading	10th Battalion The Royal West Kent Regiment April 1918		
War Diary	Ablainzeville	01/04/1918	02/04/1918
War Diary	Thievres	03/04/1918	03/04/1918
War Diary	Bonnieres	04/04/1918	04/04/1918
War Diary	Eecke	05/04/1918	07/04/1918
War Diary	St Jean	08/04/1918	07/05/1918
War Diary	Siege Camp	08/05/1918	10/05/1918
War Diary	Foster Camp	11/05/1918	14/05/1918
War Diary	Foster & "B" Camps.	14/05/1918	16/05/1918
War Diary	East Of Ypres	17/05/1918	31/05/1918
Operation(al) Order(s)	10th Battn R.W. Kent Regt. Operation Order No. 2.	02/05/1918	02/05/1918
War Diary	Ramparts Ypres (Sheet 28 N.W)	01/06/1918	02/06/1918
War Diary	Proven (Hazebrouck) 5a	03/06/1918	03/06/1918
War Diary	St Momelin (Hazebrouck) 5a	04/06/1918	05/06/1918
War Diary	St Momelin	06/06/1918	10/06/1918
War Diary	Cormette	11/06/1918	11/06/1918
War Diary	Quelmes	12/06/1918	15/06/1918
War Diary	Quelmes (Hazebrouck) 5.A	16/06/1918	24/06/1918
War Diary	St Momelin	25/06/1918	25/06/1918
War Diary	Ledringhem (Hazebrouck 5.A)	26/06/1918	30/06/1918
Operation(al) Order(s)	Operation Order No 9 By Major C.F. Stallard M.C. Comdg 10th Bn R.W. Kent Regt	01/06/1918	01/06/1918
Operation(al) Order(s)	Operation Order No 10 By Major F.A. Wallis Comdg 10th Bn. R. West Kent Regt	03/06/1918	03/06/1918

Operation(al) Order(s)	Operation Order No 11 By Lt Col. The Hon. E.R. Thesiger Comdg 10th Bn. Royal West Kent Regt	10/06/1918	10/06/1918
Operation(al) Order(s)	10th. Bn. Royal West Kent Regt. Operation Order No. 12.	18/06/1918	18/06/1918
Operation(al) Order(s)	10th Bn Royal West Kent Regt Operation Orders No 13	24/06/1918	24/06/1918
Operation(al) Order(s)	Operation Orders No 14 10th Bn Royal West Kent Regt	24/06/1918	24/06/1918
Operation(al) Order(s)	10th Bn. R. West Kent Regt Operation Order No 15	25/06/1918	25/06/1918
Operation(al) Order(s)	Operation Order No 16 10th Bn Royal West Kent Regiment.	29/06/1918	29/06/1918
War Diary	Abeele Sheet 27	01/07/1918	01/07/1918
War Diary	Reninghelst Sheet 28 N.W.	02/07/1918	05/07/1918
War Diary	Laclytte	06/07/1918	12/07/1918
War Diary	La Clytte (Sheet 28 S.W.1 Kemmel)	12/07/1918	31/07/1918
Miscellaneous	Reference Operation Order No 17	01/07/1918	01/07/1918
Operation(al) Order(s)	10th Bn. Royal West Kent Regt Operation Order No 17.	01/07/1918	01/07/1918
Operation(al) Order(s)	10th Battn. Royal West Kent Regt. Operation Orders No. 18	06/07/1918	06/07/1918
Operation(al) Order(s)	10th Battn Royal West Kent Regt. Operation Orders No 19	15/07/1918	15/07/1918
Operation(al) Order(s)	Royal West. Kent Regt. Operation Orders No. 20.		
Miscellaneous	Addendum To O.O. No 21.	26/07/1918	26/07/1918
Operation(al) Order(s)	10th Bn. Royal West Kent Regt Operation Order No 21.	26/07/1918	26/07/1918
Operation(al) Order(s)	10th Bn R.W. Kent Regt Operation Order No 22	26/07/1918	26/07/1918
Operation(al) Order(s)	10th Bn. R.W. Kent Regt Operation Order No 23.	27/07/1918	27/07/1918
Operation(al) Order(s)	10th Bn Royal West Kent Regt Operation Order No 24	28/07/1918	28/07/1918
Operation(al) Order(s)	10th Bn R.W. Kent Regt O.O. No. 25	30/07/1918	30/07/1918
Miscellaneous	Reference O.O. No 24	30/07/1918	30/07/1918
War Diary	Kemmel	01/08/1918	02/08/1918
War Diary	Dallington Camp	03/08/1918	07/08/1918
War Diary	Zevecoten	08/08/1918	10/08/1918
War Diary	Near Murrumbridge	11/08/1918	20/08/1918
War Diary	Zevecoten	21/08/1918	25/08/1918
War Diary	Scherpenberg-Dickebusch	26/08/1918	29/08/1918
War Diary	Wizernes	30/08/1918	31/08/1918
Operation(al) Order(s)	10th Bn. R.W. Kent Regt Operation Order No. 26	01/08/1918	01/08/1918
Operation(al) Order(s)	10th. Battn Royal West Kent Regt. Operation Order No 27.	08/08/1918	08/08/1918
Operation(al) Order(s)	10th Bn. Royal West Kent Regt. Operation Order No. 28	11/08/1918	11/08/1918
Operation(al) Order(s)	10th Bn. Royal West Kent Regt. Operation Order No. 31.	25/08/1918	25/08/1918
Operation(al) Order(s)	10th Bn. Royal West Kent Regt. Operation Order No. 32.	28/08/1918	28/08/1918
War Diary	Wizernes	01/09/1918	02/09/1918
War Diary	Sheet 28 3.F. G 24.b.7.6	03/09/1918	04/09/1918
War Diary	Dickebusch Area	05/09/1918	17/09/1918
War Diary	Lappe Area Sheet 27 L.29.	18/09/1918	22/09/1918
War Diary	Lappe Area	23/09/1918	26/09/1918
War Diary	Dominion Camp Sheet 28 (3) G17.a.-G11.c	27/09/1918	29/09/1918
War Diary	Houthem	29/09/1918	30/09/1918
Operation(al) Order(s)	Operation Order No. 33.	01/09/1918	01/09/1918
Operation(al) Order(s)	10th Bn. Royal West Kent Regt. Operation Order No. 35.	03/09/1918	03/09/1918

Operation(al) Order(s)	10th Bn. Royal West Kent Regt. Operation Order No. 38	05/09/1918	05/09/1918
Operation(al) Order(s)	10th Bn. Royal West Kent Regt. Operation Order No. 36.	05/09/1918	05/09/1918
Operation(al) Order(s)	10th Bn. Royal West Kent Regt. Operation Order No. 37.	07/09/1918	07/09/1918
Operation(al) Order(s)	10th Bn. Royal West Kent Regt. Operation Order No. 40	11/09/1918	11/09/1918
Operation(al) Order(s)	10th Bn. Royal West Kent Regt. Operation Order No. 39	11/09/1918	11/09/1918
Operation(al) Order(s)	10th Bn. Royal West Kent Regt. Operation Order No. 41.	13/09/1918	13/09/1918
Operation(al) Order(s)	10th Bn. Royal West Kent Regt. Operation Order No. 42.	18/09/1918	18/09/1918
Operation(al) Order(s)	10th Bn. Royal West Kent Regiment. Operation Order No. 46.	27/09/1918	27/09/1918
War Diary	Houthem	01/10/1918	16/10/1918
War Diary	North Of Gulleghem	16/10/1918	26/10/1918
War Diary	Coutrai	27/10/1918	31/10/1918
War Diary	Courtrai (Sheet 29) 1/40,000	01/11/1918	01/11/1918
War Diary	Knokke	02/11/1918	03/11/1918
War Diary	Langestraat	04/11/1918	08/11/1918
War Diary	Meerche	09/11/1918	10/11/1918
War Diary	Segelsem	10/11/1918	13/11/1918
War Diary	Sarlardinge	14/11/1918	17/11/1918
War Diary	Vollezeel	18/11/1918	20/11/1918
War Diary	Les Deux Acren	21/11/1918	30/11/1918
Miscellaneous	Scheme For Practice Attack	03/11/1918	03/11/1918
Operation(al) Order(s)	Operation Order No. 52 Sheet 29 S.E.	04/11/1918	04/11/1918
Operation(al) Order(s)	Operation Order No. 53	10/11/1918	10/11/1918
Operation(al) Order(s)	Operation Order No. 54.	12/11/1918	12/11/1918
Operation(al) Order(s)	Operation Order No 55.	17/11/1918	17/11/1918
Operation(al) Order(s)	Operation Order No 56	18/11/1918	18/11/1918
Operation(al) Order(s)	Operation Order No 57	20/11/1918	20/11/1918
War Diary	Les Deux-Acren	01/12/1918	11/12/1918
War Diary	St Pierre-Capelle	12/12/1918	12/12/1918
War Diary	Lembecq	13/12/1918	13/12/1918
War Diary	Braine L'Alleud	14/12/1918	16/12/1918
War Diary	Baisythy	16/12/1918	16/12/1918
War Diary	Sombreffe	17/12/1918	17/12/1918
War Diary	Longchamps	19/12/1918	19/12/1918
War Diary	Ville-En-Hesbaye	20/12/1918	31/12/1918
Operation(al) Order(s)	10th Bn. Royal West Kent Regt. Operation Order No 58	08/12/1918	08/12/1918
Miscellaneous	March Table To Accompany Operation Order No 58		
Operation(al) Order(s)	Operation Order No 59 By Lt Col The Hon E.R Thesiger Comdg 10th R. West Kent Regt	12/12/1918	12/12/1918
Miscellaneous	All Recipients Of O.O. 58. D/9.12.18.	10/12/1918	10/12/1918
Miscellaneous	All Recipients Of O.O. 58. D/9.12.18	10/12/1918	10/12/1918
Operation(al) Order(s)	Operation Order No 60 By Lieut Col The Hon. E.R. Thesiger Comdg 10th R.W. Kent Regt.	13/12/1918	13/12/1918
Miscellaneous	All Recipients Of O.O. 58	15/12/1918	15/12/1918
Operation(al) Order(s)	10th Bn. R. West Kent Regt. Operation Order No. 62	16/12/1918	16/12/1918
Operation(al) Order(s)	10th Bn. Royal West Kent Regt. Operation Order No. 63.	17/12/1918	17/12/1918

Operation(al) Order(s)	10th Bn. Royal West Kent Regt. Operation Order No 64	18/12/1918	18/12/1918
Operation(al) Order(s)	Operation Order No. 65. 10th Bn. Royal West Kent Regt.	19/12/1918	19/12/1918
Heading	10th Bn Roy. West Kents Jan-Feb 1919		
War Diary	Ville-en-Hesbaye	01/01/1919	08/01/1919
War Diary	Lohmar	09/01/1919	23/01/1919
War Diary	Seelschied	24/01/1919	29/01/1919
War Diary	Lind	30/01/1919	30/01/1919
War Diary	Coln-Kalk	31/01/1919	31/01/1919
Operation(al) Order(s)	10th Bn. Royal West. Kent Regt. Operation Order No 1	08/01/1919	08/01/1919
Operation(al) Order(s)	10th Bn. Royal West Kent Regt. Operation Order No 2.	21/01/1919	21/01/1919
Operation(al) Order(s)	10th Bttn. Royal West Kent Regt. Operation Order No 3	29/01/1919	29/01/1919
Operation(al) Order(s)	10th Bn. R.W. Kent Rgt O.Order No 4	31/01/1919	31/01/1919
War Diary	Coln-Kalk	01/02/1919	28/02/1919

41ST DIVISION

123RD INFY BDE

10TH BN ROY.WEST KENTS

MAY 1916-~~DEC 1918~~ OCT 1917

MARCH 1918 - 1919 FEB

TO 34 DIV 101 BDE

IN ITALY 1917 NOV - 1918 FEB

WO 95/2638 (1)

10/Queen's Own (R.W.Kents)

May '16 – Oct '17

Army Form C. 2118

10 West Kent

Vol. 1

123 / 41 XLI

Instructions regarding War Diaries and Intelligence Summaries are contained in F. S. Regs., Part II. and the Staff Manual respectively. Title Pages will be prepared in manuscript.

WAR DIARY
or
~~INTELLIGENCE SUMMARY~~
(Erase heading not required.)

Place	Date	Hour	Summary of Events and Information	Remarks and references to Appendices
ALDERSHOT	25-4-16	–	Bn. warned to hold itself in readiness for Embarkation "Overseas" for Active Service.	
— " —	3-5-16	–	Bn. left ALDERSHOT in three parties entraining at FARNBOROUGH for SOUTHAMPTON as under:- Dept. ALDERSHOT. Dept. FARNBORO. 1st Party. 5.30 a.m. 8.30 a.m. 2nd Party. 6.30 a.m. 9.30 a.m. 3rd Party. 7.30 a.m. 10.30 a.m. } Bn. concentrated at Southampton at 12-30 p.m. Each party constituted a Trainload and had its complement of Transport Vehicles & Animals.	
SOUTHAMPTON.	3.5.16	4 p.m.	H.Q personnel, "A" "C" "D" and 1½ Platoons "B" Coy. embarked in S.S. St. TUDNO., arrived HAVRE 10-15 a.m. 4th May. Remainder of "B" Coy & Transport embarked in S.S. "City of BENARES", sailing at 7 a.m. 4th May 1916 & arriving at HAVRE about 2 p.m. A Heavy mist held up the St TUDNO in Mid-channel for about 4 or 5 hours. Strength embarking 34 Officers 917 O.R Transport complete. 53 Horses One Other Rank casualty embarking. – kicked by horse in stomach. – evacuated SOUTHAMPTON Mil. Hosp.	
HAVRE	4.5.16	11.15 a.m.	"A" "C" "D" and 1½ Platoons "B" Coy disembarked and proceeded by March Route to No. 2 Camp, at SANDVICK, about 4½ miles S.E. of HAVRE, arriving about 3 p.m. Remainder of "B" Coy & Transport disembarked arriving at No. 2 Camp at SANDVICK at 10 p.m. Strength of Bn arriving at No. 2 Camp SANDVICK - HAVRE. 34 Officers 916 Other Ranks 52 Horses One ~~Other Rank~~ HORSE Casualty here, handed over to A.S.C.	

1875 Wt. W593/826 1,000,000 4/15 J.B.C. & A. A.D.S.S./Forms/C. 2118.

Instructions regarding War Diaries and Intelligence Summaries are contained in F. S. Regs., Part II. and the Staff Manual respectively. Title Pages will be prepared in manuscript.

WAR DIARY

or

~~INTELLIGENCE SUMMARY~~

(Erase heading not required.)

Army Form C. 2118

Place	Date	Hour	Summary of Events and Information	Remarks and references to Appendices
HAVRE.	4.5.16.	3.15 pm	Orders received for Bn. less 6 Officers. 250 O. Ranks to proceed by train from Point 4. GARE de MERCHANDISE HAVRE at 18.00 hours on 5.5.16. Destination not given. 6 Officers 250 Other Ranks. to entrain Point 6 GARE MARITINE at 20 hours. Destination not given. Ordy Room Sergt. proceeded to D.A.Q.M.G., HAVRE Base for Entrainment on being posted to D.A.G. 3rd. Echelon for duty. Strength leaving HAVRE 34 Officers 914 O. Ranks. Casualties 1. O. Rank to 3rd Echelon & 1 O. Rank to Hosp'l (Sunstroke).	
HAVRE.	5.5.16	6 pm.	Bn less 6 Officers 250 O. Rks. entrained as above. Train left at 9 pm. arriving at GODEWAERSWELDE. (Re. Map BELGIUM & part of FRANCE) Sheet 27 1/40,000. Q. 12. d. 4.0., about 5 pm. 6.5.16. Bn detrained and proceeded by march Route to "MOOLENACHER" (Re Map of BELGIUM & part of FRANCE) Sheet 27 1/40,000., X.19. to Billets.	
HAVRE.	5.5.16	8 pm.	6 Officers and 250 O. Ranks entrained at Pt. 6. GARE MARITINE at 20 hours, arriving at GODEWAERSWELDE Re. Map as above) about 10 pm. 6.5.16, detrained and proceeded by march route to MOOLENACHER. (Re-Map as above) to billets. Bn. billeted at MOOLENACHER as follows:- Re. Map as above). H.Q. & A. Coy. X.19.a.2.7 Machine Gun Section. X.19.a.5.9. Transport. X.13.c.7.2. "B" Coy. X.13.d.0.5½. "C" Coy. W.18.d.0.6 "D" Coy. W.24.a.4.7. Strength no alteration.	
MOOLENACHER.	6/5/16 to 27/5/16.		During this period the Bn. remained at MOOLENACHER, Training etc.	

1875 Wt. W593/826 1,000,000 4/15 J.B.C. & A. A.D.S.S./Forms/C. 2118.

3

Instructions regarding War Diaries and Intelligence Summaries are contained in F. S. Regs., Part II. and the Staff Manual respectively. Title Pages will be prepared in manuscript.

WAR DIARY
or
~~INTELLIGENCE SUMMARY~~
(*Erase heading not required.*)

Army Form C. 2118

Place	Date	Hour	Summary of Events and Information	Remarks and references to Appendices
MOOLENACHER			Bn held in readiness to re-inforce 1st. ANZACS. Bn Operation Order No. 1. – Attached –	Appdx. 1.
— " —	27.5.16	3 p.m.	Bn. moved from MOOLENACHER at 3 p.m. by March Route via BAILLEUL (billetting at BAILLEUL for the night) to relieve Bde of the 9th Div. in the Right Sector of the DIVISIONAL LINE. Bn Order no. 2. attached. Strength Officers 34 Other Ranks 1002 (93 O. Ranks transferred from 4 1st. Div. Cyclist)	Appdx. 2.
BAILLEUL	28.5.16	3.40 p.m.	The Bn marched from BAILLEUL by march route to LE BIZET. (Re MAP BELGIUM & part of FRANCE) Sheet 36 1/40,000 C.13.b.3.4. There were no casualties on the march. All ranks were heavily laden, pace very slow hence no men fell out. Bn arrived at LE. BIZET about 8 p.m. and billetted, relieving 3rd. Bn. S.A. Infy Rgt. and assumed duties of Reserve Battn to the 4th Bn. S.A. Infy Rgt (Scottish) in the front line. LEFT SUB SECTOR.	
LE. BIZET			Bn immediately began to dig itself in and erecting Dug-outs etc as protection from SHELL FIRE. Periodical bursts of Heavy shell fire while in Reserves, but sustained no Casualties.	
— " —	30.5.16	8 p.m.	The Bn under orders of the 1st. S.A Infy BDE. proceeded to relieve the 4th Bn. S.A. Infy (Scottish) in the front line Trenches from (Re. MAP ARMENTIERES) 36. N.W. 2.1/10,000 C.4.a. 4.7. to C.4.c. 9.2½. with Bn. H.Q. at DESPIERRE FARM C. 3. c. ~~[illegible]~~ 7½.7. The Relief was carried out by Platoons at 5m. intervals with their feet encased in Sandbags to prevent noise. Relief completed by 1 a.m. 31.5.16. The 4th S.A. Infy (Scottish) moving into Reserves at LE. BIZET. Bn. on the Right in the front line 20th. D.L.I. with the 23rd Bn. Middx in Reserve. Bn. on the left in front line. 12th. East Surrey Rgt with 10th Bn R.W. Surrey Rgt in Reserve. 3 Officers and 268 O.R. of Bn. were left at LE BIZET as Details – accommodation insufficient for whole Bn. in the front line. Bn. Operation Order. No. 3 with Defence Scheme and sketch of Trenches, attached	Appdx ~~3~~ 3 & 4
H.Qrs FRONT LINE DESPIERRE FARM. C.3.c.8.7.	31.5.16		Situation normal.	

A. Wood-Martin Lt Col. 10th (S) Bn R.W. Kent R.

1875 Wt. W593/826 1,000,000 4/15 J.B.C. & A. A.D.S.S./Forms/C. 2118.

Appendix I.

10th Bn Royal West Kent Rgt. = Operation Order No I.

Re Maps 27, 28, 36 & 36a

I On receipt of orders to move, Companies will prepare to Move at once.
Dress:- Marching order. Waterbottles filled.
Rations carried on the men.
(1) Iron Ration. (2) The next day's ration, less Meat fresh or tinned.

2 Company Commanders will at once fall in their Companies, rifles & kits in hand, march clear of billets, pile arms and lay kits alongside.

Tell off fatigue parties (1) To roll blankets in tens, and place in a convenient spot for packing on G.S. Waggons on arrival. (2) To clean up billets and surrounding ground (3) Fill in latrines, and any other fatigues that may be required.

Officers' servants to collect Officers' kits and place at spot convenient for packing on G.S. Wagon.

Billets to be left scrupulously clean and any digging to be made good if time permits.

3. All Sanitary men and 1 cook per Company to be left behind to clear up and see that nothing is left behind, and to help load G.S. Wagons. They will then join Echelon B and march with it, vide Divl. W.S.O.

4. Companies will rendezvous at the Battalion Alarm Post, cross roads, W.24. b 86.
One hour after orders to move are received.

5. The Battalion will march in accordance with the attached March Table.

6. Reports to the head of the Battalion.

7. The Signalling Officer will report to the General Staff Officer at the starting point, half an hour before the Battalion is due to pass it
(10 W.S.O. [illegible]

Sheet II.

8. The Billeting Officer & party, i.e. Lieut. Pearson, each C.Q.M.S. & Sergt. Mansfield, will march in rear of the Advanced Guard, and will be under the command of the Senior Officer present. D.W.S.C. page 16.

9. The Billeting Area for the Battalion is at "DOULIEU" village of.

10. S.A.A. limbers must fill from the nearest D.A.C. in the Concentration Area, the position of which will be notified as soon as known.

11. Water carts to be kept filled.

12. With reference to para 5 of these Orders, in the event of the Battalion having plenty of time before moving off on receipt of orders to move, it will not be necessary to leave behind the two men as detailed, unless the Baggage Wagon does not arrive, when they will help to pack it and march with it. On short notice being given to move, these men will be left behind for cleaning up purposes, etc. and will then report to the Divisional Train, the position of which will be notified.

B. A. Kennedy [illegible]
C/W.K

Copy No. 1. Filed
" 2 War Diary
" 3. C.O.
" 4 2nd i/c Command.
" 5. O.C. 'A' Coy.
" 6 O.C. B. Coy
" 7 O.C. C. Coy
" 8 O.C. D. Coy
" 9 Transport Officer.
" 10. Q.M.
" 11. M.G. & Snipers.

Appendix 2.   Copy No. 13. War Diary

10TH BN. R.W.KENT REGT. SPECIAL BATTALION ORDER No.2. Copy No. 13

Reference Maps:- 1/40,000; Sheets 27,28,36 & 36 A.

---

1. The Battalion will relieve a Battalion of the 1st South African Infantry Brigade in the Left Sub-sector, Front Line, in accordance with the attached Time & March Table.

2. The completion of the relief by each Company will at once be reported to the Adjutant at Battalion Headquarters by Runner.

3. On moving into the 9th Division Area, i.e., after leaving BAILLEUL, the Battalion will march by Platoons at 200 yards distance, and will take precautions against observation by hostile aircraft. These distances are to be strictly maintained.
Time to be synchronised with the Adjutant's watch at 9 am. daily.

4. Guides for the Battalion as it moves to LE BIZET will meet Platoons at the Brigade Head Quarters of the 1st S.A. Infantry Brigade. There is to be no checking at these points. Platoons are to move straight on to their billets and ABSOLUTE SILENCE is to be maintained during the Relief.

5. Lieut. G. F. DRAYSON will precede the Battalion on leaving BAILLEUL, and report at the Head Quarters of the 1st S.A. Infantry Brigade to assemble the Guides. He should know the exact order of march of the Battalion. He should report to the Adjutant, before leaving, for instructions.

6. 1st Line Transport will march 500 yards in rear of the Batt. Any wagons of the 1st Line Transport which are actually required to take stores, etc, to the billets at LE BIZET will be split up & march behind each Company. The Machine Gun Sections will march in rear of the Battn. The remainder of the 1st Line Transport, which will be all together, will move direct to its Transport Lines and NOT go through LE BIZET. A guide will meet 1st Line Transport at PONT d' ACHELLES, (sheet 36 N.W. 1/20,000) & guide it to its position. The Transport Officers must arrange to collect the wagons of their Transport which have accompanied the Companies to LE BIZET, and have them taken to the Transport Lines when empty.

7. Baggage and Supply wagons will march behind the 1st Line Transport, and a Guide will meet them at the 1st S.A.Brigade Head Quarters. Company Commanders will arrange for a hot meal to be served before moving from BAILLEUL, and the Cookers will march empty. The unexpired portion of the day's rations will be carried on the man.

8. When the relief is complete, Company Commanders will render to the Adjutant the Reports attached to these orders at the times stated. Times to be strictly adhered to.

9. No. 28 Machine Gun Company, 9th Division, will remain in its position in the Right Sector.

10. Billeting Party will parade as under at Battalion Headquarters at 7 am on the 27th inst. and proceed to BAILLEUL to make all arrangements for billeting the Battalion.
Lieut. A.J.S.Pearson.
All Company Quartermaster Sergts.
Sergt. Mansfield "B" Coy. and
1 other N.C.O. to be selected by
Company Commanders.

An N.C.O. of each Company of the above party will meet his Company before it enters BAILLEUL and guide it to its Billets.

CONTINUED ON SHEET NO. 2.

SHEET NO. 2.

11. All Blankets will be rolled in tens and dumped with Officers' baggage at Company Headquarters by 11 a.m. on Saturday 27th inst. ready to be picked up by a Motor Lorry which will carry them. Blankets to be neatly rolled, tied and labelled, shewing Company, Platoon and Section.

12. The exact amount of baggage Officers will take into the trenches with them is as follows:-

What can be carried on the person only.

Anything that is found necessary to have afterwards can be sent for to the Rest Billets.

13. The use of the telephone between Front Line and Battalion Headquarters is strictly prohibited, except only in case of emergency S.O.S. call.

14. The Battalion will march in the following order from Billeting Area on the 27th inst.

ADVANCE GUARD	1 Platoon of "A" Coy.
MAIN BODY	"A" Coy. less 1 Platoon.
	"B" "
	"C" "
	"D" " less 1 Platoon.
REAR GUARD	1 Platoon of "D" Coy.

Signallers and Snipers, Head of Main Body. Stretcher Bearers with their Companies.

May 26th 1916.

Captain.
Adjutant 10 (s) Bn. R.W.Kent Regt.

Issued through Orderly:

Copy No. 1 Filed
2. Commanding Officer.
3. 2nd i/Command
4. O.C. "A" Coy.
5. O.C. "B" "
6. O.C. "C" "
7. O.C. "D" "
8. Transport Officer.
9. Machine Gun Officer.
10. Sniping Officer.
11. Quartermaster.
12. Signalling Officer.
13. War Diary.

DAILY REPORTS.

Reports required by Company Commanders at Battalion Head Quarters.

Nature.	Due at Bn. H.Q. at.	
Morning Situation & Wind Report.	3.30 a.m.	Giving:(1) General Situation, Normal or otherwise. (2) Any events of the night as far as is known, such as a raid or a minor enterprise, successful or otherwise. Further details ascertained during the day should be given in the "Evening Report".
Shell Report.	6 am.	No. of Shells fallen in each Company's Sect. Description if possible, and damage done etc.
Intelligence Report. for previous 24 hrs. 6 am to 6 am.	6am.	Due from Intelligence Officer.
Daily State	6 am.	
Wind Report	10.30 am.	
Casualty Report	12.30 pm.	
Evening Situation & Wind Report	3 pm.	Vide remarks "Morning Situation".
Report on any alteration in disposition since 7.30 am and forecast of any alterations likely to occur after report has been rendered and before 7.30 am on the following morning.	6.30 pm.	In addition change of Reliefs to be reported when complete.
Details of any inventions, trench tricks, or contrivances, resorted to, to defeat the enemy information about which may be useful to other formations.	As they occur.	

SHEET NO. 4.

TIME TABLE.

Date	Brigade	Unit	From	To	Remarks.
27th May	123rd Inf.Bri.	20th D.L.I. 10/R.W.Kent	Billeting Area	NOOTE BOOM (via MERRIS) BAILLEUL via MOOLENACKER.	Not to enter NOOTE BOOM until after 8.30 am
28th May	123rd Inf.Bri.	20th D.L.I.	NOOTE BOOM	LE BIZET	Relief to commence at 6 pm.
		10/R.W.Kent	BAILLEUL	do	Take over Billets of Reserve to Right Sector from "C"&"D" Bns. 1st S.A.I.Bri.
	1st S.A. Inf.Bri.	"C" & "D" Bns.	LE BIZET	BAILLEUL and NOOT BOOM	
29th May	123rd Inf.Bri.	20th D.L.I.	LE BIZET	Right Sub-Sector, FRONT LINE	Under orders of 1st S.A.I.Bri.
	1st S.A. Inf.Bri.	"A" Bn.(C.P.S. from Sub-Sector, FRONT LINE)	FRONT LINE	LE BIZET	Past Reserve to Right Sector.
30th May	123rd Inf.Bri.	10/R.W.Kent	LE BIZET	Left Sub-sector FRONT LINE	Under orders of 1st S.A.I.Bri.
	1st S.A. Inf.Bri.	"B" Bn.	FRONT LINE	LE BIZET.	Reserve to Right Sector. G.O.C. 1st S.A.I.Bri. will continue to command Right Sector.

MARCH TABLE 10/Royal West Kent Regt.

Date.	Unit	From	To	Route	Time	Distance.
27th May	10/ West Kent Rgt.	Billet-ing Area	BAILLEUL	MOOLEN-ACKER - BAILLEUL	To leave Billeting Area at 3 pm.	3 miles.

REMARKS:- Billeting parties to go over in the morning & have all arrangements made. Guides from the Billeting Parties will meet each Company before it enters BAILLEUL, & guide it to its Billets.

Date.	Unit	From	To	Route	Time	Distance.
28th May	10/ West	BAILLEUL	LE BIZET ~~Nieppe~~	BAILLEUL - NIEPPE - PONT DE NIEPPE - LE BIZET	Leading platoon to leave BAILLEUL at 3.50 pm	8 miles

REMARKS:- Guides will meet Platoons at Hd.Qrs.1st S.A.INF.BRI.on arrival. Guides will meet 1st Line Transport at PONT d' ACHELLES. A lorry will carry blankets to a point on the outskirts of PONT DE NIEPPE to be selected by the C.O. Baggage wagons when empty must take the blankets up to LE BIZET.

Date.	Unit	From	To	Remarks
30th May	10/ West Kent Rgt.	LE BIZET	FRONT LINE	REMARKS:- Under orders of 1st South African Brigade.-

Appendix 3.

War Diary

SECRET.

Copy No. 15

10th BN. ROYAL WEST KENT REGT. - OPERATION ORDER NO. 3.

Reference Maps 1/40,000.
Sheets Nos. 28.36.

---

1. The Battalion will relieve the 4th South African Infantry in the trenches (Left Sub Sector Front Line) to-night, 30th inst.

2. Dress - Marching Order, every N.C.O. and man to carry two sandbags to be worn on the feet fastened at the knee.

3. The Battalion will parade at 7.45 p.m., each complete unit falling in outside its own Billets. Reports to Major W. F. Soames, who will report the Battalion present or otherwise to the Adjutant on arrival at the trenches.

4. The Battalion will move into the trenches via NICHOLSONS AVENUE by Platoons at intervals of at least five minutes, in the following order - A. Coy., B. Coy., C Coy., D Coy., the leading Platoon of A. Coy. to move off at 8 p.m. Major W. F. Soames will regulate the move

5. All Trench Stores will be handed over and receipts in duplicate obtained.

6. Company Commanders are responsible for the rendering of all reports and returns due at Battalion Headquarters as per list of returns etc. issued to all Company Commanders.

7. (i) Company Officers' kits to be stored in their own Company Stores.
(ii) Headquarters in Battalion H. Q. Stores.
(iii) Blankets to be rolled in tens, labelled, and handed in to Battalion Qr. Mr. Stores.
(iv) Tools in possession of Companies to be returned to Qr. Mr. Stores and receipts obtained from Quartermaster.

8. Before moving off Platoon Commanders will ensure that nothing is left behind in Billets.

9. Immediately on completion of relief Company Commanders will report to the Adjutant by runner.

10. Officers and other ranks not proceeding to the trenches will be billited together under arrangements made by Capt. H. I. Jones, and will be und r the command of that officer. He will rend r to tge Adjutant by [illegible] a.m. daily a Daily State and report.

11. To-morrow's rations will be carried up to the trenches to-night by the men under arrangements of Company Commanders.

12. Artillery and Infantry on either flank must be informed when patrols are going out. This information must never be sent over the wire from the front line.

13. Every Officer and N.C.O. and man is to know exactly what position he is to occupy underthe following circumstances:-
(a) Bombardment.
(b) Gas attack.
(c) Attack.
All men should be frequently questioned with regard to this.

14. Equipment will be worn during the day and night in the front line trenches and support trenches. (This does not include the pack).

All working parties are to take their rifles and equipment with them. Application has been made for permission for the men to work in shirt sleeves during the hot weather, provided every man has a handkerchief with his Gas Helmet, to tie round the neck. This is not to be done until orders arereceived sanctioning it.

15. All Gaps will be patrolled, and patrols will start from eitherend of the gap every half hour. They will report to the men holding the trench at the opposite end of the Gap and will then return.

16. The tops of the parapet in a great many places, especially in the Gaps, is at present too smooth, and must be made more irregular.

17. There is to be a thorough understanding of the action taken by the front and support lines.
There is to be no withdrawal should the enemy gain a footing in any of the defended parts of the front line. Counter attacks with bombs from both flanks is the immediate reply to entry by the enemy.

18. The position of listening posts should be changed every two nights, otherwise the enemy know exactly where they are.

19. There is to be an organised system of tricks in the gaps by day and night (e.g., flares, sniping, smoke, and alteration of the appearance of the top of the parapet).

20. Places where the wire in front overlaps to allow of patrols going out, should be marked inside the parapet by a board, in order that patrols may know exactly where they can get out.

21. The enemy's action lately has been to heavily bombard the front line, and then lift the bombardment at a certain point of the line, keeping up the bombardment on the front line on both sides of the part lifted, and the attack has taken place on the part lifted before the defenders realised that it was coming.
All officers, N.C.O's and men should be instructed that directly the bombardment lifts they should immediately ascertain if the enemy is attacking, and every man must be ready to fire over the parapet the moment the bombardment lifts from his particular trench.

22. Artillery support should not be asked for at night unless absolutely necessary, as nothing gives the position of the guns away so much as firing at night.

23. The rockets which are in the front line now are only to be used as an alternative if the telephone is broken. Company Commanders and Platoon Commanders must be made to clearly underH stand this, and if a rocket is sent up a runner must immediately be sent to the nearest telephone whichx is working, to say why the rocket was sent up and from which trench, as it is extremely difficult for the artillery to see exactly where the support is needed.
If the enemy sends up rockets of the same colour as our own a telephone message should immediately be sent to the artillery to say that it was theenemy's rocket and not our own.
If Battalion H.Q. see a rocket of our own colour go up, they should immediately test telephones to Companies. This will also be a check on who sent the rocket up.

24. Lewis Guns must be mounted every night and ready to fire

25. The best positions for the bombers should be worked out, and they should be in positions where they can work best in the event of the enemy gaining a footing in any part of our line, and should have a sufficient supply of bombs with them.

26. Flash Obscurers for the Lewis Guns should be indented for by Regiments, also Knobkerri Heads for entrenching tools (about 50 per Company) and each Company should indent for the Dial Instrument for marking down enemy gun flashes.

27. The Rifles and Periscopes used with the Sniperscope should be covered with sacking, but this should be done so as not to interfere with the sights. All other periscopes should also be disguised with sacking.

28. An organised system of warning Machine Guns and Trench Mortar Batteries if the enemy should penetrate into a Gap or Locality should be worked out by Battalions. The only way that this can be done satisfactorily, appears to be by Company runners.

29. All Vermorel Sprayers should be inspected by the Divisional Gas Expert, Lt. Cook of the 11th Queen's and a report should be rendered as soon as this is done; stating if they are in proper working order.

F. R. Slaney [signature]
Captain & Adjt.
10/Bn. Royal West Kent Regt.

Issued through Orderly

Copy No, 1 Filed.
2 O. C.
3 2/in Command.
4 O. C. A Coy.
5 O. C. B Coy.
6 O. C. C Coy.
7 O. C. D Coy.
8 M. G. Officer.
9 Signalling Officer.
10 Transport Officer.
11 Quartermaster.
12 Bombing Officer.
13 Intelligence Officer.
14 Medical Officer.
15. War Diary.

SECRET. **Appendix 4.** Copy No 2. War Diary

11th Bn Royal West Kent Regt.

DEFENCE SCHEME.

Reference: Maps 28 + 36 [illegible]

BRIGADE AREA. 1. The Area held by the 123rd Infantry Brigade, forming the Right Sector of 41st Divn Line is as follows:-

Front Line:- Trenches 90-102 (both incl.)

Northern Line:- SUFFOLK AVENUE (incl.) - CALVAIRE (excl.) - MORTELETTE CHAPELLE. (excl:).

Southern Boundary:- RIVER LYS.

DEFENCES. 2. (a) The Front Line is divided up into DEFENDED LOCALITIES with GAPS in between, vide attached Map. These GAPS are wired behind the Parados, and will be maintained as Covered Communications between DEFENDED LOCALITIES. They are to be patrolled at frequent intervals during the night and every effort made to keep enemy under the impression that they are still occupied.

DEFENDED LOCALITIES. Defended Localities are:-

CARTERS FARM Locality.
TOUQUET "
RAILWAY "
GLASGOW REDOUBT.

DEFENDED POSTS. (b) Defended Posts:-

STATION REDOUBT.
7 TREES "
RESERVE FARM.
FORT PAUL.

N.B. These Posts are defended by a system of Machine Guns which cover the ground in front of the POSTS and the GAPS between the Posts.

SUBSIDIARY LINE. (c) The portion of the Subsidiary Line within the area, i.e., from RIVER LYS - (C.8.b.3.8.) CALVAIRE WORK (excl.)

NORMAL DISTRIBUTION OF TROOPS. 3. LEFT BATTALION:-

Right Coy: { Left of Gap "C" to left of No 96 incl: finding own support in 96 S.

Centre Coy: { Left of 96 (excl.) to Right of Gap "D" (incl.) finding own support in 98 S & Parade.

Sheet 2.

Left Coy:	3 Platoons (less 1 Section) GLASGOW REDOUBT. finding own support in 102 S. 1 Section FORT PAUL. 1 platoon RESERVE FARM.	
Local Reserve:- Coy:	1½ Platoons	PATERNOSTER ROW.
	1½ "	7 TREES REDOUBT.
	1 "	Trench 98 S.

DISTRIBUTION of BATTALION.

A. Coy. Left of Gap "C" to left of 97 incl: finding own support in 96 S.

B. Coy. Left of 97 (excl.) to right of Gap "D" (incl.) finding own support in 97 S & Parade.

C. Coy. 3 Platoons (less 1 Section) Glasgow Redoubt. finding own support in 102 S. 1 Section in FORT PAUL. 1 Platoon in Reserve Farm.

D. Coy. 1½ Platoons Paternoster Row.
1½ " 7 Trees Redoubt.
1 " 98 S.

DISTRIBUTION of LEWIS GUNS.

1 at junction of Trenches 95 & 96.
1 " Trench 97.
1 " " 98
1 " junction of Trenches 99 & 100 (com^dg. Gap D.)

If others available:-
1 at Glasgow Redoubt.
1 " 7 Trees Farm.
2 " Paternoster Row.

NORMAL DISTRIBUTION OF M.G. (Vickers) FRONT LINE.

(a) 1 gun right flank of Trench 96.
1 " Centre of " 102
1 " left flank of " 102
3

SUPRORT. (b) 1 " junction of Harrians Avenue & Paternoster Row.
1 " " " Screen Avenue & Long Avenue.
2

SUBSIDIARY LINE. (c) 2 Guns on each side of Railway near LA FLENCQUE FM. (XIV Post.)
2 " at CALVAIRE.

N.B. 2 4·5" Howitzers are detailed to cover the Gap between Trenches 93-96.

Sheet 3.

BATTLE H.Q. 123rd Infy B'de CONVENT, LE BIZET.

BATTALION PATERNOSTER ROW.

GENERAL PRINCIPLES. 1. Defended Localities & Posts to be held at all costs.

2. In pushing up Reserves, the lines of Defence next in rear of threatened Sector must be left with a Nucleus Garrison.

3. Close co-operation of Artillery always to be ensured.

4. Constant touch to be kept with our own troops all round.

5. All unit Commanders must think out plans to meet the various contingencies that may arise.

6. Every Officer & N.C.O. must know his Battle position and exact routes to Defended Localities.

7. TRENCH STANDING ORDERS 8A as amended will be rigidly carried out.

8. Returns called for will be punctually rendered.

ACTION IN CASE OF ATTACK. There are four cases to be considered:-

(a) When the line held by the Brigade on the Right, South of the RIVER LYS, is broken.

In this case no offensive action is possible owing to the River.

(b) When the enemy gains a footing in one of the Defended Localities.

(1) GLASGOW REDOUBT. Should be immediately reinforced by Fighting Section from FORT PAUL. FORT PAUL Garrison being made good automatically ~~by~~ from Garrison of RESERVE FARM, under orders of Company Commander.

Further assistance will be given, if required, from the Local Reserve Company in PATERNOSTER ROW, under orders of Battalion Commander.

Sheet 4.

These reinforcements will all move on GLASGOW REDOUBT by SUFFOLK AVENUE.

(c) When the enemy gains a footing in one of the Gaps:–

(1) GAP "C". The Fighting Section from HIGH COMMAND should immediately take action & bomb inwards. The Battalion on the Right should take similar action:–

All available Lewis & M. Guns to be trained on the Gap.

STOKES GUNS to be removed to safer position.

HIGH COMMAND to be reinforced from 98.S. automatically, who will be replaced by Troops from PATERNOSTER ROW. moving by HARNIANS AVENUE. & AMEN CORNER.

(2) GAP "D" Fighting Sections from adjacent Companies to bomb inwards at once.

(3) GAP "E". A Fighting Section from GLASGOW REDOUBT to be reinforced from Trench 102 S, FORT PAUL, & RESERVE FARM in succession, will bomb inwards. If enemy has established himself a counter attack under orders of the Battalion Commander will be made by way of SUFFOLK AVENUE & CHESHIRE AVENUE, a bombing party from the latter being detailed to deal with enemy endeavouring to cross the wire. The Lewis & M. Guns should be trained on the Gap at once and artillery fire asked for to deal with enemy reinforcements, by barrage, or direct fire on Gap when Infantry should be withdrawn.

NOTE:– It is found by experience that too large parties are sent as reinforcements, causing congestion and delay when smaller well organized Fighting Parties can do the work & more expeditiously.

ENEMY GENERAL ATTACK ALONG WHOLE FRONT.

(a.) With Gas.

1. Helmets to be at once put on.
2. Warning to be given at once to all

Sheet 5.

3. All dug outs cleared.

4. The parapet to be manned & every gun & rifle turned on enemy.

5. Artillery S.O.S. call given at once.

(b). Without Gas.

(1) Men to take cover lying as close to the 1st line parapet as possible.

(2) Men in support trenches to move as quickly as possible to adjacent AVENUES, but remain in readiness to re-man their trenches immediately on the fire being "lifted".

WORKING PARTIES. In case of sudden attack:—

(a) All working parties from the Support & Local Reserve Coy. working in the firing line, come automatically under control of the Company Commanders of the Trenches and Localities where they are working.

(b) The Local Reserve Coy. will immediately send one Officer to act as Liason Officer to Brigade Headquarters for orders.

S.A.A.
GRENADES.
TRENCH STORES.

The amounts alloted to —

1. Companies.
2. The Battalion.

will be maintained in accordance with instructions issued to all concerned by the Brigade.

SIGNALS
TELEPHONE

(1) are forbidden from Battalion H.Q. to Fire Trenches, Support Trenches & Strong Points, and vice versa except in emergency, such as S.O.S. call. Runners to be substituted.

(2) To Brigade or Units in rear of Battalion H.Q. as seldom as possible. Runners used whenever possible.

CASUALTIES. To be immediately reported to M.O. and conveyed at once to Regimental AID POST with rifle & equipment. In this connection Platoon Commanders must satisfy themselves by frequent inspection that the men carry Field Dressing always.

(Sgd.) A. Wood Martyn
Lieut. Colonel.
10th Bn Royal West Kent Regt.

Copy No 1. Filed.
2. War Diary
3. G.O.C. 123rd Infy. Bde.
4. O.C. "A" Coy.
5. O.C. "B" "
6. O.C. "C" "
7. O.C. "D" "
8. 2nd i/c Command.
9. Bombing Officer
10. Sniping Officer
11. M.G. Officer.
12. 189th F.A. Bde.
13. 20th D.L.I.
14. 12th East Surreys.
15. 11th Queens.
16.
17.
18.

ADDENDUM TO BATTALION DEFENCE SCHEME.

Action to be taken if Enemy penetrates:-

(a) Any defended locality.
(b) Any Gap between the defended localities.

(a) Should the Enemy penetrate into any defended locality the responsibility for ordering our Artillery to open fire on this locality will rest with the Infantry Brigade Commander concerned.

(b) In the event of the Enemy penetrating any of the Gaps between the defended localities the responsibility for ordering Artillery fire to be opened on the Gap will rest with the nearest Company Commander.

The order will be in the form of the Code Message "Q.Q.Q. Gap E" and will be sent to the Battery with which the Company Commander is in direct communication.

The Battery Commander will at once inform the Artillery Group Commander who will, if the Battery already warned does not cover the Gap in question, direct the Battery detailed to open fire.

The ~~Battery~~ Artillery Group Commander will at once inform the C.R.A. & Divisional H.Q. of the situation.

Since it is intended that Gaps should be fired on by Artillery, Trench Mortars, M.G. & rifles on receipt of Code Message "Q.Q.Q. Gap E" it must be distinctly understood that there can be no question of sending bombers to work down the Gaps from the flank of the defended locality on each side.

The action of the Bombers on the flanks of the defended localities will, in such cases be confined to preventing the hostile bombers & Infantry coming within effective throwing distance of the defended locality.

In connection with the action to be taken to meet cases (a) & (B) above, Brigade, Battalion & Company Commanders should at once organise means of rapid communication to Light Trench Mortar Batteries, & M.G. in supporting points behind localities & Gaps, detailed to open fire on the gaps.

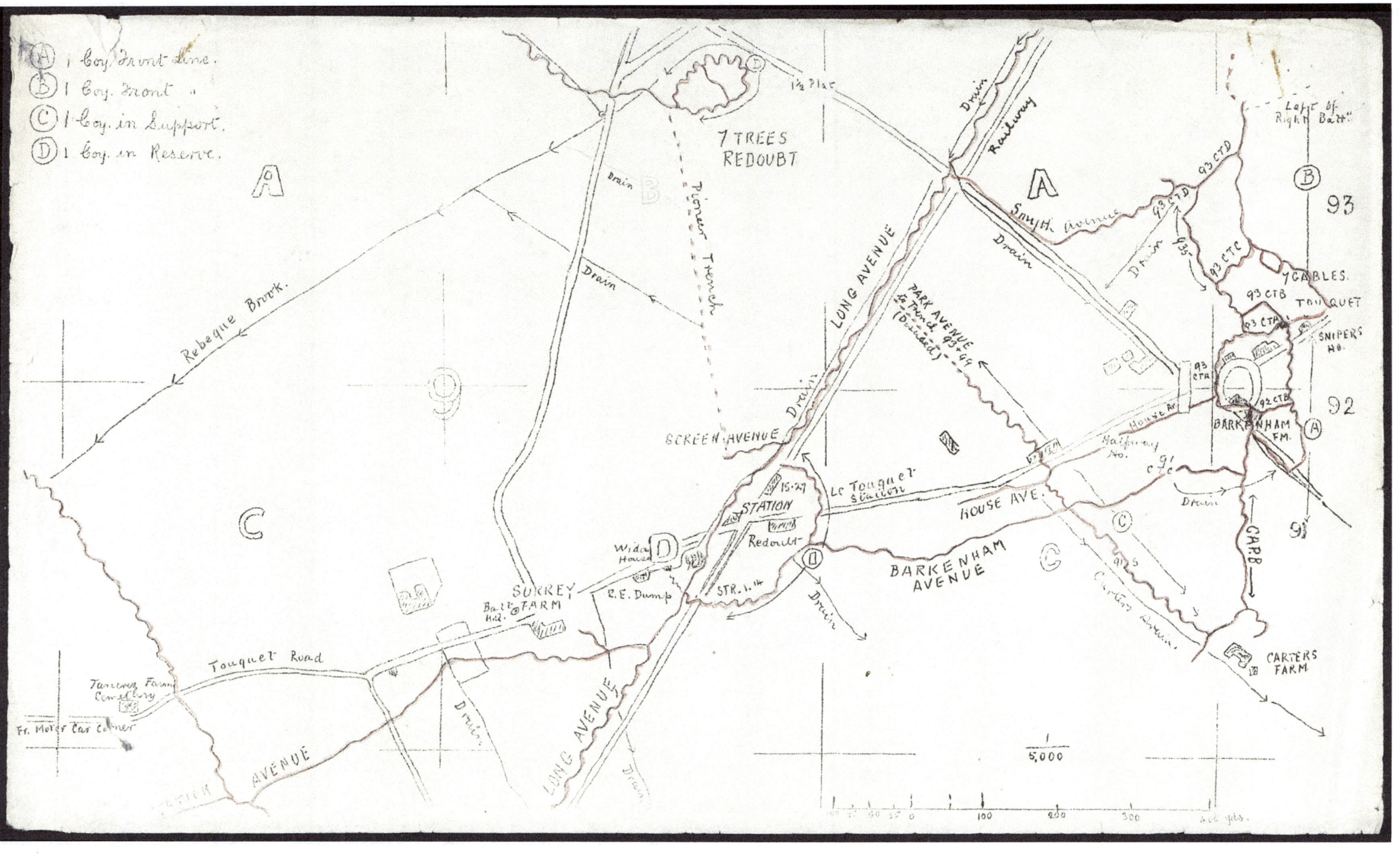
A 1 Coy. Front Line.
B 1 Coy. Front "
C 1 Coy. in Support.
D 1 Coy. in Reserve.
7 TREES REDOUBT
1½ Plat
Railway
Drain
Pioneer Trench
Left of Right Batt."
93 CTD
Smyth Avenue
93 CTC
7 GABLES.
93 CTB
TOUQUET
93 CTA
SNIPERS HO.
93
92
91
BARKENHAM FM.
92 CTB
House Av.
Halfway Ho.
LONG AVENUE
PARK AVENUE
Le Touquet Station
HOUSE AVE.
SCREEN AVENUE
STATION
Redoubt
STR. 1. 14
BARKENHAM AVENUE
CARB
Carters Drain
CARTERS FARM
Rebeque Brook
R.E. Dump
SURREY FARM
Batt. Hd.
Touquet Road
Tancrez Farm Cemetery
Fr. Motor Car Corner
AVENUE
1/5,000
100
200
300
400 yds.

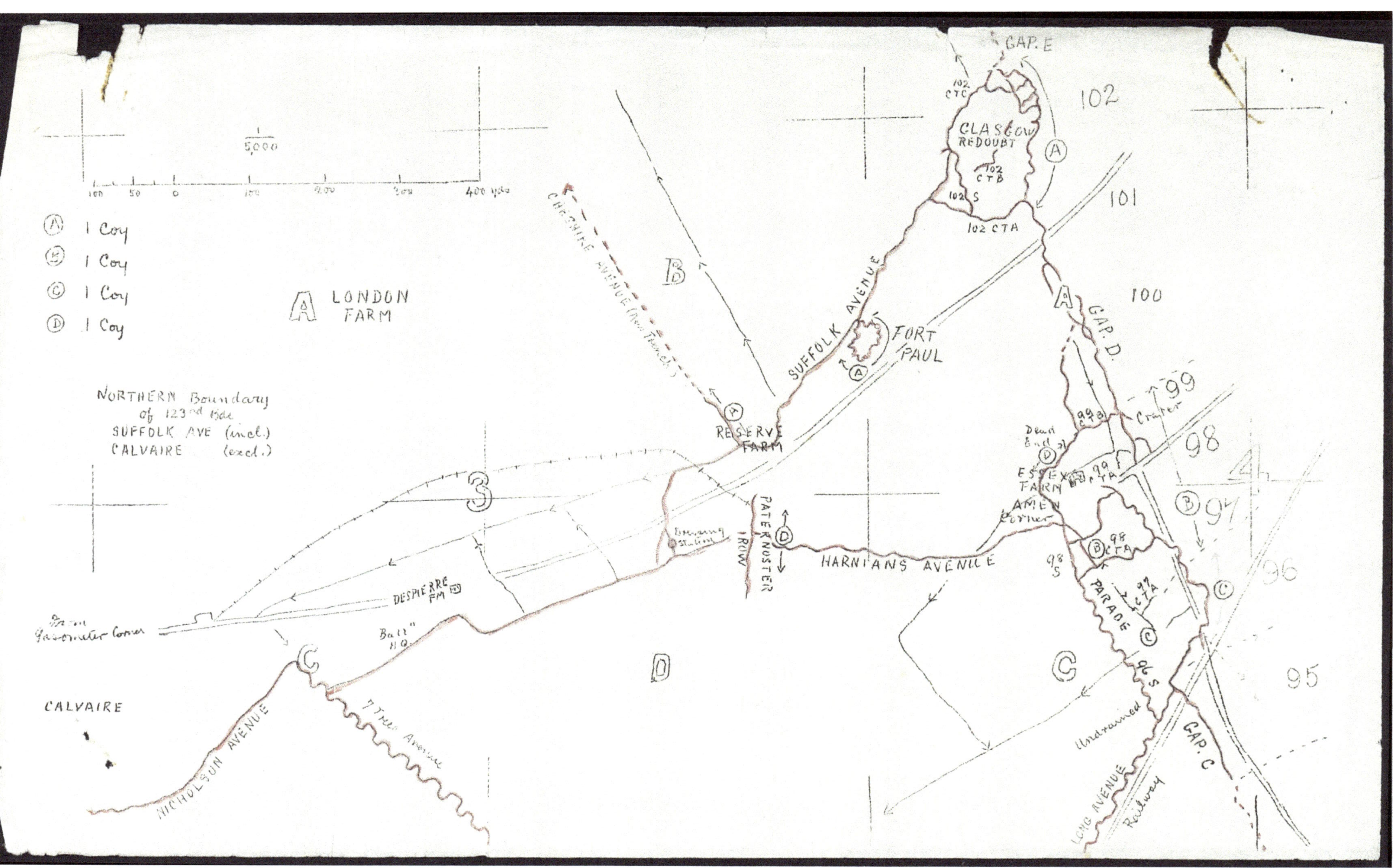

1/5,000
100 50 0 100 200 300 400 yds
(A) 1 Coy
(B) 1 Coy
(C) 1 Coy
(D) 1 Coy
A LONDON FARM
NORTHERN Boundary of 123rd Bde
SUFFOLK AVE (incl.)
CALVAIRE (excl.)
GAP. E
102 CTC
GLASGOW REDOUBT
102 CTB
102 S
102 CTA
102
101
100
99
98
97
96
95
GAP. D.
Crater
B
CHESHIRE AVENUE (New Trench)
SUFFOLK AVENUE
FORT PAUL
RESERVE FARM
Dead End
ESSEX FARM
99 CTA
99 CTB
AMEN Corner
PATERNOSTER ROW
HARNIANS AVENUE
98 CTA
98 S
PARADE
97 CTA
96 S
GAP. C
Undrained
LONG AVENUE
Railway
3
DESPIERRE FM
Ball" H.Q.
From Gasometer Corner
D
C
CALVAIRE
NICHOLSON AVENUE
7 Trees Avenue

Sheet. I

XLI

Army Form C. 2118

Instructions regarding War Diaries and Intelligence Summaries are contained in F. S. Regs., Part II. and the Staff Manual respectively. Title Pages will be prepared in manuscript.

WAR DIARY
or
~~INTELLIGENCE~~ SUMMARY
(Erase heading not required.)

10th Bn. R. W. Kent. R.

June

Vol 2

Place	Date	Hour	Summary of Events and Information	Remarks and references to Appendices
Bn. H.Q. DESPIERRE Fm. Ref. Map 36. N.W. 3 1/10000 C.3.c 8.7.) Front line)	1.6.16		Situation normal. Casualties nil.	
	2.6.16		—"— Casualties 1 killed 7 wounded O.R.	
	3.6.16		—"— 9 other ranks wounded.	
	4.6.16		—"— Casualties nil.	
	5.6.16		—"— At 8 pm the Bn was relieved by the 11th Bn. Queens in the left sector front line Trenches. Relief carried out by platoons and completed. Bn returned to LE BIZET and remained in reserve to 11th Bn Queens. Operation order No 4 attached. App x. Casualties 1 wounded O.Rks.	App x. 4
Billets LE BIZET	6.6.16 to 11.6.16.		Situation normal. Casualties nil. At 8 pm on the 11/6/16 the Bn. relieved the 11th Bn. Queens in the left sector front line Trenches. Relief carried out in usual manner. Queens relieved the Bn. as Bn. in Res. at LE BIZET. Casualties nil. Operation order No. 5 attached.	App x 5.
DESPIERRE Fm.	12.6.16 to 15.6.16		Situation normal. Casualties O.Rks. 3 killed 3 wounded.	
	16.6.16		At 12 mn a "Gas alarm" was ordered and normal conditions were not resumed until 3 a.m. During this period very heavy shelling took place on both sides. Casualties 1 O.R. wounded. The Bn received a draft of 17 men from 23rd Bn. R. Fusiliers.	
	17.6.16		Situation normal. Gas alarm 5am to 6am. No effects. At 8 pm the Bn was relieved by 11th Bn Queens in the front line and proceeded to LE BIZET as Res. Bn. Relief carried out. Operation order No 6 attached. Casualties 2 O.Rks. wounded.	App x. 6.
LE BIZET.	18.6.16		Normal.	
	19.6.16.		" At 9 pm a wiring party under Major Beattie went out. Casualties during the night out of this party were 1 officer killed 1 officer wounded, 1 O.R. killed [illegible] O.Rks. wounded.	
	20.6.16 to 23.6.16		Normal.	
Bn. H.Q. DESPIERRE Fm.	24.6.16	8 p.m. 9.30.	The Bn. proceeded to relieve the 11th Bn "Queens" in the front line trenches and were relieved as Res. Bn. by 11th Bn Queens. Time for relief was stated as 9.30 pm but the completion of same was delayed considerably owing	

1875 Wt. W593/826 1,000,000 4/15 J.B.C. & A. A.D.S.S./Forms/C. 2118.

Sheet 2.

10/ R W Kent Rt.

Instructions regarding War Diaries and Intelligence Summaries are contained in F. S. Regs., Part II. and the Staff Manual respectively. Title Pages will be prepared in manuscript.

WAR DIARY ~~or~~ INTELLIGENCE SUMMARY

(Erase heading not required.)

Army Form C. 2118

Place	Date	Hour	Summary of Events and Information	Remarks and references to Appendices
			to very heavy shelling by the enemy of our ~~own~~ front line support and communication trenches. The front line trenches (98S. – 97) were considerably damaged and many traverses blown in causing some casualties by men being buried by falling parapets and sandbags. Trench mortar Battery and M. Gunners of 11th Bn Queens suffered most. Fatigue parties worked all night digging out bodies and repairing the trenches as far as possible. One Coy. of the 11th Bn Queens remained on duty with the Bn. as a 5th Coy. but "C" Coy [illegible] no Reserve. Operation order No 7. attached.	[illegible] x. 7.
			Very heavy shelling continued throughout the night by both sides.	
			Casualties At LE BIZET. (through shelling) 1 O.R. killed 7 O.R. wounded 1 Offr. Shell Shock.	
			In TRENCHES. 1 Offr. Shell Shock. 7 O.Rs. wounded.	
	25.6.16	–	Situation normal. Rebuilding and repairing of trenches continued. Cas 1 O.R. killed.	
	26.6.16 to 28.6.16	–	— " — wounded 2 O.Rs. killed 1 O.Rk.	
	29.6.16	–	— " — Killed 1 Offr. 1 O.Rk. wounded 3 O.Rks.	
	30.6.16	–	During the day a heavy bombardment of enemy's wire and trenches took place to [illegible] and clear the way for a Bn Raiding Party under Capt. R. L. [illegible] during the night of the 30th inst. During the day the artillery shelled and cut the enemy's wire at:- (Ref. Map. 36. N.W. 2.) C. 4. a. 7½. 3¾ – C. 4. a. 7½. 4. – C. 4. a. 7½. 5. – C. 4. d. 1. 5½ — During this bombardment a few of our shells fell short into our support trenches. 97S. and 97L. This fire appeared to come from a battery from LE BIZET – [illegible]. Fire was then stopped. No casualties through this mishap. The Medium Trench Mortar Battery was used at this stage but had to be withdrawn as the Enemy bombarded and damaged the Emplacements. The Trench Mortars however did good work with the demolition of the enemy's wire.	
		10.43 pm	At this hour 2/Lt [illegible] and 7 other ranks. went over parapet and entered the enemy's trenches. Enemy's wire was well cut and no difficulty was experienced in entering & quitting his trenches. Parapets had been completely smashed. The party found the enemy's trenches 8'–9' deep and 3' wide – sides revetted with wire and corrugated iron wired back with stiff stakes supported with angle iron. Fire steps – [illegible] planks – reached by steps. Trenches were smashed to pieces but had been of an excellent type.	

1875 Wt. W593/826 1,000,000 4/15 J.B.C. & A. A.D.S.S./Forms/C. 2118.

Sheet. 3

Instructions regarding War Diaries and Intelligence Summaries are contained in F. S. Regs., Part II. and the Staff Manual respectively. Title Pages will be prepared in manuscript.

WAR DIARY 10/R. W. Kent Rt.
or
~~INTELLIGENCE SUMMARY~~

(Erase heading not required.)

Army Form C. 2118

Place	Date	Hour	Summary of Events and Information	Remarks and references to Appendices
			from doors or from saps where they cut through trenches. Doors [illegible] Stairs went to support uprights. 3 Dugouts seen empty but appeared to have been recently used. These dugouts were partially underground and roofed with 10 layers of sandbags supported by crossed girders. No enemy were met either dead or alive. At this period the enemy bombarded their own trenches. Enemy M. Guns fired all the time and the patrol met fire from the flanks and support trenches. An electric telephone wire was cut and two of the party were slightly electrified. These wires were cased red & black. Owing to the trenches being [illegible] no identifications were secured. The patrol were in the trenches over 10 minutes. The movement over "No Man's Land" were hampered rather with Gas and Smoke. One man was wounded in the enemy's trenches and one slightly gassed on return. On recrossing "No Man's Land" a want of support from [illegible] was felt. The operation on the whole and all were disappointed at such [illegible] result. The conduct of this patrol and its safe return reflects great credit on 2Lt. Kingsell who it is agreed showed great coolness in leading men and observation on matters to be reported. The casualties during the day were 5 wounded & killed and after operations 23 of whom 9 were gassed.	
			As soon as our operations commenced our trenches were immediately bombarded by all kinds of Trench missiles and artillery. Damage caused was slight except in Sub. 'C' where several breaches were dealt with. A Gas Cylinder was smashed at the commencement by Enemy fire which caused trouble and accounted for some of the gassed casualties. The Smoke screen worked admirably. A second emission of gas brought on a fierce bombardment by the enemy especially on the Saps. A certain amount of damage was done by the enemy's bombardment during the day and night to the various AVENUES, but as it occurred the damage was immediately repaired. All telephone wires were cut by the fire and were rendered useless during operations.	
			Total Casualties during day and night of 30th inst. were:- Killed 10 O.Ranks Wounded 21 -"-	
			Strength of Bn. on 30/6/16 30 Offrs. 934 O.Ranks.	
			A. Wood-Martyn Lieut. Col. Comdg. 10/R. W. Kent Rt.	

1875 Wt. W593/826 1,000,000 4/15 J.B.C. & A. A.D.S.S./Forms/C. 2118.

S E C R E T.   Copy No. 17 ....

10TH BN. ROYAL WEST KENT REGT. -- OPERATION ORDER NO. 4

1. The Battalion will be relieved in the FRONT LINE on the night of 5th/6th inst. by the 11th Battalion "The Queen's", moving into Reserve at LE BIZET according to the attached Relief Table.

2. Lewis Gun Section, Trench Mortar Battery, Observers, Snipers, Battalion Pioneers and Watermen will be relieved at intervals of one hour between each in the order named above, commencing at 10.30 a.m. on the morning of the day of relief.

3. Company Commanders and Sentries of the Relieving Unit will come into the portion of the line they are to take over at 3 p.m. on the afternoon of the Relief, and the Sentries will take over their duties at 8.30 p.m. from the Sentries of this Battalion.

4. Officers commanding Companies will hand over to relieving Company Commanders all details of work in hand and to be done in the Front and Support Trenches, and will hand over and check all Trench Stores.

5. All documents relating to the portion of the line taken over by the relieving Unit to be handed over.

6. The relief will be carried out by Platoons, which will move at intervals of at least 5 minutes.

Officers commanding Companies will send a Guide per Platoon to report to the Battalion Head Quarters of the 11th "Queen's" at LE BIZET by 6.30 p.m. Each guide is to be given a slip of paper stating number of trench and bay (not Company). Officers commanding Companies will send a runner or N.C.O. to report to the Adjutant that these Guides have been sent by 6.30 p.m.

7. Companies will not leave their positions in the line under any circumstances until properly relieved.

Companies will move off on relief in the following order:-

"D" Company) first, followed by -
"B" ") via HARNIAN AVENUE.
"A" ")
"C" " via SUFFOLK AVENUE.

8. The Adjutant will remain at Battalion Head Quarters, DESPIERRE FARM, until all Companies are relieved, and Officers commanding Companies will report to him on their way out.

9. Companies will move direct to their billets when the Relief is complete.

10. The Billeting Officer (Lieut. Pearson) with the Company Quarter Master Sergts. and one Other Ranks per Platoon, Machine Gun Section, Snipers and Signallers, will proceed to LE BIZET at 10 a.m. to take over the Billets of the relieving Unit. Officers commanding Companies will detail the above to meet Lieut. Pearson at the Battalion Head Quarters, ~~XXXXXXXX XXXXX~~ of the 11th "Queen's", VILLA DE ROSE, by 11 a.m. Billeting Officer to report to the Adjutant before leaving the Front Line.

11. No articles held on Company Charge (i.e., Very Pistols, Saws, Periscopes, etc.) will be handed over. A.F. W.3405 will be handed in to the Adjutant when completed and agreed by both Company Commanders.

SHEET 2.

12. Special measures in case of alarm during relief should be arranged, and Platoon Commanders to act according to their positionat the time.

13. Officer Commanding "D" Company will send 1 Platoonto relieve the Platoon of the 11th "Queen's" at PETIT REBECQUE FARM, relief to take place at 5.30 p.m.

14. The following Guards will be sent to relieve those of the 11th "Queen's" by 6.30 p.m.

"D" Coy.	1 N.C.O. & 5 men	Head Quarters Guard.
"D" "	1 N.C.O. & 3 "	On the Gong.
"A" "	1 N.C.O. & 3 "	Company Guards.
"B" "	1 N.C.O. & 3 "	
"C" "	1 N.C.O. & 3 "	
"D" "	1 N.C.O. & 3 "	

15. The Transport Officer will have the Company Cookers brought to LE BIZET and placed in position under cover for each Company. Officers' Mess Cart at Gunners Farm at 4 p.m.

16. Officers commanding Companies will report to the Adjutant when their Companies are settled in their Billets, by runner.

F. R. Slaney Capt. &
Adjutant.
10th/Bn. R.W.K Regt.

Copy No. 1. Filed
2. War Diary.
3. C.O.
4. 2nd i/Command.
5. 123rd Infantry Brigade.
6. O.C. "A" Coy.
7. O.C. "B" "
8. O.C. "C" "
9. O.C. "D" "
10. M.G. Officer.
11. Sniping "
12. Signalling "
13. Transport "
14. Quartermaster.
15. O.C. Trench Mortar Battery.
16. War Diary (duplicate).
17.
18.
19.
20.

TABLE OF RELIEFS.

DATE Night of	UNIT IN TRENCHES	RELIEVING UNIT	TRENCHES OCCUPIED	COMMUNICATION TRENCHES FOR RELIEVING UNIT.
5th/6th	10th R.W. Kent Rgt.	11th Queen's	LEFT SUB-Sector 123rd Bde. Line.	SHELL AVENUE -NICHOLSONS AVENUE

COMMUNICATION TRENCHES FOR RELIEVED UNIT.	STARTING POINT	TIME THE LEADING PLATOON PASSES STARTING POINT.	REMARKS.
NICHOLSONS AVENUE - GASOMETER CORNER	Commencement of SHELL AVENUE.	8.15 p.m.	Relieved Battn. to RESERVE LE BIZET on completion of Relief.

S E C R E T.   Copy No. 2, War Diary

10TH BN. ROYAL WEST KENT RGT. OPERATION ORDER NO. 5.

1. The Battalion will move from Reserve at LE BIZET to relieve the 11th Battalion "The Queen's" in the Front Line Left Sub Sector, on the night of the 11th/12th inst., in accordance with the attached Relief Table.

2. Dress: Marching Order without Blankets, each man to carry two Sandbags.

3. Signallers, Lewis Gun Teams, Trench Mortar Batteries, Observers, Snipers, Battalion Pioneers and Watermen will relieve those of the 11th "Queen's" at intervals of one hour between each in the order named above, commencing at 10.30 a.m. to-morrow, 11th inst. Officers & N.C.Os. in charge of the above parties will report to the Adjutant 5 minutes before their time for marching off.

4. Company Commanders, Sentries and 1 N.C.O. per Platoon will go into the Trenches at 3 p m on the afternoon of the relief; the Sentries will take over their duties at 8.30 p.m. Company Commanders will ascertain what work his Company has to complete in the Front and Support Trenches, and will take over and check all trench Stores.

5. The Relief will be carried out by Platoons. Platoons will move at intervals of at least 5 minutes in the following order:-

Platoons of "D" Company.
" " "A" "
" " "B" "
" " "C" "

Reports to Major W. F. Soames, who will report the Battalion present or otherwise to the Adjutant on arrival at the trenches. Major W. F. Soames will regulate the move.

6. All documents relating to the portion of the line taken over will be handed over by the relieved Unit, including a statement of the new work completed.

7. The 11th "Queen's" will take over the billets the Battalion vacates. Before moving off Platoon Commanders will ensure that nothing is left behind in billets. Billets are to be left clean, and a report to be rendered to the Adjutant to that effect.

8. No portion of any Unit is to leave its position in the line under any circumstances until properly relieved.

9. Rations for the 12th inst. will be carried up to the front line by the men under arrangements of Company Commanders.

10. The two Sandbags carried by N.C.Os and men will be worn on the feet, tied at the ankle and knee, to deaden the noise of walking on the duck boarding.

11. Every Officer, N.C.O. and man is to know exactly what position he is to occupy under the following circumstances:-

(a) Bombardment.
(b) Gas Attack.
(c) Attack.

All men should be frequently questioned as to this.

12. Attention is called to Battn. Order No. 3 dated 30/5/16.

13. Company Commanders will ensure that all reports and returns are rendered to Battalion Head Quarters at the times stated on the Schedule issued to them.

CONTINUED ON SHEET NO. 2.

SHEET 3.

14. (i) Company Officers' Kits will be stored in their own Company Stores.
(ii) Headquarters in Battalion Head Quarter Stores.
(iii) Blankets to be rolled in tens, labelled and placed in Company Stores, with Tools etc. on Company charge not required to be taken up to the Front Line.

15. A.F.W. 3405 will be handed in to the Adjutant when completed and agreed by both Company Commanders.

16. Immediately on completion of relief Company Commanders will report to the Adjutant by runner.

10/6/1916.

E. P. Slaney Capt.
Adjutant 10/Bn. Royal West Kent Regt.

Copy No. 1. Filed.
2. War Diary.
3. C.O.
4. 2nd i/Command.
5. 123rd Infantry Brigade.
6. O.C. "A" Coy.
7. O.C. "B" "
8. O.C. "C" "
9. O.C. "D" "
10. M.G.Officer.
11. Sniping Officer.
12. Signalling "
13. Transport "
14. Quartermaster.
15. O.C. T.M.Battery.
16. O.C. 11th Bn. "The Queen's"
17. War Diary (Duplicate).
18.
19.
20.

SHEET 3.

RELIEF TABLE.

Date.	Unit in Trenches.	Relieving Unit.	Trenches Occupied.	Communication Trench for Relieving Unit.
11/12th	11th Queen's	10th R.W. Kent Regt.	Left Sub-sector 123rd Bde. Line.	SHELL AVENUE - NICHOLSONS AV.

Communication Trench for Relieved Unit.	Starting Point.	Time the Leading Platoon passes starting point.	Platoon Guides.
NICHOLSONS AV.- GASOMETER CORNER.	Commencement of SHELL AV.	8.15 p.m.	To be at Bn.H.Q. at 6.30 p.m.

S E C R E T.   Copy No..........

10TH BN. ROYAL WEST KENT REGT. - OPERATION ORDER NO. 6.

1. The Battalion will be relieved in the FRONT LINE on the night of the 17th/18th inst. by the 11th Battalion "The Queen's", moving into Reserve at LE BIZET according to the attached Relief Table.

2. Signallers, Lewis Gun Section, Trench Mortar Battery, Snipers, and Pioneers, Water Party and Bombers, will be relieved at intervals of one hour between each in the order named above, commencing at 10.30 a.m. on the morning of the day of Relief.

3. Company commanders and Company Sergeant Majors of the relieving Unit will come into the portion of the line they are to take over at 3.15 p.m. on the afternoon of the Relief, and will check and take over all Stores etc.

4. Officers commanding Companies will hand over to relieving Company Commanders all details of work in hand and to be done in the Front and Support Trenches.

5. All documents relating to the portion of the Line taken over by the relieving Unit to be handed over.

6. The Relief will be carried out by Platoons, which will move at intervals of at least 5 minutes.

7. Companies will not leave their positions in the Line under any circumstances until properly relieved.
Companies will move off on relief in the following order:-

"A" Company)
"B" ") via MOTOR CAR CORNER.
"D" " via HARNIAH AVENUE.
"C" " via SUFFOLK AVENUE.

8. The Adjutant will remain at Battalion Head Quarters DESPIERRE FARM, until all Companies are relieved, and Officers commanding Companies will report to him on their way out. "A" and "B" Company Commanders will report by runner.

9. Companies will move direct to their billets when the Relief is complete.

10. The Billeting Officer (Lieut. Pearson) with the Company Quarter Master Sergeants will proceed to LE BIZET at 6 p.m. to take over the billets of the relieving Unit. Lieut. Pearson to report to the Adjutant before leaving the Front Line.

11. No articles held on Company Charge (i.e., Very Pistols, Saws, Periscopes, etc.) will be handed over. A.F.W.3405 will be handed in to the Adjutant when completed and agreed by both Company Commanders.

12. Special measures in case of alarm during relief should be arranged, and Platoon Commanders to act according to their position at the time.

(CONTINUED ON SHEET 2).

(SHEET 2).

13. Officer commanding "D" Company will send 1 Platoon to relieve the Platoon of the 11th "Queen's" at PETIT REBECQUE FARM, relief to take place at 5.30 p.m.

14. The following Guards will be sentbto relieve those of the 11th "Queen's" by 6.30 p.m.

"D" Coy.	1 N.C.O. & 6 men	Head Quarters Guard.
"D" "	1 N.C.O. & 3 "	Company Guards.
"A" "	1 N.C.O. & 3 "	
"B" "	1 N.C.O. & 3 "	
"C" "	1 N.C.O. & 3 "	
"D" "	1 N.C.O. & 3 "	On the Gong.

15. The Transport Officer will have the Company Cookers brought to LE BIZET and placed in position under cover for each Company.
Officers' Mess Cart and Maltose Cart to be at GUNNERS FARM at 9 p.m.

16. Officers commanding Companies will report to the Adjutant when their Companies are settled in their Billets, by runner.

R. P. Slaney
Capt. &
Adjutant.
10th Bn.Royal West Kent Regt.

16th June 1916.

Copy No. 1. Filed.
2. War Diary.
3. C.O.
4. 2nd in Command.
5. 123rd Infantry Brigade.
6. O.C. "A" Company.
7. O.C. "B" "
8. O.C. "C" "
9. O.C. "D" "
10. M. G. Officer.
11. Sniping Officer.
12. Signalling "
13. Transport "
14. Quartermaster.
15. O.C. T.M.Battery.
16. O.C. 11th Bn. "The Queen's"
17. War Diary (Duplicate)
18.
19.
20.

TABLE OF RELIEFS.

DATE night of.	UNIT IN TRENCHES.	RELIEVING UNIT.	TRENCHES OCCUPIED	COMMUNICATION TRENCHES FOR RELIEVING UNIT.
7th/18th	10th R.W. Kent Rgt.	11th Queen's	LEFT SUB-SECTOR – 123rd Bde. Line	SHELL AVENUE –NICHOLSONS AVENUE

COMMUNICATION TRENCHES FOR RELIEVED UNIT.	STARTING POINT.	TIME THE LEADING PLATOON PASSES STARTING POINT	REMARKS.
"A" & "B" COYS. via MOTOR CAR CORNER "C" & "D" via NICHOLSONS AVENUE & GASOMETER CORNER.	Commencement of SHELL AVENUE.	8.15 p.m.	Relieved Battalion to RESERVE LE BIZET on completion of Relief.

S E C R E T. Copy No. 2. War Diary.

10TH BN. ROYAL WEST KENT RGT. OPERATION ORDER NO. 7.

1. The Battalion will move from Reserve at LE BIZET to relieve the 11th Battalion "The Queen's" in the Front Line Left Sub Sector, on the night of the 24th/25th inst.

2. Dress: Marching Order without Blankets, each man to carry two Sandbags.

3. Signallers, Lewis Gun Teams, Trench Mortar Batteries, Observers, Snipers, Battalion Pioneers and Watermen will relieve those of the 11th "Queen's" at intervals of one hour between each in the order named above, commencing at 10.30 a.m. to-morrow, from Billets, 24th inst. Officers & N.C.Os. in charge of the above parties will report to the Adjutant 5 minutes before their time for marching off.

4. The Battalion will move into the Trenches via NICHOLSON'S AVENUE by Platoons at intervals of at least five minutes, in the following order:- "A" Coy, "B" Coy., "D" Coy., "C" Coy., the leading Platoon of "A" Company to move off at 9.30 p.m. Platoons will fall in outside their billets under their Platoon Commanders five minutes before their time due for marching off. Reports to the 2nd in command, who will regulate the move, informing the Adjutant on arrival at the trenches, Battalion present or otherwise. Companies will occupy the portion of the line they held during the last period of occupation.

5. Company Commanders with their Company Sergeant Majors will move into the portion of the line they are to take over at 3.15 p.m. on the afternoon of Relief, check and take over all Stores etc. and will ascertain all details of work in hand and to be done in the Front and Support Line Trenches, especially urgent work ordered by the Brigade during the week.

6. All documents relating to the portion of the line taken over will be handed over by the relieved Unit, including a statement of the new work completed.

7. The 11th "Queen's" will take over the Billets the Battalion vacates. Before moving off Platoon Commanders will ensure that nothing is left behind in Billets. Billets are to be left clean, and a report to be rendered to the Adjutant to that effect.

8. No portion of any Unit is to leave its position in the line under any circumstances until properly relieved.

9. Rations for the 25th inst. will be carried up to the front line by the men under arrangements of Company Commanders.

10. Every Officer, N.C.O. and man is to know exactly what position he is to occupy under the following circumstances:-
    (a) Bombardment.
    (b) Gas Attack.
    (c) Attack.

    All men should be frequently questioned as to this.

11. Attention is called to Battalion Operation Order No.3. dated 30/5/16.

12. Company Commanders will ensure that all reports and returns are rendered to Battalion Head Quarters at the time stated on the Schedule issued to them.

13. (i) Company Officers' kits will be stored in their own Company Stores.
    (ii) Headquarters in Battalion Head Quarter Stores.

(CONTINUED ON SHEET 2)

SHEET 2.

(iii) Blankets to be rolled in tens, labelled and placed in Company-Stores, with Tools etc. on Company charge not required to be taken up to the Front Line.

14. A.F.W. 3405 will be handed in to the Adjutant when completed and agreed by both Company Commanders.

15. The Detachment at PETIT MEBECQUE FARM will be relieved by the 11th "Queen's" at 5.30 p.m. on the afternoon of the Relief.

16. The following Guards will be relieved by the 11th "Queen's" at 6.30 p.m.on the afternoon of Relief:-

1 N.C.O. & 6 men	Head Quarters Guard.
1 N.C.O. & 3 "	Company Guards.
1 N.C.O. & 3 "	
1 N.C.O. & 3 "	
1 N.C.O. & 3 "	
1 N.C.O. & 3 "	On the Gong.

17. The Transport Officer will arrange to take Company Cookers away from Reserve billets when finished with by Companies, and and for the Officers' Mess Cart and one limber to be at Battalion Head Quarters by 3 p.m.

18. Immediately on completion of relief Company Commanders will report to the Adjutant by runner.

F. A. Slaney

23/6/1916.

Captain
Adjutant 10/Bn. Royal West Kent Regt.

Copy No. 1. Filed.
2. War Diary.
3. C.O.
4. 2nd i/Command.
5. 123rd Infantry Brigade.
6. O.C. "A" Company.
7. O.C. "B" "
8. O.C. "C" "
9. O.C. "D" "
10. M.G.Officer.
11. Sniping "
12. Signalling Officer.
13. Transport "
14. Quartermaster.
15. O.C. T.M.Battery.
16. O.C. 11th Bn. "The Queen's"
17. War Diary (Duplicate)
18.
19.
20.

10/R.W. Kent. Rgt. **WAR DIARY** ~~or~~ ~~INTELLIGENCE~~ **SUMMARY**

(*Erase heading not required.*)

SHEET. I. 41

Army Form C. 2118

10 WKR VOL 3

Instructions regarding War Diaries and Intelligence Summaries are contained in F. S. Regs., Part II. and the Staff Manual respectively. Title Pages will be prepared in manuscript.

Place	Date	Hour	Summary of Events and Information	Remarks and references to Appendices
BN. H.Q. DESPIERRE. FARM.	1/7/16	–	Very quiet during the day. Damage done during previous night was repaired and emplacements rebuilt. Very little sniping or shelling on either side. Strength. 30 Offcs. 932 O. Ranks.	
G.3.c	2/7/16		Situation normal. Very little firing on either side. It was noticed that considerable damage had been done by our artillery to the enemy's lines. They had repaired a lot of it and mended much of the broken wire during the night. Our repairing continued. Strength 30 – 932	wounded. 6. O. Ranks
	3/7/16.		As on 2nd instant. Strength 30 – 925. Casualties. K. 4. O.R. W. 6 O.R. Evac. Sick. 1. O.R.	
	4/7/16	9.30pm	The Bn was relieved by 11th. Bn. Queen's in the front line and took up its position as Res. Bn. at LE BIZET in the usual manner. Relief completed satisfactorily. Strength 30-920. Evac. Sick. 3 O.R.	Off x 8.
LE-BIZET.	5/7/16 to		Situation normal. Enemy's Artillery shelled LE BIZET but caused no casualties. At 5.30 A.M. on 6/7/16. 'D' Coy moved to FUSILIER TERRACE. U.27a Strength 30-917. Evac. Sick. 11. O.R.	
C.13.d	7/7/16	10.30pm	Under instructions from 123rd Infy. Bde a change in Bn. H.Qrs and situation of the Bn. in Reserve was carried out. Time and move was under arrangement between O.C. 10/R.W. Kent and 11th Bn. East Surrey ~~Quarters~~ Regt. who vacated our new quarters.	
			At 10-30pm. H.Qrs. moved off to SOYER FARM. (Ref. Map. B.b.d	
		11.30pm	'A' Coy moved to SOYER FARM to occupy quarters with H.Qrs.	
		10.30pm	'B' Coy moved to DELENELLE FM. (Ref. Map. C.1.d.	
		11. Pm	'C' Coy moved to TILLEUL FARM (1½ Platoons) & 1½ Platoons to GRAND REBECQUE FARM & 1 Platoon to PETITE REBECQUE FARM Moves carried out successfully. Strength 30 – 917. O2c. C.T.c.d C.T.c respectively.	
SOYER FARM. H.Qrs.	8/7/16.		Situation normal. A few enemy shells dropped in "D" Coys lines causing 4 casualties. Strength 30 – 915. Casualties 1. Offcr. W. (on patrol duties) K. 1. O.R. W. 5. O.R.	
B.b.d.	8/7/16.	11.35pm	A Raiding party previously arranged under Capt. R.L. Pillman, and consisting of himself – 2 NCOs & 16 men left the parapet of the front line at 11.35 pm. and successfully reached the enemy parapet after cutting the wire themselves. They lay upon the parapet for sometime listening and as they were getting into the German front line trench fire was opened on them apparently from riflemen firing through loopholes concealed on the ground close to a communication trench. Capt. R.L. Pillman was badly wounded and died next morning at 8. a.m. Sgt. Cramp was wounded in the back. The party returned about 1-15 pm. carrying the Captain. Under these circumstances a demolition party did not go out.	

1875 Wt. W593/826 1,000,000 4/15 J.B.C. & A. A.D.S.S./Forms/C. 2118.

Instructions regarding War Diaries and Intelligence Summaries are contained in F. S. Regs., Part II. and the Staff Manual respectively. Title Pages will be prepared in manuscript.

– 10/ R. W. Kent Rgt. –

WAR DIARY

~~or~~

~~INTELLIGENCE SUMMARY~~

(Erase heading not required.)

Sheet. II

Army Form C. 2118

Place	Date	Hour	Summary of Events and Information	Remarks and references to Appendices
			Immediately our party went over our parapet they were fired on but went on with their mission. From this it will be seen that the party was seen and the spot they left watched. Fortunately on their return they went to the right and left of the spot and so escaped casualties on return. Captn. Pilman being unable to make a report this detail was obtained from the men. No retaliation took place after this raid. Casualties. 1. Offcr. D. of W. & 1. O.R. W.	
Soyer Farm. H.Q. B.b.d.	9/7/16.		Normal Strength. 29 – 913. Evac. Sick. 1.	
– " –	10/7/16		Normal. A few Enemy shells dropped near Bn. H Qrs. but no casualties caused. The men at once took cover. Strength 28 – 913. O.R.	
– " –	11/7/16		Normal. Delenelle Farm was shelled rather heavily between 10 am. and 11 am. but no casualties occurred. Strength 28 – 908. Evac. Sick. 3.	
– " –	12/7/16		Situation normal. Very quiet during the day. At 11 pm. our guns opened a heavy fire. The Enemy retaliated and sent shells in vicinity of Soyer and Delenelle Farms. No Casualties. Shelling on both sides ceased at 3.30 am 13/7/16. Strength. 28 – 909.	
– " –	13/7/16.		Normal. About 10 pm. our artillery immediately in rear of Soyer Fm. commenced a heavy bombardment of the German trenches. No retaliation took place. Cessation of bombardment at 11-20 pm. Strength 28 – 908. Evac. Sick 5.	
– " –	14/7/16		Normal during the day. Relief as per attached Bn. order took place successfully at 10 pm. Strength 28 – 908.	Appx. 9.
Despierre Farm. C.3.c	15/7/16		Normal. The day was spent by all in studying the new positions in the line. Much work was done in repairing trenches which had previously been neglected. Snipers were quiet on both sides. During the day our artillery kept up a vigorous bombardment of Enemy's wire to prepare the way for a minor Enterprise by the D.L. Infy. on our right. The Enemy did not retaliate and were quiet in every respect. During the night a message shewing English and French victories on the Western Front at this date was exhibited for information of Enemy at dawn and during the day. Although placed in a conspicuous place in the front line the Enemy did not attempt to destroy it in any way.	

1875 Wt. W593/826 1,000,000 4/15 J.B.C. & A. A.D.S.S./Forms/C. 2118.

Instructions regarding War Diaries and Intelligence Summaries are contained in F. S. Regs., Part II. and the Staff Manual respectively. Title Pages will be prepared in manuscript.

— 10/R.W. Kent. Rgt. — **WAR DIARY** ~~or~~ ~~INTELLIGENCE SUMMARY~~

(Erase heading not required.)

SHEET. III

Army Form C. 2118

Place	Date	Hour	Summary of Events and Information	Remarks and references to Appendices
DESPIERRE FM. H.Q. C.3.c	15/7/16	10pm.	During the night our artillery vigorously bombarded the Enemy's lines but brought forth no retaliation. The M.G. Sect. were active in preventing enemy from working. (2/Lt. Allen joined the Bn. from 12th Res. Bn.) Strength. 29 - 907. Cas. 1.W. O.R. Evac. Sick 2 O.R.	
— " —	16/7/16	—	Normal. During the day our Artillery bombarded the Enemy's front line trenches but the Enemy retaliated very feebly (about 50 shells against 500). At 10pm. Our Artillery again bombarded them and this time brought rather more retaliation than during the day. Sniping very moderate on both sides through lack of targets. Machine Guns very active again in preventing Enemy from working. Our work progressed very favourably. The vicinity of DESPIERRE FM. was shelled by the Enemy between 10.30 pm & 11 pm but little material damage was done. Strength. 29 - 907. K. 1. O.R. 2. W. Evac. Sick 1. O.R.	
— " —	17/7/16	—	Artillery Bombardment (moderate) continued - Feeble retaliation by the enemy in the vicinity of CHESHIRE AVENUE. U.27.d. Snipers on both sides were very quiet during the day but more active during the night. Our M.G. Section was active during the night - Enemy's M.G. quiet. Patrols during the night report nothing unusual. - A quiet day. Strength 29 - 912. W. 2. O.R. Evac. 2. O.R.	
— " —	18/7/16	—	Normal. The intermittent bombardment of the Enemy's wire and support trenches continued. Patrols during the night encountered nothing unusual. Our Machine Guns were very active during the night on the points where the M.G. Enemy's wire required repairs. Sniping on both sides quiet. Enemy's retaliation of our bombardment - very feeble - a few shots only falling in our lines and doing no material damage. About 20 Minnenwerfers were shot into our front line near AYR STREET U.27.b. Enemy reported to be working hard at repairs to their damaged trenches. Strength. 29 - 910. W. 1. O.R. Evac. Sick. 1. O.R.	
— " —	19/7/16		Normal. Our bombardment continues with feeble retaliation in our lines but the enemy heavily bombarded places in rear. Our M.G. Sect. effective and active in preventing Enemy working parties.	

1875 Wt. W593/826 1,000,000 4/15 J.B.C. & A. A.D.S.S./Forms/C. 2118.

Instructions regarding War Diaries and Intelligence Summaries are contained in F. S. Regs., Part II. and the Staff Manual respectively. Title Pages will be prepared in manuscript.

– 10/R.W. KENT. Rgt –

SHEET. IV.

WAR DIARY

~~or~~

~~INTELLIGENCE SUMMARY~~

(Erase heading not required.)

Army Form C. 2118

Place	Date	Hour	Summary of Events and Information	Remarks and references to Appendices
			progressing with their repairs. Our Snipers were fairly active as more targets than usual were exposed through Enemy working parties. Our patrols saw nothing unusual. At various times during the morning and evening the Enemy lit fires or smoke columns. White lights were also sent up during the night in rear of the enemy's lines but no result was observed of their signals. An enemy aeroplane shelter was observed in rear of their lines and 3 Aeroplanes left the cover and attempted to cross our lines but were prevented by our Anti Aircraft guns. One of them dropped or shewed a red light about 2.20 am on 20th instant. Enemy also had 4 observation balloons up during the day and evening. At 12-45 am. an Enemy smoke bomb was thrown out from the German lines, 5 minutes afterwards 2 double yellow lights were sent up close to the same spot. They were visible for 3 minutes.	
DESPIERRE F.M. / L.R.			Strength 29 – 903. Cas. Nil	
C.2.e	20/7/16	✓	Intermittent bombardment of Enemy's wire and trenches continued. Enemy retaliated with a few shells in our front and communication trenches. H. Qrs also received a few about mid-day. Patrols reported nothing unusual. M. Guns on both sides more active than yesterday. During the early morning more smoke columns were seen coming from the Enemy's lines it died away after about 10 minutes but was resumed again shortly afterwards but this time lasted about ½ hour. About 9-45 pm. an incendiary bomb was thrown out by the Enemy into "No mans land". On examining it from the parapet it was seen that a mist was concentrating round it, and floating gradually towards the German lines. A Mills Hand Grenade was thrown into it and immediately an explosion followed ~~fire~~ by flames which shot about 20 ft in the air. Volumes of light smoke floated towards the German lines causing their Gas alarms to be sounded. Flames came from the place for some time after. The ground was afterwards patrolled and small pieces of phosphorous were found which ignited when thrown to the ground. Two Enemy Aeroplanes rose from their ground in rear but failed to cross our lines. Strength 35 – 899. A draft of 6 Offrs joined the Bn. from the 9th Res. Bn.	

1875 Wt. W593/826 1,000,000 4/15 J.B.C. & A. A.D.S.S./Forms/C. 2118.

— 10/R W Kent Rgt. — Sheet V.

Army Form C. 2118

Instructions regarding War Diaries and Intelligence Summaries are contained in F. S. Regs., Part II. and the Staff Manual respectively. Title Pages will be prepared in manuscript.

WAR DIARY
or
INTELLIGENCE SUMMARY
(Erase heading not required.)

Place	Date	Hour	Summary of Events and Information	Remarks and references to Appendices
DESPIERRE FM. C.3.c	21/3/16	–	Normal. Artillery normal much less active than on 3 previous days. Sniping was more active on both sides during day & night. The enemy exposed themselves more than usually. Hand Grenades were thrown in the direction of our snipers. Patrols went out in the night to a point from which enemy "Very" lights were emanating and encountered an enemy party and observed that the Germans were driving in stakes and wiring along the front of their lines & repairing other wire. On return of the patrol our M.G. Sect. opened fire on the enemy working points and stopped their work from progressing. At 7.45 pm. one of our airmen attacked and drove off a hostile aeroplane from over our lines. During the morning an enemy aeroplane dropped bombs on our supports evidently to draw fire from our forward batteries but without success. Communication — at 11.15 pm lights were sent up by the enemy near TILLEUL FARM (N.W.) they were sent up in 2 groups of 5 & 3. There was a regular interval between each light and a long one between each group. A patrol of ours went to the vicinity but discovered nothing unusual. Strength 34 – 897.	
— " —	22/3/16	—	Normal. At 9.30 am the enemy art. opened fire on our H.Qrs. firing about 16 shells in all. No casualties occurred. In the lines both art. fire normal. Sniping on both sides quiet. Patrols reported nothing unusual. The enemy had two observation balloons up during the day but quickly hauled them down on the approach of our aircraft. Strength 34 – 897.	
— " —	23/3/16	—	Normal. Artillery on both sides normal with exception of a few enemy shells directed in vicinity of CHESHIRE AVENUE. Enemy trench mortar missiles were hurled into our front line trenches between 6-30 pm & 8.0 pm. Two S.R. Bays in 'C' Coy lines were pushed in and levelled to the ground. A Lewis M. Gun Dugout & Emplacement were wrecked and a gun buried. The enemy snipers fired from screens in front of their parapet but with no success as we spotted them and silenced their fire. During the evening relief took place as per attached Bn. Order. Relief completed successfully. Strength 35 – 896.	Appx. 10
SOYER. FM. H.Qrs.	24/3/16	–	Normal. Strength 35 – 896.	
	25/3/16	–	Normal — " — 35 – 898.	
B.6.d	26/3/16	–	Normal. At 11 pm. Artillery in rear of H.Qrs. opened up a severe bombardment without retaliation of any activity. The Bn. "Stood to" but were not required. Normal conditions were resumed at 3-20 am. Strength 35 – 893	

1875 Wt. W593/826 1,000,000 4/15 J.B.C. & A. A.D.S.S./Forms/C. 2118.

Instructions regarding War Diaries and Intelligence Summaries are contained in F. S. Regs., Part II. and the Staff Manual respectively. Title Pages will be prepared in manuscript.

10/ R.W. KENT. RGT. –

WAR DIARY or ~~INTELLIGENCE SUMMARY~~

(Erase heading not required.)

SHEET. VI.

Army Form C. 2118

Place	Date	Hour	Summary of Events and Information	Remarks and references to Appendices
LE BIZET. H.Qrs. C.13.k.	27/7/16	–	Normal. At 3 pm. the Bn moved back under Coy. arrangements to the former billets at LE BIZET under instructions of the Brigade as Res. BN. to the 11th Bn. QUEEN'S who had taken over during the day the original front line sector. Move completed successfully. Strength – 35 – 898.	
– " –	28/7/16	–	Normal. During the morning the enemy sent a few shells into LE BIZET. Damage nil. Strength – 35 – 887. Casualties since 20/7/16. Offrs. nil. O.R. K.1. W.3. Evac. Sick 13.	
– " –	29/7/16	–	Normal. Very quiet during the day. Strength. 35 – 882 – Evac. Sick. 6. O.R.	
– " –	30/7/16	–	Normal. Strength 35 – 881. Evac. Sick. 2.	

30/7/16

[signature] Lieut Col
Commdg 10/ R.W. Kent. Rgt.

1875 Wt. W593/826 1,000,000 4/15 J.B.C. & A. A.D.S.S./Forms/C. 2118.

War Diary (Duplicate).

14.

S E C R E T.

Copy No..............

1 OTH BN. ROYAL WEST KENT REGT. - OPERATION ORDER NO. 8.

1. The Battalion will be relieved in the FRONT LINE on the night of the 3 rd/4th inst. by the 11th Battalion "The Queen's", moving into Reserve at LE BIZET.

2. Signallers, Lewis Gun Section, Trench Mortar Battery, Snipers and Pioneers, Water Party and Bombers, will be relieved at intervals of one hour between each in the order named above, commencing at 10.30 a.m. on the morning of the day of Relief.

3. Company Commanders and Company Sergeant Majors of the relieving Unit will come into the portion of the line they are to take over at 3.15 p.m. on the afternoon of the Relief, and will check and take over all Stores etc.

4. Officers commanding Companies will hand over to relieving Company Commanders all details of work in hand and to be done in the Front and Support Trenches.

5. All documents relating to the portion of the line taken over by the relieving Unit to be handed over.

6. The Relief will be carried out by Platoons, which will move at intervals of at least 5 minutes.

7. Companies will not leave their positions in the Line under any circumstances until properly relieved, and no N.C.O. or man is to be allowed to leave the Front Line in advance of his Company, e.g., Cooks, Servants, etc.
Companies will move off on relief in the following order:-

"B" Company }
"A" " } via HARNIAN AVENUE.
"D" " }
"C" " via SUFFOLK AVENUE.

8. The Adjutant will remain at Battalion Head Quarters DES PIERRE FARM, until all Companies are relieved, and Officers commanding Companies will report to him on their way out.

9. Companies will move direct to their billets when the relief is complete.

10. The Billeting Officer (Lieut. Pearson) with the Company Quarter Master Sergeants will proceed to LE BIZET at 6 p.m. to take over the billets of the relieving Unit. Lieut. Pearson to report to the Adjutant before leaving the Front Line.

11. No articles held in Company Charge (i.e., Very Pistols, Saws, Periscopes, etc.) will be handed over. A.F.W. 3405 will be handed in to the Adjutant when completed and agreed by both Company Commanders.

12. Special measures in case of alarm during relief should be arranged, and Platoon Commanders to act according to their position at the time.

(CONTINUED ON SHEET 2).

(SHEET 2)

13. Officer commanding "D" Company will send 1 Platoon to relieve the Platoon of the 11th "Queen's" at PETIT REBECQUE FARM, relief to take place at 5.30 p.m.

14. The following Guards will be sent to relieve those of the 11th "Queen's" by 6.30 p.m.

("B" Coy.	1 N.C.O. & 6 men	Head Quarters Guard.
("D" "	1 N.C.O. & 3 ")	
"A" "	1 N.C.O. & 3 ")	Company Guards.
"B" "	1 N.C.O. & 3 ")	
"C" "	1 N.C.O. & 3 ")	
("D" "	1 N.C.O. & 3 "	On the Gong.

15. The Transport Officer will have the Company Cookers brought to LE BIZET and placed in position under cover for each Company.
Officers' Mess Cart and Maltese Cart to be at GUNNERS FARM at 9 p.m.

16. Officers commanding Companies will report to the Adjutant when their Companies are settled in their Billets, by runner.

[signature]
Capt. &
Adjutant.
2/7/16 10th Bn. Royal West Kent Regt.

Copy No.1. Filed.
2. War Diary.
3. C. O.
4. 2nd in Command.
5. 123rd Infantry Brigade.
6. O. C. "A" Company.
7. O. C. "B" "
8. O. C. "C" "
9. O. C. "D" "
10. M. G. Officer.
11. Sniping Officer.
12. Signalling Officer.
13. Transport "
14. Quartermaster.
15. O.C. T.M.Battery.
16. O.C. 11th Bn. "The Queen's"
17. War Diary(Duplicate)
18.
19.
20.

SECRET. Copy No. 18.

10TH BN. ROYAL WEST KENT REGT. - OPERATION ORDER NO. 8.

1. The Battalion will be relieved in the FRONT LINE on the night of the 3 rd/4th inst. by the 11th Battalion "The Queen's", moving into Reserve at LE BIZET.

2. Signallers, Lewis Gun Section, Trench Mortar Battery, Snipers and Pioneers, Water Party and Bombers, will be relieved at intervals of one hour between each in the order named above, commencing at 10.30 a.m. on the morning of the day of Relief.

3. Company Commanders and Company Sergeant Majors of the relieving Unit will come into the portion of the line they are to take over at 3.15 p.m. on the afternoon of the Relief, and will check and take over all Stores etc.

4. Officers commanding Companies will hand over to relieving Company Commanders all details of work in hand and to be done in the Front and Support Trenches.

5. All documents relating to the portion of the line taken over by the relieving Unit to be handed over.

6. The Relief will be carried out by Platoons, which will move at intervals of at least 5 minutes.

7. Companies will not leave their positions in the Line under any circumstances until properly relieved, and no N.C.O. or man is to be allowed to leave the Front Line in advance of his Company, e.g., Cooks, Servants, etc.

Companies will move off on relief in the following order:-

"B" Company)
"A" ") via HARNIAN AVENUE.
"D" ")
"C" " via SUFFOLK AVENUE.

8. The Adjutant will remain at Battalion Head Quarters DES PIERRE FARM, until all Companies are relieved, and Officers commanding Companies will report to him on their way out.

9. Companies will move direct to their billets when the relief is complete.

10. The Billeting Officer (Lieut. Pearson) with the Company Quarter Master Sergeants will proceed to LE BIZET at 6 p.m. to take over the billets of the relieving Unit. Lieut. Pearson to report to the Adjutant before leaving the Front Line.

11. No articles held in Company Charge (i.e., Very Pistols, Saws, Periscopes, etc.) will be handed over. A.F.W. 3405 will be handed in to the Adjutant when completed and agreed by both Company Commanders.

12. Special measures in case of alarm during relief should be arranged, and Platoon Commanders to act according to their position at the time.

(CONTINUED ON SHEET 2).

(SHEET 2)

13. Officer commanding "D" Company will send 1 Platoon to relieve the Platoon of the 11th "Queen's" at PETIT REBECQUE FARM, relief to take place at 5.30 p.m.

14. The following Guards will be sent to relieve those of the 11th "Queen's" by 6.30 p.m.

("B" Coy.	1 N.C.O. & 6 men	Head Quarters Guard.
("D" "	1 N.C.O. & 3 ")	
"A" "	1 N.C.O. & 3 ")	Company Guards.
"B" "	1 N.C.O. & 3 ")	
"C" "	1 N.C.O. & 3 ")	
"D" "	1 N.C.O. & 3 "	On the Gong.

15. The Transport Officer will have the Company Cookers brought to LE BIZET and placed in position under cover for each Company.
Officers' Mess Cart and Maltese Cart to be at GUNNERS FARM at 9 p.m.

16. Officers commanding Companies will report to the Adjutant when their Companies are settled in their Billets, by runner.

Capt. &
Adjutant.
2/7/16 10th Bn. Royal West Kent Regt.

Copy No.1. Filed.
2. War Diary.
3. C. O.
4. 2nd in Command.
5. 123rd Infantry Brigade.
6. O. C. "A" Company.
7. O. C. "B" "
8. O. C. "C" "
9. O. C. "D" "
10. M. G. Officer.
11. Sniping Officer.
12. Signalling Officer.
13. Transport "
14. Quartermaster.
15. O.C. T.M.Battery.
16. O.C. 11th Bn. "The Queen's"
17. War Diary(Duplicate)
18.
19.
20.

SECRET. Copy. No. 2.........

10TH BN. ROYAL WEST KENT REGT. OPERATION ORDER NO. 6.

1\. The Battalion will move from Reserve Billets to relieve the 11th Battalion "The 'Queen's" in the Front Line, Left Sub Sector, on the night of the ~~XXXX/XXXXX~~ 14th/15th inst.

2\. Dress: Marching Order without blankets, each man to carry two sandbags. These sandbags will be filled by each man the same night and stacked "in reserve".

3\. Signallers, Lewis Gun Teams, Trench Mortar Battery, Observers, Snipers, Battalion Pioneers and Watermen, will relieve those of the 11th "Queen's" at intervals of one hour between each in the order named above, commencing at 10.30 a.m. to-morrow 14th inst., from billets. Officers and N.C.Os. in charge of Signallers, Snipers, Battalion Pioneers and Watermen in billets at SOYER FARM will report to the Adjutant 5 minutes before their time for marching off. The remainder will report by wire as follows: L.G.T.R.C., L.T.M.B.R.C. Detail of Relief and Routes attached.

4\. The Battalion will move into the Trenches in the following order. Detail of Relief and Routes attached.

"A" COMPANY. First to move, relieving "A" Company 11th "Queen's" at 7 p.m., 3 Platoons in CHESHIRE AVENUE, 1 Platoon at ~~LAWRENCE FARM~~ Lancashire Support. Guides from the 11th "Queen's" will be waiting in Communication Trench at LAWRENCE FARM.

"D" COMPANY. After being relieved by 11th "Queen's", to relieve "B" Company 11th "Queen's", Trenches 108 to Trench 111, both inclusive, finding its own immediate support.

"C" COMPANY. Will relieve "D" Company "The Queen's", leaving billets at 10 p.m. Trenches to be taken over - GLASGOW REDOUBT, and 102S to 107 inclusive. Two Guides will meet the two Platoons for left of GAP E. at GLADGOW REDOUBT end of Gap.

"B" COMPANY. Relieving "C" Company 11th "Queen's", march off from Billets at 10 p.m.

Trench 99	1 Platoon.
Part of 98 S. & BATCHELORS WALK	1 "
PATERNOSTER ROW (To find garrison of 1 N.C.O.) & 6 men for FORT PAUL)	1½ "
RESERVE FARM	½ "

Companies to move off by platoons of at least 5 minutes interval.

5\. Officers Commanding Companies, Light Trench Mortar Battery, and Lewis Machine Gun Officer to reconnoitre their positions before taking overthe line.

6\. Company Commanders, with their Company Sergeant Majors, will move into the portion of the line they are to take over at 3.15 p.m. on the afternoon of the Relief, check and take over all Stores etc., and will ascertain all details of work in hand and to be done in the front and Support line trenches, especially urgent work ordered by the Brigade during the week.

7\. All documents relating to the portion of the line taken over will be handed over by the relieved Unit, including a statement of new work completed.

SHEET 2.

8. Every Officer, N.C.O. and man is to know exactly what position he is to occupy under the following circumstances:-
(a) Bombardment.
(b) Gas attack.
(c) Attack.
All men should be frequently questioned as to this.

9. Company Commanders will ensure that all Reports and Returns are rendered to Battalion Headquarters at the times stated on the Schedule issued with these Orders.

10. A.F.W.3405 will be handed in to the Adjutant when completed and agreed by both Company Commanders.

11. The Detachment at PETIT REBECQUE FARM will be relieved by the 11th "Queen's" at 5.30 p.m. on the afternoon of Relief.

12. The 11th "Queen's" will take over the billets the Battalion vacates. Before moving off Platoon Commanders will ensure that nothing is left behind in billets. Billets are to be left clean and a Report to be rendered to the Adjutant to that effect.

13. (i) Company Officers' kits will be stored in their own Company Stores.
(ii) Head Quarters with ~~Battalion~~ Quartermasters' Stores.
(iii) Blankets to be rolled in tens, labelled and placed in Company Stores, with Tools etc on Company charge not required to be taken up to the Front Line.

14. The Transport Officer will arrange to take Company Cookers and Water Carts back to the Transport Lines when finished with by Companies.
One limber to be at Battalion Headquarters by 3 p.m. and Officers' Mess Cart at Battalion Headquarters by 9 p.m.

15. Rations for 15th inst:-

"C" and "D" Company will be carried by the men under arrangements of Company Commanders.
"B" Company Rations will be dumped at Gunners Farm and arranged by Platoons by the C.Q.M.S. As each Platoon passes through Gunners Farm it will pick up its rations and proceed on to NICHOLSONS AVENUE.
"A" Company rations will be dumped at MAISON 75., the Company Commander sending sufficient men to pick them up as they pass the dump.

16. Immediately on completion of ~~XX~~ Relief Company Commanders will report to the Adjutant, "B" and "C" Companies by runner, "A" and "D" Companies by wire, thus:-
A.R.C.
D.R.C.

17. Attention is called to B.O.O. No. 3 dated 30/5/16 which can be seen at Battalion Headquarters if necessary.

13/7/16.

[signature]
Capt. & Adjt.
1?/Bn. Royal West Kent Regt.

Copy No. 1. Filed
2. War Diary.
3. C.O.
4. 2nd in Command
5. 123rd Infantry Brigade.
6. O.C. "A" Company
7. O.C. "B" "
8. O.C. "C" "
9. O.C. "D" "
10. M.G.Officer
11. Sniping Officer.
12. Signalling "
13. Transport "
14. Quartermaster.
15. O.C. T.M.Battery.
16. O.C.11th Bn. "The Queen's"
17. War Diary (Duplicate)
18. M.O.
19
20

TABLE OF RELIEFS, ROUTES, ETC.

10TH BN. ROYAL WEST KENT REGIMENT.

Date.	Unit.	Route	Starting Point.	Time first Platoon or Party passes starting Point
14/7/16	Signallers	LE BIZET, SHELL PATH NICHOLSONS AVENUE	Entrance NICHOLSONS AVENUE.	11.15 a.m.
"	Lewis Gun Team	do.	do.	12.15 p.m.
"	Light Trench Mortar Batty.	do.	do.	1. 15 p.m.
"	Observers & Snipers	do	do.	2. 15 p.m.
"	Battn. Pioneers & Watermen	do.	do.	3. 15 p.m.
"	"A" Company	SOYER FARM to DELENELLE FARM turning right at road junction C.1.d.3.5. to BORDER AVENUE.	BORDER AVENUE	6 p.m.
"	"B" Company	DELENELLE FARM GASOMETER CORNER GUNNERS FARM NICHOLSONS AVENUE	GUNNERS FARM	10.45 p.m.
"	"C" Company	GUNNERS FARM NICHOLSONS AVENUE, SUFFOLK AVENUE.	GUNNERS FARM	10.5 p.m.
"	"D" Company	From FUSILIER TERRACE via most direct route to position in Line.		

War Diary (Dup.)

S E C R E T.

Copy No......18.....

10BN. ROYAL WEST KENT REGIMENT - OPERATION ORDER NO. 10.

1. The Battalion will be relieved in the Front Line on the night of the 23rd/24th instant by the 11th Battalion "The Queens"

2. Signallers, Lewis Gun Section, Trench Mortar Battery, Snipers and Observers, Pioneers and Watermen will be relieved at intervals of 1 hour between each in the order named above, commencing at 10.30 a.m.

3. Company Commanders and Company Sergeant Majors of the relieving Unit will come into the portion of the Line they are to take over at 3.15 p.m., and will check and take over all Stores etc.

4. Officers Commanding Companies will hand over to the relieving Company Commanders all details of work in hand and to be done in the Front Line and Support Trenches.

5. All documents relating to the portion of the line taken over by the relieving Unit to be handed over.

6. The relief will be carried out by Platoons which will move at intervals of at least five minutes, as follows:-

"A" Coy. 11th "Queen's" will relieve "A" Coy. 10 R.W.K. in LANCASHIRE SUPPORT and CHESHIRE AVENUE at 6.15 p.m.
"A" Coy. 10th Royal West Kent Rgt. moving into FUSILIER TERRACE.
"B" Coy. 11th "Queen's" will relieve "D" Coy. 10 R.W.K. at 6.30 p.m.
"D" Coy. 10th Royal West Kent Rgt. will move to billets at SOYER FARM.
Two Platoons of "D" Coy. 11th "Queen's" will relieve the two Platoons of "C" Coy. 10th R.W.Kents in 106 and 107 at 7 p.m.
The two Platoons of "C" Coy. 10th Royal West Kent Rgt.mocing into billets at DELENELLE FARM.

All the above moving via BORDER AVENUE.

"C" Coy. 11th "Queen's" will relieve "B" Coy. 10th R.W.K. in 99 - 98 S - PATERNOSTER ROW - FORT PAUL - and RESERVE FARM at 9.30 p.m.
"B" Coy. 10th Royal West Kents moving into billets at TILLEUL FARM.
Two Platoons of "D" Coy. 11th "Queen's" will relieve the two Platoons of "C" Coy. 10th R.W.Kents in GLASGOW REDOUBT at 9.45 p.m., the latter moving into billets at DELENELLE FARM.
The last two reliefs via NICHOLSONS AVENUE.

A Platoon of "C" Coy. 11th "Queen's" will relieve the Platoon of "B" Coy. 10th R.W.Kents in PATERNOSTER ROW at 5.30 p.m., the Platoon of "B" Coy. 10th R. W.Kents relieving the PETIT REBECQUE GARRISON by 6.30 p.m.

SHEET 2.

The Guard at GUNNERS FARM will be relieved by "A" Coy. 11th "Queen's" at 6.30 p.m.

7. Companies will not leave their ~~portion of the~~ positions in the Line under any circumstances until properly relieved, and no N.C.O. or man is to be allowed to leave the Front Line in advance of his Company, e.g., Cooks, Servants, etc.

8. The Adjutant will remain at Battalion Headquarters, DES-PIERRE FARM until all Companies are relieved. The Officer commanding "A" and "D" Companies will report when relief is complete by runner. Officer commanding "B" and "C" Companies will report to the Adjutant on their way out.

9. Companies will move direct to their billets when the relief is complete.

10. No articles held on Company charge will be handed over to the relieving Unit. Sniperscopes and Periscopes, other than "Vigilant" pattern, are not to be removed from the Trenches. They are Trench Stores and will be taken on charge in Trench Inventories, and handed over on relief. A.F.W. 3405 will be handed in to the Adjutant when completed and agreed by both Company Commanders.

11. Special measures in case of alarm during relief to be arranged, and Platoon Commanders will act according to their position at the time.

12. The Transport Officer will have the Company Cookers taken to the Companies at their billets to-night after dark, and the Water Carts to Battalion Headquarters. He will arrange to have one limber and the Officers' Mess Cart at GUNNERS FARM by 10.15 p.m.

13. Officers Commanding Companies will report to the Adjutant by runner when their Companies are settled in their billets.

G. R. Stanley

23/7/16.

Capt. & Adjt.
10th Bn. Royal West Kent Regt.

Copy No. 1. Filed.
2. War Diary.
3. C.O.
4. 2nd in Command.
5. 123rd Infantry Brigade.
6. O.C. "A" Coy.
7. O.C. "B" "
8. O.C. "C" "
9. O.C. "D" "
10. Lewis Rifle Gun Officer.
11. Intelligence Officer.
12. Signalling Officer.
13. Transport Officer.
14. Quartermaster.
15. O.C. L.T.M.B.
16. M.O.
17. O.C. 11th "Queen's"
18. War Diary (duplicate).
19.
20.

War Diary (Dup)

SECRET. Copy No. 17

10TH BN. ROYAL WEST KENT REGT. OPERATION ORDER NO. 11.

1. The Battalion will move from Reserve at LE BIZET to relieve the 11th Bn. "The Queen's" in the Front Line Left Sub Sector, on the night of the 1st/2nd August.

2. Dress: Marching Order without Blankets, each man to carry two sandbags.

3. Signallers, Lewis Gun Teams, Trench Mortar Batteries, Observers, Snipers, Battalion Pioneers and Watermen will relieve those of the 11th "Queen's" at intervals of one hour between each in the order named above, commencing at 10.30 a.m. to-morrow, ~~XXXX~~ 1st prox., from Billets. Officers & N.C.Os. in charge of the above parties will report to the Adjutant 5 minutes before their time for marching off.

4. The Battalion will move into the Trenches in the following order:- "B" Coy., "D" Coy., "A" Coy., "C" Coy., "B", "D" & "C" Companies moving via NICHOLSONS AVENUE and HARNIANS AVENUE. "A" Company via NICHOLSONS AVENUE and SUFFOLK AVENUE.

"B" Company will take over Trenches 95 to 97 both inclusive, finding its own supports in 96 S. + 97 S.

"D" Company will take over trenches left of 97 (exclusive) to right of Gap "D" (inclusive), finding its own support in 98 S. & Parade. + Bachelors Walk.

"A" Company. Three Platoons, less 1 Fighting Section, in GLASGOW REDOUBT, finding its own supports in 102 S.

(+101) 1 Fighting Section in FORT PAUL.
1 Platoon at RESERVE FARM.

"C" Company (LOCAL RESERVE):-
2 ~~1½~~ Platoons PATERNOSTER ROW
2 ~~1½~~ " 7 TREES REDOUBT.
~~1 " 98 S.~~

Companies will move by Platoons at intervals of at least 5 minutes, the leading Platoon of "B" Company to move off at 9.30 p.m.

Platoons will fall in outside their billets under their Platoon Commanders five minutes before their time due for marching off. Reports to the 2nd in Command, who will regulate the move, and inform the Adjutant on arrival at the trenches, Battalion present or otherwise.

5. Company Commanders with their Company Sergeant Majors will move into the portion of the line they are to take over at 3.15 p.m. on the afternoon of Relief, check and take over all Stores etc., and will ascertain all details of work in hand and to be done in the Front and Support Line Trenches, especially urgent work ordered by the Brigade during the week.

6. All documents relating to the portion of the line taken over will be handed over by the relieved Unit, including a statement of the new work completed.

7. The 11th "Queen's" will take over the Billets the Battalion vacates. Before moving off Platoon Commanders will ensure that nothing is left behind in billets. Billets are to be left clean, and a report to be rendered to the Adjutant to that effect.

8. [illegible]

9. Rations forthe 2nd prox. will be carried up to the front line ~~XXXXX~~ by the men under arrangements of Company Commanders.

(CONTINUED ON SHEET 2)

SHEET 2.

10. Every Officer, N.C.O. and man is to know exactly what position he is to occupy under the following circumstances:-

(a) Bombardment.
(b) Gas Attack.
(c) Attack.

All men should be frequently questioned as to this.

11. Company Commanders will ensure that all reports and returns are rendered to Battalion Head Quarters at the time stated on the Schedule issued to them.

12. (i) Company Officers' Kits will be stored in their own Company Stores.
(ii) Headquarters in Battalion Head Quarter Stores.
(iii) Blankets to be rolled in tens, labelled and placed in Company Stores, with Tools etc. on Company charge not required to be taken up to the Front Line.

13. A.F.W. 3405 will be handed in to the Adjutant when completed and agreed by both Company Commanders.

14. The Detachment at PETIT REBECQUE FARM will be relieved by the 11th "Queen's" at 5.30 p.m. on the afternoon of Relief.

15. The following Guard will be relieved by the 11th "Queen's" at 6.30 p.m. on the afternoon of Relief:-

1 N.C.O. and 6 men - Headquarters Guard.

16. The Transport Officer will arrange to take Company Cookers and Water Carts away from Billets when finished with by Companies, and for the Officers' Mess Cart and one limber to be at Battalion Headquarters by 3 p.m.

17. Immediately on completion of Relief Company Commanders will report to the Adjutant by runner.

F. R. Sleeney[signature]
Captain.
Adjutant 10/Bn Royal West Kent Regt.

31/7/16.

Copy No. 1. Filed.
2. War Diary.
3. C.O.
4. 2nd i/Command.
5. 123rd Infantry Brigade.
6. O.C. "A" Company.
7. O.C. "B" "
8. O.C. "C" "
9. O.C. "D" "
10. M. G. Officer.
11. Sniping "
12. Signalling Officer.
13. Transport "
14. Quartermaster.
15. O.C. T.M.Battery.
16. O.C. 11th Bn. "The Queen's"
17. War Diary (Duplicate)
18. M.O.
19.
20.

10th R W Kent Regt — August 1916 — Sheet 1

WAR DIARY
or
INTELLIGENCE SUMMARY
(Erase heading not required.)

Army Form C. 2118

10 W Ken

Instructions regarding War Diaries and Intelligence Summaries are contained in F. S. Regs., Part II. and the Staff Manual respectively. Title Pages will be prepared in manuscript.

Place	Date	Hour	Summary of Events and Information	Remarks and references to Appendices
LE BIZET	31/7/16		Normal Strength 35–881 Casualties Nil	
	1/8/16		During the day situation normal, Relief as per Appendix 11 carried out successfully.	APPX 11
H.Q. DESPIERE FARM			Strength 31–872, Casualties nil.	
	2/8/16		Situation normal Artillery on both sides very quiet. Sniping normal. Our Machine Guns prevented a German working party progressing at 11.30 P.M. At 8 A.M. four Germans got over their parapet presumably to get in some wounded, our Machine Guns drove them back.	
			Strength 36–875, Evacuated O.R. 3, Casualties Nil.	
	3/8/16		Situation Normal, Our Patrols encountered nothing unusual. At 1.30 A.M. Enemy shot a Very Light across our lines in an unusual manner, It was fired like a rifle bullet.	
			Strength 36–875, Casualties O.R. 1 K, O.R. 1 W	
	4/8/16		Situation Normal unusually quiet throughout the day	
			Strength 31·874 Evacuated O.R. 3 Casualties O.R. 1 W.	
	5/8/16		Situation Normal. Our operations very quiet in all respects, Patrols met nothing unusual, Enemy Operations:-	
		10.30 AM	A few Enemy shells 7.7 were fired into our Communication Trenches, no damage done. The Enemy tried to tempt our Snipers with a dummy figure, Our men did not fire.	
		11.15 PM	A red rocket was fired which broke into four red balls, no result was observed of this signal.	
			Strength 31–871 Casualties Nil.	
	[illegible]		Situation normal. In the morning the Enemy fired more 7.7 Shells into Our trenches but were silenced by Our Guns. Enemy's Machine Guns much more active than during last few days. Enemy's attitude is generally nervous and unsettled. Our Patrols report nothing unusual.	
			Strength 31–871 Casualties nil	
	7/8/16		Situation normal. Our Artillery bombarded rear of Enemy's lines from 7.30 to 8 P.M. firing about 200 Shells, Our Snipers were fairly active and succeeded in breaking 5 Enemy periscopes, Patrols met nothing unusual. Our Aeroplanes dropped smoke bombs over Enemy's trenches evidently for Ranging purposes, Enemy very inactive in all respects.	
			Strength 31–867, Evacuated O.R. 4 Casualties Nil.	

1875 Wt. W593/826 1,000,000 4/15 J.B.C. & A. A.D.S.S./Forms/C. 2118.

10th Bn R. W. Kent Reg — August 1916 — Sheet 2

Army Form C. 2118

WAR DIARY
or
INTELLIGENCE SUMMARY
(Erase heading not required.)

Instructions regarding War Diaries and Intelligence Summaries are contained in F. S. Regs., Part II. and the Staff Manual respectively. Title Pages will be prepared in manuscript.

Place	Date	Hour	Summary of Events and Information	Remarks and references to Appendices
H.Q. DE SPIERRE FARM	8/8/16		Normal, the enemy sniper was located at 6.30 AM. He was firing from a V [illegible] plate and was [illegible]. He had an observer watching the effect of his fire through a periscope. We opened fire with Rifle Grenades and eventually put them out of action. No retaliation was given to our Grenades. Both Enemy and ourselves very quiet in all respects otherwise. Our Patrols met nothing unusual. Strength 36-844. Evacuated OR 1. Casualties OR K. OR 1 W.	
	9/8		Normal, very quiet. Nothing unusual reported by Patrols. Strength 36-856 Evacuated OR 7. Casualties Nil	
	10/8/16		Normal. At 3 PM a heavy trench mortar projectile was shot into the locality of D Company 98 R.T. but did no damage. Our Trench Mortars retaliated and directed one gun on to a sniper post and succeeded in knocking it out. Patrols met nothing unusual. Strength 36-852 Casualties OR 4	
	11/8 12/8/16		Normal. The [illegible] on both sides were much quieter than usual. Our Patrols encountered nothing unusual. Strength 36-851, Evacuated OR 1 Casualties 1 W.	
	13/8		Normal. At [illegible] PM the Battalion was relieved in the front line by the 11th Bn [illegible] Regt and took up billets as per Bn Order No. [illegible] (Appendix 12) Strength 36-857 Casualties Nil	APPX 12
H.Q. LE BIZET	13/8		Normal. Officer joined Lt. F. [illegible] from R.S.M. Strength 37-857 Casualties Nil	
	14/8		Normal. Officer joined Lt. F. C. Evans from Marlborough House Sted St [illegible]. Strength 37-850 Casualties 1 OR	
	15/8/16		Normal. Strength 37-850 Casualties Nil	
	16/8		Normal. Battalion was relieved by 11th Bn Northumberland Fusiliers (68th Brigade 23rd Div.) and proceeded by route march to LA CRECHE (Ref. Map Belgium & France Sheet 36 N.W. 1/20000 A5d88) en route to BERTHEN. Strength 38-844 Casualties Nil.	APPX 13
H.Q. LA CRECHE	17/8/16		Normal. Battalion marched from LA CRECHE to BERTHEN and billeted. Sheet 27 1/40000	
H.Q. BERTHEN			H.Q. R27b88, A Co R27a18, B Co R33b80, C Co R27a49, D Co R27c50. Strength 38-846 Casualties Nil	
	18/8/16		Normal. Battalion began training for Open Warfare after long tour of Trenches. Strength 38-846 Evacuated OR 1 Casualties Nil.	

1875 Wt. W593/826 1,000,000 4/15 J.B.C. & A. A.D.S.S./Forms/C. 2118.

10th Royal W. Kent Regt — August 1916 — Sheet 3

WAR DIARY
or
INTELLIGENCE SUMMARY
(Erase heading not required.)

Army Form C. 2118

Instructions regarding War Diaries and Intelligence Summaries are contained in F. S. Regs., Part II. and the Staff Manual respectively. Title Pages will be prepared in manuscript.

Place	Date	Hour	Summary of Events and Information	Remarks and references to Appendices
BERTHEN	19/8/16		Normal. Strength 35 – 845 Casualties nil	
	[illegible]		Normal. [illegible] evacuated [illegible] 2Lt [illegible] and 2Lt [illegible], Strength 35 – 844 Casualties [illegible] Casualties nil.	
	[illegible]		Normal, Strength 39 – 844 Casualties nil	
	[illegible]		Normal, Strength 39 – 844 Casualties nil	
	[illegible]		Normal. Battalion proceeded by route march to BAILLEUL & entrained for LONG PRE (Ref Map France 1/100000 Abbeville 14, L6) as per App. 14. Strength 39 – 845 Casualties nil	APPX 14
H.Q. BUSSUS BUSSUEL	[illegible]		Normal. Battalion arrived at LONG PRE about 2.45 AM detrainment completed by 5.30 AM proceeded by route march to BUSSUS BUSSUEL (Ref Map France, Sheet LENS 11 1/100000 A5) Billet. Strength 39 – 845 Casualties nil.	
	[illegible]		Normal. Continuation of training for Open Warfare, Strength 39 – 845 Casualties nil.	
	[illegible]		Normal Strength 39 – 841 Transferred to [illegible] 3 Transferred to England 1 Casualties nil	
	[illegible]		Normal Strength 39 – 841 Casualties nil	
	[illegible]		Normal Strength 39 – 841 Casualties nil	
	[illegible]		Normal Strength 39 – 841 Casualties nil	
	[illegible]		Normal Strength 39 – 841 Casualties nil	
	[illegible]		Normal Strength 39 – 840 Evacuated 1 Casualties nil	

[illegible signature]
Lt Col
Comm^dg 10th Bn Royal West Kent Regt

1875 Wt. W593/826 1,000,000 4/15 J.B.C. & A. A.D.S.S./Forms/C. 2118.

SECRET. Copy No...17 WD (Dup)........

10TH BN. ROYAL WEST KENT REGIMENT - OPERATION ORDER NO.12.

1. The Battalion will be relieved in the Front Line on the night of the 12th/13th inst. by the 11th Bn. "The Queen's" Regt. moving into reserve billets as detailed below.

2. Signallers, Lewis Gun Section, Trench Mortar Battery, Snipers and Pioneers, Water Party and Bombers, will be relieved at intervals of one hour between each in the order named above, commencing at 10.30 a.m. on the morning of the day of Relief.

3. Company Commanders and Company Sergeant Majors of the relieving unit will come into the portion of the Line they are to take over at 3.15 p.m. on the afternoon of the Relief, and will check and take over all Stores etc.

4. Officers Commanding Companies will hand over to relieving Company Commanders ~~[struck out]~~ the Log Book with all details of work in hand and to be done in the Front and Support Trenches.

5. All documents relating to the portion of the Line taken over by the relieving Unit to be handed over.

6. The Relief will be carried out by Platoons, which will move at intervals of at least five minutes.

7. Companies will not leave their positions in the Line under any circumstances until properly relieved, and no N.C.O. or man is to be allowed to leave the Front Line in advance of his Company, e.g., Cooks, Servants, etc.

Companies will move off on relief in the following order:-

"D" Company) via HARNIAN AVENUE and NICHOLSONS AVENUE.
"B" "
"C" "
"A" " via SUFFOLK AVENUE and NICHOLSONS AVENUE.

8. The Adjutant will remain at Battalion Headquarters, DESPIERRE FARM, until all Companies are relieved, and Officers commanding Companies will report to him on their way out.

9. Companies will move direct to their Billets on completion of relief as follows:-

"A" Company	LE BIZET	Only rooms facing WEST are to be occupied, and as thinly as possible.
"B" "	LE BIZET	
"C" "	PETIT REBECQUE FARM	
"D" "	GRAND REBECQUE FARM	

Snipers, Lewis Gun Section, and Light Trench Mortar Battery will billet with their respective Companies.

10. Officers Commanding Companies will send 1 N.C.O. or man per Platoon to their Company Quartermaster Sergeant by 6.30 p.m. 12th inst. to ascertain where their Platoons will be billeted. These men will meet their Platoons as they come out of the Line at the entrance of NICHOLSONS AVENUE, and guide them to their billets.

11. No articles held on Company Charge will be handed over to the relieving Unit. Sniperscopes and Periscopes, other than "Vigilant" pattern, are not to be removed from the Trenches. They are Trench Stores and will be taken on charge in Trench Inventories.

(Continued on Sheet 2.)

and handed over on relief. A.F.W.3405 will be handed in to the Adjutant when completed and agreed by both Company Commanders.

12. Special measures in case of alarm during relief to be arranged and Platoon commanders will act according to their position at the time.

13. The Officer Commanding "C" Company will send 1 Platoon to relieve the Platoon of the 11th "Queen's" at PETIT REBECQUE FARM. This Platoon will be taken from SEVEN TREES REDOUBT. Relief to take place at 5.30 p.m. The Officer Commanding 11th Queen's will send a Platoon to relieve this Platoon for this purpose.

14. The following Guards will be sent to relieve those of the 11th "Queen's" by 6.30 p.m.

"A" Company 1 N.C.O. & 6 men - Hd.QR.Guard LE BIZET.
"D" " 1 N.C.O. & 3 " - Coy. Guard GRAND REBECQUE FARM.

15. The Transport Officer will have the Company Cookers taken to the Billets of the Companies - 1 Water Cart to GRAND REBECQUE FARM and 1 to LE BIZET.
Officers' Mess Cart and Maltese Cart to be at GUNNERS FARM by 9 p.m.

16. Officers Commanding Companies will see that Cookers are screened from view from the air, and as little smoke as possible allowed to issue from them.

17. Attention is called to instructions issued in 123rd Infantry Brigade letters A/1210 dated 10/8/16 and S.413 dated 10/8/16, passed to Company Commanders yesterday. These instructions are to be strictly complied with; also the necessary arrangements to be made for sentries to be provided with whistles to give warning of Aeroplanes and Hostile Artillery Fire. In the latter case all ranks will take cover in their allotted places.

18. Officers Commanding Companies will report to the Adjutant when their Companies are settled in their Billets, by runner.

F. R. Slessey
Capt.
11/8/16. Adjutant 10/Bn.Royal West Kent Regt.

Copy No.1. Filed.
2. War Diary.
3. C.O.
4. 2nd in Command.
5. 123rd Ingantry Brigade.
6. O.C. "A" Company.
7. O.C. "B" "
8. O.C. "C" "
9. O.C. "D" "
10. Machine Gun Offider.
11. Sniping Officer.
12. Signalling "
13. Transport "
14. Quartermaster.
15. O.C., Trench Mortar Battery.
16. O.C. 11th Bn. "The Queen's"
17. War Diary (Duplicate).
18. Medical Officer.
19.
20.

War Diary (Duplicate.)

SECRET. Copy No. 3 ....

10TH (S) BN. ROYAL WEST KENT RGT. - OPERATION ORDER NO. 13.

Reference Maps 27 and 36, 1/40,000.

1. The Battalion will be relieved by A. Battalion, 68th Infantry Brigade of the 23rd Division, and proceed to Reserve Billeting Area in accordance with the attached Time Table.

2. Dress: Marching Order. Water Bottles filled.

3. (a) The completion of Relief of each Company will at once be reported to the Adjutant at Battalion Headquarters, by runner.

(b) As each Company is relieved, platoons will move off at 200 yards interval, proceeding by the following route:-

> LE BIZET - CHAPELLE ROMPUE - Junction Main Road
> B.18.a. - OOSTHOVE FARM to junction road B.5.c. -
> West to B.15.b. - thence to main road junction
> ~~B.8.a. Road S.W. to B.7.d. thence main road~~
> ~~along road N.W. to Billets~~
> B.1.a. - Road S. to road junction B.1.c. thence main road to A.5.

(c) Distances to be strictly maintained.

(d) The 2nd in Command will be at the Head of the Column.

(e) The first Platoon to move off will form the "Advance Guard", and the last Platoon "Rear Guard".

Platoon Commanders will take precautions against observation by Hostile Aircraft, and be responsible for the protection of their Platoons.

The Machine Gun Section will march as such, in rear of the Column.

Snipers in front of the leading Platoon.

(f) Halts at 10 minutes to the Clock Hour, resuming march at Clock Hour exactly. Watches to be synchronised with the Adjutant's at 8 p.m. 16th inst. and 9 a.m. 17th inst.

4. The Telephone personnel of the Battalion will not move until 24 hours after the in-coming Unit has taken over.

Al Signalling Equipment in excess of Mobilization Equipment, i.e., Buzzers, Exchanges, Daylight Signalling Lamps, extra Telephones etc., will be regarded as Trench Stores and handed over to the in-coming Unit.

5. The Billeting Officer, with Billeting Party as under, will parade at Battalion Headquarters at 8 a.m. tomorrow and proceed to LA CRECHE to make all arrangements for billeting the Battalion.

> Captain F.A.Wallis.
> 2/Lieut. V.Holden.
> All Company Quartermaster Sergeants.
> Sergt. Mansfield "B" Company, and
> 1 other N.C.O. or man to be selected by
> Company Commanders from each Platoon.

These latter will act as Guides, and will be instructed to meet their Platoons at the CHURCH A.5.a. (sheet 36) and guide them to their Billets.

(Continued on Sheet 2)

6. Immediately on arrival at new Billets Officers Commanding Companies are held strictly responsible that adequate sanitary arrangements are made.

7. Officers and men when in billets or bivouac must always be ready to turn out at a moment's notice.

8. First Line Transport will move direct from its present lines to new billets. The Transport Officer will send a Guide to the Billeting Officer to ascertain where his new billets are situated, instructing the Guide where to meet him to conduct the Transport there. Cookers to be sent to Company new billets on arrival.

9. Officers' Baggage to be at Battalion Headquarters by 4 pm to-morrow, ready to be loaded in Transport.

(a) Transport Officer will send Baggage Wagons to Battalion Headquarters, and Officers' Mess Cart to each Company Mess, commencing at "B" Company at 7.30 p.m. and finishing at Battalion Headquarters Mess.

(b) Company Cookers, Watercarts and Baggage Wagons to be taken away to Transport Lines after teas to-morrow. All Cooks accompanying Cookers and acting as Baggage Guard to Transport.

10. (a) Rations for the 17th inst. will be taken by Quartermaster to LA CRECHE from Ration Dump, and will be issued to Companies on arrival at new Billets. Company Quartermaster Sergeants to report to Quartermaster immediately on arrival, with statement of numbers of Officers and Other Ranks, including all Specialists belonging to their Companies.

(b) Rations for the 18th will be drawn by Quartermaster from Ration Dump and will accompany the Battalion to Billets at MONT DES CATS, and will be issued on arrival. Company Quartermaster Sergeants will report to Quartermaster as above.

(c) Quartermaster to arrange for a supply of hot Tea for the Battalion on arrival at new Billets to-morrow night.

11. Officers Commanding Companies will have their Billets and surroundings thoroughly cleaned to-morrowready to be handed over to in-coming Unit scrupulously clean. A Certificate to this effect is to be handed to the Adjutant by ~~xxx~~ 8 p.m. to-morrow. The above also applies to to the Transport Officer respecting his lines.

12. Officers Commanding Companies will report to the Adjutant on arrival at new Billets, Present or otherwise.

13. The Billeting Officer, and Company Quartermaster Sergeants will proceed to MONT DES CATS on the 17th inst. parading at 6.30 a.m., to arrange the billeting of the Battalion at R.20.d.8.7. Sheet 27, 1/40,000.

14. The Battalion will march in the following order from Billeting Area on the 17th inst., time to be notified later:-

(Continued on Sheet 3.)

Sheet 3.

ADVANCE GUARD - 1 Platoon of "A" Company.

MAIN BODY - "A" Company less 1 Platoon.
"B" "
"C" "
"D" " less 1 Platoon.

REAR GUARD - 1 Platoon "D" Company.

Signallers and Snipers will march at head of Main Body.
Stretcher Bearers with their Companies.
LEWIS Rifle Gun Section in rear of Battalion.
Companies will move at 200 yards interval.
1st Line Transport 500 yards in rear of MAIN BODY.

15. The attention of all Officers is called to 41st Division Standing Orders.

[signature]
Captain.
15-8-16. Adjutant 10/Bn. Royal West Kent Regiment.

Copy No. 1. Filed.
2. War Diary.
3. " " (Duplicate).
4. O.C.
5. 2nd in Command.
6. O.C. "A" Company.
7. O.C. "B" "
8. O.C. "C" "
9. O.C. "D" "
10. Signalling Officer.
11. Transport Officer.
12. Lewis Rifle Gun Officer.
13. Sniping Officer.
14. Quartermaster.
15. Medical Officer.
16.
17.

MOVEMENT TABLE.

DATE	UNIT OF RELIEVING BRIGADE.	FROM	TO	UNIT OF 123rd INFANTRY BRIGADE.
Aug. 16th	A & B Battns 68th Inf.Bde.	STEENWERCK AREA.	LE BIZET & ARMENTIERES	10th R.W.Kent Regt. & 20th Durham L.I.
Aug. 17th	-	-	-	10th R.W.Kent Regt. & 20th Durham L.I.

FROM	TO	REMARKS.
LE BIZET & ARMENTIERES.	Bivouac in LA CRECHE AREA, Sheet 36,1/40,000 Squares A 3,4,5 & 6.	ARMENTIERES Battalion relief to be complete by 3 p.m. Battalion of 68th Brigade 23rd Div. not to pass Bde.H.Q. before 8.30 p.m.
LA CRECHE AREA	MONT DES CATS	10th R.W.Kent,Billets in R.20,d.8.7. 20th Durham L.I. Billets in R.32.d.7.2. Sheet 27 1/40,000

10TH BN. ROYAL WEST KENT REGT.

OPERATION ORDER NO. 14 - ADDENDUM.

Rations. The unexpended portion of the day's Ration for the 23rd August will be carried on the man, and Supply Wagons will be entrained loaded with Rations for the 24th August.

S E C R E T. Copy No. 2 War Diary

10TH BATTN. ROYAL WEST KENT REGT. - OPERATION ORDER NO. 14.

1. The Battalion will entrain on Wednesday the 23rd of August, 1916, at BAILLEUL MAIN Station for LONGPRE, according to the attached table.

2. Dress: Marching Order, Water Bottles filled.

3. (a) The train will consist of one Officers' Carriage, 14 Flat Trucks and 33 covered Trucks.
   (b) Each Flat Truck will take an average of 4 axles. Each covered truck will take 6 H.D.Horses, or 8 L.D.Horses or Mules, or 40 men.
   (c) No personnel or Stores will be allowed in the Brake vans at each end of the train.

4. (a) The Transport, including Supply and Baggage Wagons, and "A" Company will parade at 11 hours 30 minutes, and will arrive at the entraining Station three hours before the departure of the train, viz:- 14 hours 28 mins.
   (b) Battalion Signallers, Snipers, Lewis Gun Section, "B" "C" and "D" Companies will parade at 13 hours, and will arrive at the entraining Station 1½ hours before the departure of the train, i.e., 15 hrs. 58 mins. "B" and "C" Companies to be formed up in cross roads in front of "A" Company's Billets. "D" Company will join the Column passing their Billets. "B" Company will find 1 Platoon as Advance Guard and "D" Company 1 Platoon as Rear Guard.

5. (a) Officers Commanding Companies will render to the Adjutant by 9 a.m. on the 23rd inst. a complete Marching Out State of their Companies, including all Specialists, but not to include Transport and Grooms.
   (b) The Transport Officer will render a Marching Out State to the Adjutant by 9 a.m. on the 23rd inst. showing number of men (Transport and Grooms) Horses, 4 wheeled and 2 wheeled vehicles, including Lewis Gun Carts and Bicycles.
   (c) The Officer Commanding "A" Company will obtain a consolidated Marching out State for the Battalion from the Adjutant before marching off, and hand it to the R.T.O. at the station at BAILLEUL.
   (d) The Transport Officer must provide Breast ropes for Horse Trucks. These can be improvised from Picketing Ropes. The ropes for lashing vehicles on the Flat Trucks will be provided by the Railway.

6. The entrainment of the Battalion must be completed half an hour before the departure of the train, and no one is to be allowed to leave the train once the Battalion is entrained.

7. (a) At stopping places during the journey no Officer, N.C.O. or man is to be allowed to leave the train without permission of his Company Commander. This order is to be rigidly adhered to and thoroughly explained to all ranks. Severe disciplinary action will be taken with anyone who contravenes this order. No one is allowed to ride on the steps of the vehicles.
   (b) Pickets are to be detailed by the Officer Commanding "A" Company for the front of the train, and by the Officer Commanding "D" Company for the rear of the train, at all stops, to prevent troops leaving. The Provost Sergeant and two Police will also look out for the centre of the train.

(Continued on Page 2)

Sheet 2.

8. **Water Carts and Water Bottles to be full on entraining. The Quartermaster to indent for sufficient Petrol Tins to be entrained filled with water to allow of water bottles being filled at detraining station without drawing from the water carts.**

9. Station Platforms and Sidings are to be left clean. No waste paper, empty tins, etc. are to be thrown out of the train.

10. No Troops or Transport are to enter the Station Yard at BAILLEUL until permissionm is obtained from the R.T.O.
The Route is as follows:-

Route from Billets by same road to BAILLEUL as the Battalion came by, thence :
MARKET SQUARE.
Rue l'OCCIDENT
Rue de la GARE
to STATION.

11. Orders for Rations will be issued later.

Captain.
21-8-16. Adjutant 10/Bn.Royal West Kent Regt.

Copy No. 1 Filed.
2. War Diary.
3. War Diary (Duplicate)
4. O.C.
5. 2nd in Command.
6. O.C."A" Company.
7. O.C."B" "
8. O.C. C" "
9. O.C."D" "
10. Transport Officer.
11. Signalling Officer.
12. Lewis Gun Officer.
13. Sniping Officer.
14. Quartermaster.
15. Medical Officer.
16. 123rd Infantry Brigade.
17.
18.
19
20.

Type & No. of Train.	Entraining Station.	Unit.	Time of departure from entraining Station.	Date.	Detraining Station.
T.C.16.	BAILLEUL MAIN	10th R.W.Kent.	17.28	23-8-16	LONGPRE.

WAR DIARY
or
~~INTELLIGENCE SUMMARY~~
(Erase heading not required.)

Army Form C. 2118

Vol 5

Instructions regarding War Diaries and Intelligence Summaries are contained in F. S. Regs., Part II. and the Staff Manual respectively. Title Pages will be prepared in manuscript.

1-9-16 to 30-9-16.

10th BATTN ROYAL WEST KENT REGT.

Place	Date	Hour	Summary of Events and Information	Strength O	Strength OR	Casualties O	Casualties OR	Sick OR	Remarks and references to Appendices
BUSSUS BUSSUEL H.Q.	1 9/16		Normal.	38	817			2	
	2 9/16		Normal.	38	817			–	
"	3 9/16		Normal.	38	815			3	
"	4 9/16		Normal.	38	815			1	
"	5 9/16		Normal.	38	815			4	
"	6 9/16		Normal. Battalion proceeded by Route March to LONGPRE and entrained for MERICOURT, thence by Route March to BECORDEL, Map Reference:- Sheet 62D 1/40000 E.12.a.1.3. Two Officers joined: 2 Lieut. C. E. PHIPPS, 2 Lieut. N. W. AKHURST.	38	815			–	
BECORDEL	7 9/16		Normal. Draft of 50 men joined Battalion, transferred from Leicester Territorial Regt.	40	815			6	
"	8 9/16		Normal.	40	859			2	
"	9 9/16		Normal. Battalion moved from BECORDEL to FRICOURT CAMP, Map Reference by Route March.					1	
FRICOURT CAMP	10 9/16		Normal. Battalion proceeded by Route March to MONTAUBAN relieving 5th KINGS OWN LANCASHIRE REGT taking up position in Forward Area as Reserve. Map Reference: FRANCE. Sheet 57c S.W. 1/20,000. Headquarters S.27.b.5.0., "A" Coy. S.27.b.6.1., "B" Coy. S.27.b.7.5., "C" Coy. S.27.b.4.5., "D" Coy S.27.d.5.9. Reserve Specialists left behind with Transport. Officers joined: 2/Lt GADBAN V.J. 2/Lt RICHMOND A.S.	40	859			1	
MONTAUBAN	11 9/16		Normal. An Enterprise was carried out by "B" + "C" Companies, to construct six Strong Points 150 yards forward of Front Line (DELVILLE WOOD). This operation was successfully carried out, with one casualty.	42	859			2	
"	12 9/16		Normal. "C" Company were withdrawn, whilst "B" Coy. continued to occupy constructed work. At 7 pm Battalion proceeded to DELVILLE WOOD and relieved 23rd Middlesex Regt. Relief carried out successfully. Regiment on our Right 3/4th Battn South Lancs., on our Left 11th Queens Regt.	42	858			1	
DELVILLE WOOD	13 9/16		Normal. Continued in occupation. CASUALTIES: KILLED OR. 8. WOUNDED OR 17	42	851			–	

1875 Wt. W593/826 1,000,000 4/15 J.B.C. & A. A.D.S.S./Forms/C. 2118.

Instructions regarding War Diaries and Intelligence Summaries are contained in F. S. Regs., Part II. and the Staff Manual respectively. Title Pages will be prepared in manuscript.

WAR DIARY
or
~~INTELLIGENCE SUMMARY~~
(Erase heading not required.)

Army Form C. 2118

II

10th BATTn ROYAL WEST KENT REGT

Place	Date	Hour	Summary of Events and Information	Strength O	Strength OR	Casualties O	Casualties OR	Sick OR	Remarks and references to Appendices
DELVILLE WOOD	14 9/16		Normal. During the early hours of the morning the Battalion was relieved by the 10th Queens Regt. (124th Brigade) the Relief taking some considerable time owing to very heavy shell fire, the Relief not being complete until about 9 AM. Casualties 6 O.R. Battalion marched to POMMIERES REDOUBT.	42	897			-	
POMMIERES REDOUBT	15 9/16		At 12.30 am Battalion proceeded to take up position in YORK TRENCH as a Reserve Bn 41st Division to support an attack by 122nd + 124th Brigades on FLERS and GUEDECOURT. At 11 AM Battalion occupied CARLTON TRENCH, and at 1 pm moved across OPEN under Heavy Barrage, and finally reached its Objective in line, SWITCH TRENCH, SOUTH OF FLERS, with very few casualties. This position was held in defence of FLERS in case of counter attack. Officer casualties during day: Killed CAPT. H. H. LOGAN, Wounded: LIEUT-COLONEL A. WOOD MARTYN, MAJOR S. H. BEATTIE, and 2/LIEUT. A. W. EDMETT. The position was consolidated during the night. Heavy Shelling continued during the whole period. Regiment on our Left Flank 3rd New Zealanders, on our Right for a period 23rd Durham Light Infantry.	42	872			1	Appendix 15
SWITCH TRENCH	16 9/16		MAJOR W. F. SOAMES joined Battalion and took over Command. "A" + "C" Coys under 2/Lieut V. HOLDEN and 2/Lieut L. A. H. GINGELL respectively were ordered to reinforce position East of FLERS, but on receipt of Brigade Orders were withdrawn to original position, viz: SWITCH TRENCH. Battalion was then reorganized. Burial of dead, Salvage work, and consolidation of position was continued. Position heavily shelled.	42	871			-	
"	17 9/16		Continuation of work as per 16th. again heavily shelled. Casualties, Officers, Killed: 2/Lieut S. LAURENCE, 2/LIEUT. STONES., Wounded 2/Lieut A. S. F. PERCIVAL.	42	878			2	
"	18 9/16		About 3 AM. relieving unit, 1/10th LIVERPOOL SCOTTISH, arrived. Battalion relief completed by 5 AM. Casualties during relief - NIL. 9 AM. Battalion arrived at POMMIERES REDOUBT - Breakfasted. 11 AM. Battalion withdrew to Rest Camp at BECORDEL M R. Total Casualties during operations from 11-9-16 to 18-9-16 - KILLED O. 3 OR 16 WOUNDED O. 4 OR 71. MISSING OR. 7.	42	878			-	
BECORDEL	19 9/16		Rest, Training + reorganization.	35	878			2	

1875 Wt. W593/826 1,000,000 4/15 J.B.C. & A. A.D.S.S./Forms/C. 2118.

Instructions regarding War Diaries and Intelligence Summaries are contained in F. S. Regs., Part II. and the Staff Manual respectively. Title Pages will be prepared in manuscript.

WAR DIARY
or
INTELLIGENCE SUMMARY
(Erase heading not required.)

Army Form C. 2118.

111

10TH BATTN ROYAL WEST KENT REGT

Place	Date	Hour	Summary of Events and Information	Strength O	Strength OR	Casualties O	Casualties OR	Sick OR	Remarks and references to Appendices
BECORDEL	20 9/16		Inspection of Brigade by Divisional General who in a short address complimented the Battalion on the work done during recent operations. Rest, Training & Reorganization.	35	866			6	
"	21 9/16		" " " "	35	871			7	
"	22 9/16		" " " "	35	877			-	
"	23 9/16		" " " "	35	877			7	
"	24 9/16		" " " "	35	880			-	
"	25 9/16		" " " "	35	881			-	
"	26 9/16		" " " "	35	881			2	
"	27 9/16		At 6.30 pm Battalion proceeded by Route march to MONTAUBAN en route to FLERS & bivouaced for the night at POMMIERES REDOUBT.	35	880			2	
POMMIERES REDOUBT	28 9/16		At 1.30 pm Battn resumed march to FLERS via YORK TRENCH, halting at latter place until 8 pm. Battn relieving Loyal North Lancs. Regt. in FRONT LINE (Headquarters N.E. of FLERS). This operation was carried out successfully.	35	881			-	
N.E. of FLERS	29 9/16		Battalion continued in Occupation of FRONT LINE. At night an enterprise was carried out in conjunction with a working party from Pioneer Battn Middlesex Regt. to reconstruct FRONT LINE Trench. This operation was carried out successfully. During day the trenches were heavily shelled. Casualties:	35	881			-	
	30 9/16		Battn were relieved from FRONT LINE by 23rd Middlesex Regt. & withdrew to Reserve Trenches. "A" & "C" Coys. were relieved during daytime, "B" & "D" Coys. at night. Operation carried out successfully. Trenches heavily shelled both day & night.	35	880			-	

TOTAL CASUALTIES 28th to 30th inst.:- KILLED O. - O.R. 7. WOUNDED O. 1. O.R. 39. MISSING OR 5.

TOTAL REINFORCEMENTS during MONTH:

	OR
9th	50
14th	42
18th	75
22nd	7
27th	1
	175

[illegible] Major

COMDG. 10th (S) Bn. ROYAL WEST KENT REGT.

SECRET. Copy. No 1

QUIET. OPERATION ORDER No 21.

App 15

Reference Maps are:-

Special Map attached "A"

Trench Maps already issued.

LONGUEVAL 57c S.W. 3.

INFORMATION. 1. The 41st Division, in co-operation with other Divisions of the XV Corps is to attack and capture the enemy system of defences on its front on the 15th September (Z Day).

Other troops of the 4th army and French are co-operating.

The attack will be pushed home with the utmost vigour all along the line until the most distant objectives have been reached. For the last 2½ months we have been gradually wearing down the enemy. His moral is shaken, he has few, if any, fresh Reserves available, and there is every probability that a combined determined effort will result in a decisive victory.

The role of the 41st Division

is to capture the enemy's defences (including FLERS) up to & including the line Pt. N. 20. d. 5. 0. (exclusive) – N. 20. c. 3. 6. – Road Junction N. 25. b. 0. 6.

The 41st Division will be in the centre, with the 14th Div. on its right and the New Zealand Division on its left.

Dispositions & Stages of Attack. 2. The 124th & 122nd Infantry Brigades will be in the front line (124th Infantry Brigade on the Right). The 123rd Infantry Brigade will be in Divisional Reserve.

Each Infantry Brigade will have 1 Section R.E. from their affiliated Field Coys. R.E. attached.

The operations are divided into four (4) stages, and each line will be captured successively:–

1st Objective (Green Line)

The enemy's trenches 800 yards South of FLERS (SWITCH LINE), from junction with COCOA LANE (excl.) to junction with COFFEE LANE.

Infantry must follow behind the tanks, and should any Strong Point succeed in holding up the Infantry they will call for a tank to assist them. The Signal will be for "Enemy in sight", with the Rifle.

Each tank has an escort of 1 N.C.O. and 10 men, and should the tanks get in rear of the Infantry or for any reason be obliged to withdraw across ground over which infantry has passed, the escort will remove any wounded which happen to lie in the path of the tank. The escort will also protect the tank from close assault.

Should the tanks become out of action at any time and be unable to advance, (especially on the advance from FLERS TRENCH. to attack the village when the tanks are supposed to precede the Infantry by 15 minutes) the Infantry are on no account to wait for them, but will advance at the hour arranged for the

S. 6. c. 2.7. (excl:)
No halts will be made in TEA SUPPORT TRENCH.

2nd Objective, (Brown Line).
Enemy's trenches running S.E. on the S.W. and S. sides of FLERS. (FLERS LINE), from T.1.b.1.2 to M.36.d.3.4.

3rd Objective (Blue Line).
The village of FLERS and the line, Cross Roads N.31.b.4.0. – N edge of FLERS to Road Junction N.31.a.2.5. (excl:).

4th Objective (Red Line).
Establish line, N.20.d.5.0 (exclu:) – N.20.c.3.6. – Road Junction N.25.b.0.6. (Track excl).

The objectives in several cases consist of a double line of Trenches. Where this is the case the troops will be given the trench furthest away from us as their Objective, steps being taken to deal adequately with the intermediate trench.

ASSEMBLY. 3. 15. 9. 16. QUIET, YORK TRENCH. from S. 16. d. 0.5 to S. 16. d. 8.1. Hour of arrival at trenches 1.30 A.M. Hour by which relief is to be completed is 2·30

AVENUE of approach is FLARE LANE. Companies to march at 300 yards interval. Room is to be left on either side of Brigade Head Quarters in YORK TRENCH.

APPROACH AVENUES. 4. Allotted to 123rd Infantry Brigade:-

FLARE LANE
MILK LANE.

DIVIDING LINE 5. (a) Dividing Line between the Right of 124th Infantry Brigade and the Left Brigade 14th Division will be :-

The line Pt. S. 22. c. 9. 2, - S. 17. d. 9. 6. - thence COCOA LANE to its junction with SWITCH LINE - T. 1. d. 0. 2 (incl. to 14th Division) - Road junction T. 1. b. 1. 2. (incl. to 14th Division) - Road Junction N. 31. b. 4. 0. (incl. to 41st Division). Strong Pt.

N. 31. b. 5. 2. (incl. to 41st Div.) - Road junction N. 26. c. 4. 4. (incl. to 14th Div.) - Road Junction N. 26. a. 9. 1 (incl. to 14th Division) - Road Junction N. 21. c. 0. 6 (incl. to 14th Divn.)

(b) Dividing line between 124th Infantry Brigade and 122nd Infantry Brigade - S. 22. c. 8. 6. to cross roads S. 17. b. 3. 4. inclusive of FLARE LANE - thence via LONGUEVAL - FLERS ROAD to its junction at S. 6. b 9. 3. - T. 1. a. 4. 8 - N. 31. c 85. 45. - N. 31. b. 15. 15. - N. 31. b. 2. 6. thence along track to N. 20. c. 4. 4. (All incl. to 124th Inf. Bde.).

(c) Dividing Line between 122nd Infantry Brigade and the Right Brigade New Zealand Div:- S. 21. d. 8. 7. - Junction of Tracks at S. 16. d. 1. 6 - thence to S. 11. c. 0. 4. - S. 11. d. 0. 8. - Junction of PEACH. TRENCH and TEA TRENCH (incl. to 41st Div.) COFFEE LANE (incl. to N.Z. Div.) - M. 36. d. 3. 3. - Road junction at M.36.b.5.0. (incl. to N.Z. Div.) – Cross Roads at N.31.a. 2.5. (incl. to N.Z. Div.) – N.25.b. 0.6. (Track incl. to N.Z. Div.)

DIRECTING FLANK. 6. The Right of the 122nd Infantry Brigade will direct. General direction of attack 28° TRUE Bearing.

ARTILLERY. 7. The Divisional artillery will form creeping barrages as shown in APPENDIX.C. The attacking troops will advance immediately behind these barrages, and not more than 50 yards distance between waves.

HOUR OF ASSAULT. 8. At "ZERO" hour which will be notified later the 122nd and 124th Infantry Brigades advance. The 123rd Infantry Brigade will not move from its position of assembly until orders are received from Brigade Headquarters.

When orders are received to advance, units will

advance in artillery formations of Platoons. During the advance LONGUEVAL must be avoided as far as possible. Troops that have moved off their line of direction to pass LONGUEVAL must correct their direction as soon as they are clear of the village.

R.E. 9. 1 Section 233rd Field Coy. R.E. will be attached to the 10th Royal West Kent Regt. and will move with them.

~~TANKS 10 This Section will report at Brigade Headquarters at POMMIERS REDOUBT, at 8 pm 14th inst~~

TANKS. 10. TEN tanks, Heavy Section M. G. Corps, will co-operate in the attack.

The role of these tanks is to destroy the Hostile Machine Guns and Strong Points, and clear the way for the Infantry. They will usually precede the Infantry.

tanks in order that they may derive the benefit of the artillery barrage. This necessary action must be decided on by the officers in command of troops on the spot.

As soon as the final objective has been established the tanks will be withdrawn to a position South of LONGUEVAL to replenish.

The following signals will be used from tanks to Infantry and aircraft:—

FLAG Signals:-

RED FLAG = OUT OF ACTION.

GREEN FLAG = AM. ON OBJECTIVE.

Other flags are inter-tank signals

LAMP SIGNALS.

Series of "T's" = OUT OF ACTION

Series of "H's = AM ON OBJECTIVE.

Infantry must not wait for tanks that get behind time table.

OBJECTIVES & RATE OF ADVANCE.

11. The successive objectives are given in para 2. The advance will be carried out

in accordance with the attached time table.

ORGANIZATION OF BATTn 12. (1). The Battalion will parade at 12 midnight 14/15th and march to YORK TRENCH. Companies to march with 300 yards interval in the following order:- A. B. C. D. Battalion Bombers, 4 Lewis Guns under Lt. Tennyson Smith, Battalion Headquarters.

DRESS. (2) Fighting Order, 2 Sandbags, 2 Bombs, Mills, Every 3rd man to carry pick or shovel, each man to carry 170 rounds S.A.A. In addition to the 170 rounds carried above, each Company Commander detail 40 men to carry an extra bandolier. Water bottles are to be filled.

WATER (3) O.C. 'C' Coy. will detail a carrying party of 25 men to carry two full Petrol tins of water, Men are to be warned that water will be very scarce. Above men to follow the rear company.

DUMPS. 13. O.C. "C" Coy. will detail 6 men to report to Lt Deacon 20th D.L.I. at Brigade Head Quarters at 6 pm the 14th inst. who will take them to GREEN LANE Dump where they will be used as a carrying party when the Brigade advances.

CLEARING UP. 14. Each Company will detail a "Mopping Up" Party of 1 Officer & 20 men. Each man of this party will carry 1 "P" Grenade.

CONSOLIDATION. 15. Each objective will be consolidated as soon as possible after its capture, and made secure against counter attack.

COMMUNICATION TRENCHES. 16. O.C. 'D' Coy. will tell off a special party of 1 Officer + 50 O.R. to dig communication between our front line + the German lines if required.

VICKERS. GUNS. 17. 2 Vickers guns will be attached to the Battalion. O.C. "A" Coy. will detail 4 men to each Vickers Gun to carry ammunition.

LEWIS GUNS. 18. 1 with each Company, 4 in Battalion Reserve.

BOMBS. 19. The 2 Mills Bombs carried by each man are to be looked upon as a reserve for the use of Bombing Squads, and are to be dumped & collected in each line gained. Each Coy. will detail 2 Bombing Squads. Each Bombing Squad will carry 2 Buckets or Sandbags full of Bombs.

ROCKETS. 20. 6 Blue Rockets for S.O.S. will be with Battalion Hd. Qrs.

COMMUNICATION WITH AEROPLANES. 21. Every Officer & N.C.O. and 50 men per Coy. will carry 2 Red flares. These are to be lighted in the front line only, at intervals of 20 yards on gaining the line of each objective, as soon as the contact aeroplane appears (or calls for flares on the KLAXON horn) and again at 2 pm and 5 pm on Z DAY. (15th September) and at 7 am on the day following Z day 16th September. Panels & lamps will also be frequently used to report the situation.

VISUAL SIGNALLING & RUNNING.

22. Full use is to be made of Visual Signallers and runners, which may become the only available means of communication.

(a) Visual Signalling. Messages may be handed in for despatch at the under mentioned Visual Stations:-

S. 18. c. 1. 9.
S. 16. b. 5. 2
S. 16. d. 6. 1
S. 24. b. 3. 0.
POMMIERS REDOUBT.

(b). Runners relay posts have been constructed at intervals of 300 yards in FLARE and MILK LANES.

Note: If other means fail runners must be employed at whatever cost.

MEDICAL. 23. ADVANCED Dressing Station - THE QUARRY S. 22. c. 2. 6.
Divl. Collecting Station - F.6. a. 2. 0, MAMETZ - MONTAUBAN ROAD.

PRISONERS OF WAR. 24. Will be brought back to the nearest Stragglers Post. Escort 10% sufficient. Corps Cage at F.6. c (Map 62d).

TRANSPORT. 25. 1st Line Transport will be located F. 2. c. and d.

WATCHES. 26. Synchronised at 5 AM on the 15th inst.

REPORTS. 27. Reports to be sent to Battalion H.Q.s as frequently as possible. Brigade require reports from Battalion every hour

Copy No 1. Filed
2.
3. } War Diary
4. O.C. A Coy
5. O.C. B "
6. O.C. C "
7. O.C. D "
8.

14/9/16

[signature]
Capt & Adjt
QUIET.

10th S. Bn. Royal West Kent Regt [illegible] Sheet I

173/4

Army Form C. 2118

Vol 6

Instructions regarding War Diaries and Intelligence Summaries are contained in F. S. Regs., Part II. and the Staff Manual respectively. Title Pages will be prepared in manuscript.

WAR DIARY
or
INTELLIGENCE SUMMARY
(Erase heading not required.)

Place	Date	Hour	Summary of Events and Information	Remarks and references to Appendices
[illegible]	[illegible]	[illegible]	[illegible] relieved from Reserve Trenches [illegible] Middlesex Regt (12th Division) [illegible] to [illegible] MONTAUBAN [illegible] Strength 36 [illegible]	
MONTAUBAN	[illegible]		Situation normal. Divisional rest & training. [illegible] Officers [illegible] 2/Lt [illegible] Clemens, 2/Lt [illegible] Morris, 2/Lt J.M. [illegible] Strength 38 off. 831 O.R.	
	[illegible]		Situation normal. Battalion moved forward to South of MAMETZ WOOD [illegible] S19c. Bayonets [illegible] Strength 30 off. 831 O.R.	
S. of MAMETZ WOOD	[illegible]		Situation normal. Operation postponed [illegible]. Divisional rest & training. Strength 30 off. 831 O.R. Casualties [illegible]	
	[illegible]		Situation normal. Divisional rest and training. Strength 30 off. [illegible] O.R.	
	[illegible]		Situation normal. Divisional rest and training. Strength 30 off. [illegible] O.R.	
	[illegible]		Situation normal. Battalion moved forward as per [illegible] Order [illegible] App. I
[illegible]			At night Battalion advanced to BIRD TRENCH [illegible] 15th Bn. HANTS Regt [illegible] and assisted in construction of [illegible] front line. Strength [illegible]	
	[illegible]		Continuation of work. During the night Battalion [illegible] Trench. [illegible] Strength [illegible] Casualties [illegible]	
	[illegible]		Situation normal. Continuation of work. Strength 30 off. [illegible] Casualties [illegible]	
	[illegible]		Situation normal. Continuation of work. During the night [illegible] Battalion was relieved by 15th Bn. Liverpool Regt and returned to Camp S. of MAMETZ WOOD. [illegible] S16c. [illegible] carried successful. During [illegible] from 7th to 11th [illegible] total casualties [illegible] Batt.	

1875 Wt. W593/826 1,000,000 4/15 J.B.C. & A. A.D.S.S./Forms/C. 2118.

continued on Sheet II

10th (S) Bn Royal West Kent Regt

WAR DIARY
or
INTELLIGENCE SUMMARY
(Erase heading not required.)

Sheet II

October 1916

Army Form C. 2118

Instructions regarding War Diaries and Intelligence Summaries are contained in F. S. Regs., Part II. and the Staff Manual respectively. Title Pages will be prepared in manuscript.

Place	Date	Hour	Summary of Events and Information	Remarks and references to Appendices
[illegible]	[illegible]		[illegible] Strength 38 – [illegible]	
			[illegible]	
			[illegible] Strength [illegible]	
	[illegible]		[illegible]	
	[illegible]		[illegible] for [illegible] [illegible] BILLETS	[illegible]
[illegible]	[illegible]		[illegible]	
			[illegible] Divisional Commander and [illegible]	
			[illegible]	
	[illegible]		[illegible]	
	[illegible]		[illegible] OISEMONT [illegible]	[illegible]
	[illegible]		[illegible] CITERNES to. [illegible]	
	[illegible]	[illegible]	[illegible]	
[illegible]	[illegible]	[illegible]	[illegible]	
	[illegible]		[illegible]	
	[illegible]	[illegible]	[illegible]	[illegible]

1875 Wt. W593/826 1,000,000 4/15 J.B.C. & A. A.D.S.S./Forms/C. 2118.

10th S. Bn Royal West Kent Regt   **WAR DIARY** *or* **INTELLIGENCE SUMMARY**   Sheet III   October 1916   **Army Form C. 2118**

Instructions regarding War Diaries and Intelligence Summaries are contained in F. S. Regs., Part II. and the Staff Manual respectively. Title Pages will be prepared in manuscript.

(Erase heading not required.)

Place	Date	Hour	Summary of Events and Information	Remarks and references to Appendices
ALBERTA CAMP	[illegible]/10/16		Situation normal. Battalion moved off at 3PM and marched to DICKEBUSCH. Map Ref. BELGIUM Sheet 28 N.W. H28c7.1 relieving 50th Batt. Australian Infantry Regt. taking up position in Reserve to 123 Brigade APP V. Strength O. 37 O.R. 531 B, C & D Companies billeted in DICKEBUSCH. A Co at VOORMEZEELE.	APP V
DICKEBUSCH	[illegible]/10/16		Situation Normal. B, C & D Companies finding fatigue parties for various Dumps and Trenches. A Co. being employed at VOORMEZEELE in reconstruction of Dug outs and Trenches. Strength O. 37 O.R. 533 Evacuated O.R. 3	
"	[illegible]/10/16		Situation Normal. Continuation of work. Strength O. 37 O.R. 531 Evacuated O.R. 3 Two Military Medals awarded to A Co. of Battalion	
"	26/10/16		Situation normal. Continuation of work. Strength O. 37 O.R. 533	
"	27/10/16		Situation normal. Continuation of work. Strength O. 37 O.R. 534	
"	28/10/16		Situation normal. Continuation of work. Strength O. 37 O.R. 537	
"	29/10/16		Situation normal. Continuation of work. 1 Officer wounded 2Lt Gadban V.J. Strength O. 37 O.R. 537.	
"	30/10/16		Situation normal. The Battalion were relieved by the 15th Bn Kings Royal Rifles and withdrew to CHIPPEWA CAMP Map Ref. M6a1.7. APP VI. The Operation was carried out successfully. Strength O. 35 O.R. 537	APP VI
CHIPPEWA CAMP	31/10/16		Situation normal. Rest and Training. Strength O. 35 O.R. 537.	

1/XI/16   S. R. Stoney [signature] Major
~~LIEUT.-COLONEL~~
COMDG. 10th (S) Bn. ROYAL WEST KENT REGT.

1875 Wt. W593/826 1,000,000 4/15 J.B.C. & A. A.D.S.S./Forms/C. 2118.

War Diary App. 1

S E C R E T.

QUIET - WARNING ORDER.

1. The 122nd and 124th Brigades will attack the positions of GIRD & GIRD SUPPORT Trenches in front of them on October 7th 1916. Zero hour will be notified later.

2. The 123rd Brigade will be in Divisional Reserve.

3. The 10th Royal West Kent Regt. will move into SWITCH TRENCH early on the morning of October 7th ,and will be prepared to move forward into FLERS SUPPORT Trench if the 11th Queen's are called on to support either of the Brigades in the Front Line.

4. Each man will carry two Bombs and one extra Bandolier S.A.A., and will further carry a second Bandolier or an extra three Bombs, and four Sandbags.

Mopping Up Parties will carry two "P" Bombs in place of two of these extra Bombs.

5. Men will carry a Pick or a shovel - 1 Pick to 3 Shovels.

6. Each man will carry one day's rations in addition to his Iron Ration.

7. 25 cans of Water per Company will be carried, and dumped at Company Headquarters in SWITCH TRENCH.

6/10/16.

[signature] 2/Lieut.
a/Adjutant, QUIET.

LIAISON OFFICER. 2/Lieut. HOLDEN will proceed with Battalion as Liaison Officer. He will remain with his Unit until it is in position, and will then report the situation to Brigade Headquarters not later than 2 p.m.

RECONNAISANCE. All routes forward to Front Line will be reconnoitred by 10th Royal West Kent Regt.

WATER. 25 Petrol Tins of water will be carried per Company, with an additional 10 in the Battalion for Battalion Headquarters.

RATIONS. The remaining portion of the day's rations to be carried on the man.

TRANSPORT. The Transport Officer will be at "THISTLE DUMP" at 8.15 a.m. tomorrow, with necessary Tools, Ammunition, Water, Flares and Bombs, as arranged this evening.
Companies will make up their full complement from this supply at "THISTLE DUMP".

MISCELLANEOUS. Officers' Baggage and Packs of Other Ranks proceeding into action to be stacked outside Headquarters by 7 a.m.
Breakfast at 6.30 a.m.
O.C. Companies will report to the Adjutant by 7.45 a.m. that their Company Lines are left in a state of cleanliness.

H. Cowes, 2/Lieut.
A/Adjutant 10th Royal West Kent Regt.

Issued through runners at 7.35 pm 6/10/16.

Copy No. 1. Filed.
2.
3. O.C. "A" Coy.
4. O.C. "B" "
5. O.C. "C" "
6. O.C. "D" "
7. War Diary.
8. " " duplicate.

App 1

S E C R E T.   Copy No...8...

10TH BN. ROYAL WEST KENT RGT. - OPERATION ORDER NO. 84.

Reference Maps: Sheet 57^{C} S.W. 1/20,000.
GUEUDECOURT to BAPAUME 1/10,000

INFORMATION. At ZERO hour, 7th October 1916, the offensive will be continued by the Fourth Army.
The Divisional Commander intends to carry out the attack on a Two Brigade Front, the 124th Infantry Brigade on the right, and the 122nd Infantry Brigade on the left.
The 123rd Infantry Brigade will be in Divisional Reserve.

DISPOSITION The 10th Bn. Royal West Kent Regt. will leave its present bivouacs at 8 a.m. to take up its position in SWITCH TRENCH.
Dress: Fighting Order, with Great Coats "en Banderole".
Route: Same as reconnoitred by Officers on the 6th inst.
All movements N. of SWITCH TRENCH must be made by Communication Trenches by day.

VICKERS GUNS. Two Vickers Guns will be attached to the Battalion

BRIGADE H.Q. 123rd Infantry Brigade Headquarters will be at CARLTON TRENCH, to whichall Battalion Reports must be sent.

BATTALION H.Q. Battalion Headquarters will be in SWITCH TRENCH, to whichall Company reports must be sent.

BOMBS & S.A.A. Each Man will carry 4 Bombs and 2 Bandoliers of S.A.A. in addition to 120 rounds.

FLARES. Yellow Flares will be taken by the Battalion in boxes ready for issue to every Officer, N.C.O. and 50 men per Company. These are to be lighted in FRONT LINE ONLY on reaching its objective, and at 4 p.m. and 6 p.m. 7th October, and 7 a.m. 8th Octr.

RUNNERS PORTS. Battalion Signal Officer will arrange for Runner Posts (if necessary) between Battalion Headquarters and Company Headquarters. These Posts are to be clearly marked and their exact positions communicated to Battalion Headquarters.

SIGNAL STATIONS. The Signal Officer will establish a Signal Station at Battalion Headquarters, where the C.O. or his representative will always be.

DRESSING STATION. The Regimental Aid Post will be in SWITCH TRENCH from which point wounded will be evacuated.

WATCHES. All Watches will be synchronised by Brigade Signal Officer at 9.30 a.m. and 1.30 p.m. on the 7th inst.

HOUR OF ZERO. Communicated later.

REPORTS. The Situation Report will be sent by O.C. Companies to Battalion Headquarters as soon as possible after ZERO hour, and every hour afterwards. Important events will be communicated at once.

App II

Battalion Warning Order.

8.15 p.m. 12.X.16.

---

1. The Bn. will hold itself in readiness to proceed by train to DERNANCOURT at 8.30 a.m. tomorrow, Friday, 13th inst.

2. Reveille will be at 5 a.m. Breakfasts at 6 a.m.

3. All Officers' Baggage and Regimental Baggage will be stacked outside Bn. Headquarters by 7 a.m.

4. Blankets will be carried on the man.

5. The Lines must be thoroughly cleaned before departure, and a report rendered by Company Commanders to the Adjutant that this has been done, at 8.15 a.m.

6. Coy.Qr.Mr.Sgts. will see that the rations for the day are done up by Platoons after breakfast. They will be carried in sandbags by men of the Platoons.

7. The time of parade will be notified later.

8. An exact marching out state, shewing numbers of Officers and other ranks who are proceeding, will be rendered to the adjutant by 7 a.m.

(sd) F. Cozens, 2/Lt.
A/Adjutant 10th Royal West Kent Regiment.

BATTALION ORDER NO. 27.

1. The Battalion will entrain to-day at EDGEHILL Station at 14.00 hours.

2. The Battalionwill parade on Battalion Parade Ground ready to move off at 12 noon. Only personnel, packs and Lewis Gun handcarts will be entrained.

3. A picquet will be detailed at each end of the train to prevent men getting out when the train is at a standstill.

4. 2/Lieut. V. HOLDEN will meet the Battalion at the detraining Station and conduct it to the billets.

5. Two Motor Ambulances will meet the Battalion at the detraining Station to pick up any sick.

6. Billets must be left scrupulously clean, and a certificate to this effect will be rendered to the Adjutant at 11.45 a.m.

7. Acknowledge.

(sd) F. Cozens. 2/Lt.
17/10/16. A/Adjutant, 10th Bn. Royal West Kent Rgt.

APP. III/a

S E C R E T. Copy No....8/....

10TH BN. ROYAL WEST KENT REGT. - ORDER NO. 28.

The Battalion will move by rail from the 4th Army Area on the 19th October 1916, in accordance with the undermentioned instructions.

1. Entraining Station PONT REMY.

2. The Battalion will parade, ready to proceed, at 10 p.m. on the 19/10/1916, as under:-

"A" Company leading - head of column on Cross Roads near Church, followed by,

"B" Company.

"C" Company - head of column on Cross Roads S.W. of Church, followed by,

"D" Company, less 1 Officer and 50 Other Ranks.

3. Dress:- Marching Order.

4. Hour of entrainment - 2.38 a.m., 20/10/1916.

5. Rations: To be carried on the man for the 20th inst.

Rations for the 21st inst. will be carried on the Supply Wagons of the Train which accompanies the Battalion.

Rations for the 22nd inst. on the Supply Column.

6. On no account are men to leave the train after it has once started.

"A" Company will detail a picquet for one end of the train, and "D" Company for the other.

7. An Entraining State will be handed to the R.T.O. at the Station by the Adjutant.

8. Baggage. Officers' Baggage to be stacked outside Company Headquarters, ready for loading, at 4 p.m.

Officers' Mess Cart will call for Mess Utensils at 8 p.m. (It is essential that these be ready for loading at this time).

9. Transport & Machine Gun Section parade at 9 p.m. , and proceed to PONT REMY under their respectiveOfficers. They sould arrive at the Station 3 hours before the train is timed to start.

2/Lieut. G. P. Couch and 50 Other Ranks of "D" Company will report to the Transport Officer at 8.45 p.m., and will proceed with the Transport to assist in entrainment.

10. Miscellaneous. Water Bottles to be filled at 7 p.m.

Transport to take a supply of water for the Battalion in case of necessity.

Billets to be left scrupulously clean.

O. C. Companies will reportto the Adjutant at 10 p.m.

that all are present and ready to march off.

11. Acknowledge.

F. Cozens 2/Lieut.

19th Octr. 1916. a/Adjt. 10 Bn. Royal West Kent Rgt.

Copies issued to:.

O.C. "A" Company.	No. 1
O.C. "B" "	2
O.C. "C" "	3
O.C. "D" "	4
Quartermaster.	5
Transport Officer.	6
War Diary.	7
War Diary (duplicate)	8.

App IV

SECRET. Copy No. 7.....

10TH BN. ROYAL WEST KENT REGT. - ORDER NO. 29.

1. The Battalion will move to ALBERTA CAMP at Map 28, M.5.a.5.3. to-morrow morning, by Route March, via GODEWAERSVELDE.

2. "A" Company will find an advance Guard of 1 Platoon.

Remainder of "A" Company will be ready to pass the Turning into Headquarters at 7.30 a.m.

"B" Company will follow in rear of "A" Company.

"C" and "D" Companies will be ready to join the Battalion as it passes

Headquarters Section will march in rear of "C" Coy.

Transport will march in rear of Battalion.

"D" Company will find a Rear Guard of 1 Platoon.

3. Officers' Kits and Company Stores must be stacked at Company Headquarters ready for collection at 6.30 a.m.

4. The Officers' Mess Cart will call at "A" Company Headquarters at 7 a.m. , "B" Company at 7.5 a.m., "C" Coy. at 7.10 a.m., "D" Company at 7.15 a.m. Headquarters at 7.20 a.m.

5. Billets are to be left scrupulously clean.

6. Breakfasts at 6 a.m. Cookers to be withdrawn at 6.30 a.m.

[signature] 2/Lieut.

22/10/16. A/Adjt. 10th Bn.Royal West Kent Rgt.

Copy No. 1 to O.C. "A" Coy.
2 " O.C. "B" "
3 " O.C. "C" "
4 " O.C. "D" "
5 " Transport Officer.
6 " Quartermaster.
7 " War Diary.
8 " " " (duplicate).

app 5

S E C R E T. Copy No.........

10TH BN. ROYAL WEST KENT REGT. - ORDER NO. 30.

The Battalion will relieve the 50th Bn. Australian Infantry Regiment, as Reserve Battalion of the Brigade, to-morrow.

1. The Battalion will move off "A" "B" "C" "D" Companies by ½ Platoons at 300 yards interval. Connection will be kept by dropping connecting files.

2. "A" Company will move off at 3 p.m. to-morrow, to arrive at Battalion Headquarters DICKEBUSCH, at 5 p.m. They will relieve "A" Company, 50th Australian Infantry, at VOORMEZEELE.

"B" "C" and "D" Companies will be billetted in DICKEBUSCH.

"B" Company will occupy billets to be arranged by O.C. "B" Company.

"C" and "D" Companies will take over billets from "C" and "D" Companies, 50th Australian Infantry.

3. The route (which may be obtained from the Adjutant) will be reconnoitred by 1 Officer per Company, with 1 Guide per Platoon.

4. O.C. Companies, with their Company Sergeant Majors, will proceed to Headquarters of Companies of 50th Australian Infantry, to arrive at or before 3 p.m, and will prepare A.F.W.3405 in duplicate.

5. Lieut. Hinds, and Signallers of "A" Coy. and Headquarters, will proceed to relieve Signallers of 50th Australian Infantry, to arrive not later than 12.30 p.m.

6. Lieut. J.A. Tennyson-Smith, and Lewis Gunners of "A" Coy. will accompany Signallers of "A" Company, and will leave Handcarts in Archway at Battalion Headquarters in DICKEBUSCH.

7. Transport and Quartermaster's Stores will proceed to new lines at "MICMAC".
Cookers will be sent after dark to "B" "C" and "D" Coys. in DICKEBUSCH.
"A" Company dixies will go up to VOORMEZEELE WITH RATIONS AFTER dark.

8. Rations for day following will come up after dark.

9. Completion of relief will be reported by runner to Battn. Headquarters in DICKEBUSCH, and A.F.W.3405 will be rendered.

10. A return shewing numbers of STROMBOS Horns and Cylinders and their condition, will be rendered by 11 a.m. 24th Octr.

(sd) F. COZENS. 2/Lt.
22/10/16. a/Adjt. 10th Bn. Royal West Kent Rgt.

Secret

War Diary

Copy 1

Battalion Operation Orders No 31

The Bn: will be relieved by "DEVOTION to-morrow the 30th relief commencing at 9 a.m.

1. Coys will be ready to hand over & move off at 9 a.m. All men will be kept inside their billets until the relieving platoon arrives.

2. As soon as platoons are relieved they will proceed via:- HALLEBAST CORNER to CHIPPEWA CAMP (Route as previously reconnoitred) MAP REFERENCE M.6.a 1.7.

3. A list of stores etc to be handed over will be made out in duplicate & a receipt obtained for the Stores. The duplicate list will be handed in to Battalion Hd. Qrtrs; on arrival in Camp. Gum Boots must be handed over in a clean condition.

4. All Billets, dug-outs etc vacated by the Battalion must be left scrupulously clean.

5. Quartermaster & C.Q.M. Sgts. will proceed to CHIPPEWA CAMP at 7 am. & take over their respective billets. Sergt Andrews will also proceed & take over Hd: Qrtrs Billets.

6. All Baggage of "B", "C", & "D" Coys: will be ready for loading outside Coy: Hd: Qrtrs; at 8.30 a.m. including Officers' Mess Utensils.

The Transport Officer will arrange to have a G.S. Wagon & Officers' Mess Cart at "D" Coy's Hd Qrtrs at that time, & commence collecting & finish up at Head Quarters.

Arrangements for moving Qtr: Mstrs' Stores will be made by the Quartermaster.

The Cooker will be taken away at 8.30 am & proceed to CHIPPEWA CAMP. Dinners to be ready on arrival of Battalion "A" COY. All Baggage except Dixies, will be collected by Transport Officer on the night of the 29th inst. Dixies of this Coy will be carried as far as the Q.M. Stores DICKEBUSCH by the men & then handed over to Qrtr Mstr. for removal to CAMP.

7. Signallers will be relieved under arrangements to be made by Lieut G.T. Hinds with the relieving Unit.

8. Blankets will be ~~handed~~ carried on the man.

9. Completion of relief will be reported by O.C. Coys to the Adjt. at Bn: Hd. Qrtrs. DICKEBUSCH.

10. Rations "A" Coy will make their own arrangements about carrying to-morrows rations. The remainder of the Coy's rations for "B" "C" & "D" Coys will be carried on the Cooker.

Copy 1 "A" COY
2 "B"
3 "C"
4 "D"
5 WAR DIARY

No 6 War DIARY (dup)
7 QRTR: MSTR:
8 TRANSPORT OFFR
9 HD. QRTR: COPY.

J Cox Lieut
Adjt

2/Lieut BLOOD

Instructions regarding War Diaries and Intelligence Summaries are contained in F. S. Regs., Part II. and the Staff Manual respectively. Title Pages will be prepared in manuscript.

10th Royal West Kent Regt

WAR DIARY
or
INTELLIGENCE SUMMARY
(Erase heading not required.)

November 1916

Sheet 1

Vol 7

Army Form C. 2118

Place	Date	Hour	Summary of Events and Information	Remarks and references to Appendices
CHIPPEWA CAMP [illegible]	1/11		Situation normal, Rest and Training, Improvement of Camp. Strength 35 OR 833	
	2/11		Strength 35 OR 833	
	3/11		Situation normal, Battalion moved forward and relieved 15th Bn Hampshire Regt in the Centre Sub-sector of the 123rd Brigade this operation was carried out successfully, no casualties. Strength 35 OR 833	APP I
[illegible]	4/11	[illegible]	Situation normal, Patrols out night 4/5th [illegible] nothing unusual, About 3.30 PM Our Artillery bombarded Enemy's trenches, Enemy's Artillery retaliated with Whiz bangs & [illegible] shells also [illegible] trench mortars this continued for about two hours, Direct hits were observed on Enemy's front line, Our Parapet slightly damaged. Casualties wounded 4 O.R. Strength 35 OR 829	
	5/11		Situation normal, Enemy quiet, Casualties [illegible] Strength 35 OR 827	
	6/11		Situation normal, [illegible] Battalion relief in front line [illegible] APP II the operation was carried out successfully	APP II
		11 AM	Our artillery retaliated to Enemy's whiz-bangs, Machine Guns active during night. Patrols out but report nothing unusual.	
		11 PM	Enemy bombarded front line with whiz-bangs and Trench Mortars, Company Commander [illegible] retaliation, bombardment ceased at 11.40 PM, Parapet slightly damaged. [illegible] for bombardment the night quiet. Strength 35 OR 827	
	7/11	3 AM	Situation normal, 3 AM hostile [illegible] party observed, Lewis Gunners fired and dispersed party, Groans were heard. During the day three enemy periscopes smashed by our Snipers. Casualties wounded 1 O.R. Strength 35 OR 826	
	8/11		During early hours of morning the water rose in the trenches, flooding the dug-out of [illegible] In the forenoon Enemy sent over [illegible] shells many bursting in the vicinity of [illegible] Orders were received to withdraw [illegible] to Dressing Station (APP III). Patrols out during night report nothing unusual, Situation generally quiet. Casualties wounded 1 O.R. Strength 35 OR 825	APP III
	9/11	11.40 AM	Situation normal, Battalion were relieved by 15th Bn H. R. R. (APP IV) this operation was carried out successfully. Battalion on Relief marched to Chippewa Camp [illegible] Casualties killed 1 O.R. Strength 35 OR 836	APP IV

1875 Wt. W593/826 1,000,000 4/15 J.B.C. & A. A.D.S.S./Forms/C. 2118.

10th Royal West Kent Regt

WAR DIARY
or
INTELLIGENCE SUMMARY
(Erase heading not required.)

November 1916 — Sheet II

Army Form C. 2118

Instructions regarding War Diaries and Intelligence Summaries are contained in F. S. Regs., Part II. and the Staff Manual respectively. Title Pages will be prepared in manuscript.

Place	Date	Hour	Summary of Events and Information	Remarks and references to Appendices
CHIPPEWA CAMP	10/11/16		Situation normal, Rest, Training and improvement of Camp for winter Quarters. Evacuated 2 O.R. Strength 35 O. 834 O.R.	
	11/11/16		" " Strength 35 O. 834 O.R.	
M.R. M.6.a.4.7.	12/11/16		Battalion inspected by Corps Commander, presentation of Medal Ribbons to those awarded medals. Casualties Wounded 1 O.R. Evacuated 13 O.R. Strength 36 O. 820 O.R.	
	13/11/16		Situation normal, Rest & Training. Evacuated 2 O.R. Strength 35 O. 818 O.R.	
	14/11/16		" " " " Evacuated 3 O.R. Strength 35 O. 815 O.R.	
	15/11/16		" " " " 2/Lt Percival arrived. Strength 36 O. 818 O.R.	
	16/11/16		Battalion moved forward and relieved 15th Bn Hampshire Regt as Reserve Battalion Left sub-sector (as per APP V) Hd Qrs, A & C Company's DICKEBUSCH, "B" Co near the School VOORMEZEELE, "D" Co in CONVENT AREA VOORMEZEELE. This operation was carried out successfully. Strength 36 O. 818 O.R.	APP V
DICKEBUSCH Belgium Map S.28 N.28.c.1.	17/11/16		Situation normal, Battalion employed as working party, i.e. Construction and repairing of Trenches and carrying material to FRONT LINE. Strength 36 O. 818 O.R.	
	18/11/16		Situation normal. Strength 36 O. 818 O.R.	
	19/11/16		" " Evacuated 12 O.R. Strength 36 O. 806 O.R.	
	20/11/16		" " Strength 36 O. 806 O.R.	
	21/11/16		Enemy active with Artillery in vicinity of VOORMEZEELE & SCOTTISH WOOD. Lt Peacock wounded. Evacuated 3 O.R. Strength 35 O. 803 O.R.	
	22/11/16		Situation normal. Strength 35 O. 803 O.R.	
	23/11/16		Situation normal. Battalion was relieved by 18th K.R.R. (as per APP VI) This operation was carried out successfully and completed by about 3 p.m., Battalion marched to CHIPPEWA CAMP M.R. M.6.a.4.7. taking up old Quarters. During relief, Enemy bombarded vicinity of VOORMEZEELE, but no casualties. Strength 35 O. 804 O.R.	APP VI
CHIPPEWA CAMP	24/11/16		Rest and Training, working party's found for R.E. works. Evacuated 8 O.R. Strength 35 O. 796 O.R.	
	25/11/16		" " " Draft of 1 Officer & 27 O.R. joined Battn. Strength 36 O. 791 O.R.	
	26/11/16		" " Strength 36 O. 824 O.R.	
	27/11/16		" " Evacuated 4 O.R. Strength 36 O. 820 O.R.	

1875 Wt. W593/826 1,000,000 4/15 J.B.C. & A. A.D.S.S./Forms/C. 2118.

16th Royal West Kent Regt

Instructions regarding War Diaries and Intelligence Summaries are contained in F. S. Regs., Part II. and the Staff Manual respectively. Title Pages will be prepared in manuscript.

WAR DIARY
or
INTELLIGENCE SUMMARY
(Erase heading not required.)

November 1916

Sheet III

Army Form C. 2118

Place	Date	Hour	Summary of Events and Information	Remarks and references to Appendices
CHIPPEWA CAMP	22/11/16		Situation normal. The Battalion relieved 15th Hampshire Regt in the centre portion of the left sub-sector. H Elev sub sector, this operation was carried out successfully. H.Qrs at DRESSING STN. VOORMEZEELE, D Co & 2 Platoons of B Co in FRONT LINE. "A" Co and 2 Platoons B Co in OLD FRENCH TRENCH, "C" Co in VOORMEZEELE SWITCH. Relief completed at 7.5 PM. Weather fairly very cold during relief. Machine Guns active at night. No casualties, Transferred O.R. 3. Strength O. 36 O.R. 817	APP VII
TRENCHES [illegible]	23/11/16		Situation normal. Weather [illegible] between 11 AM & 2 PM Enemy fired [illegible] bombs and trench mortars on our FRONT LINE. Our M.T. Mortars & L.T. Mortars retaliated, hits observed on Enemy's parapet. Our trenches suffered damage. No casualties. Strength O. 36, O.R. 817	
	24/11/16		Situation normal. About 11.45 AM our M.T. Mortars and L.T. Mortars opened fire on Enemy's trenches, Enemy retaliated with TRENCH MORTARS and minenwerfers. This continued intermittently during the afternoon. Direct hits were observed on Enemy trenches. Casualties Nil. Strength O. 36 O.R. 816	

C. J. Soames
Lt Col
Comdg 10th Royal West Kent Regt

1875 Wt. W593/826 1,000,000 4/15 J.B.C. & A. A.D.S.S./Forms/C. 2118.

APP I

S E C R E T. Copy No. 15.

10TH BN. ROYAL WEST KENT RGT. - OPERATION ORDER NO. 32.

Reference Maps: Sheet 28 S.W.) 1/20,000.
Sheet 38 N.W.)

1. The Battalion will relieve the ~~10th King's Royal Rifle Corps~~ 15th Hampshire Regt, in the Centre Sub-sector of the 123rd Brigade Sector, to-morrow, Relief to commence at 11.30 a.m. and to be completed by 7 a.m. 4th November 1916.

2. Order of Move. Lewis Guns to move at 8.45 a.m. (Relief under arrangements of Lewis Gun Officer.).

"C" Coy. will move off at 9 a.m., by Platoons at 100 yards interval, followed by:

"B" Coy.	ditto.	ditto.	ditto.
"A" "	ditto.	ditto.	ditto.
"D" "	ditto.	ditto.	ditto.
Snipers	ditto	ditto.	ditto.
Hd. Qrs.	ditto.	ditto.	ditto.

in the order named.

Two Officers, 35 men, and 2 Lewis Guns of "D" Company will leave ECLUSE TRENCH for their position on the Left of the Line at dusk.

3. Rations. Rations will be taken by the Transport (to be at Ration Dump at 8 p.m. nightly, where they will be met by ration parties as detailed by Companies). All men will carry their to-morrow's rations.

4. Transport. A Limber will be at Battalion Hd. Qrs. at 10 a.m. to-morrow. It will proceed with its contents to be at Ration Dump by 6 p.m. 3rd November 1916.

5. Details. The following Details will proceed in rear of the Battalion under 2/Lt. A. A. Willoughby . Theynwill be quartered in spare billets at DICKEBUSCH for training, viz:-

Lewis Gunners - Sgt. Bailey & 3 men per Company.
Bombers - L/Sgt. Bull & 3 " " "
N.C.O. Class - Sgt. Commons & 2 O.R. per "

6. Blankets. All Blankets will be handed in to Company Stores by 7 a.m. to-morrow, rolled and labelled in bundles of ten. Coy. Qr. Mr. Sgts. will send one Blanket per man with the rations to-morrow night (except "C" Company, who will leave all Blankets behind)

The Regtl. Qr. Mr. Sgt. will deal with Hd. Qr. Blankets in the same manner.

7. Pumps. O.C. Companies will render a Return as soon as possible after relief, shewing the number of Pumps required in their portion of the line.

8. Trench Stores. A complete list of Trench Stores etc., taken over by each Company, must be sent to Battalion Headquarters by 9 a.m. 4th inst.

9. Headquarters Attached. The Battalion Pioneer Section and Drainage Section will be attached to Battalion Headquarters, and march off with them.

(CONTINUED ON SHEET 2)

(SHEET 2)

10. **Dress**. Marching Order.

11. **Relief**. Completion of Relief will be reported by runner to Battalion Headquarters.

12. **Wiring**. Wiring, as arranged, for each side of CONVENT LANE and SHELLY LANE, will be commenced as soon as possible.

13. Carrying, and other parties will avoid showing duckboards etc. over the tops of parapets of communication and other trenches as this draws fire.

14. Acknowledge.

H. Cozens.

2/11/16. 2/Lieut.
a/Adjt. for O.C. 10/Royal West Kent Rgt.

Copy No. 1 Filed.
2 O.C."A" Coy.
3 O.C."B" "
4 O.C."C" "
5 O.C."D" "
6. C.O.
7. M.O.
8 Intelligence Officer.
9 Lewis Gun Officer.
10 Bombing Officer.
11 Signalling Officer.
12 Quartermaster
13 Transport Officer.
14 War Diary.
15 " " (duplicate).

APPx

SECRET. Copy No..........

BATTALION ORDER NO. 33.

INTER-COMPANY RELIEF.

1. "A" Company will relieve "C" Company in the Front Line to-morrow, 6th inst., commencing at 6.30 a.m. i.e., by half Companies.

A half Company of "A" Company will relieve a half Company of "C" Company via CONVENT LANE. As soon as the relieved half Company of "C" are settled in VOORMEZEELE SWITCH, the other half of "A" Company will relieve the remainder of "C".

2. O.C. "B" Company will detail a Half Platoon (15 Rifles) to do duty with "A" Company. This party to report to O.C. "A" Company at 6.15 a.m. in VOORMEZEELE SWITCH.

The party of "B" Company which has been doing duty with "C" Company (30 Rifles) will report to O.C. "B" Company in OLD FRENCH TRENCH on relief.

3. 2/Lieut. NORRIS will arrange to relieve O.C. "B" Company (details later).

4. The Lewis Gun Officer will arrange to relieve the two Lewis Gun Teams on the left of the MUD PATCH at the same time as the relief of "D" Company takes place (Time later.)

5. Completion of Relief to be reported, viz- "B.O. No 33 complied with", by runner.

6. All Trench Stores must be handed over and a receipt obtained.

(Sd). F Cozens 2/Lieut.
a/Adjutant BLOOD

5-11-16

APPIV

ADDENDUM TO BATTALION ORDER NO. 34.

GUIDES. O.C. Companies will detail Platoon Guides to be at the Y.M.C.A., DICKEBUSCH, at 11.30 a.m. sharp. These Guides will report to the Adjutant at Battalion Headquarters, DRESSING STATION, VOORMEZEELE, at 10.30 a.m. sharp, where they will receive instructions.

8/11/16.

F. Cozens 2/Lieut.
a/Adjt. for O.C. B L O O D.

Copy No..5.....

BATTALION OPERATION ORDER NO. 34.

The Battalion will be relieved in the line to-morrow, 9th inst., by the 18th Bn. Kings Royal Rifle Corps. Relief to commence at 11.30 a.m. and to be completed by 7 a.m. 10th inst.

ORDER OF RELIEF. 1. "A" Coy. K.R.R.C. will relieve "A" Coy. 10th R.W.K.
"B" " " " " "D" " " "
"C" " " " " "B" " " "
"D" " " " " "C" " " "

Lewis Guns will be relieved, commencing at 9.30 a.m., with the exception of the two on the left of the MUD PATCH, O.3.2. O.3.3. As soon as Companies are relieved they will move off by Platoons at 100 yards interval, via CONVENT LANR. After passing STRAGGLERS POST, should the portion of CONVENT LANE by under water, Platoons will get out of the trench and follow the hedge by the tramway along the CONVENT WALL, and thence via CONVENT LANE - DICKEBUSCH - HALLEBAST CORNER OUDERDOM and CHIPPEWA CAMP.

Companies will close at HALLEBAST CORNER and proceed from there at 300 yards interval.

Limbers will be ready at the Transport Lines, where Company Commanders May have the packs of their Company loaded on passing.

The relief of the Half Company occupying ~~XXXXX~~ O.3.2. O.3.3. will move off from OLD FRENCH TRENCH about 5.30 p.m.

The relieved party returning via Trench Tramway through LILLE DUMP to Dressing Station VOORMEZEELE, where they will change their Gum Boots and socks and obtain packs. A hot drink will be supplied before moving off from Dressing Station.

Completion of Relief will be reported by Company Commanders on passing Battalion Headquarters, Dressing Station.

STORES. 2. Trench Stores will be handed over , a receipt obtained, and a list showing these articles forwarded to Battalion Headquarters on arrival in Camp.

All Stores brought in by the Companies will be taken out but care must be taken that the two new Camp Kettles taken over during the tour, are handed over as Trench Stores.

GUM BOOTS. 3. Company Commanders must be very careful that no Gum Boots are left wet about the Trenches or in dugouts. These should be sent as soon as possible to the drying room where they can be handed over to the incoming unit. Boots retained in the Trenches must be handed over and a receipt obtained.

ANKLE BOOTS. 4. O.C. "D" Company, Lewis Gun Officer, and Sniping Officer, will ensure that all Ankle Boots and packs of the men now occupying the left of the MUD PATCH are at the Dressing Station by 12 noon to-morrow, and so arrange to prevent confusion on arrivsl of party.

BLANKETS. 5. Company Commanders will ensure that no Blankets are left in their trenches or dugouts. Any not already handed in will have to be carried.

REPORT ON ARRIVAL. 6. Company Commanders will report personally to C.O. on arrival in Camp, when their Companies are housed and settled.

T. Cozens 2/Lieut.
a/Adjt. for O.C. B L-O O D.

8/11/16.

Copy No. 1 O.C. "A" Coy.
2 O.C. "B" "
3 O.C. "C" "
Copy No. 4 O.C. "D" Coy.
5 War Diary.
6 " " duplicate.

S E C R E T. Copy No. 13.....

10TH BN. ROYAL WEST KENT REGT. - ORDER NO. 35.

Refce. Maps:- 28 S.W. 1/20,000.
28 N.W. 1/20,000.

---

1. The 10th Bn. Royal West Kent Regt. will relieve the 15th Bn. Hampshire Regt. as Reserve Battalion, Left Sub-Sector, to-morrow, 16th inst., relief to be completed by 7 a.m. 17th November 1916.

2. Relief to be carried out via RENINGHELST - OUDERDOM - MILLEKAPELLEKEN FARM (H.30.c.). Leading Platoon to reach Cross Roads at DICKEBUSCH by 8.30 a.m.
"A" Companywill move off at 7.30 a.m., by Platoons at 100 yards distance, followed by "B" "C" "D" and Headquarters in the same order.

"A" Coy. 10 R.W.K. will relieve "A" Coy. 15th Hants. DICKEBUSCH.
"B" " " " " "B" " near the School VOORMEZEELE.
"C" " " " " " " DICKEBUSCH.
"D" " " " " " " in Convent Area VOORMEZEELE.

3. Maps, Trench Stores, etc., Indents for R.E. Stores, and 2nd Army Code Books are to be taken over and a complete list shewing the articles received to be forwarded to Battalion Head quarters by 7 p.m. 16th inst. A separatereturn will also be rendered by 4 p.m. punctually, shewing number of Braziers, and Soyer Stoves taken over, and No. required.

4. Specialists/(N.C.Os and Men) will move and remain with their Companies.
Handcarts will proceed under Company arrangements. "B" and "C" Coy. Handcarts must not leave DICKEBUSCH till dark.

5. 1 G.S.Wagon (Hd. Qrs.), Officers' Mess Cart, Maltese Cart, and 1 Limber per Company will be at Battalion Headquarters at 7 a.m.. All loading must be completed by 7.15 a.m.
If it is found that a second journey to DICKEBUSCH is necessary, Company Quartermaster Sergeants and two men must remain withthe unloaded portion and proceed when it is loaded.

6. Blankets to be rolled in bundles of 10, labelled, and stacked ready for loading at 6.45 a.m.
Three Cookers (with fires lighted) and 2 Water Carts (filled) will proceed in rear of the Battalion at a proper distance.

7. O.C. "A" Company will arrange to relieve the Water Guard at the Lake and Tank immediately on arrival. This guard will remain on duty for the tour.
O.C. "B" and "D" Companies will arrange for immediate relief of VOORMEZEELE Main Road Guard and ELZENWALLE STREET, respectively.
"C" Company will detail 6 men to report to the Manager, Y.M.C.A., DICKEBUSCH, as waiters and fatigue men.
Battalion Headquarter Guard, CHIPPEWA CAMP, will remain on duty until relieved by the 10th K.R.R.C., and will then proceed to DICKEBUSCH and report to Battalion Headquarters, on arrival.

8. The Quartermaster will hand over the Camp to the incoming Unit, and obtain a receipt for all Camp Property.

(CONTINUED ON SHEET NO. 2).

SHEET E.

9. Completion of relief to be reported to Battalion Headquarters by the quickest method available, as follows "B.O. No. 35 complied with".

10. Acknowledge.

[signature]

2/Lieut.

15/11/16. a/Adjutant for O.C. 10/Royal West Kent Rgt.

Copy No. 1 Filed.
2. C.O.
3. O.C. "A" Coy.
4. O.C. "B" "
5. O.C. "C" "
6. O.C. "D" "
7. Transport Officer.
8. Quartermaster.
9. Signalling Officer.
10. Intelligence "
11. Lewis Gun Officer.
12. Medical Officer.
13. War Diary.
14 " " duplicate.

SECRET. Copy No....13.......

10TH BN. ROYAL WEST KENT REGT. - OPERATION ORDER NO. 36.

APP. VI

1. The Battalion will be relieved on the 23rd inst. by the 18th Kings Royal Rifle Corps. Relief to commence at 9.30 a.m. and be completed by 7 a.m. 24th inst.

2. The Signalling Officer and Lewis Gun Officer will make all arrangements for their relief..

3. On completion of relief units will march via DICKEBUSCH - HALLEBAST CORNER - OUDERDOM to CHIPPEWA CAMP. All movements by Platoons at 100 yards distance.

4. Maps, Aeroplane Photos, Trench Stores and Second Army Codes will be handed over and a receipt obtained. All receipts are to be sent to Battalion Headquarters, CHIPPEWA. Indents for R.E.Stores will be submitted as usual, and details of these handed over to incoming units.

5. Completion of Relief to be reported at once to Battalion Headquarters, DICKEBUSCH, 23rd, by O.C. Companies, Signalling Officer and Lewis Gun Officer.

6. CHIPPEWA CAMP will be taken over by the Quartermaster at 10 a.m. 23rd inst.
O.C. "C" Company will detail 1 N.C.O. and 6 men to leave DICKEBUSCH at 8.15 a.m. and relieve the Camp Guard at CHIPPEWA. Their duties will include taking care of Camp and fittings when taken over.

7. <u>TRANSPORT</u>. A mounted orderly from the Transport Lines is to report at Battalion Headquarters, DICKEBUSCH, by 11.30 a.m. 23rd inst.
Blankets of "A" and "C" Companies must be rolled and stacked at the Quartermaster's Stores DICKEBUSCH by 9 a.m. Company limbers will convey to CHIPPEWA according to instructions given.
Blankets of "B" and "D" Companies will be carried down by the men and rolled at QR.Mr. STORES DICKEBUSCH, where they will be loaded on Company Limbers, together with the men's packs.
A G.S.Wagon to be at Headquarters at 9 a.m. for Headquarter Blankets, Orderly Room boxes, and Officers' Kits of "A" and "C" Companies and Headquarters.
The Mess Cart will collect Mess Boxes and have same loaded by 10 a.m.
Mess Boxes and Officers' kits of "B" and "D" will be brought down on the ration limbers on the evening of the 22nd and stored at Quartermaster Stores, DICKEBUSCH till following morning.
The Maltese Cart and the Medical Officer's Horse will be at DICKEBUSCH at 10.30 a.m.
The VOORMEZEELE Water Cart will be brought down on the evening of the 22nd inst.
The two water carts and all Field Kitchens are to leave DICKEBUSCH by 9 a.m. 23rd inst. All Cooks are to be in DICKEBUSCH by 9 a.m. to accompany Cookers and prepare a hot meal for men on arrival at CHIPPEWA.
All Petrol Cans not handed over are to be brought back to Camp.

[signature] 2/Lieut.
a/Adjt. for O.C. 10/Royal West Kent Rgt.

22/11/16.

Copy No. 1 Filed
2 C.O.
3 O.C."A"Coy.
4 O.C."B" "
5 O.C."C" "
No. 6 O.C. "D" Coy.
7 Medical Offr.
8 Transport Sgt.
9 Quartermaster
10 Signalling Offr.
No.11 Lewis Gun Offr.
12 War Diary.
13 " "

S E C R E T. Copy No...12.......

APP VII

OPERATION ORDER NO. 37.

1. The 10th Bn. Royal West Kent Regt. will relieve the 15th Bn. Hampshire Regt. in the centre portion of the Left Sub-Sector, to-morrow, 28th inst. The Relief to be complete by 7 a.m. 29th inst.

2. Dress:- Fighting Order, Great Coats rolled. Jerkins to be rolled on the back of the belt.
Packs will be stacked in the spare hut reserved for Company Stores.
1 Blanket per man for "A" "C" Hd.Qrs. and half "B" Coy. will be rolled in bundles of ten and stacked ready for loading on the Company Limbers at 9 a.m.
Remainder of Blankets to be stacked by Companies in the Spare Hut.

3. Signallers, Lewis Gunners and Battalion Observers will march off in separate parties, commencing at 9 a.m., followed by:

"D"	Coy.	who	will	relieve	"A"	Coy.	15th	Hants	Regt.
"B"	"	"	"	"	"C"	"	"	"	"
"A"	"	"	"	"	"B"	"	"	"	"
"C"	"	"	"	"	"D"	"	"	"	"

Movements will be by Platoons at 100 yards distance. Leading Platoon of "D" Company should be at DICKEBUSCH by 11.30 a.m.
Headquarters move off at 1.30 p.m., followed by "Details" under 2/Lieut. A.S.Richmond.

4. Rations will be taken by the Transport (to be at Ration Dump at 6 p.m. nightly) whence they will be conveyed on the trolleys to their respective Company Dumps by the Company Qr. Mr. Sergts. and any spare men not in the line.
All men will carry the remainder of to-morrow's rations.

5. Company Limbers will be at Battalion Hd. Qrs. by 9 a.m. to-morrow.
Officers' Mess Cart and 1 G.S. Waggon will be at Battalion Headquarters at 1 p.m. for Hd.Qr. Stores and Officers Kits.
These vehicles will not pass through DICKEBUSCH until 6 p.m.

6. Complete List of Trench Stores etc. taken over by each Company must be sent to Battalion Hd. Qrs. by 9 a.m.

7. Completion of Relief will be reported by wire as follows: "B"O.O. No. 37 complied with".

8. Quartermaster will hand overthe Camp to the incoming unit and obtain a receipt for all Camp Furniture handed over.

9. Cookers will be taken away at 10.30 a.m.
1 Water Cart will be taken up full every night with the rations and will ~~xx~~ remain during the next day in VOORMEZEELE.

[signature]
2/Lieut.
27/11/16. a/Adjt. for O.C. 10/RW.Kent Regt.

No. 1 Filed.
2 C. O.
3 O.C."A" Coy.
4 O.C."B" "
5 O.C."C" "
No. 6 O.C."D" Coy.
7 Medical Offr.
8 Transport Sergt.
9.Quartermaster.
10.Signalling Offr.
No.11 Lewis Gun Offr.
12 War Diary.
13 " "
14 Intelligence Offr.

Instructions regarding War Diaries and Intelligence Summaries are contained in F. S. Regs., Part II. and the Staff Manual respectively. Title Pages will be prepared in manuscript.

Army Form C. 2118.

WAR DIARY
or
INTELLIGENCE SUMMARY

(Erase heading not required.)

10th Royal West Kent Regt Sheet I Dec 1916

Vol 8

Place	Date	Hour	Summary of Events and Information	Remarks and references to Appendices
Centre Left Sub-sector	1/12/16		Situation normal, weather misty, quiet day and night. Strength O. 36. O.R. 814	
"	2/12/16		Situation normal, nothing of importance to record. Strength O. 36. O.R. 814. Evacuated O.R. 2	
"	3/12/16	12 MN	Enemy shelled our Trenches for short period, our Trench Mortars replied	
		3.30 A.M.	Enemy opened fire with Trench Mortars, Our Artillery retaliated, this lasted for about 3/4 of an hour, No damage to our trenches. Strength O. 36. O.R. 814. Evacuated O.R. 1. During the day the Battalion were relieved by the 18th K.R.Rs, as per APPX I. Battalion marched back to CHIPPEWA CAMP M6a4.7. Relief completed by about 8.30 PM. This operation was carried out successfully, no casualties	APPX I OP. ORDER 38
CHIPPEWA CAMP M6a4.7.	4/12/16		Rest & Training, Improvement of Camp. Strength O. 36 O.R. 812	
"	5/12/16		" Reinforcement O. 1. O.R. 17 Strength O. 37. O.R. 829	
"	6/12/16		" Strength O. 37. O.R. 829	
"	7/12/16		" Strength O. 37 O.R. 829	
"	8/12/16		" Strength O. 37 O.R. 828 Evacuated O.R. 1. During above period from 4th to 8th Battalion also found R.E. Working Parties	
	9/12/16		Situation normal Battalion relieved 15th Hants Regt as Reserve Battalion Left sub-sector. Battalion H.Q., "B" & "D" Coys billeted in DICKEBUSCH. "A" Coy in the School Area, VOORMEEZLE, "C" Coy CONVENT AREA, VOORMEEZLE. This operation was carried out successfully, no casualties Lt Pocock rejoined Strength O. 38 O.R. 828	APPX II OP ORDER 39

2449 Wt. W14957/M90 750,000 1/16 J.B.C. & A. Forms/C.2118/12.

Instructions regarding War Diaries and Intelligence Summaries are contained in F. S. Regs., Part II. and the Staff Manual respectively. Title Pages will be prepared in manuscript.

10th Royal West Kent Regt

WAR DIARY
or
INTELLIGENCE SUMMARY

(Erase heading not required.)

Sheet II

Dec 1916

Army Form C. 2118.

Place	Date	Hour	Summary of Events and Information	Remarks and references to Appendices
DICKEBUSCH	10/12/16		Situation normal. Battalion finding working Parties for R.E. viz Constructing Dug-outs, repair of Trenches and carrying material to front line. Strength O. 39 O.R. 882	
B.H.2. Belgium	"	4 PM	Enemy shelled VOORMEEZLE VILLAGE, no damage, Reinforcements O.R. 55, Major Beattie rejoined	
Sheet 28 N.W. H28.C.7.1	11/12/16		Situation normal Battalion employed as per above, Strength O. 39 O.R. 872. Evacuated O.R. 10	
	12/12/16		" " " " " Strength O. 39 O.R. 870. Evacuated O.R. 2	
	13/12/16		" " " " " Strength O. 39 O.R. 870	
	14/12/16	11 AM	Enemy shelled VOORMEEZLE VILLAGE, Convent Area, destroying two dug-outs but no casualties	
		6 PM	Enemys Machine Guns active in vicinity of CONVENT LANE, 3 Casualties O.R. 1 Killed O.R. 2 Wounded. Strength O. 39 O.R. 868	
	15/12/16		Situation normal, The Battalion relieved by 15th K.R.R.C. (APPX III,) and withdrawn to	APPX III
		1 PM	CHIPPEWA CAMP. M.6.a.4.7. Relief complete at 1 PM. This operation was carried out successfully 1 Casualty Wounded. Strength O. 39 O.R. 865	OP ORDER 40
CHIPPEWA CAMP M.6.a.4.7	16/12/16		Situation normal, Rest & Training. Strength O. 39 O.R. 866	
	17/12/16		" " Strength O. 38 O.R. 866	
	18/12/16		" " Strength O. 38 O.R. 866	
	19/12/16		" " Strength O. 38 O.R. 866	
	20/12/16		" " Strength O. 38 O.R. 868	
			During above period 11th to 20 The Battalion also found R.E. Working parties	
	21/12/16		Situation normal, The 123rd Brigade was inspected by the C in C Sir Douglas Haig, After inspection the Battalion "marched past" in column of Fours and returned to Camp. Strength O. 38 O.R. 868	
	22/12/16		Situation normal, The Battalion relieved the 15th Bn. Hampshire Regt in the Centre Portion of the Left sub-sector, this Operation was carried out successfully. Strength O. 38 O.R. 868	APPX IV OP ORDER 41

10th Royal West Kent Regt

Instructions regarding War Diaries and Intelligence Summaries are contained in F. S. Regs., Part II. and the Staff Manual respectively. Title Pages will be prepared in manuscript.

WAR DIARY
or
INTELLIGENCE SUMMARY
(Erase heading not required.)

December 1916
Sheet 111

Army Form C. 2118.

Place	Date	Hour	Summary of Events and Information	Remarks and references to Appendices
Centre Left Sub-sector	23/12/16		During the night Our Artillery and Trench Mortars active, Patrols out report nothing unusual. One of our Snipers shot a German on Enemy's parapet. During the day our Artillery shelled Enemys Front and Support Lines, Enemy retaliated but no damage done. Our Trench mortars were quiter than usual. Strength 38 O. 868 O.R.	
	24/12/16		Much Artillery activity, Enemy shelled VOORMEZEELE, FRONT LINE quiet, nothing special to report. Strength 38 O. 865 O.R. Evacuated 3 O.R.	
	25/12/16	7 AM	Stokes Gun fire caused Enemy to retaliate on SHELLEY LANE which was damaged.	
		8 AM	Stokes Gun fire caused much damage to Enemy's Trenches. Enemy exploded a Camouflet but only caused little damage, no casualties	
		10.45AM	Our Trench Mortars and Artillery opened fire on the Enemy's lines along the whole Front, Enemy's retaliation damaged our Front Line cook-house and spoilt the dinner	
		3 PM	Stokes Gun opened with good effect, Enemy retaliated on Front line but no damage done. Patrols out during night dispersed hostile patrol also reported on State of Enemys wire. Strength 38 O. 865 O.R.	
	26/12/16		Quiet. Our Patrols out during night report "No Mans Land" between SHELLEY LANE and CONVENT LANE impassable owing to water. Casualties Killed 1 O.R. Wounded 2 O.R. Strength 38 862 Evacuated 3 O.R.	
	27/12/16		Artillery, Trench Mortars considerably below normal, slightly increased machine Gun activity. Enemys Trench Mortars fired on Our Front-line but silenced by Stokes Gun. Enemy shells fell in neighbourhood of VOORMEZEELE. Patrols out nothing unusual to report. Strength 38. 862 O.R.	
	28/12/16		During the night our Artillery and Trench Mortars shelled Enemys Lines, A Test by us of Green and S.O.S. Rockets caused some anxiety to Enemy. During day Stokes Gun and M.T.M. active, Artillery below normal. Patrols report on state of Enemy wire. Casualties Killed 1 O.R. Wounded 1 O.R. Strength 38. 855 O.R. Evacuated 3 O.R.	
	29/12/16		During forenoon Enemy shelled VOORMEZEELE. Battalion relieved by the 18th Bn K. R. Rifles, the Operations was carried out successfully and the Battalion marched back to CHIPPEWA CAMP M.6.a.4.7. Strength 38 O. 855 O.R.	APPX V OP ORDER [illegible]
CHIPPEWA CAMP M.6.a.4.7.	30/12/16		Situation normal, rest and training. Reinforcements joined Battalion 179 O.R. Strength 38 O. 1034 O.R.	
	31/12/16		" " " Strength 38 O. 1034 O.R.	

W. F. Soames Lt Col
Comm.dg. 10th R. West Kent Regt

2449 Wt. W14957/M90 750,000 1/16 J.B.C. & A. Forms/C.2118/12.

SECRET. Copy No. 10

APP I

BATTALION ORDER NO. 38.

1. The Battalion will be relieved by the 18th K.R.R.C. on 3rd December 1916.

2. Leading Platoon of Relieving Unit to be at DICKEBUSCH by 11.30 a.m. 3.12.16.

3. On completion of Relief Companies will return to CHIPPEWA CAMP via DICKEBUSCH - HALLEBAST CORNER - OUDERDOM. Arrangements will be made for vehicles to meet the half Company of "B" from the MUD PATCH, at DICKEBUSCH Hd. Qrs. for the purposeof conveying them to Camp. A Hot Drink will also be ready for this half Company at Battalion Headquarters. VOORMEZEELE. O.C. "B" Company will send one cook to Battn. Hd. Qrs. and the Company Qr. Mr. Sergt. will have the necessary Soup Squares at Battalion Hd. Qrs. by 5 P.M. for this purpose.

4. Maps, Aeroplane Photographs, Trench Stores and Second Army Code Books will be handed over and a receipt obtained. The receipt to be sent to Bn. Hd. Qrs. immediately on arrival in Camp. Great care is to be taken in compiling these Lists. Indents for R.E. Stores to be submitted as usual and details ofthese to be handed over to the Relief.

5. Transport as follows will be at Battalion Hd. Qrs. at 5 p.m.

Headquarters - 1 G.S.Wagon and Maltese Cart.
"A" "B" "C" "D" Coys. - 1 Limber per Company.

Headquarter Officers' Horses at 9 p.m.

The whole of the Transport will then return from Camp at once to DICKEBUSCH Hd. Qrs. for conveyance of half "B" Coy. to Camp. They will awaitthe arrival of half Company of "B" at DICKEBUSCH.

6. O.C.Companies will arrange for their Blankets to be brought out in bundles of ten and dumped in the vicinity of Bn. Hd. Qrs. A man should be left in charge of each Company Dump and to assist in loading. Care must be taken that only articlestaken into the line are brought out.

7. All Trenches and Dugouts must be left as clean as possible.

8. Work in hand and work proposed must be explained to the ~~xx~~ relieving Company.

9. Completion of Relief to be reported to Bn. Hd. Qrs. by wire, as follows, and confirmed by runner :-

"B.O. No. 38 complied with."

10. Company Qr. Mr. Sergts. will arrange to have a good hot meal for every N.C.O. and man on arrival in camp.

11. Acknowledge.

2/12/16.

2/Lieut.
Adjutant BLOOD.

SECRET

Copy No...12.....

APPX II

10TH BN ROYAL WEST KENT REGIMENT.

OPERATION ORDER No 39

---

1. The 10th Bn Royal West Kent Regiment will relieve the 15th Bn Hampshire Regt as Res Bn, Left Sub-Sector to-morrow 9th inst. Relief to be completed by 7 a.m. 10th inst.

2. Relief to be carried out via RENINGHELST - OUDERDOM - MILLEKAPELLEN FARM (H.20.c.) Leading Platoon to reach DICKEBUSCH by 9.30. a.m.

3. A Coy will move off at 7.30 a.m. by Platoons at 100 yds distance, followed by "B". "C". "D" & Headquarters in the same order:-

"A" Coy will proceed to the SCHOOL AREA. VOORMEZEELE.
"B" " " " " DICKEBUSCH.
"C" " " " " CONVENT AREA "
"D" " " " " DICKEBUSCH.

The above will take over from the Coys of the 15th HANTS who are in the area to which they are proceeding.

4. Maps, Stores, Indents for R. E. Stores, & 2nd Army Code Books are to be taken over and a complete list shewing the articles received to be forwarded to Bn H.Qrs by 7 p.m. 9th inst.

5. Specialists will move and remain with their Companies. Handcarts will proceed under Coy arrangements.

6. 1 G.S.Wagon. Maltese Cart and 1 Limber per Coy will be at Bn H.Qrs at 7 a.m. All loading to be completed by 7.15.a.m. Officers' Mess Cart to be at Bn H.Qrs by 9a.m.. If it is found that a second journey to DICKEBUSCH is necessary, the C.Q.M.S. and 2 men must remain behind with the unloaded portion and proceed when it is loaded.

7. Blankets to be rolled in bundles of 10, labelled and stacked ready for loading at 6.45.a.m. 3 Cookers (with fires lighted) i.e. "B". "D". & one for H.Qrs, & 2 Water Carts (filled) will proceed in rear of the Bn at a proper distance.

8. Battalion H.Qr Guard. CHIPPEWA CAMP. will remain on dutyuntil relieved by the 18th KINGS ROYAL RIFLES and will then proceed to Battalion H.Qrs. DICKEBUSCH.

9. The Camp must be left scrupulously clean. Officers Commanding Companies must see that their lines are thoroughly clean before parading.
The Q.M. will hand over the Camp to the incoming unit and obtain a receipt for same. He should also obtain a Chit as to the cleanliness of the Camp when handed over.

10. Completion of relief to be reported toBn H.Qrs by the quickest method available. "B.O.No.39 complied with"

S. Cozens (signature)
2/Lieut & Adjt.
10th Royal West Kent Regt.

8/12/16.

No. 1. O. C.
2. 2nd i/c
3. File.
4. Int: Officer.
5. Lewis Gun Offr
6. Signalling Offr.
7. Quartermaster.
8. O.C. "A" Coy.
9. O.C. "B" "
10. O.C. "C" "
11. O.C. "D" Coy.
12. War Diary.
13. " "
14. O.C. 15th Hants
15. O.C. 18th K.R.R

S E C R E T   Copy No ....

APPX III

10th BN ROYAL WEST KENT REGIMENT.

OPERATION ORDER No. 40.

1. The Battalion will be relieved to-morrow the 15th inst. by the 18th Kings Royal Rifle Corps. Relief to commence at 9.30 a.m.

2. Companies will be ready to move by 9.15 a.m. and men will remain in their billets until their relief arrives.

3. The Signalling Officer and Lewis Gun Officer will make all arrangements for their reliefs.

4. On completion of relief units will march via DICKEBUSCH - HALLEBAST CORNER - OUDERDOM to CHIPPEWA CAMP. All movements by Platoons at 100 yards distance.

5. Maps, Aeroplane Photos, Trench Stores, and Second Army Code Books will be handed over and a receipt obtained. All receipts are to be sent to Bn Headquarters, CHIPPEWA. Indents for R. E. Stores will be submitted as usual, and details of these handed over to the relieving units.

6. Completion of Relief to be at once reported to Battalion Headquarters, DICKEBUSCH, by O.C. Companies, Signalling Officer, and Lewis Gun Officer.

7. CHIPPEWA CAMP will be taken over by the Quartermaster by 10 a.m. 15th instant.
O.C. "D" Company will detail one N.C.O. and 3 men to leave DICKEBUSCH at 8.30 a.m. and relieve the Camp Guard at CHIPPEWA.

<u>TRANSPORT.</u> A mounted orderly from the Transport Lines is to report at Battalion Headquarters, DICKEBUSCH, by 11.30.a.m. 15th inst.
Blankets of "B" and "D" Companies must be rolled and stacked at the Quartermaster's Stores, DICKEBUSCH by 9.a.m. Company limbers will then convey to CHIPPEWA according to instructions given.
Blankets of "A" and "C" Companies will be carried down by the men and rolled at Quartermaster's Stores, DICKEBUSCH, where they will be loaded on Company limbers, together with the men's packs.
A G.S.Wagon is to be at Headquarters at 9 a.m. for Headquarter Blankets, Orderly Room boxes, and Officers'Kits of "B" and "D" Companies and Headquarters.
The Mess Cart will collect Mess Boxes and have same loaded by 10 a.m.
Mess Boxes and Officers' Kits of "A" and "C" Companies will be brought down on the ration limbers this evening, 14th inst, and stored at Quartermaster's Stores, DICKEBUSCH until the following morning.
The Maltese Cart and Medical Officer's horse will be at DICKEBUSCH at 10.30 a.m.
The Water cart at VOORMEZEELE will be brought down this evening, 14th inst.
The 2 water carts and Field Kitchens are to leave DICKEBUSCH by 9.a.m. 15th inst. All Cooks are to be in DICKEBUSCH by 9.a.m to accompany cookers and prepare a hot meal for men on arrival at CHIPPEWA.
All Petrol Cans not handed over are to be brought back to Camp.

14/12/16.

[signature]
Major,
Adjutant. 10th Bn R. W. Kent Rgt.

Copy No 1. Filed.   6. O.C. "D" Coy.
2. C. O.   7. [illegible]   11. Lewis Gun Officer
3. O.C. [illegible]   [illegible] War Diary.
4. "B" " [illegible]   13. " "
5. " " " [illegible]   O.C. 18th K.R.R's.

S E C R E T.   Copy No.........16..........

10th BN. R. W. KENT REGT.

APPX V

BATTALION OPERATION ORDER No 45.

1. The Battalion will be relieved by the 18th K.R.R.C. on 29th December 1916.

2. The leading Platoon of the Relieving Unit to be at DICKEBUSCH by 11.30.a.m. 29/12/16.

3. On completion of Relief Companies will return to CHIPPEWA CAMP via DICKEBUSCH - HALLEBAST CORNER - OUDERDOM. All movements will be by Platoons at 100 yards distance.

4. Maps, Aero Plane Photographs, & Trench Stores, will be handed over and a receipt obtained. Receipt to be handed to Adjutant by O.C. Company on passing Battalion Head Quarters. Great care should be taken in compiling these lists. Indents for R.E.Stores to be submitted as usual and details of these to be handed over to the Relief.

5. O.C. Companies will arrange for their blankets to be brought out in bundles of 10 and dumped in the vicinity of the Bn Hd Qrs. An N.C.O. or reliable man should be left in charge of each Company dump, and assist in loading of transport. Care should be taken that only articles taken into the line are brought out.

6. All Trenches and Dugouts are to be left as clean as possible, and all trench boots not in use will be sent to Drying Room at Bn Head Qrs. A thorough search is to be made that none of these are left in Dugouts or anywhere about the trenches.

7. Work in hand and proposed work must be thoroughly explained to O.C. Relieving Unit.

8. Transport will be near Y.M.C.A. Hut, DICKEBUSCH to convey the Half-Company of "C" from the MUD-PATCH to CAMP. O.C."C" Company will send one Cook to Bn Hd Qrs to report to the Regimental Sergeant Major after dinner to-morrow, to make a hot drink for this Half-Company on their reaching Bn Hd Qrs. The Cook will obtain the necessary Soup Squares at Bn Hd Qrs.

9. The N.C.O. in charge of the Lewis Guns will arrange for all Lewis Guns, (with the exception of the two in the MUD-PATCH), to be placed in the Lewis Gun limbers at DICKEBUSCH and taken to CAMP. The Transport Officer will arrange for the Lewis Gun limbers to be at DICKEBUSCH by 8.p.m. The two Lewis Guns from the MUD-PATCH will be conveyed in the limbers conveying the Half-Company from DICKEBUSCH.

10. Transport as follows will be at Bn Hd Qrs by 5.p.m.
<u>Headquarters.</u> 1 G.S.Wagon, Maltese Cart, & Offrs Mess Cart
<u>"A" "B" "C" "D" Coys.</u> 1 Limber per Company.
Headquarter Officers' Horses to be at DICKEBUSCH by 7.p.m.
Limbers for conveying the Half-Company and Machine Guns from MUD-PATCH to be at DICKEBUSCH by 9.p.m.

11. C.Q.M.S. will arrange to have a good hot meal for their Companies on arriving in Camp.

12. Completion of Relief to be reported to Bn Hd Qrs by wire, viz:- "B.O.No.45 complied with", and Coy Commanders will report in person on passing Bn Hd Qrs.

13. Acknowledge.

[signature]
Capt. & Adjt.

1. Filed.	5. O.C."B"	9. L.G.Officer.	13. Medical Officer.
2. C.O.	6. O.C."C"	10. Signal: "	14. O.C. 18th. K.R.R.C.
3. 2nd i/c	7. O.C."D"	11. Transport "	15. War Diary.
4. O.C."A"	8. Int: Offr.	12. Quartermaster.	16. " "

S E C R E T. Copy No................

10TH BN ROYAL WEST KENT REGT.

OPERATION ORDER No.41.

APP IV

1. The 10th Bn Royal West Kent Regt. will relieve the 15th Bn. Hampshire Regt. in the centre portion of the Left Sub-Sector, to-morrow, 22nd inst. The Relief to be complete by 7 a.m. 23rd inst.

2. Dress:- Fighting Order, Great Coats rolled. Jerkins to be rolled on the back of the belt.
One blanket per man for "A" and "D" Companies, Headquarters, and those N.C.O's and men of "C" Company not occupying the Locality, to be rolled in bundles of 10 and stacked ready for loading on Company limbers by 9 a.m.
The remainder of blankets and Packs of all Companies to be stacked by Companies and placed in the Reserve Store of the 11th Queens Quartermaster's Stores.

3. Signallers, Lewis Gunners, & Battalion Observers, will march off in separate parties, commencing at 9 a.m. under arrangements to be made by the Signalling Officer, Lewis Gun Officer, and Intelligence Officer.
The Battalion Lewis Gun Officer will arrange with the Transport Officer for the transport of his Guns.

4. The Battalion will move from the Camp in the following order:- "B" Coy who will occupy the front line. O.2.5. - O.2.8., followed by "C" Coy, who will occupy the Old French Trench and the Locality., followed by "D" Coy, 2 Platoons occupying Old French Trench from Convent Lane, & 2 Platoons in Ecluse Trench., followed by "A" Coy, who will occupy Voormezeele Switch.
Battalion Lewis Gun Officer will detail 3 guns for Front Line, 2 guns for Old French Trench, 2 guns for Locality, 3 guns for Voormezeele Switch, and 2 guns for September Post.
The leading Platoon of "B" Coy will move off from Camp so as to reach DICKEBUSCH by 11.30.a.m.
Movements will be by Platoons at 100 yards distance. Headquarters will move off at 1.30.p.m.

5. Rations will be taken by the Transport (to be at Ration Dump at 7.p.m. nightly) whence they will be conveyed on the trolleys to their respective Company Dumps by the Company Qr Mr. Sergts. and any spare men not in the line.
All men will carry the remainder of to-morrow's rations.

6. Company Limbers will be at Battalion Hd.Qrs. by 9.a.m. to-morrow.
Officers' Mess Cart and 1. G.S. Wagon will be at Bn Headquarters at 1.p.m. for Hd. Qr. Stores and Officers Kits.
These vehicles will not pass through DICKEBUSCH until dark.

7. Complete List of Trench Stores etc. taken over by each Company must be sent to Bn Hd Qrs. by 9.a.m.

8. Completion of Relief will be reported by wire as follows:- "B.O.O. No. 41 complied with".

9. Quartermaster will hand over the Camp to the incoming unit and obtain a receipt for all Camp Furniture handed over.

10. Cookers will be taken away at 10.30.a.m.
1 Water Cart will be taken up full every night with the rations and will remain during the next day in VOORMEZEELE.

[signature]
Captain.
Adjt. for O.C. 10th R.W.Kent Rgt.

21/12/16.

No.1. Filed.
2. C. O.
3. O.C."A" Coy.
4. O.C."B" "
5. O.C."C" "
No. 6. O.C."D"Coy.
7. Medical Offr.
8. Transport Sergt.
9. Quartermaster.
10. Signalling Offr.
No. 11. Lewis Gun Offr.
12. War Diary.
13. " "
14. Intelligence Offr.

Army Form C. 2118.

10th Royal West Kent Regt

Sheet I

10 R W Kent Regt

Vol 9

Instructions regarding War Diaries and Intelligence Summaries are contained in F. S. Regs., Part II. and the Staff Manual respectively. Title Pages will be prepared in manuscript.

WAR DIARY
or
INTELLIGENCE SUMMARY

(Erase heading not required.)

Place	Date	Hour	Summary of Events and Information	Remarks and references to Appendices
CHIPPEWA CAMP M 6 a 4.7	1/1/17		Rest. Battalion keep up Xmas day. Strength 38 offs 1028 O.R.	
	2/1/17		Rest & Training, improvement of Camp. Evacuated 1 O.R. Strength 38 offs 1027 O.R.	
— " —	3/1/17	7.30AM	Situation normal. Battalion proceeded to relieve 15th Battalion Hampshire Regt as Reserve Battalion, Left sub-sector, APPX I. "Hd Qrs" "A" & "C" DICKEBUSCH, H.28.c.7.6. "B" to CONVENT SCHOOL, VOORMEZEELE, "D" to CONVENT AREA VOORMEZEELE, this Operation was carried out successfully and completed by 12.30 P.M. Strength 38 offs 1027 O.R.	APPX I
DICKEBUSCH Map Ref. Belgium 28 S.W. H.28.c.7.6.	4/1/17		Situation normal. Casualties 1 O.R. wounded. Evacuated 2 O.R. Strength 38 offs 1019 O.R.	
	5/1/17		" Reinforcements 2 O.R. Strength 38 offs 1024 O.R.	
	6/1/17		" Evacuated 1 O.R. Strength 38 offs 1023 O.R.	
	7/1/17		" Reinforcements 5 O.R. Evacuated 1 O.R. Strength 38 offs 1025 O.R.	
	8/1/17	12 noon	Enemy shelled VOORMEZEELE AREA rather more than usual. Battalion relieved by 18th Bn King's Royal Rifles and marched back to CHIPPEWA CAMP M 6 a 4.7. This operation was carried out successfully. During period from 3/1 to 8/1 the Battalion whilst in Reserve were employed as R.E. working and carrying parties to FRONT LINE. Strength 38 offs 1025 O.R.	APPX II
CHIPPEWA CAMP M 6 a 4.7	9/1/17		Rest, Training, improvement of Camp. Two officers joined 2Lt Tabb, 2Lt Collins.	
	10/1/17		" Evacuated 1 O.R. Strength 40 offs 1026 O.R.	
— " —	11/1/17		" Strength 40 offs 1025 O.R.	
— " —	12/1/17		" Evacuated 1 O.R. Strength 40 offs 1027 O.R.	
— " —	13/1/17		" Strength 40 offs 1027 O.R.	
— " —	14/1/17		" Evacuated 1 O.R. Strength 40 offs 1026 O.R.	
			Evacuated 3 O.R. Strength 40 offs 1021 O.R.	
	15/1/17	11.30AM	Battalion relieved 15th Battalion Hampshire Regt in centre portion of Left sub-sector, this operation was carried out successfully.	APP III
		3.30PM	Our Artillery and T.M. carried out a shoot on Enemy's front line damaging Enemy's trenches badly. Enemy retaliated with Minenwerfer and Field Guns blowing in a little of our front line and CONVENT LANE.	

2449 Wt. W14957/M90 750,000 1/16 J.B.C. & A. Forms/C.2118/12.

10th R West Kent Regt

Army Form C. 2118.

WAR DIARY
or
INTELLIGENCE SUMMARY

(Erase heading not required.)

Sheet II

Instructions regarding War Diaries and Intelligence Summaries are contained in F. S. Regs., Part II. and the Staff Manual respectively. Title Pages will be prepared in manuscript.

Place	Date	Hour	Summary of Events and Information	Remarks and references to Appendices
Centre. Left Sub-sector	15/1/17		During evening Enemy made sudden bursts of fire. Patrols out during night but weather conditions adverse to gaining information. Captain Vatrey transferred to a Labour Battalion. Evacuated 1 O.R. Strength 39 Offrs 1025 O.R.	
	16/1/17		During the night there was a Trench Mortar duel on our right	
		2 PM.	Our Trench Mortars fired with good effect on Enemy's wire and Trenches. Enemy replied with shells and Trench Mortars which finished in a Trench Mortar duel in which we had the last word. A few shells fell in neighbourhood of VOORMEZEELE. Snipers active during day. Patrol out during night but weather conditions bad. Casualties 1 O.R. Killed, Evacuated 2 O.R. Strength 39 Offrs 1022 O.R.	
	17/1/17	7.15AM	Our Artillery shelled the Craters for half an hour.	
		11 AM.	Our Trench Mortars bombarded Enemy's Front line, Enemy retaliated with Trench Mortars and Rifle grenades. Our Snipers active. Patrols out during night but snow prevented much movement. Casualties 1 O.R. wounded Strength 39 Offrs 1021 O.R.	
	18/1/17		Situation Normal. Enemy Artillery quiet. Trench Mortars active.	
		3.20PM	Stokes Gun shelled the Craters, Enemy replied with Rum-jars on CONVENT LANE & SHELLEY LANE. Patrols out during night but nothing unusual to report. 3 Officers joined 2Lt Crombie 2Lt Shrimpton 2Lt Hodges. Casualties 1 O.R. Killed 1 O.R. Wd. Evacuated 5 O.R. Strength 42 Offrs 1019 O.R.	
	19/1/17		Situation normal. Enemy shelled VOORMEZEELE during afternoon.	
		11.20PM	Our Artillery bombarded whole of Enemy's Front line, this was followed by a Raid on Enemy's trenches by the Battalion on our left. The raid was successful. Enemy's retaliation was very feeble. Patrols out later but report everything quiet. Evacuated 2 O.R. Strength 42 Offrs 1019 O.R.	
	20/1/17		Situation normal. Stokes-guns active. Patrols out during night nothing unusual to report. Evacuated 2 O.R. Strength 42 Offrs 1019 O.R.	
	21/1/17	7.30AM	Stokes-guns fired a few rounds on Enemy's Front line, Enemy retaliated with Heavy Minenwerfer, Rum-jars and 77.mm shells. Our Artillery retaliated and silenced Enemy. Our Front-line was blown in in two places. Enemy Sniper wounded one of our Stretcher-bearers who was attending a man blown out of the trench. One of our Snipers saw the German and shot him, also another German shortly afterwards. Patrols out, nothing unusual to report. Reinforcements 22 O.R. Casualties 9 O.R. Wd. Strength 42 Offrs 1029 O.R.	

2449 Wt. W14957/M90 750,000 1/16 J.B.C. & A. Forms/C.2118/12.

Army Form C. 2118.

10th R. West Kent Regt

WAR DIARY
or
INTELLIGENCE SUMMARY

(Erase heading not required.)

Sheet 111

Instructions regarding War Diaries and Intelligence Summaries are contained in F. S. Regs., Part II. and the Staff Manual respectively. Title Pages will be prepared in manuscript.

Place	Date	Hour	Summary of Events and Information	Remarks and references to Appendices
Centre left sub-sector	[illegible]/17	[illegible]	Situation normal. Battalion were relieved by 18th Bn Kings Royal Rifles Bn [illegible] and marched to CHIPPEWA CAMP M6.a.4.7. The operation was carried out successfully. Strength 42 Offrs 1028 O.R.	APPX IV
CHIPPEWA CAMP M6.a.4.7	[illegible]/17		Situation normal. Rest, Training, Improvement of Camp. Evacuated 3 O.R. Strength 42 Offrs 1027 O.R.	
	[illegible]/17		Evacuated 3 O.R. Strength 42 Offrs 1027 O.R.	
	[illegible]/17		Strength 42 Offrs 1027 O.R.	
	[illegible]/17		Evacuated 1 O.R. Strength 42 Offrs 1026 O.R.	
	[illegible]/17		Strength 42 Offrs 1026 O.R.	
	[illegible]/17		Situation normal. Battalion relieved 15th Battalion Hampshire, as Reserve Battalion left sub-sector. Battn H.Q. "B" & "D" Coys DICKEBUSCH, H.25.c.7.1. "A" Coy CONVENT AREA "C" Coy CONVENT SCHOOL, VOORMEZEELE. The operation was carried out successfully. During evening the enemy shelled DICKEBUSCH YPRES Rd. Casualties 1 O.R. slightly wd. Strength 42 Offrs 1026 O.R.	APPX V
DICKEBUSCH	[illegible]/17		Situation normal. Strength 42 Offrs 1026 O.R.	
O.P. Belgian War [illegible]	[illegible]/17		Evacuated 4 O.R. Strength 42 Offrs 1022 O.R.	
H.25.c.7.1.	[illegible]/17		Strength 42 Offrs 1022 O.R.	
			During period in Reserve Battalion found R.E. parties and carrying parties for front line.	

R. A. [illegible] Major
Comm'dg
10th Royal West Kent Regt

2449 Wt. W14957/M90 750,000 1/16 J.B.C. & A. Forms/C.2118/12.

APPX I

S E C R E T. Copy No......12....

10TH BN ROYAL WEST KENT REGIMENT.

OPERATION ORDER No 46.

1. The Battalion will relieve the 15th Bn Hampshire Regt as Reserve Bn, Left Sub-Sector, to-morrow 3rd inst. Relief to be completed by 7.a.m. 4th inst.

2. Relief to be carried out via:- RENINGHELST - OUDERDOM - MILLEKAPELLEN FARM (H.20.c) Leading Platoon to reach DICKEBUSCH by 9.30.a.m..

3. The Battalion will move off by Platoons at 100 yards distance in the following order:-
"A" Coy Leading Platoon move off at 7.30.a.m. followed by "B", "C", and "D" Companies.
Headquarters move off at 1.30.p.m.

"A" Coy will relieve Company of the 15th Hants at DICKEBUSCH.
"B" " " " " " " " CONVENT SCHOOL VOORMEZEELE
"C" " " " " " " " DICKEBUSCH (Brasserie)
"D" " " " " " " " CONVENT. VOORMEZEELE

4. Maps, Stores, & Indents for R.E. Stores. are to be taken over and a complete list shewing the articles received to be forwarded to Bn H.Qrs by 7.p.m. 3rd inst.

5. Specialists will move & remain with their Coys, with the exception of the Pioneer Section, who will be billetted together under arrangements to be made by the Pioneer Officer.

6. Blankets are to be rolled in bundles of 10, labelled, & stacked ready for loading at 6.45.a.m. 3 Cookers (with fires lighted).i.e. "A" & "C" Coys, & one for Hd Qrs, & 2 Water Carts (filled) will proceed in rear of the Battalion at 300 yards distance. Dixies will be taken by "B" & "D" Coys for cooking in VOORMEZEELE.

7. One G.S.Wagon. Maltese Cart and 1 Limber per Coy will be at Bn H.Qrs at 7.a.m. All loading to be completed by 7.30 a.m.. Officers Mess Cart to be at Bn.H.Qrs by 9.a.m. Transport Officer will make necessary arrangements, if it is found necessary to make a second journey to DICKEBUSCH, and C.Q.M.S. & 2 men per Coy will remain behind to load up the second journey. Lewis Gun Carts to be at Bn. Hd. Qrs at 7.a.m. to convey Lewis Guns.

8. Bn.Hd.Qr. Guard. CHIPPEWA CAMP. will remain on duty until relieved by the 18th K.R.R.'s, & will then proceed to Bn. Hd. Qrs. DICKEBUSCH. and report to R.S.M.

9. The Camp must be left scrupulously clean. Officers Commanding Companies must see that their lines are thoroughly clean before parading.
The Q.M. will hand over the Camp to the incoming unit and obtain a receipt for same. He should also obtain a Chit as to the cleanliness of the Camp when handed over.

10. Completion of relief to be reported to Battalion Head Quarters by the quickest method available. viz:- "B.O.No.46 complied with".

D. H. Slaney Capt
Adjutant
BL00

2/1/17.

16 Transport OFFICER

No. 1. O. C.
2. 2nd i/c
3. File.
4. Intge Officer.
5. Lewis Gun Officer.
6. Signalling Offr.
7. Quartermaster.
8. O.C. "A" Coy.
9. O.C. "B" "
10. O.C. "C" "
11. O.C. "D" Coy.
12. War Diary.
13. " "
14. O.C. 15th Hants.
15. O.C. 18th K.R.R.

APPX II

SECRET.

Copy No....12.......

10th ROYAL WEST KENT REGIMENT.

OPERATION ORDER No 47.

1. The Battalion will be relieved to-morrow the 8th inst, by the 18th Kings Royal Rifle Corps. Relief to commence at 9.30.a.m.

2. Companies will be ready to move off by 9.15 a.m. and men will remain in their billets until their relief arrives.

3. The Lewis Gun Officer and Signalling Sergeant will make all arrangements for their reliefs.

4. On completion of relief, units will march via DICKEBUSCH HALLEBAST CORNER - OUDERDOM to CHIPPEWA CAMP. All movements by Platoons at 100 yards distance.

5. Maps, Aeroplane Photos, and Trench Stores will be handed over and a receipt obtained. All receipts are to be sent to Bn Hd Qrs, CHIPPEWA. Indents for R.E. Stores will be submitted as usual, & details of those handed over to the relieving units.

6. Completion of Relief to be at once reported to Bn Hd Qrs DICKEBUSCH, by O.C. Companies, Lewis Gun Officer, and Sig: Sergt.

7. CHIPPEWA CAMP will be taken over by the Quartermaster by 10.a.m. 8th inst.
O.C. "A" Coy will detail one N.C.O., and 6 men to leave DICKEBUSCH at 8.30.a.m. and relieve the Camp Guard at CHIPPEWA.

8. TRANSPORT. A mounted orderly from the Transport Lines is to report at Bn Hd Qrs DICKEBUSCH, by 11.30.a.m. 8th inst.
Blankets of "A" and "C" Companies must be rolled & stacked at the Quartermaster's Stores, DICKEBUSCH, by 9.a.m. Company limbers will then convey to CHIPPEWA according to instructions given.
Blankets of "B" and "D" Companies will be carried down by the men and rolled at Quartermaster's Stores DICKEBUSCH where they will be loaded on Company limbers, together with the mens packs.
A G.S.Wagon is to be at Headquarters at 9.a.m. for Hd Qr blankets, Orderly Room boxes, and Officers' kits of "C" and "A" Companies and Headquarters.
The Mess Cart will collect Mess Boxes and have same loaded by 10.a.m.
Mess Boxes and Officers' kits of "B" and "D" Companies will ~~the~~ be brought down on the ration limbers this evening, 7th inst and stored at Quartermaster's Stores, DICKEBUSCH, until the following morning.
The Maltese Cart is to be at DICKEBUSCH by 10.30.a.m.
Field Kitchens and Water Cart are to leave DICKEBUSCH by 9.a.m. 8th inst. All Cooks are to be in DICKEBUSCH by 9.a.m. to accompany cookers and prepare a hot meal for men on arrival at CHIPPEWA.
All Petrol Cans not handed over are to be brought back to Camp.

7/1/17.

R.R. Steward [signature]
Capt. & Adjt.
10th R. W. Kent Regt.

Copy No.					
1.	Filed.	6.	O.C. "D" Coy.	11.	Lewis Gun Officer
2.	C.O.	7.	Medical Officer.	12.	War Diary.
3.	O.C."A"Coy.	8.	Quartermaster.	13.	" "
4.	" " "B" "	9.	~~Quartermaster.~~ Transport Offr.	15.	O.C. 18th K.R.R's.
5.	" " "C" "	10.	Signalling Sergt.		

SECRET. Copy No ......1.........

APPX III

10TH ROYAL WEST KENT REGT.

BATTALION ORDER No 46.

1. The 10th Bn Royal West Kent Regt, will relieve the 15th Bn. Hampshire Regt. in the centre portion of the Left Sub-Sector, to-morrow, the 15th inst. The Relief to be complete by 7.a.m. 15th inst.

2. Dress:- Fighting Order, Great Coats rolled. Jerkins to be rolled on the back of the belt.
One blanket per man for "B" and "D" Companies, Hd. Qrs. and one blanket per man for "A" Coy (except the portion of "A" Coy occupying the LOCALITY) to be rolled in bundles of 10 and stacked ready for loading on Company Limbers by 9.a.m.
– The remainder of blankets and Packs of all Companies to be stacked by Companies ~~and placed~~ in a place to be notified later.

3. Signallers, Lewis Gunners, & Battalion Observers, will march off in separate parties, commencing at 9 a.m. under arrangements to be made by the Signalling Officer, Lewis Gun Officer, and Intelligence Officer.
The Battalion Lewis Gun Officer will arrange with the Transport Officer for the transport of his Guns.

4. The leading Platoon of "C" Coy will move off from Camp so as to reach DICKEBUSCH by 11.30.a.m., followed by "A". "B". and "D" Coys.
Movements by Platoons at 100 yards distance.
Headquarters will move off at 1.30.p.m.

5. Rations will be taken by the Transport (to be at Ration Dump at 7.p.m.nightly) whence they will be conveyed on the trolleys to their respective Company Dumps by the C.Q.M.S. and any spare men not in the line.
All men will carry the remainder of to-morrow's rations.

6. Company Limbers will be at Bn Hd. Qrs. by 9.a.m. to-morrow.
Officers'Mess Cart and one G.S.Wagon will be at Bn Hd. Qrs at 1.p.m. for Hd. Qr. Stores and Officers Kits.
These vehicles will not pass through DICKEBUSCH until dark.

7. Complete Lists of Trench Stores, etc, taken over by each Company to be sent to Bn. Hd. Qrs. by 9.a.m.

8. Completion of Relief will be reported by wire as follows:- "B.O.O. No 46" complied with".

9. Quartermaster will hand over the Camp to the incoming Unit and obtain a receipt for all Camp Furniture handed over.

10. Cookers will be taken away at 10.30.a.m.
1 Water Cart will be taken up full each night with the rations and will remain during the next day in VOORMEZEELE.

[signature] Capt. & Adjt.
10th R. W. Kent Regiment.

14/1/17.

No.1. Filed.
2. C.O.
3. O.C."A"Coy.
4. " " "B" "
5. " " "C" "
6. O.C."D"Coy.
7. Transport Officer.
8. Quartermaster.
9. Signal: Officer.
10. Lewis Gun "
11. Intelligence Officer.
12. Medical Officer.
13. 18th K.R.R.C.
14. 15th Hants. Regt.
15. War Diary.
16 " "

S E C R E T. Copy No....15.......

10th BN. R. W. KENT REGT.

APPX IV

BATTALION OPERATION ORDER No 52.

1. The Battalion will be relived by the 18th K.R.R.C. on 22nd January 1917.

2. The leading Platoon of the Relieving Unit to be at DICKEBUSCH by 11.30.a.m. 22/1/17.

3. On completion of Relief Companies will return to CHIPPEWA CAMP via DICKEBUSCH - HALLEBAST CORNER - OUDERDOM. All movements will be by Platoons at 100 yards distance.

4. Maps, Aeroplane Photographs, and Trench Stores, will be handed over and a receipt obtained. Receipt to be handed to Adjutant by O.C. Company on passing Battalion Headquarters. Great care should be taken in compiling these lists. Indents for R.E.Stores to be submitted as usual and details of these to be handed over to the Relief.

5. O.C.Companies will arrange for their blankets to be brought out in bundles of 10 and dumped in the vicinity of Bn.Hd.Qrs. An N.C.O. or reliable man should be left in charge of each Company dump, and assist in loading of transport. Care should be taken that only articles taken into the line are brought out.

6. All Trenches and Dugouts are to be left as clean as possible and all trench boots not in use will be sent to Drying Room at Bn Head Qrs. A thorough search is to be made that none of these are left in Dugouts or anywhere about the trenches.

7. Work in hand and proposed work must be thoroughly explained to O.C. Relieving Unit.

8. Transport will be near Y.M.C.A. DICKEBUSCH to convey the Half Company of "A" from the MUD-PATCH to CAMP. O.C. "A" Coy will send one Cook to Bn. Hd. Qrs to report to the R.S.M. after dinner to-morrow, to make a hot drink for this Half-Coy on their reaching Bn. Hd. Qrs. The Cook will obtain the necessary Soup Squares at Bn Hd Qrs.

9. The Lewis Gun Officer will arrange for all Lewis Guns, (with the exception of the three in the MUD-PATCH) to be placed in the Lewis Gun limbers at DICKEBUSCH and taken to Camp. The Transport Officer will arrange for the Lewis Guns limbers to be at DICKEBUSCH by 2.p.m. The three Lewis Guns from the MUD-PATCH will be conveyed in the limbers conveying the Half-Company from DICKEBUSCH.

10. Transport as follows will be at Bn. Hd. Qrs by 6 p.m.:-
<u>Headquarters.</u> 1 G.S.Wagon, Maltese Cart, & (Officers Mess Cart. 5 p.m.)
<u>"A" "B" "C" "D" Coys.</u> 1 Limber per Company.
Headquarter Officers' Horses to be at DICKEBUSCH by 7.p.m.
Limbers for conveying the Half-Company and Machine Guns from MUD-PATCH to be at DICKEBUSCH by 9 p.m.

11. The Pioneer Officer will make arrangements for the party of 42 Pioneers. Their blankets etc will be loaded at Bn Hd Qrs.

12. C.Q.M.S. will arrange to have a good hot meal for their Companies on arriving in Camp.

13. Completion of Relief to be reported to Bn Hd Qrs by wire, viz:- "B.O.52 complied with", and Coy Commanders will report in person on passing Bn Hd Qrs.

[signature] Capt & Adjt.

21/1/17.

1. Filed.
2. C.O.
3. 2nd i/c
4. O.C. "A"
5. O.C."B"
6. O.C."C"
7. O.C."D"
8. Int: Offr.
9. L.G.Officer.
10. Signal "
11. Transport "
12. Quartermaster.
13. Medical Officer
14. O.C.18th K.R.R.C
15. War Diary.
16. " "
17. Pioneer Officer.

APPX II

SECRET. Copy No ..141.....

10TH BN ROYAL WEST KENT REGIMENT.

BATTALION OPERATION ORDER. No. 53.

1. The Battalion will relieve the 15th Bn Hampshire Regt as Reserve bn, Left Sub-Sector, to-morrow 28th inst. Relief to be completed by 7.a.m. 28th inst.

2. Relief to be carried out via:- RENINGHELST - OUDERDOM - MILLEKAPELLEN FARM (H.1.20.c.) Leading Platoon to reach DICKEBUSCH by 9.30.a.m.

3. The Battalion will move off by Platoons at 100 yards distance in the following order:-
"B" Coy. Leading Platoon move off at 7.30.a.m. followed by "D". "C" and "A" Companies.
Headquarters move off at 1.30.p.m.
"A" Coy will relieve Coy of 15th Hants at CONVENT. VOORMEZEELE.
"B" " " " " " " " DICKEBUSCH.
"C" " " " " " " " CONVENT SCHOOL "
"D" " " " " " " " DICKEBUSCH (Brasserie)

4. Maps, Stores, & Indents for R.E.Stores are to be taken over and a complete list shewing the articles received to be forwarded to Bn. Hd. Qrs by 7.p.m. 28th inst.

5. Specialists will move and remain with their Coys, with the exception of the Pioneer Section, who will be billetted together under arrangements to be made by the Pioneer Officer.

6. Blankets are to be rolled in bundles of 10, labelled, and stacked ready for loading at 6.45.a.m. 3 Cookers (with fires lighted) i.e."B" & "D" Coys, & one for Hd Qrs, & 2 Water Carts (filled) will proceed in rear of the Battalion at 300 yards distance. Dixies will be taken by "A" and "C" Coys for cooking in VOORMEZEELE.

7. One G.S.Wagon, Maltese Cart, and 1 Limber per Company will be at Bn. Hd. Qrs at 7.a.m. All loading to be completed by 7.30.a.m. Officers Mess Cart to be at Bn Hd Qrs by 9.a.m. Transport Officer will make necessary arrangements, if it is found necessary to make a second journey. Lewis Gun Carts to be at Bn Hd Qrs at 7.a.m. to convey Lewis Guns.
C.Q.M.S. and 2 men per Coy will remain behind to load up if a second journey is found necessary.

8. Bn.Hd.Qr.Guard CHIPPEWA CAMP will remain on duty until relieved by the 18th K.R.R's., and will then proceed to Bn. Hd. Qrs. DICKEBUSCH and report to R.S.M.

9. The Camp must be left scrupulously clean. Officers Commanding Companies must see that their lines are thoroughly clean before parading.
The Q.M. will hand over the Camp to the incoming unit and obtain a receipt for the same. He should also obtain a Chit as to the cleanliness of the Camp when handed over.

10. Completion of relief to be reported to Bn. Hd. Qrs. by the quickest method available. viz:- "B.O.No.53 complied with"

27/1/17.

[signature] Capt & Adjt.
10th R. W. Kent Regiment.

No.1. O.C.
2. 2nd i/c
3. File.
4. Int: Officer.
5. Lewis Gun "
6. Signalling"
7. Quartermaster.
8. O.C. "A" Coy.
9 " "B" "
10. " "C" "
11. " "D" "
12. Pioneer Officer.
13. Transport Officer.
14. War Diary.
15 " "
16. O.C. 15th Hants.
17. O.C. 18th K.R.R.C.

10th Royal West Kent Regt

WAR DIARY
or
INTELLIGENCE SUMMARY

(Erase heading not required.)

Sheet I February 1917

Vol 10

Army Form C. 2118.

Instructions regarding War Diaries and Intelligence Summaries are contained in F. S. Regs., Part II. and the Staff Manual respectively. Title Pages will be prepared in manuscript.

Place	Date	Hour	Summary of Events and Information	Remarks and references to Appendices
Reserve Battn DICKEBUSCH H26.c.7.1	1.2.17		Situation normal, Artillery fire in DICKEBUSCH AREA above normal. Strength Offs 42. O.R. 1025.	
	2.2.17		" " Offs 42. O.R. 1025.	
	3.2.17		" " During above period The Battn found R.E. working partys and carrying partys to Front Line	
		12 noon	The Battalion relieved by 18th Bn King. Royal Rifles and withdrawn by Platoons to CHIPPEWA CAMP M6a4.7. This operation was carried out successfully. Casualties 1 O.R. wounded. Strength Offs 42. O.R. 1024 Evacuated Sick O.R. 1	APPX I
CHIPPEWA CAMP M6a4.7	4.2.17		Situation normal, Rest and Training, improvement of Camp. Draft joined 15. O.R. Strength Offs 42. O.R. 1030. Evacuated Sick O.R. 9.	
	5.2.17		" " Strength Offs 42. O.R. 1031.	
	6.2.17		" " Strength Offs 42 O.R. 1031.	
	7.2.17	4.30 PM	A Fire broke out in the Officers hut although immediate action was taken it was impossible to extinguish. Constant flooding of the huts in near vicinity prevented the fire spreading. The Hut was completely destroyed and several officers kit. Strength Offs 42 O.R. 1031	
	8.2.17		Situation normal Rest & Training Strength Offs 42. O.R. 1031	
	9.2.17		" " Strength Offs 42. O.R. 1021 Evacuated Sick O.R. 10	
	10.2.17	7 AM	Situation normal, The Battalion relieved 15th Battn Hampshire Regt in the Centre portion of Left Subsector APPX II This operation was carried out successfully. 'A' Co Front-line, 'B' Co. VOORMEZEELE SWITCH, 'C' Co ECLUSE TRENCH, 'D' Co OLD FRENCH TRENCH & LOCALITY. Quiet day. Wounded 1. O.R. Strength Offs 42 O.R. 1014. Evacuated Sick O.R. 6	APPX II
Centre Left Sub-sector	11.2.17		Situation normal, Patrols out during night and reported hostile working party which was dispersed, Machine guns active during night.	
		11 AM	Stokes Gun fired on an Enemy Snipers post, the shooting was good, Enemy retaliated heavily with minenwerfer on our Front line. Enemy snipers less active, Killed O.R. 2 Wounded O.R. 2 Strength Offs 42. O.R. 1013. Evacuated O.R. 1.	
	12.2.17		Situation normal, Patrols out during night reported an Enemy wiring party, this was dispersed by Rifle fire.	
		3.30 Am	Enemy blew up a Camouflet which caused little damage beyond cracking a few struts, no action followed. During the morning Our Artillery fired on Enemy Front line to which Enemy retaliated with 20. 77 m/m. A Stokes gun shoot caused Enemy to retaliate with rum-jars.	
		2 PM	Enemy fired Minenwerfer on Our Front line Stokes gun replied with 60 Rds which silenced Enemy	
		6 PM	C Co relieved 'A' Co in FRONT LINE Killed O.R. 1 Strength Offs 42 O.R. 1005	
	13.2.17		Situation normal, Patrols out during night located Enemy machine guns and Sentries, Our machine guns active with indirect fire. Early in the morning a party of nine Germans crossed No mans land and attempted to enter Our Trench, the Sentry grappled with the first man and tried to capture him but he escaped, The whole party was fired on and ran back through the mist.	

2449 Wt. W14957/M90 750,000 1/16 J.B.C. & A. Forms/C.2118/12.

10th Royal West Kent Regt

Instructions regarding War Diaries and Intelligence Summaries are contained in F. S. Regs., Part II. and the Staff Manual respectively. Title Pages will be prepared in manuscript.

WAR DIARY
or
INTELLIGENCE SUMMARY
(Erase heading not required.)

Sheet II February 1917

Army Form C. 2118.

Place	Date	Hour	Summary of Events and Information	Remarks and references to Appendices
Centre Left Sub-sector	13/2/17	1.30 PM	Stokes Gun opened fire on suspected Snipers posts, Enemy retaliated with Minenwerfer and Shrapnel. Stokes Gun continued to fire and our Artillery also retaliated. Killed O.R. 2 Wounded O.R. 2 Strength 42 Officers 1008 O.R.	
– " –	14/2/17		Situation normal. Patrols out during night report all quiet, Machine Guns active on Enemys Dumps and Communications, much counter-battery work during day.	
		4 PM	Enemy fired Shrapnel over OLD FRENCH TRENCH to which our Artillery replied. "A" Co relieved "B" Co in FRONT LINE. Wounded O.R. 7. Strength 42 Offs 988 O.R. Evacuated Sick O.R. 12.	
– " –	15/2/17		Situation normal. Patrols out but nothing unusual to report. Night quiet	
		9 Am	Enemy fired four 77 mm on FRONT LINE, and shrapnel on OLD FRENCH TRENCH, Our Snipers active. Strength 42 Offs 988 O.R.	
	16/2/17		Situation normal, Patrols out during night and report on Enemys wire. Enemy fired Minenwerfer and [illegible] on front line, otherwise quiet during the day	
		4 PM	"C" Co relieved "A" Co in front line. Strength 42 Offs 988 O.R.	
	17/2/17	12 Noon	Situation normal, The Battalion relieved by 15th Bn Hampshire Regt and withdrawn by Platoons as relieved to CHIPPEWA CAMP M.6.a.4.7. this operation was carried out successfully. Wounded 1 O.R. Strength 42 Offs 988 O.R.	APPX III
CHIPPEWA CAMP M.6.a.4.7	18/2/17		Situation normal, Rest & Training, Lt Col Wood-Martyn rejoined Battalion and resumed Command. Draft of 27 O.R. joined. Strength 42 Offs 1002 O.R. Evacuated 13. O.R.	
	19/2/17		Situation Normal. Rest & Training, Draft joined 35 O.R. Strength 42 Offs 1035 O.R. Evacuated 2. O.R.	
	20/2/17		" " 2/Lt. Dillon & Draft of 7 OR joined. Strength 43 Offs 1040 O.R. Evacuated 2. O.R.	
	21/2/17		" " Strength 43 Offs 1039 O.R. Evacuated 1. O.R.	
	22/2/17	5 AM	Situation normal. Battalion relieved 15th Battalion Hampshire Regt in Centre portion of Left Sub-sector APPX IV This operation was carried out successfully. "A" Co ECLUSE TRENCH, "B" Co OLD FRENCH TRENCH & LOCALITY, "C" Co VOORMEZEELE SWITCH, "D" Co FRONT LINE. Day exceptionally quiet, Wounded 1 O.R. Strength 43 Offs 1039 O.R.	APPX IV
Centre Left Sub-sector	23/2/17		Situation normal, Patrols out during night returned with useful information, Quiet during morning, During afternoon our Artillery bombarded the Craters with good effect, Enemy retaliated with minenwerfer and Shrapnel, no damage done. Killed 2. O.R. Strength 43 Offs 1037 O.R.	
– " –	24/2/17	5 AM	Situation normal, "A" Co relieve "D" Co in FRONT LINE, Our Artillery bombarded CRATERS with good effect.	
		4 PM	In accordance with pre-arranged plan Our Front Line troops withdrawn to OLD FRENCH TRENCH.	

2449 Wt. W14957/M90 750,000 1/16 J.B.C. & A. Forms/C.2118/12.

10th Royal West Kent Regt

Instructions regarding War Diaries and Intelligence Summaries are contained in F. S. Regs., Part II. and the Staff Manual respectively. Title Pages will be prepared in manuscript.

WAR DIARY
or
INTELLIGENCE SUMMARY

(*Erase heading not required.*)

Sheet III February 1917

Army Form C. 2118.

Place	Date	Hour	Summary of Events and Information	Remarks and references to Appendices
Centre Left Sub-Sector	24/2/17	4.25 PM	Enemy heavily bombarded our FRONT & OLD SUPPORT LINE.	
		4.55 PM	Our Artillery barraged CRATERS to cover the Raid on Our right, The Raid was very successful, Our front line and Old Support lines was under heavy Enemy barrage. The disposition of Company preventing casualties. The movement of our men in front line had evidently led Enemy to expect the Raid to come from our front. Our Patrol out last night dispersed Enemy patrol with bombs. 2/Lt J.C. Brown, slightly wounded, 1. O.R. slightly wounded. Strength 43 Offs 1032 O.R. Evacuated 3. O.R.	
	25/2/17		Situation normal. Patrol out during night report all quiet. Quiet during day. 1. O.R. slightly wounded. Strength 43 Offs 1032 O.R.	
	26/2/17		Situation normal. Enemy shelled VOORMEZEELE. Our Artillery retaliated and silenced Enemy.	
		5 AM	"D" Co relieved "A" Co in FRONT LINE. State of No Mans Land prevented useful patrol work during night. 2/Lt H. Harris joined, 2. O.R. wounded, Strength 43 Offs 1032 O.R.	
	27/2/17	12 Noon	Situation normal. The Battalion relieved by 15th Battn Hampshire Regt and Platoons as relieved marched back to CHIPPEWA CAMP M.6.a.4.7. this operation was carried out successfully. Strength 44 Offs 1027 O.R. Evacuated 3 O.R.	APPX V
	28/2/17		Situation normal. Rest & Training. Strength 44 Offs 1037. O.R.	

A Wood [illegible] Lt Col
Comm dg 10th Royal West Kent Regt

2449 Wt. W14957/M90 750,000 1/16 J.B.C. & A. Forms/C.2118/12.

APPX I

S E C R E T

Copy No....14.....

10th ROYAL WEST KENT REGIMENT.

OPERATION ORDER No 54.

1. The Battalion will be relieved to-morrow the 3rd inst, by the 18th Kings Royal Rifle Corps. Relief to commence at 9.30.a.m.

2. Companies will be ready to move off by 9.15.a.m. and men will remain in their billets until their relief arrives.

3. The Lewis Gun Officer and Signalling Officer will make all arrangements for their reliefs.

4. On completion of relief, units will march via DICKEBUSCH HALLEBAST CORNER -OUDERDOM to CHIPPEWA CAMP. All movements by Platoons at 100"yards distance.

5. Maps, Aeroplane Photos, and Trench Stores will be handed over and a receipt obtained. All receipts are to be sent to Bn Hd Qrs, CHIPPEWA. Indents for R.E.Stores will be submitted as usual, and details of these handed over to the relieving unit.

6. Completion of Relief to be at once reported to Bn Hd Qrs DICKEBUSCH, by O.C. Companies, Lewis Gun Officer, and Sig: Officer.

7. CHIPPEWA CAMP will be taken over by the Quartermaster by 10. a.m. 3rd inst.
O.C."B" Coy will detail one N.C.O.., and 6 men to leave DICKEBUSCH at 8.30.a.m. and relieve the Camp Guard at CHIPPEWA.

8. TRANSPORT. A mounted orderly from the Transport Lines is to report at Bn Hd Qrs DICKEBUSCH, by 11.30.a.m. 3 rd inst.
Blankets of "B" and "D" Companies must be rolled and stacked at the Quartermaster's Stores, DICKEBUSCH, by 9.a.m. Company limbers will then convey to CHIPPEWA according to instructions given.
Blankets of "A" and "C" Companies will be carried down by the men and rolled at Quartermaster's Stores, DICKEBUSCH, where they will be loaded on Company limbers.
A G.S. Wagon is to be at Headquarters at 9.a.m. for Hd. Qr. blankets, Orderly Room boxes, and Officers' kits of "B" and "D" Companies and Headquarters.
The Mess Cart will collect Mess Boxes and have same loaded by 10.a.m.
Mess Boxes and Officers' kits of "A" and "C" Companies will be brought down on the ration limbers this evening, 2nd inst, and stored at Quartermaster's Stores, DICKEBUSCH, until the following morning.
The Maltese Cart is to be at DICKEBUSCH by 10.30.a.m.
Field Kitchens and Water Cart are to leave DICKEBUSCH by 9.a.m. 3rd inst. All Cooks are to be at DICKEBUSCH by 8.a.m. to accompany cookers and prepare a hot meal for men on arrival at CHIPPEWA.
All Petrol Cans not handed over are to be brought back to Camp.

[signature] 2nd Lieut.
for Capt. & Adjt.
10th R.W.Kent Regiment.

2/2/17.

No.1. Filed.	7. Quartermaster.	13. Pioneer Officer.
2. C.O.	8. Medical Officer.	14. War Diary.
3. 2nd i/c.	9. O.C. "A" Coy.	15. " "
4. Int. Officer.	10. " "B" "	16. O.C. 18th K.R.R.C.
5. Lewis Gun "	11. " "C" "	Transport Officer.
6. Signalling "	12. " "D" "	

APPX: II

S E C R E T. Copy No......15....

10TH ROYAL WEST KENT REGIMENT.

OPERATION ORDER No 55.

1. The Battalion will relieve the 15th Hants Regt in the centre Portion of the Left Sub-Sector, tomorrow, the 10th inst. Relief to be complete by 7.a.m. 11th inst.

2. Dress:- Fighting Order, Great Coats rolled. Jerkins to be rolled on the back of the belt.
One Blanket per man to be taken(with the exception of "A" Coy and the portion of "D" Coy occupying the LOCALITY) to be rolled in bundles of 10 and stacked ready for loading on Company Limbers by 7.a.m.- The remainder of blankets and Packs of all Coys to be stacked by Companies in a place to be notified later.

3. Signallers, Lewis Gunners, & Battalion Observers, will march off in separate parties, commencing at 7.30 a.m. under arrangements to be made by the Signalling Officer, Lewis Gun & Int Officer. The Bn Lewis Gun Officer will arrange with the Transport Officer for the transport of his guns.

4. The leading Platoon of "A" Coy will move off from Camp so as to reach DICKEBUSCH by 9.30.a.m., followed by "D", "C" and "B"Coys. Movements by Platoons at 100 yards distance.
Headquarters will move off at 11.30.a.m.

5. Rations will be taken by the Transport (to be at Ration Dump at 7.p.m. nightly) whence they will be conveyed on the trolleys to their respective Company Dumps by the C.Q.M.S. & any spare men not in the line. All men will carry the remainder of to-morrow's rations.
Coy Limbers will be at Bn Hd Qrs by 7.a.m. to-morrow.
Officers' Mess Cart and one G.S.Wagon will be at Bn Hd Qrs at 11.30.a.m. for Hd. Qr. Stores and Officers Kits.
Vehicles will not pass through DICKEBUSCH until dark.
Complete Lists of Trench Stores, etc, taken over by each Coy to be sent to Bn Hd Qrs by 9.a.m. 11/3/17.
Quartermaster will hand over Camp to the incoming Unit and obtain a receipt for all Camp Furniture handed over, including the Prisoners of War Coy Camp.

9. Cookers will be taken away at 9.30.a.m. 1 Water Cart to be taken up full each night with the rations and will remain during the next day in VOORMEZEELE.

10. The Pioneer Officer will arrange for the billotting of the party of Pioneers as before, and see that they get their blankets and rations.

11. Completion of Relief to be reported by wire as follows:- "B"O"O" No 55 complied with".

[signature]
2/Lieut.
for Capt. & Adjt.
10th R.W.Kent Regiment.

/17.

1. Filed.	7. Transport Officer.	13. O.C.18th K.R.R.C.
2. C. O.	8. Quartermaster.	14. O.C.15th Hants Regt
3. O.C."A"Coy.	9. Signal: Officer.	15. War Diary.
4. " "B" "	10. Lewis Gun & Int. O.	16. " "
5. " "C" "	11. Medical Officer.	
6. " "D" "	12. Pioneer Officer.	

APPX III

S E C R E T. Copy No....16....

10th R. W. Kent Regt.

BATTALION OPERATION ORDER No.50.

1. The Battalion will be relieved by the 15th Hants Regt on 17th February 1917.

2. The leading Platoon of the Relieving Unit to be at DICKEBUSCH by 9.30.a.m. 17/2/17.

3. On completion of Relief Coys will return to Chippewa Camp via DICKEBUSCH -HALLEBAST CORNER - OUDERDOM. All movements will be by Platoons at 100 yards distance.

4. Maps, Aeroplane Photographs, and Trench Stores, will be handed over and a receipt obtained. Receipt to be handed to Adjutant by O.C. Coy on passing Bn Hd Qrs. Great care should be taken in compiling these lists. Indents for R.E.Stores to be submitted as usual and details of these to be handed over to the Relief.

5. O.C. Companies will arrange for their blankets to be brought out in bundles of 10 and dumped in the vicinity of Bn.Hd.Qrs. An N.C.O. or reliable man should be left in charge of each Coy dump, and assist in loading of transport. Care should be taken that only articles taken into the line are brought out.

6. All Trenches and Dugouts are to be left as clean as possible and all trench boots not in use will be sent to Drying Room at Bn Hd Qrs. A thorough search is to be made that none of these are left in Dugouts or anywhere about the trenches.

7. Work in hand and proposed work must be thoroughly explained to O.C. Relieving Unit.

8. Transport will be ~~near Y.M.C.A.~~ at old Q.M. stores DICKEBUSCH to convey the LOCALITY GARRISON back to Camp. O.C. "D" Coy will send one Cook to Bn. Hd. Qrs. to report to R.S.M. to-morrow, to make a hot drink for the LOCALITY GARRISON on their reaching Bn Hd Qrs

The Lewis Gun Officer will arrange for the relief of all his Lewis Gunners.

Transport Officer will arrange for the following:-
Headquarter Officers' Horses to be at DICKEBUSCH at 1.30.p.m.
Mess Cart & Maltese Cart to be at VOORMEZEELE as soon as light~~s~~ permits.
Coy Limbers & Hd. Qrs. G.S.Wagon for all blankets & stores to be at VOORMEZEELE by 7.p.m., or before if light permits.
1 Lewis Gun Limber to be at VOORMEZEELE at 7.p.m.
Remaining Lewis Gun Limbers to be at DICKEBUSCH at 1.30.p.m. outside old Q.M.Stores.
2 G.S.Wagons to be at DICKEBUSCH at 8.30.p.m. outside old Q.M.Stores for carrying LOCALITY GARRISON.

11. C.Q.M.S. will arrange to have a good hot meal for their Coys on arriving in Camp.

12. Completion of Relief to be reported to Bn Hd Qrs by wire viz:- "B.O.O.50 complied with", and Coy Commanders will report in person on passing Bn Hd Qrs.

[signature]
2/Lieut.
for Capt & Adjt.

16/2/17.

1. Filed.
2. C.O.
3. 2nd i/c
4. O.C. "A"Coy.
5. O.C. "B" Coy.
6. " "C" "
7. " "D" "
8. L.G.& Int Offr
9. Signal. Offr.
10. Transport "
11. Quartermaster.
12. Medical Offr.
13. O.C.15th Hants.
14. Pioneer Officer.
15. War Diary.
16. " "

APPX. IV

S E C R E T. Copy No..14........

10TH ROYAL WEST KENT REGIMENT.

OPERATION ORDER No 80.

1. The Battalion will relieve the 15th Hants Regt in the centre portion of the left Sub-Sector, to-morrow, the 22nd inst. Relief to be complete by 7.a.m. 23rd inst.

2. Dress:- Fighting Order, Great Coats rolled. Jerkins to be rolled on the back of the belt.
One blanket per man to be taken (with the exception of "D" Coy and the portion of "B" Coy occupying the LOCALITY). to be rolled in bundles of 10 and stacked ready for loading on Company Limbers at 7.a.m. The remaining blankets of all Coys to be stacked in bundles in Shoemaker's Store, with the exception of 10 blankets per Coy which will be sent to the Quartermaster's Stores for medical huts. Packs will be stored by Coys in separate tents (1 tent per Coy) set apart for that purpose.

3. Signallers, Lewis Gunners, & Battalion Observers, will march off in separate parties, commencing at 7.30.a.m. under arrangements to be made by the Signalling Officer, Lewis Gun & Intelligence Officer. The Bn Lewis Gun Officer will arrange with the Transport Officer for the transport of his guns.

4. The leading Platoon of "D" Coy will move off from Camp so as to reach DICKEBUSCH by 9.30.a.m., followed by "B" "A" and "C" Coys. Movements by Platoons at 100 yards distance.
Headquarters will move off at 11.30.a.m.

5. Rations will be taken by the Transport (to be at Ration Dump at 7.p.m. nightly) whence they will be conveyed on the trolleys to their respective Coy Dumps by the C.Q.M.S., & any spare men not in the line. All men will carry the remainder of to-morrow's rations.

6. Coy Limbers will be at Bn Hd Qrs by 7.a.m. to-morrow. Officers' Mess Cart and one G.S.Wagon will be at Bn Hd Qrs at 11.a.m. for Hd Qr Stores and Officers Kits.
Vehicles will not pass through DICKEBUSCH until dark.

7. Complete Lists of Trench Stores, etc. taken over by each Coy to be sent to Bn Hd Qrs by 9.a.m. 23/3/17.

8. Quartermaster will hand over Camp to the incoming Unit and obtain a receipt for all Camp Furniture handed over, including the Prisoners of War Coy Camp.

9. Cookers will be taken away at 9.30.a.m. 1 Water Cart to be taken up full each night with the rations and will remain during the next day in VOORMEZEELE.

10. The 12 Pioneers of "C" Coy will march off with Hd Qrs and be billetted with them at VOORMEZEELE.

11. Completion of Relief to be reported by wire as follows:- "B.C.O.80 complied with".

12. CHIPPEWA CAMP and all billets to be left scrupulously clean and certificates to be rendered by O.C. Coys to that effect.

[signature] 2/Lieut.
A/Adjutant.
10th R.W.Kent Regt.

22/3/17.

No.1. Filed.	6. Transport Officer.	11. Medical Officer.
2. C.O.	7. O.C."D" Coy.	12. Pioneer "
3. O.C."A"Coy.	8. Quartermaster.	13. O.C.15th Hants.
4. " "B" "	9. Signal Officer.	14. War Diary.
5. " "C" "	10. Lewis Gun & Int O.	15. " "

APPX V

S E C R E T. Copy No......16...

10th BN R. W. KENT REGT.

BATTALION OPERATION ORDER No 63.

1. The Battalion will be relieved by the 15th Hants Regt on 27th February 1917.

2. The leading Platoon of the Relieving Unit to be at DICKEBUSCH by 9.30.a.m. 27/2/17.

3. On completion of Relief Coys will return to CHIPPEWA CAMP via DICKEBUSCH -HALLEBAST CORNER - CUDERDOM. All movements will be by Platoons at 100 yards distance.

4. Maps, Aeroplane Photographs, and Trench Stores, will be handed over and a receipt obtained. Receipt to be handed to Adjutant by O.C. Coy on passing Bn Hd Qrs. Great care should be taken in compiling these lists. Indents for R.E.Stores to be submitted as usual and details of these handed over to the Relief.

5. O.C. Coys will arrange for their blankets to be brought out in bundles of 10 and dumped in the vicinity of Bn Hd Qrs. An N.C.O. or reliable man should be left in charge of each Coy dump, and assist in loading of transport. Care should be taken that only articles taken into the line are brought out.

6. All Trenches and Dugouts are to be left as clean as possible and all trench boots not in use will be sent to Drying Room at Bn Hd Qrs. A thorough search is to be made that none of these are left in Dugouts or anywhere about the trenches.

7. Work in hand and proposed work must be thoroughly explained to O.C. Relieving Unit.

8. 2 G. S. Wagons will be at CAFE BELGE at 8.30.p.m. to convey the LOCALITY GARRISON back to Camp. O.C. "B" Coy will send one Cook to Bn Hd Qrs to report to R.S.M. tomorrow, to make a hot drink for the LOCALITY GARRISON on their reaching Bn Hd Qrs.

9. The Lewis Gun Officer will arrange for the relief of his Lewis Gunners.

10. Transport Officer will arrange for the following:-
Headquarter Officers' Horses to be at DICKEBUSCH at 1.30.p.m.
Mess Cart and Maltese Cart to be at VOORMEZEELE as soon as light permits.
Coy Limbers and Hd. Qrs. G. S. Wagon for all blankets and stores to be at VOORMEZEELE as soon as light permits.
1 Lewis Gun Limber to be at VOORMEZEELE at 7.p.m.
Remaining Lewis Gun Limbers to be at DICKEBUSCH at 1.30.p.m. outside old Q.M.Stores.

11. C.Q.M.S. will arrange to have a good hot meal for their Coys on arriving in Camp.

12. Completion of Relief to be reported to Bn Hd Qrs by wire, viz:- "B.O.O. 63 complied with", and Coy Commanders will report in person on passing Bn Hd Qrs.

[signature]
2/Lieut.
for O.C.BLOOD.

26/2/17.

Filed.	5. O.C. "B" Coy.	9. Signal Offr.	13. O.C.15th Hants.
C.O.	6. " "C" "	10. Transport "	14. Pioneer Officer.
2nd i/c.	7. " "D" "	11. Quartermaster.	15. War Diary.
O.C."A"Coy.	8. L.G.& Int.Offr.	12. Medical Offr.	16. " "

Army Form C. 2118

Instructions regarding War Diaries and Intelligence Summaries are contained in F. S. Regs., Part II. and the Staff Manual respectively. Title Pages will be prepared in manuscript.

WAR DIARY or INTELLIGENCE SUMMARY

(Erase heading not required.)

10th Bn Royal West Kent Regt March 1917 Sheet No I

Vol XI

Place	Date	Hour	Summary of Events and Information	Remarks and references to Appendices
CHIPPEWA CAMP M6.a.4.7	1/3/17		Rest & Training. Strength Offs 44. O.R. 1029.	
"	2/3/17		" " Offs 44. O.R. 1029.	
"	3/3/17		" " Offs 44. O.R. 1029.	
"	4/3/17		" " Offs 44. O.R. 1029.	
DICKEBUSCH H26.c.7.1	5/3/17	7 AM	Situation normal. The Battalion relieved the 18th Battn King's Royal Rifle Corps as Reserve Battalion Left sub-sector. This operation was carried out successfully. (Battalion H.Q. 'A' & 'C' Coys at DICKEBUSCH 'B' Coy CONVENT, VOORMEZEELE. 'D' Coy ECLUSE TRENCH (Left) Evacuated sick OR 3. Strength Offs 44. O.R. 1026.	OP. O. No 64 APPX I
"	6/3/17		Situation normal. Strength Offs 44. O.R. 1026.	
"	7/3/17	7 AM	Situation normal. Lt Tennyson Smith wounded whilst on Special Reconnaissance, he was carried in by Cpl Wallis under Enemy's fire, but expired 15 minutes afterwards. Strength Offs 43. O.R. 1026.	
"	8/3/17		Situation normal. Strength Offs 43. O.R. 1026.	
"	9/3/17		Situation normal. Casualties Killed. O.R. 1. Wounded O.R. 2. Evacuated Sick O.R. 6. Strength Offs 43. O.R. 1017.	
"	10/3/17		Situation normal. Strength Offs 43. O.R. 1018.	
"	11/3/17		Situation normal. During above period whilst in Reserve the Battalion furnished Working Party for R.E. constructing and reclaiming Trenches carrying parties to Front Line.	
		11.30 AM	The Battalion relieved by 15th Battn Hampshire Regt. this operation was carried out successfully. Platoons as relieved marched back to CHIPPEWA CAMP. Strength Offs 43. O.R. 1018.	OP. O. No 65 APPX II
CHIPPEWA CAMP M6.a.4.7	12/3/17		Situation normal. Rest & Training. Strength Offs 43. O.R. 1018.	
"	13/3/17		" " Lt F.W. Roberts rejoined. Strength Offs 43. O.R. 1018.	
"	14/3/17		" " Strength Offs 44. O.R. 1018.	
"	15/3/17		" " Strength Offs 44. O.R. 1018.	
"	16/3/17		Strength Offs 44. O.R. 1018.	
	17/3/17	0.30 AM	Situation normal. The Battalion relieved the 18th Bn Kings Royal Rifle Corps in the centre portion of Left sub-sector. This operation was carried out successfully. 'B' Coy FRONT LINE, 'C' Coy LOCALITY & OLD FRENCH TRENCH, 'A' Coy VOORMEZEELE SWITCH, 'D' Coy ECLUSE TRENCH. Casualties W. O.R. 2. rejoined O.R. 7. Strength Offs 44. O.R. 1023.	OP. O. No 66 APPX III
Centre Left sub-sector	18/3/17		Situation normal. During the night enemy fired 77 cm at about one hour interval on VOORMEZEELE SWITCH. PATROLS out during night inspecting our own wire. At dawn our Snipers fired on Enemy's working party causing two certain casualties. Our Artillery active during day. Casualties K O.R. 1 W O.R. 2. Strength Offs 44. O.R. 1021	
"	19/3/17		Situation normal. Our Patrols out during night inspect and report on Enemy's wire. Our Snipers account for one man of hostile working party. Enemy's Machine guns active during the night on Our Communications	
		5 AM	Enemy fired 77 cm on Our FRONT LINE no damage done. this was in reply to Our Artillery.	
		6 PM	'D' Coy relieve 'B' Coy in FRONT LINE. Casualties W O.R. 2 Strength Offs 44 O.R. 1018.	

1875 Wt. W593/826 1,000,000 4/15 J.B.C. & A. A.D.S.S./Forms/C. 2118.

Instructions regarding War Diaries and Intelligence Summaries are contained in F. S. Regs., Part II. and the Staff Manual respectively. Title Pages will be prepared in manuscript.

10th Bn Royal West Kent Regt

WAR DIARY or INTELLIGENCE SUMMARY

(Erase heading not required.)

March 1917 Sheet II

Army Form C. 2118

Place	Date	Hour	Summary of Events and Information	Remarks and references to Appendices
Centre Left Sub-Sector	20/3/17		Situation normal, Our Machine guns and Lewis guns active during the night. Patrols out, one of our Patrols mistook enemys wire for our own and tried to get into No3 CRATER. Enemy bombed them, one was killed and one wounded. After several attempts to bring back his wounded comrade, the unwounded man returned to our Trenches.	
		11 AM.	A Party of about five germans attempted to enter our trenches at O.2.d.7.8. They were dispersed by rifle fire. Two of them remained behind in a shell hole, one was unwounded and surrendered, the other died of his wounds. Three others were hit whilst getting back to their Trenches. Casualties W & M. O.R. 2 Strength Offs 44. O.R. 1016.	
"	21/3/17		Situation normal. Machine guns active on both sides during the night. Patrols out report all quiet.	
		5 to 10 AM	Our Artillery fired continually on enemy's support lines. During the afternoon our Stokes gun fired 100 Rds on Enemy's Front Line. Hostile Trench mortars fired a few rounds on to the LOCALITY. ~~6 PM~~	
		6 PM	"B" Coy relieve "D" Coy in FRONT-LINE. Strength Offs 44. O.R 1014.	
"	22/3/17		Situation normal Machine guns active. Patrols report on Enemys wire. Artillery activity above normal	
"	22/3/17		Casualties K. O.R. 1 Strength Offs 44, O.R. 1014	
	23/3/17		Situation normal, Quiet during the night, Patrols out report all quiet.	
		11 AM	The Battalion was relieved by the 15th Bn Hampshire Regt. Platoons as relieved withdrew and marched back to CHIPPEWA. This operation was carried out successfully.	OP. O. No 69 APPX IV
			Officers joined 2Lt J. H. Dodson, 2Lt D. F. Anderson. Evacuated Sick O.R. 18. Strength Offs 44. O.R. 995.	
CHIPPEWA CAMP M.6.a 4.7.	24/3/17		Situation Normal, Rest & Training. Strength Offs 46. O.R. 995.	
	25/3/17		" " " " Strength Offs 46. O.R. 995.	
	26/3/17		" " " " Evacuated Sick O.R. 1 Strength Offs 46. O.R. 995.	
	27/3/17		" " " " Reinforcements joined O.R. 9. Strength Offs 46. O.R. 994.	
	28/3/17		" " " " Officers joined. 2Lt H. Hopkins 2Lt C. G. Cheal, Lt G. R. Bunyard	
			Reinforcements O.R. 10 Strength Offs 46 O.R. 1002.	
	29/3/17		Strength Offs 49. O.R. 1012.	
	30/3/17	7.30 AM	Situation normal. The Battalion relieved 18th Bn Kings Royal Rifle Corps as Reserve Battalion left sub-sector. This operation was carried out successfully. Bn H.Q. "B" & "D" Coy. DICKEBUSCH, "A" Coy ECLUSE TRENCH (left) "C" Coy CONVENT, VOORMEZEELE. Strength Offs 49. O.R. 1012.	OP. O. No 70 APPX V
	31/3/17		Situation normal. During period 30th 31st. The Battalion furnished parties for R.E. work and carrying parties. Strength Offs 49. O.R. 1012.	

A. Wood Martyn
Lt Col
Commdg. 10th Royal West Kent Regt.

1875 Wt. W593/826 1,000,000 4/15 J.B.C. & A. A.D.S.S./Forms/C. 2118.

APPX I

S E C R E T. Copy No. 14

10TH BN ROYAL WEST KENT REGT.

BATTALION OPERATION ORDER No. 64.

1. The Battalion will relieve the 18th K.R.R.C. as Reserve Battalion, Left Sub-Sector, to-morrow, 5th inst.

2. Relief to be carried out via:- RENINGHELST -OUDERDOM - MILLEKAPELLEN FARM (H.20.c.) Leading Platoon to reach DICKEBUSCH by 11.30.a.m.

3. The Bn will move off by Platoons at 100 yards distance in the following order:-

"A" Coy. Leading Platoon move off at 9.30.a.m. followed by "B". "C" and "D" Companies. Headquarters move off at 1.30.p.m.

"A" Coy will relieve Coy of 18th K.R.R.C. at DICKEBUSCH.
"B" " " " " " " " " CONVENT. VOORMEZEELE.
"C" " " " " " " " " DICKEBUSCH (Brasserie)
"D" " " " " " " " " CONVENT SCH. VOORMEZEELE

4. Maps, Stores, & Indents for R.E.Stores are to be taken over and a complete list shewing the articles received to be forwarded to Bn. Hd. Qrs. by 7.p.m. 5th inst.

5. Specialists will move and remain with their Companies, excepting Pioneers who will parade with Headquarters and be billetted in DICKEBUSCH to form special wiring parties for machine gun emplacements. The Lewis Gun Officer will make the necessary arrangements for the conveyance of his Lewis Guns.

6. Blankets are to be rolled in bundles of 10, labelled , and stacked ready for loading at 8.45.a.m. 3 Cookers (with fires lighted)and 2 Water Carts (filled) will proceed in rear of the Battalion at 300 yards distance. - Dixies will be taken by "B" and "D" Coys for cooking in VOORMEZEELE.

7. One G.S.Wagon, Maltese Cart, and 1 Limber per Coy will be at Bn. Hd. Qrs.at 9.a.m. All loading to be completed by 9.30.a.m. Officers Mess Cart to be at Bn. Hd. Qrs by 12.noon.

Transport Officer will make necessary arrangements if it is found that a second journey is required, and C.Q.M.S. & 2 men per Coy will remain behind to load up.

8. Bn. Hd. Qr. Guard CHIPPEWA CAMP will remain on duty until relieved by the 18th K.R.R.C., and will then proceed to Bn Hd Qrs. DICKEBUSCH and report to R.S.M.

9. The Camp must be left scrupulously clean. Officers Commanding Companies must see that their lines are thoroughly clean before leaving.

The Quartermaster and Handing Over Committee, will hand over the Camp to the incoming unit and obtain a receipt for the same as well as a Chit as to the cleanliness of the Camp when handed over.

10. Completion of Relief to be reported to Bn Hd Qrs by quickest method available. viz:- "B.O.O.64 complied with".

Atty [signature]
2/Lieut.
A/Adjutant.

4/5/17.

No.1. C.O.	6. Quartermaste	11. Pioneer Officer.
2. 2nd i/c.	7. O.C. "A" Coy	12. Transport Officer.
3. File.	8. " "B" "	13. War Diary.
4. Int.Officer.	9. " "C" "	14. " "
5. Signalling O.	10. " "D" "	15. O.C.18th K.R.R.C.

APPX II

SECRET.

Copy No. 15

OPERATION ORDER No 65.

1. The Battalion will be relieved to-morrow the 11th inst, by the 15th Hants Regt. Relief to commence at 11.30.a.m.

2. Companies will be ready to move off by 11.15 a.m. and men will remain in their billets until their relief arrives.

3. The Signalling Officer and Lewis Gun Sergeant will make all arrangements for their reliefs.

4. On completion of relief , units will march via DICKEBUSCH HALLEBAST CORNER -OUDERDOM- to CHIPPEWA CAMP. All movements by Platoons at 100 yards distance.

5. Maps, Aeroplane Photos, and Trench Stores will be handed over and a receipt obtained. All receipt are to be sent to Bn Hd Qrs, CHIPPEWA. Indents for R.E.Stores will be submitted as usual, and details of these handed over to the relieving unit.

6. Completion of relief to be at once reported to Bn Hd Qrs DICKEBUSCH, by O.C.Coys, Signalling Officer, & Lewis Gun Sergt.

7. CHIPPEWA CAMP will be taken over by the Quartermaster by 12 noon 11th inst.
- O.C. "A" Coy will detail one N.C.O.., and 3 men to leave DICKEBUSCH at 10.30.a.m. and relieve the Camp Guard at CHIPPEWA.

8. TRANSPORT. Blankets of "A" and "C" Coys must be rolled & stacked at C.Q.M.S. DICKEBUSCH by 10.a.m.
Blankets of "B" and "D" Coys will be carried down by the men and rolled at C.Q.M.S. DICKEBUSCH.
Coy limbers will convey same to CHIPPEWA CAMP, and O.C. Coys will detail men to assist in loading.
1 G.S.Wagon is to be at H.Q. at 12 noon for H.Q. blankets, Orderly Room boxes, Stores, and Officers Kits of "A" & "C" Coys.
Any Mess boxes and Officers' kits with "B" & "D" Coys will be brought down on Ration limbers on the evening of the 10th inst.
Kitchens and Water Carts to leave DICKEBUSCH by 10.30.a.m. All cooks are to be at DICKEBUSCH by 10.30.a.m. to accompany cookers and prepare a hot meal for men on arrival at CHIPPEWA.
Mess Cart will collect and take away mess boxes at 12.30 p.m.
Maltese Cart to be at DICKEBUSCH by 11.a.m.

A. Richmond
2/Lieut.
A/Adjutant.
BLOOD.

10/3/17.

No.1. Filed.
2. C.O.
3. 2nd i/c
4. Int. Officer.
5. Signalling "
6. Quartermaster.
7. Medical Officer.
8. Transport Officer.
9. O.C. "A" Coy.
10. " "B" "
11. " "C" "
12. " "D" "
13 Pioneer Officer.
14. Lewis Gun Sergt.
15. War Diary.
16. " "
17. O.C. 15th Hants.

APPX III

SECRET. Copy No. 15.

10TH. ROYAL WEST KENT REGIMENT.

OPERATION ORDER NO. 66.

1. The Battalion will relieve the 18th. K.R.R.C. in the centre portion of the left Sub-Sector, tomorrow the 17th. inst.

2. Dress:- Fighting Order, Great Coats rolled. Jerkins to be rolled on the back of the belt.
One blanket per man to be taken (with the exception of "B" Coy. and the portion of "C" Coy. occupying the LOCALITY). to be rolled in bundles of 10 and stacked ready for loading on Company Limbers at 7 a.m. The remaining blankets of all Coys. to be stacked in bundles in Shoemaker's Store. Packs will be stored by Coys. in separate tents (1 tent per Coy.) set apart for that purpose.

3. Signallers, Lewis Gunners, & Battalion Observers, will march off in separate parties, commencing at 7.30 a.m. under arrangements to be made by the Signalling Officer, Lewis Gun & Intelligence Officer. The Bn. Lewis Gun Officer will arrange with the Transport Officer for the transport of his guns.

4. The leading Platoon of "B" Coy. will move off from Camp so as to reach DICKEBUSCH by 9.30 a.m., followed by "C" "D" and "A" Coys. Movements by Platoons at 100 yards distance.
Headquarters will move off at 11.30 a.m.

5. Rations will be taken by the Transport (to be at Ration Dump at 7 p.m. nightly) whence they will be conveyed on the trolleys to their respective Coy. Dumps by the C.Q.M.S., & any spare men not in the Line. All men will carry the remainder of to-morrows rations.

6. Coy. Limbers will be at Bn. Hd. Qrs. by 7 a.m. tomorrow. Officers' Mess Cart and one G.S. Wagon will be at Bn. Hd. Qrs. at 11 a.m. for Hd. Qrs. Stores and Officers' kits.
Vehicles will not pass through DICKEBUSCH until dark.

7. Complete list of Trench Stores etc. taken over by each Coy. to be sent to Bn. Hd. Qrs. by 9 a.m. 18/3/17.

8. Quartermaster and Handing over Committee will hand over Camp to the in-coming Unit and obtain a receipt for all Camp Furniture handed over., on the prescribed forms "A" and "B".

9. Cookers will be taken away at 9.30 a.m. 1 Water Cart to be taken up full each night with the rations and will remain during the next day in VOORMEZEELE.

10. Completion of relief to be reported by wire as follows:- "B.O.O. 66 complied with".

11. CHIPPEWA CAMP and all billets to be left scrupulously clean and certificates to be rendered by O.C.Coys to that effect.

[signature]
2/Lieut.
A/Adjutant,
10th. R.W.KENT REGT.

16.3.17.

No. 1. Filed.
2. C.O.
3. 2nd.i/C.
4. Qr.Master.
5. Sig.Officer
6. Transport Officer.
7. O.C."A" Coy.
8. O.C."B" Coy.
9. O.C."C" Coy.
10. O.C."D" Coy.
11. Medical Officer.
12. Lewis Gun & Int. Officer
13. Pioneer Officer.
14. O.C. 18th. K.R.R.C.
15. War Diary.
16. " ".

APPX. IV

S E C R E T.

Copy No.....15....

BATTALION OPERATION ORDER No 69.

---

1. The Battalion will be relieved by the 15th Hants Regt on 23rd March 1917.

2. The leading Platoon of the Relieving Unit to be at DICKEBUSCH by 8.30.a.m. 23/3/17.

3. On completion of Relief Coys will return to CHIPPEWA CAMP via DICKEBUSCH - HALLEBAST CORNER - OUDERDOM. All movements will be by Platoons at 100 yards distance.

4. Maps, Aeroplane Photographs, and Trench Stores, will be handed over and a receipt obtained. Receipt to be handed to Adjutant by O.C. Coy on passing Bn Hd Qrs. Great care should be taken in compiling these lists. Indents for R.E. Stores to be submitted as usual and details of those handed over to the Relief.

5. O.C. Coys will arrange for their blankets to be brought out in bundles of 10 and dumped in the vicinity of Bn Hd Qrs. An N.C.O. or reliable man should be left in charge ofeach Coy dump, and assist in loading of transport. Care should be taken that only vehicles taken into the line are brought out.

6. All Trenches and Dugouts are to be left as clean as possible and all trench boots not in use will be sent to Drying room at Bn Hd Qrs. A thorough search is to be made that none of these are left in Dugouts or anywhere about the trenches.

7. Work in hand and proposed work must be thoroughly explained to O.C. Relieving Unit.

8. O.C. "C" Coy will send one Cook to Bn Hd Qrs to report to R.S.M. to-morrow, to make a hot drink for the LOCALITY GARRISON on their reaching Bn Hd Qrs.

9. The Lewis Gun Officer will arrange for the relief of his Lewis Gunners.

10. Instructions as to transport will be given to the Transport Officer at Bn Hd Qrs on the evening of the 22nd inst.

11. C.Q.M.S. will arrange to have a good hot meal for their Coys on arriving in Camp.

12. Completion of Relief to be reported to Bn Hd Qrs by wire, viz:- "B.O.O.69 complied with", and Coy Commanders will report in person on passing Bn HdQrs.

A. Richmond
2/Lieut.
for O.C. BLOOD.

22/3/17.

1. Filed.	5. O.C."B" Coy.	9. Signal Offr.	13. O.C.15th Hants
2. C.O.	6. " "C" "	10. Transport Offr.	14. Pioneer Offr
3. 2nd i/c	7. " "D" "	11. Quartermaster.	15. War Diary.
4. O.C. "A" Coy.	8. L.G. & Int.Offr.	12. Medical Offr.	16. " "

APPX V

S E C R E T. Copy No....14....

BATTALION OPERATION ORDER No 70.

1. The Battalion will relieve the 18th K.R.R.C. as Reserve Battalion, Left Sub-Sector, to-morrow, 30th inst.
2. Relief to be carried out via:- RENINGHELST - OUDERDOM - MILLEKAPELLEN FARM (H.20.c.) Leading Platoon to reach DICKEBUSCH by 8.30.a.m.
3. The Battalion will move off by Platoons at 100 yards distance in the following order:-

"A" Coy will relieve Coy of 18th K.R.R.C. in ECLUSE TRENCH (LEFT) & SEPTEMBER POST.
"B" " " " " " " K.R.R.C in DICKEBUSCH.
"C" " " " " " " " " CONVENT. VOORMEZEELE.
"D" " " " " " " " " DICKEBUSCH.
Headquarters.

The following rules in regard to traffic in DICKEBUSCH are to be strictly observed:-
No lorry is to halt within ½ mile of either end of the village.
No body of troopslarger than a platoon is to march through or halt in the village
Men are not to loiter in the streets.

4. Maps, Stores, & Indents for R.E.Stores are to be taken over and a complete list shewing the articles received to be forwarded to Bn. Hd. Qrs. by 7.p.m. 30th inst.
5. Specialists will move and remain with their Companies and the Lewis Gun Officer will make the necessary arrangements for the conveyance of his Lewis Guns.
6. Blankets are to be rolled in bundles of 10, labelled, and stacked ready for loading at 7.a.m. 4 Cookers (3 with fires lighted) and 2 water carts filled will proceed in rear of the Battalion at 300 yards distance. Dixies will be taken by "A" and "C" Coys for cooking in VOORMEZEELE. & ECLUSE.
7. One G.S.Wagon, Maltese Cart, and 1 Limber per Coy will be at Bn Hd Qrs at 9.a.m. All loading to be completed by 9.30.a.m. Officers Mess Cart to be at Bn Hd Qrs by 11.a.m.
Transport Officer will make necessary arrangements if it is found that a second journey is required, and C.Q.M.S. & 2 men per Coy will remain behind toload up.
8. The camp must be left scrupulously clean. Officers Commanding Companies must see that their lines are thoroughly clean before leaving.
The Quartermaster and Handing Over Committee, will hand over the Camp to the incoming unit and obtain a receipt for the same as well as a Chit as to the cleanliness of the Camp when handed over.
9. Completion of Relief to be reported to Bn Hd Qrs by quickest method available. viz:- "B.O.O.70 complied with".

[signature]
2/Lieut.
A/Adjutant.
10th R.W.Kent Regiment.

29/3/17.

No 1. C.O.	6. Quartermaster.	11. Pioneer Officer.
2. 2nd i/c.	7. O.C. "A" Coy.	12. Transport Officer.
3. File.	8. " "B" "	13. War Diary.
4. Int. Officer.	9. " "C" "	14. " "
5. Signal. "	10. " "D" "	15. O.C. 18th K.R.R.C.

Army Form C. 2118.

10th Royal West Kent Regt

WAR DIARY
or
INTELLIGENCE SUMMARY

(Erase heading not required.)

April 1917 Sheet No 1

Vol 12

Instructions regarding War Diaries and Intelligence Summaries are contained in F. S. Regs., Part II. and the Staff Manual respectively. Title Pages will be prepared in manuscript.

Place	Date	Hour	Summary of Events and Information	Remarks and references to Appendices
DICKEBUSCH BELGIUM SHEET 28. N.W. H28. c 7.1.	1/4/17		Situation normal, HdQ. "B" & "D" Coys DICKEBUSCH, "A" Coy ECLUSE TRENCH, "C" Coy CONVENT AREA, VOORMEZEELE. Strength Offs 49. O.R. 1008.	
— " —	2/4/17		" " Strength Offs 49 O.R. 1007. Evacuated O.R. 1	
— " —	3/4/17		" " Strength Offs 49 O.R. 1007.	
— " —	4/4/17		" Major Beattie rejoined from COURSE in ENGLAND Strength Offs 49 O.R. 1007.	
— " —	5/4/17		" During above period from 1st to 5th the Battalion furnished R.E. working parties for construction and repair of Trenches etc also carrying parties to FRONT LINE.	
— " —	"	11.30 AM	The Battalion relieved by 15th Bn Hampshire Regt, this operation was carried out successfully OP.O.71. APPX I. Strength Offs 48, O.R. 1007.	OPR. OR. 71 APPX I
CHIPPEWA CAMP. M6 a 4.7	6/4/17	8.30 AM	Situation normal, The Battalion proceeded by route march to STEENVOORDE en route for WANSPETTE. OPR. OR. No 72 APPX II, arriving about 1 P.M. and billeting for the night. Strength Offs 48, O.R. 1002. Evacuated O.R. 5.	OPR. OR. No 72 APPX II
STEENVOORDE SHEET 28. B & FRANCE. Q. 4. c. 2. 6.	7/4/17	6.30 AM	Situation normal The march continued to ARNEKE, arriving about 2.30 P.M. billeted for the night. Strength Offs 48, O.R. 1005.	
ARNEKE. SHEET 27. B & FRANCE H. 12. a 9.3½	8/4/17	7. AM.	Situation Normal The march continued arriving at MOULLE about 4.30 P.M. Billets Bn H.Q Q 11. c. 8.6., "A" Coy Q 17 b 2.5., "B" Coy Q 10 c 9½.8., "C" Coy Q 16 b 7.3, "D" Coy Q 10. c. 8½. 1. Reinforcements O.R. 2. Strength Offs 48, O.R. 1007.	
MOULLE. FRANCE S.E. SHEET 27 A. Q 11. c. 8. 6	9/4/17		Situation normal, The Battalion commenced training for open warfare. Strength Offs 48, O.R. 1006. Evacuated O.R. 1	
— " —	10/4/17		" Strength Offs 48, O.R. 1006.	
— " —	11/4/17		" Strength Offs 48, O.R. 1006.	
— " —	12/4/17		" Strength Offs 48, O.R. 1006.	
— " —	13/4/17		" Strength Offs 48, O.R. 1006.	
— " —	14/4/17		" Strength Offs 48, O.R. 1006.	
— " —	15/4/17		" Lt N.W. Awkshurst proceeded to M.G.C. Strength Offs 47, O.R. 1006.	
— " —	16/4/17		" 2Lt E.M. Peacock & 2Lt K.R. Sayer, proceeded to R.F.C. Strength Offs 47, O.R. 1006.	
— " —	17/4/17		" Strength Offs 47 O.R. 1006.	
— " —	18/4/17		" Five officers joined the Battalion, 2Lt W.V. Edwards 2Lt D.V. Gray, 2Lt H.G. Brown, 2Lt D.G. Piggott 2Lt A.H. Woodriffe Strength Offs 46, O.R. 1006.	
— " —	19/4/17		Situation normal. Strength Offs 51 O.R. 1006.	

2449 Wt. W14957/M90 750,000 1/16 J.B.C. & A. Forms/C.2118/12.

10th Royal West Kent Regt

Instructions regarding War Diaries and Intelligence Summaries are contained in F. S. Regs., Part II. and the Staff Manual respectively. Title Pages will be prepared in manuscript.

WAR DIARY
or
INTELLIGENCE SUMMARY
(Erase heading not required.)

April 1917 Sheet 2

Army Form C. 2118.

Place	Date	Hour	Summary of Events and Information	Remarks and references to Appendices
MOULLE FRANCE, S.E. SHEET 27A, Q.11.c.8.6.	20.4.17		Situation normal Strength Offs 51. O.R 995. Evacuated O.R. 11	
	21.4.17		Situation normal, Final day of Training. During the above-period from 9th to 21st inst. all ranks were exercised in the various method for Attack and Defence for open warfare. The Training was progressive from the elementary stages, Section and Platoon to Brigade movements. Musketry was chiefly confined to Rapid Fire, firing at Disappearing Targets, Firing from the hip whilst advancing, very good practice was made with the latter. Bombing. Every man threw live bombs and fired Rifle grenades. Lewis gun every man fired at Targets. Bayonet Fighting and Physical Training carried out daily under Battalion Instructors. Battalion and Brigade training for the attack was carried out on selected ground similar in formation to that on our front when in the Line. Skeleton Enemy were employed and the Barrage carried out by Signallers. Both the Divisional Commander and Corps Commander visited the training area whilst the troops were at work. On the final day of Training the Army Commander viewed the troops when carrying out the attack and other manoeuvres. The Army Commander expressed his high opinion of the work done and the fitness of both Officers and men for the work to be carried out in the near future. Strength Offs 51. O.R. 1000.	
— —	22.4.17		Situation normal, Lecture by Brigadier, Holiday. Strength Offs 51. O.R 998. Evacuated O.R. 2	
— —	23.4.17	6.30 AM	Situation normal, The Battalion proceeded by Route march to ARNEKE en route for RENINGHELST (CHIPPEWA CAMP) arriving about 1.30 PM, billeted for the night. OPR OR 73 APPX III. Strength Offs 51. O.R. 998.	OPR. OR. 73 APPX III
ARNEKE SHEET 27 B.A.P. M12 a. 9.3	24.4.17	8.15 AM	Situation normal. The march continued to STEENVOORDE arriving about 1. PM. billeted for the night. Strength Offs 51. O.R 998.	
STEENVOORDE SHEET 27 B.B.F. Q.4c 8.6.	25.4.17	7.40 AM	Situation normal. The march continued to RENINGHELST (CHIPPEWA CAMP) arriving about 1 PM. Strength Offs 51, O.R 998.	
CHIPPEWA CAMP	26.4.17		Situation normal. Rest & Training Strength Offs 51, O.R 995 Evacuated O.R. 3	
M6 a. 4.7.	27.4.17		Situation normal, Strength Offs 51, O.R 995	
— —	28.4.17		" " " " Lt H.L. Foster joined Strength Offs 51, O.R 997	
— —	29.4.17		" " " " Strength Offs 52. O.R 998.	
— —	30.4.17		" " " " Officers evacuated sick struck off strength 9. Strength Offs 43 O.R. 998	

A Wood Martyn Lt Col

Commdg 10th Royal West Kent Regt.

2449 Wt. W14957/M90 750,000 1/16 J.B.C. & A. Forms/C.2118/12.

APPX I

SECRET. Copy No. 15

OPERATION ORDER No 71.

---

1. The Battalion will be relieved to-morrow the 5th inst, by the 15th Hants Regt. Relief to commence at 11.30.a.m.

2. Companies will be ready to move off by 11.15.a.m. and men will remain in their billets until their relief arrives.

3. The Signalling Officer and Lewis Gun Officer will make all arrangements for their reliefs.

4. On completion of relief, units will march via DICKEBUSCH HALLEBAST CORNER - OUDERDOM - to CHIPPEWA CAMP. All movements by Platoons at 100 yards distance.

5. Maps, Aeroplane Photos, and Trench Stores, will be handed over and a receipt obtained. All receipts are to be sent to Bn Hd Qrs, CHIPPEWA. Indents for R. E. Stores will be submitted as usual, and details of these handed over to the relieving unit.

6. Completion of relief to be at once reported to Bn Hd Qrs DICKEBUSCH, by O.C. Coys, Signalling Officer, and Lewis Gun Officer.

7. CHIPPEWA CAMP will be taken over by the Quartermaster by 12 noon 5th inst.
O.C. "B" Coy will detail one N.C.O., and 3 men to leave DICKEBUSCH at 10.30.a.m. and relieve the Camp Guard at CHIPPEWA.

8. <u>TRANSPORT.</u> Blankets of "B" and "D" Coys must be rolled and stacked at Q.M.S. DICKEBUSCH by 10.a.m.
Blankets of "A" and "C" Coys will be carried down by the men and rolled at Q.M.S. DICKEBUSCH.
Coy limbers will convey same to CHIPPEWA CAMP, and O.C. Coys will detail men to assist in loading.
1 G. S. Wagon is to be at H.Q. at 12 noon for H.Q. blankets, Orderly Room boxes, Stores, and Officers' Kits with "B" and "D" Coys.
Any Mess Boxes and Officers' Kits with "A" and "C" Coys will be brought down on Ration limbers on the evening of the 4th inst.
Kitchens and Water Carts to leave DICKEBUSCH by 10.30.a.m. All cooks are to be at DICKEBUSCH by 10.30.a.m. to accompany cookers and prepare a hot meal formen on arrival at CHIPPEWA.
Mess Cart will collect and take away mess boxes at 12.30.p.m.
Maltese Cart to be at DICKEBUSCH by 11.a.m.

A. Richmond
2/Lieut. A/Adjt.
BLOOD.

4/4/17.

No.1. Filed.
2. C.O.
3. 2nd i/c.
4. Int. Officer.
5. Signalling "
6. Quartermaster.
7. Medical Officer.
8. Transport Officer.
9. O.C. "A" Coy.
10. " "B" "
11. " "C" "
12. " "D" "
13. Pioneer Officer.
14. War Diary.
15. " "
16. O.C. 15th Hants.

APPX II

S E C R E T   Copy No.........

10th ROYAL WEST KENT REGIMENT.

OPERATION ORDER No 78.

Reference Map - HAZEBROUCK 5a. 1/100,000.

1. The 123rd Infantry Brigade Group will proceed from RENINGHELST to GANSPETTE on the 6th, 7th, & 8th April.

2. The Battalion will march from CHIPPEWA in the following order:-

Headquarters.
"A" Company.
"B" "
"C" "
"D" "

O.C. "A" Coy will arrange to send out connecting files to keep in touch with 11th Queens.

O.C. "D" Coy will drop connecting files to keep in touch with 23rd Middlesex.

The Battalion will parade on road outside CHIPPEWA CAMP at 8.30.a.m. 6/4/17 in order to pass starting point (Road Junction G.34.d.8.3. Sheet 28 N.W.) at 9.a.m.

50 yards distance between Coys is to be maintained.

3. __Dress:-__ Fighting Order. Waterproof sheets will be strapped on the back of the belt - Steel helmet must be strapped on the haversack so that it does not swing loosely.

4. __Halts.__ The usual clock-hour halts will be observed.

5. Marching-out states to be rendered by O.C. Coys to Orderly Room by 7.a.m. 6/4/17.

6. __Transport.__ The Battalion will be accompanied by the whole of its transport. Baggage wagons will report to the Bn at 2.p.m. 5th inst and remain until the evening of the 8th inst. They will then return to No. 3 Coy of the Train. Lorries will accompany the column and be available for packs and blankets only.

7. __Billeting.__ A/Capt. A. J. S. Pearson, the C.Q.M.Sergts, and Sergt House, will report to Staff Captain at the billeting rendezvous, The Bandstand, STEENVORDE, at 10.a.m. April 6th.

8. __Sick.__ The Regimental Medical Officer will make the necessary arrangements for dealing with any cases.

No man will be allowed to fall out unless in possession of a chit stating his number, rank, name& initials, unit, and reason for falling out, which must be signed by his Platoon or other Officer.

9. Coys will have Progress Reports, stating condition of men, delivered to the Adjutant by 10.30.a.m., 11.30.a.m., and subsequently at 2 hour intervals until the destination is reached.

10. Watches will be synchronized daily at 7. a.m.

11. O.C. Coys will report to Adjutant, present or otherwise on arrival at the billets, and send pin prick map references of their Coy Hd Qrs

ADMINISTRATIVE ORDERS.

1. HANDING OVER. Handing Over Committee. - Major S.H. Beattie., and Hon.Lieut E.H.Jarrett. (Quartermaster).

All Camps, Camp Stores, and Transport Lines, are to be handed over, and inventories made and checked; Camp Wardens will be present. Receipts on Form "A" must be rendered to Bn Hd Qrs by 6.p.m. 6th inst.

2. SURPLUS KIT. "Surplus Kit" will be stored in a hut in CHIPPEWA CAMP. This hut will close at 7.30.a.m. 6/4/17 and an Inventory of all Surplus Stores deposited is to be rendered to Bn Hd Qrs by 6.p.m. 6th inst. One man to be detailed by R.S.M. to be left to help take charge of these Stores.

Officers are asked to lighten their Kits as much as possible but to ensure that they have with them every requisite for moving anywhere at ant time.

3. Transport of Blankets and Packs. Two lorries will be at the disposal of the Battalion for transport of packs and blankets.

Blankets must be rolled and labelled in bundles of 10 and loaded at 7.15.a.m. 6/4/17.

Packs, containing great coats, cardigans, and leather jerkins, will be loaded first

4. Rations. The unexpired portion of rations for the 6th inst will be carried in the haversack and on the cookers.

Iron rations and biscuits must be carried in the haversack .

Water bottles must be filled overnight.

Kitchens will proceed with the transport, and dinners for men must be ready on arrival at billets in STEENVORDE.

O.C. Coys will ensure that the men carry a good haversack ration.

5. Inoculation. The Medical Officer will inoculate a number of men on the 5th inst. These will proceed later by train on the 7th inst and take their blankets and packs with them.

The following Officers will also remain behind:-

2/Lieut. L. A. Panchaud.
" F.E.E.Norris.
" G. G. Samuel.
" E. M. Pocock.
" C.E.M.Dillon.
" K. R. Sayers..

to assist in entrainment of the detachment of inoculated men on the 7th inst. A Field Officer of the 11th Queens will be O.C. Detachment.

[signature]
2/Lieut.
A/Adjutant.
10th R. W. Kent Regt.

No. 1. Filed.
2. 123rd Inf. Bde.
3. C. O.
4. 2nd in Command.
5. O.C. "A" Coy.
6. O.C. "B" "
7. O.C. "C" Coy.
8. " "D" "
9. Quartermaster.
10. Transport Officer.
11. Signalling Officer.
12. Int & Lewis Gun O.
13. Medical Officer.
14. War Diary.
15. " "

APPX III

S E C R E T. Copy No....15....

10th ROYAL WEST KENT REGIMENT.

OPERATION ORDER No 73.

Ref. Map. - HAZEBROUCK. 5a 1/100,000.

---

1. The 123rd Infantry Brigade Group will proceed from GANSPETTE to RENINGHELST on the 23rd. 24th. and 25th April and will march as an Advance Guard. Vanguard commanded by Lieut. Col. P.W.North will be found by the 20th Durham Light Infantry with 1 Battery 190th Brigade R.F.A., and 1 Sect. of 123rd M. G. Coy.

2. The Battalion will form part of the Main Guard and march immediately behind 123rd Infantry Brigade Headquarters & Signal Section.

The Battalion will march from MOULLE in the following order:-

Headquarters.)
"A" Coy.)
"B" ") in column of threes.
"C" ")
"D" ")

The Battalion will parade at Cross Roads Q.11.c.5.7 near Headquarters at 6.30.a.m. 23/4/17 in order to pass the starting point (CROSS ROADS L.14.c.4.6. E. END OF WATTEN) at 8.36.a.m.

3. Dress:- Fighting Order. Waterproof sheets to be strapped on the back of the belt - Steel Helmet must be strapped on the haversack so that it does not swing loosely.

4. Marching out states will be rendered by O.C. Coys to Orderly Room by 8 p.m. 22/4/17.

5. Halts. All Units will halt from 10 minutes before each hour until the hour.

6. Transport. Cookers, water and mess carts will be in rear of the Battalion. The remainder of the Transport will be brigaded. O.C. "D" Coy will drop guides to ensure the Bn Transport following when the Bn leaves the column.

7. Capt. A.J.S.Pearson and billeting party - 5. N.C.O's - will meet the Staff Captain at the rendezvous (CROSS ROADS, LE HENEGAT) at 10.a.m.

8. Sick. The Regimental Medical Officer will make the necessary arrangements for dealing with any cases. No man will be allowed to fall out unless in possession of a chit stating his number, rank, name and initials, unit, and reason for falling out, which must be signed by his Platoon or other Officer.

9. Progress Reports. Companies will render progress reports, staing condition of men, to the Adjutant by 10.30.a.m. 11.30.a.m. and subsequently at 2 hour intervals until the destination is reached.

10. Watches will be synchronised daily.

11. O.C. Coys will report to the Adjutant, present or otherwise, on arrival at the billets, and send pin prick map references of their Coy H.Q.

22/4/17.

A. Richmond ?/Lt a/adjt
10th R. W. Kent Regt.

10th Royal West Kent Regiment.

ADMINISTRATIVE ORDERS.

1. Blankets to be rolled in bundles of 10 and labelled. These with Packs will be stacked at various Coy etc Hd Qrs.

2. Water bottles must be filled over night. - Iron Rations carried. - Unexpired portion of rations for the 23rd inst will be carried by the men and on the Coy Cookers.

3. Headquarter rations are to be cooked by "A" Coy's Cooker.

3. Men are to avoid, if possible, wearing new boots on the march.

All men are to carry a clean dry pair of sicks in their haversacks.

O.C. Coys are responsible for foot inspections and necessary foot washing after each days march.

4. 2/Lieut. H. L. Shrimpton will remain behind to superintend loading of lorries, as follows:-

1 Lorry to load up ~~H.Q.~~ outside "A" Coy H.Q. at 5.15.a.m., packs (with blankets strapped on) and 1 Officers Valise, of the party proceeding to ST OMER.

This Lorry will return and load up Blankets and Officers Kits of "A" and "B" Coys.

1 Lorry to load up H.Q. blankets and Packs, Q.M. Stores, H.Q. Officers Valises, Orderly Room Boxes, and Transport Packs, at 6.15.a.m.

1 Lorry to collect blankets and Officers' Kits of "C" and "D" Coys at 6.15.a.m.

On the return from ARNEKE to MOULLE the three Lorries will collect Packs of "A" "B" "C" and "D" Coys.

The Mess Cart will collect Mess Boxes at 5.30.a.m.

2/Lieut. A/Adjt.
10th R. W. Kent Regiment.

22/4/17.

10th Royal West Kent Regt

Instructions regarding War Diaries and Intelligence Summaries are contained in F. S. Regs., Part II. and the Staff Manual respectively. Title Pages will be prepared in manuscript.

WAR DIARY
or
INTELLIGENCE SUMMARY
(Erase heading not required.)

May 1917 Sheet I

Army Form C. 2118

Vol 13

Place	Date	Hour	Summary of Events and Information	Remarks and references to Appendices
CHIPPEWA CAMP. M6a97	1/5/17		Situation normal. During the evening a good many hostile shells fell in the neighbourhood of the camp this continued at intervals throughout the night, very little material damage done. Strength Offs 43. O.R. 995. 3 O.R. from C.C.S.	
	2/5/17	7 am	Situation normal. The Battalion relieved the 26th Bn Royal Fusiliers in Left Battalion Sector this Operation was carried out successfully. 'A' Coy OLD FRENCH TRENCH (left) & LOCALITY, 'B' Coy OLD FRENCH TRENCH (right) 'C' Coy FRONT LINE, 'D' Coy ECLUSE TRENCH & VOORMEZEELE SWITCH, Bn H.Q. VOORMEZEELE SWITCH. Strength Offs 43, O.R. 1001.	OP OR No 74 APPX I
LEFT BATTALION SECTOR.	3/5/17		Situation normal. About 9 PM last night a gas alarm sounded, no gas observed on our front. During the alarm Enemy sent up Green lights. Patrols out during the night report on our wire. Strength Offs 43 O.R. 1001.	
	4/5/17		Situation normal. Patrols out report no sign of Enemy Patrols. Early this morning loud explosion heard in rear of Enemy lines. During the afternoon Our Heavy Artillery shelled the DAMM STRASSE. Enemy retaliated with 7.7 cm for Rifle Grenades fired from our front. Strength Offs 43. O.R. 1001	
	5/5/17		Situation normal. Distinct increase of Enemy M.G. fire during the night. One patrol of ours out during the night whilst ascertaining condition of Enemy's wire, were caught by M.G. fire. 2Lt Hodges and 2 O.R. killed 1 O.R. wounded. Increased Aerial activity and Enemy movement. Apparently Enemy relief has taken place. Strength Offs 42 O.R. 998	
	6/5/17		Situation normal. Patrols out during the night, nothing unusual to report. Enemy Artillery fire [illegible] and [illegible] both day and night. Our Stokes Guns fired on Craters in retaliation for 7.7 cm shelling. Casualties 1 O.R. killed, Strength Offs 42 O.R. 997.	
	7/5/17		Situation normal. Enemy Artillery active on VOORMEZEELE & SCOTTISH WOOD. 'B' Coy relieved 'C' Coy in FRONT LINE. Good practice made by our Artillery on CRATERS, Our Artillery carried out a Shoot [illegible] 5 minutes at 5.45 PM & 11.15 PM [illegible] slight retaliation from Enemy Artillery. Casualties 3 O.R. wounded. Strength Offs 42 O.R. 994	
	8/5/17		Situation normal. After our Artillery Bombardment of last night, Enemy Artillery very quiet. Our machine guns carried out indirect fire practice on DAMM STRASSE. Enemy shelled VOORMEZEELE during the morning. A few Fish tail bombs and one [illegible] were put over behind our front line. Casualties 2 O.R. killed. Strength Offs 42. O.R. 992.	
	9/5/17		Situation normal. VOORMEZEELE shelled during the night. Our Machine Guns active.	
		9.20 PM	Left [illegible] of [illegible] sent up S.O.S. by rocket, same time Enemy heavily shelled OLD FRENCH TRENCH, CONVENT LANE & FRONT LINE. Our Artillery fire on S.O.S. targets was prompt and accurate. The bombardment lasted 30 minutes. Enemy sent up three red rockets [illegible] O.26 a.2.4 Strength Offs 42 O.R. 992.	
	10/5/17	4 AM	Situation normal from 4 am to 7.30 am. Enemy heavily shelled new battery position at N.6 b.2.55 destroying two Gun pits and the road for about fifty yards.	
		6 AM	'C' Coy relieved 'B' Coy in FRONT LINE. 8.30 AM Enemy sent over [illegible] to the LOCALITY the first time during this tour. Strength Offs 42. O.R. 992.	

1875 Wt. W593/826 1,000,000 4/15 J.B.C. & A. A.D.S.S./Forms/C. 2118.

Army Form C. 2118.

10th Royal West Kent Regt

WAR DIARY
or
INTELLIGENCE SUMMARY

(Erase heading not required.)

May 1917

Sheet II

Instructions regarding War Diaries and Intelligence Summaries are contained in F. S. Regs., Part II. and the Staff Manual respectively. Title Pages will be prepared in manuscript.

Place	Date	Hour	Summary of Events and Information	Remarks and references to Appendices
Left Battalion Sector	11/5/17	2 PM	Situation normal. Our Machine guns carried out indirect fire on DAMM STRASSE during the night. VOORMEZEELE shelled at intervals during the day. Enemy obtained two direct hits on OLD FRENCH TRENCH, putting one of our Lewis guns out of action. Casualties 3 O.R. wounded. Strength Offs 42 O.R. 969.	
	12/5/17	2 PM	Situation normal. Artillery fire much less during the night from 5 to 6 A.M. Our Artillery shelled the Craters with good effect. Battalion relieved by the 11th Bn Queens Regt and withdrawn by Platoons (OP. ORD. No 79.) to G.H.Q. Lines as Battalion in Support. This operation was carried out successfully. Strength O/s 42 O.R. 969. Evacuated Sick 11 O.R.	OP. ORD No 79 APPX II
Batt'n Support G.H.Q. Lines	13/5/17		Situation normal. Lt. 2nd Lt McFarrell struck off Strength sick in England. Strength Offs 41 O.R. 970, Casualties [illegible]	
"	14/5/17		" " Evacuated Sick 8 O.R. Strength Offs 41 O.R. 962	
"	15/5/17		" " Capt. G. Drayson struck off Strength for duty in England. 3 O.R. wounded. Strength Offs 40. O.R. 962.	
"	16/5/17		" " Strength Offs 40. O.R. 962.	
"	17/5/17		" " Strength Offs 40 O.R. 962	
"	18/5/17		" " 2/Lt Norris struck off strength sick in England, Evacuated sick O.R. 1 Strength Offs 39 O.R. 961	
"	19/5/17		" " Strength Offs 39. O.R. 961	
"	20/5/17	8 am	Situation normal. The Battalion relieved by the 15th Bn Hampshire Regt (OP ORD No 80). This operation was carried out successfully. The Battalion on withdrawal marching back to CHIPPEWA CAMP B. Bn HQ. B & C Coy. MICMAC CAMP A & D Coys. During above tour of duty from 13th to 20th incl. the Bn furnished working parties for R.E. and carrying parties to FRONT LINE every available man being employed. Strength Offs 39 O.R. 961	OP ORD No 80 APPX III
CHIPPEWA CAMP MICMAC	21/5/17		Situation normal. Rest & Training. Bn furnishing working parties, Evacuated Sick 2 O.R. Strength Offs 39 O.R. 959	
	22/5/17		" " Strength Offs 39 O.R. 957	
"	23/5/17		" " 2/Lt Henson-Smith joined Strength Offs 40 O.R. 961, 2 O.R. from C.C.S.	
"	24/5/17		" " Strength Offs 40 O.R. 961	
"	25/5/17		" " Strength Offs 40 O.R. 961	
	26/5/17	9 AM	Situation normal. The Bn relieved the 12th Kings Royal Rifles in the Left Battalion Sector (OP ORD No 81). This operation was carried out successfully. "A" Co FRONT LINE & OLD FRENCH TRENCH (centre). "B" Coy OLD FRENCH TRENCH (right). "C" Coy ECLUSE & VOORMEZEELE SWITCH. "D" Coy OLD FRENCH TRENCH (left). Bn H.Q. GORDON LANE. Our Artillery throughout the day bombarded the DAMMSTRASSE & back Areas. Evacuated sick 1 O.R. Strength Offs. 40. O.R. 960	OP. ORD No 81 APPX IV
Left Battalion Sector	27/5/17		Situation normal. About 2 a.m. we blew a Camouflet opposite O.S.E. No action by Enemy followed. Our Artillery active throughout the day on Enemy Support and Reserve Lines. At 4.30 PM, Stokes & Medium Mortars carried out a shoot on CRATERS no retaliation followed. 8.30 PM, Enemy's Artillery shelled our Reserve Lines & Back Areas of the whole of the Brigade, many gas shells were used. Our Artillery shelled Enemy back Areas and communications, the bombardment continued throughout the night. Strength Offs 40. O.R. 960	

2449 Wt. W14957/M90 750,000 1/16 J.B.C. & A. Forms/C.2118/12.

10th Royal West Kent Regt

WAR DIARY
or
INTELLIGENCE SUMMARY
(Erase heading not required.)

May 1917
Sheet III

Army Form C. 2118.

Instructions regarding War Diaries and Intelligence Summaries are contained in F. S. Regs., Part II. and the Staff Manual respectively. Title Pages will be prepared in manuscript.

Place	Date	Hour	Summary of Events and Information	Remarks and references to Appendices
Left Battalion Sector	28/5/17		Situation normal. Our Artillery continued bombardment of Enemy back Areas. Hostile Artillery active on OLD FRENCH TRENCH whence it crept to ECLUSE TRENCH and afterwards appeared to concentrate on VOORMEZEELE. Our Aircraft active no enemy machines observed. Enemys Artillery continued active during the night damaging several dumps in the back Area. Casualties 4 O.R. Wounded Strength Offs 40. O.R. 956	
	29/5/17	6 am	Situation normal. "C" Coy relieved "A" Coy in FRONT LINE. Our machine guns active during the night. The bombardment of Enemy back Area continued but not quite so active as previously.	
		9 am	Enemy put bursts of Shrapnel over his own FRONT LINE apparently registering at that particular spot.	
		12.30 PM	Enemy fired Rum Jars and Fishtails on O26 & O27. Stokes gun retaliated and silenced Enemy. Evacuated sick 6 O.R. Wounded 5 O.R. Strength Offs 40. O.R. 945.	
	30/5/17		Situation normal. Machine guns active during the night. Artillery on both sides active throughout the night and early hours. 4.30 am CONVENT LANE shelled and some damage done to the Trench. Our Aircraft active. Evacuated sick 3 O.R. 2Lt Harding & 4 OR wounded. Strength Offs 39. O.R. 938.	
	31/5/17		Situation normal. During the night Enemy shelled VOORMEZEELE, SCOTTISH WOOD & CAFE BELGE, but much less than of late. Our heavy Artillery active	
		3.30 PM	The Battalion relieved by 15th Bn Hampshire Regt (OP ORDER No 82 APPX V) this operation was successfully carried out and Platoons as relieved marched back to CHIPPEWA CAMP M.6.a.4.7. Casualties 2 O.R. wounded. Strength Offs 39 O.R. 936	OP. ORD. No 82 APPX V

[signature]
Lt Col.
Comm'dg 10th Royal West Kent Regt

2449 Wt. W14957/M90 750,000 1/16 J.B.C. & A. Forms/C.2118/12.

APPX I

S E C R E T.

Copy No....14.

10th ROYAL WEST KENT REGT.

OPERATION ORDER No 74.

1. The Battalion will relieve the 26th Royal Fusiliers in the Left Battalion Sector on May 2nd 1917.

2. Dress:- Fighting Order, Great Coats rolled, Jerkins to be strapped on back of belt.
Officers Valises and mens blankets will not be taken but will be stored in the hut set apart for that purpose, together with the mens Packs.

3. C.S.M's, Signallers, Lewis Gunners,& Battalion Observers, will march off in separate parties commencing at 6.30.a.m.
The leading Platoon of "D" Coy will move off from Camp in time to reach DICKEBUSCH by 8.a.m., followed by "C". "A" and "B" Coys. All movements will be by Platoons at not less than 100 yds distance. Troops will not halt in DICKEBUSCH and must move in File there.
Headquarters will move off at 10.a.m.

4.

"D" Co	will relieve	"A"	Coy of	26th R. F.
"C" "	" "	"B"	" "	" "
"A" "	" "	"C"	" "	" "
"B" "	" "	"D"	" "	" "

5. Rations:- Water bottles must be filled over night. Rations will be taken by Transport whence they will be conveyed on the trolleys to their respective Coy Dumps by the C.Q.M.S., and any spare men not in the line. All men will carry the remainder of to-morrows rations.

6. Transport:- Coy Limbers will be at Bn Hd Qrs by 7.a.m. Officers Mess Cart, Maltese Cart, and 1 G.S.Wagon, for Hd Qr Stores, to be at BnHd Qrs by 9.a.m. Cookers will be taken away at 8.a.m. One Water Cart to be taken up full each night, with rations, and remain during the next day in VOORMEZEELE. Lewis Gun Limbers must be loaded over night (1st inst).

7. All Maps, Aeroplane Photographs, Defence Schemes, Trench Stores, and Dumps, will be taken over by Relieving Units. A Complete List of Trench Stores &c taken over by each Coy is to be sent to Bn Hd Qrs immediately on taking over.

8. Completion of relief to be reported at once "B.O.O. No 74" complied with".

9. The Quartermaster and Handing Over Committee will hand over the Camp to the Incoming Unit and obtain a receipt for all camp furniture handed over, on the prescribed Form "A".

10. CHIPPEWA CAMP and all billets to be left scrupulously clean and certificates to be rendered by O.C. Coys that this has been done.

H.W. Walker Capt
for
Lieut. A/Adjt.
10th R. W. Kent Regiment.

1/5/17.

No. 1. Filed.
2. C.O.
3. 2nd i/c.
4. Qr.Master.
5. Signal. Offr.
6. Transport Officer.
7. O.C. "A" Coy.
8. " "B" "
9. " "C" "
10. " "D" "
11. Medical Officer.
12. Lewis Gun & Int. Offr.
13. O.C. 26th Royal Fusiliers.
14 & 15. War Diary.

War Diary Copy II

APPX II

Battalion Operation Order 79.

The Bn. will be relieved by 11 Queens Regt. starting at 2 pm. 12.5.17.

Coys will be relieved in the following order — C. B. D. A.

Guides from both Bns. will rendezvous at junction of VOORMEZEELE SWITCH and CONVENT LANE at 1 pm.

"C" Coy will send 13 guides (1 per sentry post) other Coys. 2 per Coy.

Coys will pick up their guides at junction of VOORMEZEELE Switch and CONVENT Lane and will be led by them to their new positions.

Aeroplane Maps Trench Stores etc are to be handed over and a receipt obtained. Every care must be taken in compiling these lists and a copy sent at once to Orderly Room.

All trenches & dug outs to be left quite clean. Trench Boots not in use will be sent to STRAGGLERS POST.

Work in hand and proposed work must be thoroughly explained to relieving unit.

Completion of relief to be reported to Bn. H.Q. "BOO 79 Complied with"

2

C Coy will be relieved by CONVENT ~~SHELLY~~ LANE. and will come out by ~~CONVENT~~ SHELLY LANE.

O.C. D Coy will detail an Officer to guide garrison for the LOCALITY. This Officer will report to O.C. Supports in OLD FRENCH TRENCH 9 pm. on 12th.

12/8/17

[illegible]
a/Capt
BLOOD

SECRET   Copy No. 17.

Battalion Operation Order No 80   APPX III

1. The Bn will be relieved on May 20th by the 15th Hants whose first relieving Platoon will arrive at DICKEBUSCH at 8 am.

2. On completion of relief Coys will return to Camps as follows.

Headquarters & "C" Coy CHIPPEWA CAMP B

A B D Coy   MICMAC CAMP

by the overland route via the new trench between ENGLISH and SCOTTISH WOOD across DICKEBUSCH ROAD and thence to Camps as per track marked out. All movements will be by Platoons at 200 yds distance. Troops will not halt in DICKEBUSCH.

Bn Hd Qrs at present with Coys will, on arrival at MICMAC, return to Bn Hd Qrs.

3. Maps Aeroplane photographs and trench Stores will be handed over and a receipt obtained. These lists must be correct and a copy sent to Orderly Room by 10 pm on the 19th inst. Indents for RE Stores will be issued as usual & details of those handed over to the Relief. O C Coys will send back by Ration Limbers

on the night of the 19th inst any Stores to be taken down by transport.

4. All Trenches and Dugouts are to be left quite clean and any work in hand or proposed work must be thoroughly explained to the Relieving Unit.

5. The Lewis Gun & Signalling Officers will arrange for the relief of their Sections

6. Instructions as to transport will be given separately to the Transport Officer

7. C.Q.M.S will arrange for a good hot meal for their Coys on arrival at Camp.

8. Completion of relief to be reported to Bn Hd Qrs by the quickest method available viz. "BOO SO complied with".

[illegible]
Lieut. & A/Adjt
10th R.W. Kent Regt

15/5/17

No					
1	File	6.	Transport O	11	Medical O
2.	C.O	7	O.C. A Coy	12	Lewis Gun O
3.	2 Master	8	" B "	13	[illegible]
4	Lewis G	9	" C "	14	[illegible]
5.	Signal Off.	10	" D "	15.	[illegible]
				16 17	[illegible]

APPX V

M 10.

SECRET

Copy No 10

OPERATION ORDER No 82

1. The Battalion will be relieved in the Left Sub-Sector on May 31st by the 15th Hants.

2. Aeroplane photographs, Trench Stores, Gum Boots &c, are to be handed over on relief and a copy receipt sent to Bn. Hd Qrs.

3. All trenches, dugouts, latrines, &c to be left perfectly clean and a certificate obtained from O.C. Relieving Coy that this is so.

4. Tea rations will not be sent up to the trenches, but will be left back at CHIPPEWA CAMP. Each Coy will send 2 Cooks back at 1.30 pm to prepare teas at CHIPPEWA CAMP. Transport Officer will arrange for Cookers to be at Camp by 2.30 pm

5. The first Platoon of the Relieving Unit will arrive at DICKEBUSCH at 2.30 p.m. On relief Coys will proceed to CHIPPEWA CAMP "A" by Overland Track by Platoon at 200 yds distance; movements as far as DICKEBUSCH to be in file.

6. Transport Officer will arrange for 3 Limbers to be at DICKEBUSCH (Overland Track) at 4.30 p.m. to take Lewis Guns, ammunition, &c &c

7. Officers Kits and other articles which were not sent down on Limbers on the night of 30th/31st May will be sent down to DICKEBUSCH and placed on Lewis Gun Limbers.

Maltese Cart will be sent to R.A.P. VOORMEZEELE as early as possible on the night of 31st May/June 1st.

8. O.C. "B" Coy will detail 1 Officer and 35 OR and O.C. "C" Coy 35 OR for work during night 31st May/June 1st. On relief this Party will be distributed round N + NW portions of the BUND of DICKEBUSCH LAKE until they proceed to work. One Cooker of 20th D.L.I. will be in Avenue leading to Brigade Headquarters DICKEBUSCH from which teas will be served. Tea/Rations are being sent from CHIPPEWA to this Cooker.

9. Details of Working Party will follow. On completion of this Work Party will return to CHIPPEWA CAMP

10. Completion of Relief to be notified to this Office "O.O. No 82 completed with"

[signature]
Capt + A/Adjt
10th R. W. Kent Regt

31/5/17.

No							
1.	Filed	4.	O.C. "C" Coy	8	Quartermaster	11.	War Diary
2.	O.C. "A"	5	" "D" "	9.	Transport Offr	12.	123rd Inf Bde
3	" " "B"	7	Medical Offr	10	Lewis Gun Offr		

APPX IV

10th ROYAL WEST KENT REGIMENT.

NO 15

OPERATION ORDER No.81.

1. The Battalion will relieve the 18th K.R.R.C. in the Left Battalion Sector on May 26th 1917.

2. Dress - Fighting Order, & Great Coats rolled on back of belt.
Officers Valises and mens blankets and packs will not be taken but will be stored in a hut set apart for that purpose.
Limbers will be at MICMAC CAMP at 7.30.a.m. to collect these from "A" and "D" Coys.

3. Signallers, Lewis Gunners, and Battalion Observers, will march off in separate parties commencing at 8.30.a.m.
Transport Officer will arrange for Pack Ponies to carry Lewis Gun Magazines, and Panniers, on Overland track as far as DICKEBUSCH. These will be at CHIPPEWA and MICMAC respectively at 8.30.a.m.

4. The leading Platoon of "C" Coy will move off from Camp in time to reach DICKEBUSCH by 10.a.m, followed by "D" "A" and "B" Coys.
Movements by Platoons at 200 yds interval, after passing DICKEBUSCH to move in file.
"C" Coy will relieve "D" of 18th K.R.R.C. in ECLUSE & VOORMEZEELE SWITCH.
"D" " " " "B" " " " " O.F.TRENCH LEFT.
"A" " " " " C" " " " { FRONT LINE AND OLD FRENCH TRENCH CENTRE. TRAM TRACK to CONVENT L.
"B" " " " "A" " " " O.F.TRENCH RIGHT CONVENT LANE TO NEW C.L.

Headquarters will move off at 10.30.a.m.

5. Rations - All men will carry the remainder of to-morrows Rations, and Water bottles must be filled over night. Rations will be taken up nightly by Transport to VOORMEZEELE DUMP whence they will be conveyed to their respective Coy Dumps by the C.Q.M.S. Special care must be taken that the trolleys are kept in good repair and not left lying about.

6. Transport:- Officers' Mess Utensils and Rations, and Signalling Outfit and Orderly Room boxes will be sent by transport at 8.p.m. on the 25th inst. and dumped at R.A.P. VOORMEZEELE.
Cookers will be taken away at 9.a.m. on the 26th inst. One water cart will be taken up full each night and remain during the next day in VOORMEZEELE.

7. Working Parties. Working Parties supplied by the Battalion after noon on the 26th inst will be found by the 122nd Brigade. Parties reporting before that time will be found by this Bn and arrangements must be made for these Parties to rejoin their Coys on completion.

8. All Maps, Aeroplane Photographs, Defence Schemes, Trench Stores, and Dumps, will be taken over. A complete List of these to be sent to Bn Hd Qrs immediately on taking over.

9. Completion of Relief to be reported at once "B.O.O. 81 complied with".

10. The Quartermaster and Handing Over Committee will hand over the Camps to the Incoming Unit and obtain a receipt for all camp furniture handed over, on the prescribed Form "A".

11. CHIPPEWA CAMP and MICMAC CAMP all billets to be left scrupulously clean and certificates to be rendered by O.C. Coys that this has been done.

[signature]
Capt& A/Adjt.
10th R. W. Kent Regiment.

25/5/17.

No.1. Filed.
2. C.O.
3. 2nd i/c.
4. Qr Master.
5. Signal Offr.
6. Transport Officer.
7. O.C. "A" Coy.
8. " "B" "
9. " "C" "
10. " "D" "
11. Medical Officer.
12. Lewis Gun & Intelligence Offr.
13. O.C. 18th K.R.R.C.
14 & 15. War Diary.

Instructions regarding War Diaries and Intelligence Summaries are contained in F. S. Regs., Part II. and the Staff Manual respectively. Title Pages will be prepared in manuscript.

9

WAR DIARY
or
~~INTELLIGENCE SUMMARY~~
(Erase heading not required.)

123/41 Vol 14

Army Form C. 2118

For month Ending June 30th 17. 10th (S) Bn R West Kents.

Place	Date	Hour	Summary of Events and Information	Remarks and references to Appendices
CHIPPEWA CAMP M6a47.	1-6-17 To 5-6-17		The Battn were resting & fitting out ready for operations	
	5-6-17	9-30am	"A" Coy & 1 platoon of "B" Coy proceeded to OLD FRENCH TRENCH. This was carried out by platoons at 10 minutes interval & no casualties were incurred	
LEFT SUB SECTOR.	5-6-17	11-30pm	Remainder of the Battn marched up to the trenches by platoons & were disposed in the following order.	
			'C' Coy & 2 platoons of 'B' in GORDON STREET & 'D' Coy in the G H Q. Line (advanced) Battn Hd Qrs. were in OLD FRENCH TRENCH.	APPdx No 4 OO No 83.
			Our artillery were very active during the whole day & a barrage was practiced during the afternoon.	
	6-6-17	12-30am To 1-30 "	A Patrol was sent out from "A" Coy & entered the enemy front line which was found to be unoccupied & very much damaged.	
	6-6-17	10PM	A Party under 2Lt DAVIES & 2Lt DONALDSON marked out the Battn assembly area. This was completed without casualties	
	7-6-17	12.15am	The Battn commenced forming up on the tapes behind O 34. & O.35. A Coy on the left supported by 'C' Coy & 'B' on the right supported by 'D'	APPdx No 4 PARA 5
	7 "	3.10am	Was ZERO. HOUR & the Battn advanced under the barrage & reached the DAMMSTRASSE capturing 1 Officer & 37 OR of the enemy.	Appdx No 1
			The Battn then commenced to consolidate line beyond the DAMMSTRASSE from 100 Yds left of PHEASANT. WOOD. To OAR AVENUE	APPDX. No 5 MAP

G H Sutton (?) Major Cmdg 10th (S) Bn RW Kent.

1875 Wt. W593/826 1,000,000 4/15 J.B.C. & A. A.D.S.S./Forms/C. 2118.

Army Form C. 2118

Instructions regarding War Diaries and Intelligence Summaries are contained in F. S. Regs., Part II. and the Staff Manual respectively. Title Pages will be prepared in manuscript.

WAR DIARY
or
~~INTELLIGENCE SUMMARY~~
(Erase heading not required.)

Sheet No 2. 10th (S) Bn R W Kent Rgt

Place	Date	Hour	Summary of Events and Information	Remarks and references to Appendices
BLUE LINE [illegible]			The 11th Bn QUEENS attacked on the left & the 23rd MIDDLX on the right & men were detailed to keep touch with these units as far as possible.	
	8.6.17	2 AM	The line was extended to Right Edge of PHEASANT. WOOD. & the Battn continued to wire & generally consolidate the position. The enemys artillery was beginning to search for our positions but not much damage was caused	
"	9.6.17 & 10th "		The Batt continued to work on their lines & only 2 Casualties were incurred by enemy Shell fire.	
	11 "	6.0 P.M.	Battn was relieved By the 26th ROYAL FUSILERS. & returned by platoons to VOORMELEELE. SWITCH	
VOORMEZEELE SWITCH	June 12th		The Batth was resting, cleaning up & finding fatigue parties.	
			Casualties incurred between June 6th & June 11th — Officers: Killed 5, Wounded 4. OR: Killed 30, Wounded 188, Doubtful 10	APPDX No 2

[illegible] Major Cmdg 10th (S) Bn. R W Kent Rgt.

1875 Wt. W593/826 1,000,000 4/15 J.B.C. & A. A.D.S.S./Forms/C. 2118.

Instructions regarding War Diaries and Intelligence Summaries are contained in F. S. Regs., Part II. and the Staff Manual respectively. Title Pages will be prepared in manuscript.

WAR DIARY

or

~~INTELLIGENCE SUMMARY~~

(Erase heading not required.)

10th (S) Bn R West Kent Rgt.

Army Form C. 2118

Place	Date	Hour	Summary of Events and Information	Remarks and references to Appendices
VOORMEZEELE SWITCH	June 12th to 19th		The Battn. was resting & finding fatigue parties for burying cable & salvage work etc. The enemys artillery was fairly active & we had one casualty.	
	June 19th	5 P.M.	The first platoon moved off to relieve the 11th Bn R. West. Kents. who were in support lines. Batt. Hd Qtrs moved up later in the evening to Spoil Bank. The Battn found fatigue parties for the Regmt in front line both by day & night. Later all fatigue work had to be done by night owing to the activity of enemy artillery & aircraft.	APPX No 6 BOO. No 90
LEFT. SUB. SECTOR.	" 23rd	8 P.M.	The Battn commenced to relieve the 20th D.L.I. "A" & "D" Coys taking over the front line & "B" & "C" Coys moving up in close support. while Hd Qtrs advanced up to Sap in NORFOLK. ROAD	APPDX. No 7 BOO 91
	" 27th	10 P.M.	The DLI again relieved the Battn who came back to the positions held by them four days previously. Enemy artillery was very active during the whole time & "Spoil Bank" was very heavily shelled.	
	30th	2 P.M.	Relief of the Battn was commenced by the 15th LONDON. REGT & was carried out without any casualties. The Battn reached ONTARIO CAMP, (Q 30 c 1.5.) about 9 P.M.	
			Casualties incurred between June 19 & June 30th — Officers Wounded 1; OR Killed 3, Wounded 15	APP No 3

1875 Wt. W593/826 1,000,000 4/15 J.B.C. & A. A.D.S.S./Forms/C. 2118.

S H Beattie Major
COMDG. 10th (S) Bn. ROYAL WEST KENT REGT.

—— Div Boundaries —·—·— Batt^n Boundaries

Legend :- Machine Gun .... △
Anti Tank Empt .... ⊡
Strong Point ...... ⌑
Wire ....

St. Eloi
Shelley Farm
The Mound
Crater Lane
Middlesex Lane
Bois Confluent
Rainged Fm
Elkhof Fm
Oosthoek Estaminet
White Ch.
Signal Station
Piccadilly Fm
Oaten Wood
Damm Strasse
Pheasant Wood
H.Q.
Damm Wood
Denys Wood
Ravine Wood
Delbske Fm
Verhaest Fm
Rose Wood
Engelbrier
Estaminet
In den Jager Ct.
Bouwen Fm
Lesigne Fm
Nouffen Fm
Bonduille Fm
Goudezeune Fm
In de Sterkte Cab.
Denys Fm
Bug Wood
Marle Fm
Zero Wood
Zero Hd. Qrs
Renty Fm
Onraet Fm
Evans Fm
Grand Bois
Bois Quarante
Crobnoget Chapel
Colteau Fm
Lonewhege Fm

41st Divn
15-5-17

13 14 15 16

—— BLACK LINE —— BLUE LINE —— GREEN LINE —— RED LINE

PRINTED BY No 2 ADVANCED SECTION A.P.&S.S.

Appd X

No 5

Showing position held by Battalion

Message

......DIVISION.

Map reference or Mark on Map at back.

1. My {Company / Platoon} has reached..................
2. My {Company / Platoon} is at.............. and is consolidating.
3. My {Company / Platoon} is at.................and has consolidated.
4. Am held up by M.G. at..................
5. I need:—Ammunition.
   Bombs.
   Rifle Grenades.
   Water.
   Very lights.
   Stokes shells.
6. Counter attack forming up at..................
7. I am in touch with..................on Right / Left at............
8. I am not in touch with.................. on Right / Left
9. I am being shelled from..................
10. I estimate my present strength at..............rifles.
11. Hostile {Battery / Machine Gun / Trench Mortar} active at..................

Time............ m. Name..............................

Date.................. Platoon..............................

Company..............................

Battalion..............................

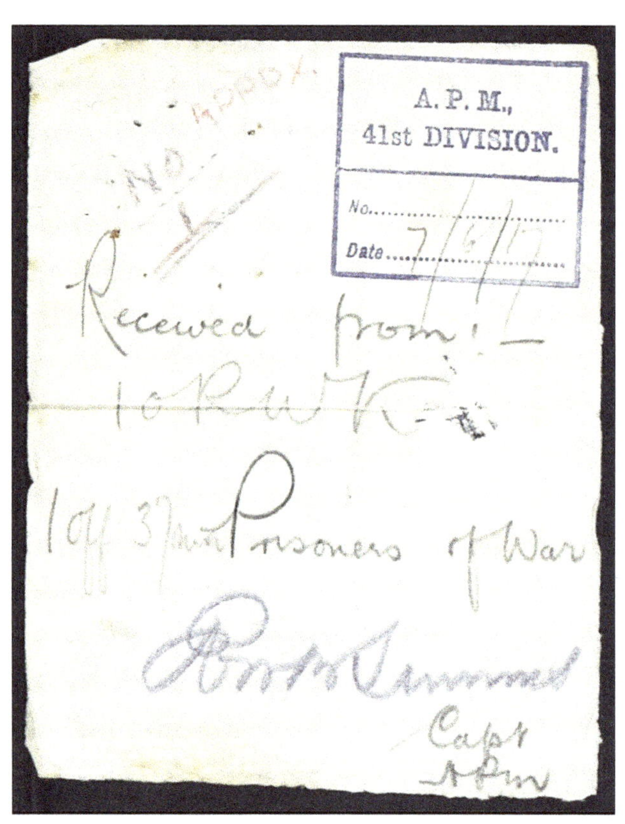
A. P. M.,
41st DIVISION.

No.

Date 7/6/17

NO APPROX.

Received from: 10 R W K

1 off 37 men Prisoners of War

Capt
APM

S E C R E T. Copy No....2....

10TH BATTN. ROYAL WEST KENT REGIMENT.

APPdx N 4

OPERATION ORDER NO. 83.

Reference Maps (Sheet 28 N.W.) 1/20,000.
(Sheet 28 S.W.)

---

1. **INTENTION.** The 123rd Infantry Brigade is to be prepared to assume the offensive after the 31st May 1917.

2. **DISPOSITION OF BRIGADE FOR BATTLE.**

Right Battalion	-	23rd Middlesex Regt.
Centre "	-	10th R.W.Kent Regt.
Left "	-	11th "Queen's" Regt.
In Support	-	20th Durham Light Infy.

3. **DAYS PRIOR TO ASSAULT.** The attack will take place on Zero Day, which will be referred to as "Z" Day, and the preceding 5 days as Y, X, W, V, U. Days before "U" Day will be known as "Z" minus 6, "Z" minus 7, etc. Days after ZERO as "A" "B" and "C" days. Days after "C" Day as "Z" plus 4, "Z" plus 5, etc.

4. **DISPOSITION PREVIOUS TO ATTACK.** The Battalion will enter the line on W/X and X/Y nights, and be prepared to attack at ZERO hour on second day.

"A" Company and 1 Platoon of "B" Company will move up on W/X night, and the remainder of the Battalion on X/Y night. The Battalion will then be disposed as follows:-

"A" Company and 1 Platoon of "B" Company in OLD FRENCH TRENCH from I.32.d.7.3½. to I.32.d.1.3.

2 Platoons of "B" Company, and "C" Company in GORDON STREET, and

"D" Company in G.H.Q. Line Advanced (from road at H.36.b.7½.5½. to H.36.b.4½.2½.)

Headquarters at I.32.d.5.2.

"A" Company will hold the FRONT LINE on the Battalion Battle Front with outposts at night only.

At 1½ hours before ZERO the Battalion will be in position on their assembly Area, which has already been reconnoitred and will be marked out with tapes and Notice Boards.

5. **BATTALION BATTLE ORDER.** The Battalion will attack on a double Company Front, with 1 Platoon of each Company in the first Wave.

"A" Company, supported by "C", on the LEFT.
"B" " " " "D" " " RIGHT.

Each Company will be formed up in three waves of 2 lines each, there being a distance of 20 yards between waves and 10 yards between lines.

6. **BATTALION BOUNDARIES.** Right Boundary - OAR AVENUE.inclusive.
Left Boundary - TRAM TRACK, including EIKHOF FARM.

7. **BATTALION OBJECTIVES.** Enemy system of Trenches between Boundaries, Right Boundary being inclusive to the Battalion up to and including the DAMSTRASSE (known as the BLUE Line).

8. **ASSEMBLY & ASSAULT.** The Battalion will move from its position of assembly to within 75 yards of enemy parapet by

SHEET 2.

ZERO hour. At ZERO plus 3" the Artillery will lift off enemy Front Line, and immediately the first Wave, followed by remaining waves, will dash to the assault.

The first wave will halt in enemy Support Line with its section of "Durham" Moppers, and make the line good immediately.

The 2nd, 3rd, 4th & 5th, 6th, 7th and 8th waves will continue to advance with no halt until the RED Line is reached. Moppers must deal with all Trenches, Dug-outs and Strong Points met with. The special work of each party of Moppers being arranged between O.s. C. attacking and Support Companies prior to the assault as far as it is possible to do so.

The 7th and 8th waves, consisting of D.L.I. halt in enemy Front and Support Lines, and mop and dig in. When the 7th wave arrives and takes over the SUPPORT TRENCH, the first wave re-forms and follows the attack.

The 5th wave, (carrying wave) dumps material in SUPPORT LINE, passing through as quickly as possible, and becomes a fighting wave.

At ZERO plus 35" the Barrage will move forward from in front of the RED Line and waves 2, 3, 4, 5, and 6 follow it.

The 2nd wave halts in the new enemy RESERVE TRENCH and mops it. This wave becomes a RESERVE at the call of the troops in the DAMSTRASSE.

If possible the 6th wave passes on and forms a line of outposts in front of the DAMSTRASSE, as close as possible under the STANDING BARRAGE. These Outposts will be reinforced by Troops in DAMSTRASSE.

9. BATTALION HEADQUARTERS. Will move with the 6th wave, and establish itself in the vicinity of the enemy Support Line, until the DAMSTRASSE is taken, when it will move there. The Pioneers under Sergt. TURNER will continue to move with the 6th wave, and assist in forming the outpost line.

10. CONSOLIDATION. As enemy Front Line Trenches are cleared, Companies must consolidate on the best line, but not less than 60 yards in front of enemy's trench.

11. STRONG POINTS. Will be established in the vicinity of:-

0.3.c.4.0.
0.3.c.8.3.
0.3.d.3.5.
0.3.d.65.70.

and be garrisoned by a section of Infantry from the Battalion in whose area the STRONG POINTS are established, together with the Vickers Gun detailed for the purpose.

12. ARTILLERY TIME TABLE.

ZERO plus 3 minutes - FRONT LINE.
ZERO plus 20 " - SUPPORT LINE.
ZERO plus 45 " - DAMSTRASSE.

Note: Whether BARRAGE is STANDING or CREEPING the most advanced line of Infantry must keep close under it. On no account must they allow the BARRAGE to creep away from them.

13. VICKERS GUNS. Move behind 6th wave. O.C. Section with Battalion Headquarters.

SHEET 3.

14. STOKES GUNS. Moves with Battalion Headquarters.

15. CONCENTRATION MARCH TABLES. Will be issued sep rately.
O.s. C. Companies are responsible that sufficient Guides are trained to lead Platoons on W/X night, X/Y night, and Y/Z night, as soon as these tables are received.

16. DRESS. As laid down in Battalion Order No. 166 para 29 dated 20.5.17.

17. MUNITIONS CARRIED ON THE MAN. As laid down in Battalion Order No. 166 dated 20.5.17., obtainable from Battalion Reserve Dump at I.32.d.3.2. OLD FRENCH TRENCH on left of Tram Track Bridge.

18. DUMPS. AMMUNITION. I.32.d.3.2. for arming men prior to the assault.
O.3.c.4.8. (LOCALITY Left) Advanced Reserve Dump.

RATIONS. For "Y" day to be brought up on the man.
For "Z" day from Dump at I.31.d.50.80.
For "A" day from Reserve Dump O.3.d.4.8.

WATER. For "Y" day)
For "Z" day) from Dump at I.31.d.50.80.
All water bottles must be taken up full and kept filled.

19. CONTACT AEROPLANES. Every man will carry two green ground flares, which will be lit in groups of five, only when called for by an aeroplane showing a white light and sounding a KLAXON horn roughly at the following times :-

Zero plus 30
Zero plus ~~XXXX~~. 1.20.
Zero plus 4.30.
Zero plus 5.30.

These flares will only be lit by the most advanced troops.

20 GENERAL DIRECTION OF ATTACK. 157° True.

21. LEWIS GUNS. Three with each Company. Only 2 trained Gunners to be taken per gun. 4th Gun with Battalion Headquarters in Reserve.

22. PICKS & SHOVELS. As many as are obtainable to be carried in ratio of 3 Shovels to 1 Pick.

23. MEDICAL. Regimental Aid Post at I.32.d.1.1½. (OLD FRENCH TRENCH) This will be pushed forward as soon as the situation permits.
Divisional Collecting Post at VOORMEZEELE.
Advanced Dressing Station at DICKEBUSCH.

24. REGIMENTAL STRETCHER BEARERS. As many reserve Stretcher Bearers as possible with Companies to render first aid. All other Stretcher Bearers with Stretchers to follow 6th wave and work up from Rear to Front.

25. **REPORTS.** Situation Reports when practicable and necessary.
Estimated Casualties, as soon as any Company has suffered 10 casualties.
Battalion Headquarters, to which reports should be sent, will be marked whenever possible with a sign in large letters BLOOD.

26. **RUNNER POSTS.** Divisional Communication Post SHELLEY LANE - SHELLEY FARM - RUINED FARM - DIKHOF FARM - DAMSTRASSE.

27. **BATTLE STOPS.** Provost Sergeant and 4 men will patrol BOLLAERTBEEK between Brigade Boundaries.

28. **PRISONERS OF WAR.** To be evacuated to Brigade Marshalling Point (Junction of CONVENT LANE and VOORMEZEELE-YPRES road) Ration Dump I.31.a.4.1.

29. **LIAISON.** O.C. "A" Company will detail 1 selected N.C.O. for 11th "Queen's" and O.C. "B" Company 1 selected N.C.O. for 23rd Middlesex Regt. to report to Battalion Headquarters on Y/Z night at 9 p.m.

30. **SALVAGE.** All parties and individual men returning from the Front Line must carry back some salvaged article with them.

31. **R.E.STORES.** From SHELLEY LANE Dump.
From "Z" Day inclusive Stores may be drawn from all dumps by any unit and no indent or authority will be necessary.

32. **TRANSPORT.** First Line Transport will remain in its position ready to move at two hours notice. Details of roads, tracks etc. to be used will be issued separately to the Transport Officer.

33. **TIME.** Watches will be synchronised daily at 9 a.m.

34. **ORGANISATION OF CAPTURED GROUND.** A Front Line in vicinity of BLACK line to be held by 3 Battalions of the 122nd Infantry Brigade within the Brigade Boundaries.
Reserve Line along BLUE line, held by 23rd Middlesex on the right, 10th R.W.Kents in the centre, and 11th Queens on the left.
A line of strong points in rear of BLUE line.
"B" Company will be responsible for the construction of a Strong Point at about O.9.b.1.9.
A Communication Trench in continuation of OAR AVENUE will be dug forward from the BLUE line, for which "D" Company will be responsible.

H. Wallis Capt a/adjt

1st June 1917. 10th Bn. Royal West Kent Regt.

Copy No.		Copy No.	
1.	Filed.	11.	Intelligence Officer.
2.	War Diary.	12.	Transport Officer.
3.	" " (Dup.)	13.	123rd Infantry Bde.
4.	C. O.	14	O.C. 23rd Middlesex Rgt.
5.	Second in Command.	15.	O.C. 11th "Queen's"
6.	O.C. "A" Coy.	16.	O.C. 20th D.L.I.
7.	O.C. "B" "	17.	Spare.
8.	O.C. "C" "	18.	"
9.	O.C. "D" "	19.	"
10.	Signalling Officer.	20	"

War Diary

appdx. No 2

Casualties of the Batt OFFICER.

Killed. 2LT. DAVIES. C.T.
" " SAMUELS, G.G.
" " MOTHERSELL. J.N.
" " DODGHSON. J.H.
" " FOSTER. H.L.

Wounded. Capt. GINGELL. L.A.H.
LT HOPKINS. H.C.
2LT. HARRIS. H.E.
" " FABB P.J.

SHEET 4.

25. REPORTS. Situation Reports when practicable and necessary.
Estimated Casualties, as soon as any Company has suffered 10 casualties.
Battalion Headquarters, to which reports should be sent, will be marked whenever possible with a sign in large letters BLOOD.

26. RUNNER POSTS. Divisional Communication Post SHELLEY LANE - SHELLEY FARM - RUINED FARM - EIKHOF FARM - DAMSTRASSE.

27. BATTLE STOPS. Provost Sergeant and 4 men will patrol BOLLAARTBEEK between Brigade Boundaries.

28. PRISONERS OF WAR. To be evacuated to Brigade Marshalling Point (Junction of CONVENT LANE and VOORMEZEELE-YPRES road) Ration Dump I.31.a.4.1.

29. LIAISON. O.C. "A" Company will detail 1 selected N.C.O. for 11th "Queen's" and O.C. "B" Company 1 selected N.C.O. for 23rd Middlesex Regt. to report to Battalion Headquarters on Y/Z night at 9 p.m.

30. SALVAGE. All parties and individual men returning from the Front Line must carry back some salvaged article with them.

31. R.E. STORES. From SHELLEY LANE Dump.
From "Z" Day inclusive Stores may be drawn from all dumps by any unit and no indent or authority will be necessary.

32. TRANSPORT. First Line Transport will remain in its position ready to move at two hours notice. Details of roads, tracks etc. to be used will be issued separately to the Transport Officer.

33. TIME. Watches will be synchronised daily at 9 a.m.

34. ORGANISATION OF CAPTURED GROUND. A Front Line in vicinity of BLACK line to be held by 3 Battalions of the 122nd Infantry Brigade within the Brigade Boundaries.
Reserve Line along BLUE line, held by 23rd Middlesex on the right, 10th R.W.Kents in the centre, and 11th Queens on the left.
A line of strong points in rear of BLUE line.
"B" Company will be responsible for the construction of a Strong Point at about O.9.b.1.9.
A Communication Trench in continuation of OAR AVENUE will be dug forward from the BLUE line, for which "D" Company will be responsible.

H.W.Whiller Capt. a/Adjt.

1st June 1917. 10th Bn. Royal West Kent Regt.

Copy No. 1. Filed.
2. War Diary.
3. " " (Dup.)
4. C. O.
5. Second in Command.
6. O.C. "A" Coy.
7. O.C. "B" "
8. O.C. "C" "
9. O.C. "D" "
10. Signalling Officer.

Copy No. 11. Intelligence Officer.
12. Transport Officer.
13. 123rd Infantry Bde.
14 O.C. 23rd Middlesex Rgt.
15. O.C. 11th "Queen's"
16. O.C. 20th D.L.I.
17. Spare.
18. "
19. "
20 "

APPDX No 6

SECRET. Copy No......... 8

BATTALION OPERATION ORDER No 90.

---

1. The Battalion will relieve the 11th Bn R. W. Kent Regt in Support on the 19th inst.

2. Companies will take over trenches from the opposite number.- They will march by Platoons at 10 minutes interval and will be met by guides at BLIGHTY BRIDGE, the first Platoon to arrive at 5.30.p.m.
"A" Coy will move off first followed by "B". "C" and "D" Coys.
Headquarters will follow the last Platoon of "D" Coy at 10 minutes interval and proceed to SPOILBANK. Pioneers, Snipers, and Bombers will proceed with H.Q.

3. Transport Officer will arrange for 2 limbers for Lewis Guns, and 1 limber for S.A.A. and Bombs, collect these from dump near STRAGGLERS POST commencing at 3.30.p.m. (limbers at 10 minutes interval), and dump same at SPOILBANK.
Bombing Officer will arrange for 1 N.C.O. and 3 men to proceed with first limber and act as guard.
60 Petrol tins will be filled with water at Transport Lines, and sent up in limber at 4.30.p.m., and dumped with the S.A.A.

4. Officers Valises, mens packs, and all empty Petrol tins to be stacked on roadside VOORMEZEELE SWITCH by 10.a.m.
Officers Mess Cart will collect mess utensils &c from dump near STRAGGLERS POST at 5.30.p.m.
Cookers will be taken away at 5.30.p.m.

5. Rations for the 20th inst will be sent direct to the Battalion Dump at SPOILBANK.
All water bottles to be filled before leaving camp and kept filled.

6. All dugouts and bivouacs will be left clean and a certificate to this effect rendered by O?C. Coys before departure.

7. Completion of relief to be notified to this Office, "B.O.O. 90 complied with".

8. The Lewis Gun Officer will take over 1 Lewis Gun A.A. Post.

9. List of any Trench Stores taken over to be sent to Headquarters as soon as possible.

[signature] Capt & A/Adjt.
10th R. W. Kent Regiment.

18/6/17.

1. C.O.
2. File.
3. O.C. "A" Coy.
4. " "B" "
5. O.C. "C" Coy.
6. " "D" "
7. Transport Officer & Quartermaster.
8. War Diary.

APPDX No 7

SECRET. Copy No....8.......

BATTALION OPERATION ORDER No 91.

1. The Battalion will relieve the 20th D.L.I. in the left sub-sector on the night 23rd/24th June 1917.

2. "A" Coy will take over the left of the FRONT LINE including the S.P. at O.5.d.4.5.

"D" " " " " " right " " " "

"C" " " " " " left " " SUPPORT LINE.

"B" " " " " " right " " " "

Headquarters will be at Norfolk Road.

1 Guide per Platoon will be sent to Bn H.Q. at 9.p.m., and these will then be sent direct to the Companies whom they are to guide.

3. Rations for the 24th will be carried on the man. On subsequent days rations will be carried up by special carrying parties at night, these parties being supplied by the Support Battalion.

4. Water All water bottles to be filled. Water will be sent up at 7.a.m. daily in Petrol tins. 40 tins of water will be taken over as reserve.

5. Patrol. O.C. "B" Coy will detail 1 Officer or selected N.C.O. and 20 picked men (including Lewis Gun team as covering party) as a permanent fighting patrol. These will live in the OLD BRITISH SUPPORT LINE by day and operate by night. Patrols on wire, and those to communicate with units on flank, will be found by the Companies in the line.

6. Disposition by day. "A" and "D" Coys will each have 4 Lewis Gun teams with 3 bombers attached and Company H.Q. (Signallers, Runners, etc), and "B" and "C" Coys will each have 2 Lewis Gun teams with 3 bombers attached and Coy H.Q. (Signallers, Runners, etc), in their respective lines by day. Remainder will come back after "stand down" in very small parties, and remain during the day in the OLD BRITISH [illegible] LINE between O.5.c.0.7. and O.5.b. central (ap[illegible] One Officer from the 2 Coys in the FRONT LINE and 1 Officer from the [illegible] Coys in the SUPPORT LINE will come back with this Party daily. These parties will return in time to arrive in their respective tr[illegible] half-an-hour before "stand to" at night.

7. O.C. Coys will take full particulars, of Defence Schemes, S.[illegible] Signals. &c, of the line taken over.

8. A List of Trench Stores taken over will be forwarded to this Office as soon as possible.

9. Completion of the relief to be reported to this Office "B.O.O. 91 complied with".

[signature]

Capt & A/Adjt.
22/6/17. 10th R. W. Kent Regiment.

No. 1. O.C. "A" Coy. 5. Transport Officer
2. " "B" " 6. Q.M.
3. " "C" " 7. War Diary.
4. " "D" " 8. File.

To — M. O
Lt. Donaldson Adjt.
Lt. Panchaud
Lt. Anderson

For information

[illegible]
Capt.
Adjt.

23/6/17

10th Royal West Kent Regt. Sheet I July 1917

123/41

10 R W Kent Vol 15

WAR DIARY
or
INTELLIGENCE SUMMARY
(Erase heading not required.)

Army Form C. 2118.

Instructions regarding War Diaries and Intelligence Summaries are contained in F. S. Regs., Part II. and the Staff Manual respectively. Title Pages will be prepared in manuscript.

Place	Date	Hour	Summary of Events and Information	Remarks and references to Appendices
Caluric Camp RENINGHELST	1.7.17	11 AM	Situation normal. The Battalion proceeded by Route March to FLETRE arriving about 3.30 P.M. Headquarters billeted remainder of Battalion Encamped Strength Off.33. O.R.700 Evacuated Sick O.R.5	
FLETRE Sheet 27 S.E. W.12 d 5.6.	2.7.17		Situation normal, rest & training Organization Strength Off 33. O.R 700	
	3.7.17		" " " Strength Off 35 O.R 696 Transferred O.R. 4 2 Officers joined 2/Lt Phillips 2/Lt Godfrey.	
	4.7.17		" " " Reinforcement O.R. 3, Strength Off.35. O.R.699	
	5.7.17		" " " Lt Cheal transferred to L.T.M.B. Lt & H Brown evacuated sick to England Reinforcement O.R. 57, Strength Off 33. O.R 753 Evacuated Sick O.R.2	
	6.7.17		" " " Strength Off 33. O.R.753	
	7.7.17		" " " Lt Col Wood-Martyn awarded D.S.O. Major Beattie, Capt Wallis Lt Roberts awarded M.C. CSM Cooper D.C.M. 15.O.R. M.M.	
	8.7.17		Strength Off 33. O.R.753	
	9.7.17		" " " Strength Off 33. O.R.739 transferred 6.O.R. Evacuated Sick 8.O.R.	
	10.7.17		" " " Strength Off 33. O.R.738 transferred 1.O.R. " Reinforcement 15 O.R. 2/Lt Coston H.W. joined transferred 1 O.R. Strength Off 34. O.R 751.	
	11.7.17		" " " Strength Off 34. O.R.751	
	12.7.17		" " " Strength Off 34. O.R.757	
	13.7.17		" " " Strength Off 34. O.R.748, transferred O.R.2 Evacuated Sick O.R.1	
	14.7.17		" " " During the night Enemy plane dropped bombs in neighbourhood of Camp but no damage done. Strength Off 34. O.R.749	
	15.7.17		" " " Strength Off 34. O.R.736. Evacuated Sick O.R.13.	
	16.7.17		" " " Strength Off 34. O.R.732 transferred O.R.2 Evacuated Sick O.R.2	
	17.7.17		" " " Strength Off 34. O.R 732	
	18.7.17		" " " Strength Off 34 O.R 732	
	19.7.17		" " " Strength Off 34 O.R 731 Evacuated Sick O.R.1	
	20.7.17		" " " Strength Off 34 O.R 731.	
		2.30 PM	The Battalion was inspected by the G.O.C. and the ribbon of D.S.O. presented to Lt Col. Wood Martyn	

2449 Wt. W14957/M90 750,000 1/16 J.B.C. & A. Forms/C.2118/12.

10th Bn Royal West Kent Regt

WAR DIARY
or
INTELLIGENCE SUMMARY

(Erase heading not required.)

Sheet II July 1917

Army Form C. 2118.

Instructions regarding War Diaries and Intelligence Summaries are contained in F. S. Regs., Part II. and the Staff Manual respectively. Title Pages will be prepared in manuscript.

Place	Date	Hour	Summary of Events and Information	Remarks and references to Appendices
FLETRE M.R. Sheet 27 S.E. W.12 d.5.9.	21/7/17	9 AM 2 PM	Situation normal. The Battalion moved forward by route march to RENINGHELST AREA, CARNARVON CAMP M.10 b.6.6. arriving in Camp about 2 PM. During the Period from 1st to 20th the Battalion was trained and organized for forthcoming Operations. Sports were held frequently, every opportunity being taken of the fine weather for the men to indulge in outdoor recreation. Both the G.O.C. and Brigade Commander frequently visited the Training Area whilst the men were at exercise. Strength Off 34. O.R. 731	
CARNARVON CAMP	22/7/17		Situation normal. Reinforcements joined O.R. 227. Strength Off 34. O.R. 958	
M.R. HARLEBEKE [?] S.A. M.10.b.6.5.	23/7/17		" Reinforcements inspected by the Brigadier. Strength Off 33. O.R. 964. Lt Edwards wounded. Reinforcements O.R. 6	
	24/7/17		" " Strength Off 33 O.R. 966 Reinforcements O.R. 2	
—	25/7/17	3.30 PM 8.30 PM	Situation normal. The Battalion moved forward to RIDGE WOOD preparatory to taking up Battle position. From RIDGE WOOD the Battalion proceeded to relieve 22 Battalion London Regt 47th DIV. in IMPACT Support Area. The relief being complete about 2 AM. 26/7/17, this Operation was carried out successfully. Strength Off 33 O.R. 968 Reinforcements O.R. 2	
	26/7/17		Situation normal. During both day and night Enemy continually shelling position. Position of Assembly Area reconnoitred. Reinforcements O.R. 7. Strength Off 33. O.R. 974	
	27/7/17	5 PM	Situation normal. A Practice Barrage was arranged and carried out by Our Artillery. Strength Off 33. O.R. 974	
	28/7/17	10 PM	Situation normal. Inter-Company Relief. "D" Co relieving "A" Co in FRONT LINE. Strength Off 33. O.R. 974	
	29/7/17		Situation normal. A Practice Barrage carried out by Our Artillery at Dawn. Strength Off 33. O.R. 974	
	30/7/17	10 PM	Situation normal. The Battalion moved forward to take up position at Assembly Area on the Tapes. Strength Off 33 O.R. 974	
	31/7/17	2 AM 3.50 AM	Battalion reported in position on Tapes for attack. Barrage opened and attack commenced. The Battalion gained two Objectives consolidated and held the same. Casualties will be included in next months War Diary on completion of Operations. Strength Off 33. O.R. 974	

[signature] Capt. & Major
Comm'dg 10th Bn Royal West Kent Regt

2449 Wt. W14957/M90 750,000 1/16 J.B.C. & A. Forms/C.2118/12.

S E C R E T. WAR DIARY Copy No.....2....

123rd INFANTRY BRIGADE OPERATION ORDER No. 102.

Reference Map 1/10,000 - Attached.

123rd Inf. Bde. H.Q.
12th July 1917.

1. INTENTION.

The 41st Division will attack on a date to be notified later in conjunction with the 19th Division of the IXth Corps on the Right and the 24th Division of the IInd Corps on the Left.

The Front of attack for the 41st Division will be from FORRET FARM on the Right to the KLEIN ZILLEBEKE Road on the Left.

The Objectives are shown on attached Map.

The 122nd Infantry Brigade will attack South, and the 123rd Infantry Brigade North of the YPRES - COMINES CANAL.

The 72nd Infantry Brigade will be on the Right of the 24th Division, with Headquarters in LARCH WOOD.

2. DISPOSITIONS OF DIVISION.

On the Right. 122nd Infantry Brigade, - Headquarters SPOIL BANK.
1 Section 228th Field Coy. R.E.

On the Left. 123rd Infantry Brigade - Headquarters BLUFF TUNNELS.
2 Battalions 124th Infantry Brigade attached to 123rd Infantry Brigade. (26th R. Fusiliers & 21st K.R.R.C.)
1 Section 233rd Field Coy. R.E.

Divisional Reserve. 124th Infantry Brigade (less 2 Battalions).
228th Field Coy. R.E. (less 1 section).
233rd Field Coy. R.E. (less one section).
237th Field Coy. R.E.
19th Middlesex Regt. (Pioneers).

The Divisional Reserve will be located East of the VIERSTRAAT - YPRES Road, in the VOORMEZEELE DEFENCES and G.H.Q. Advanced Line.

The Field Artillery will be formed into 6 Groups.

The Right Double Group, Heavy Artillery, will be affiliated to 41st Division for the operation.

3. DISPOSITIONS OF BRIGADE.

Dispositions of 123rd Infantry Brigade one hour before Zero, Headquarters, Boundaries, Overland Tracks, Tramway Tracks, R.A.P's, Objectives and Barrage Lines are given on attached Map.

The Ground shaded in Green is allotted to the 24th Division for assembly prior to the attack.

The 21st Bn. K.R.R.C. will be in Support, and the 26th Bn. Royal Fusiliers, in Reserve.

One Section 233rd Field Coy., H.Q. 123rd M.G. Coy. and H.Q. 123rd L.T.M. Battery will be established in the BLUFF TUNNELS.

4. PREVIOUS TO ATTACK.

There will be a preliminary Bombardment lasting several days.

The Division at present holding the line is working on a programme formulated by this Division in accordance with these orders.

Attacking Battalions will, on returning to the line, take over their respective fronts, echeloned in depth.

Officers Commanding these Battalions, Coy. Commanders, guides and markers will reconnoitre the Assembly Area very carefully every night until "Z" day, from the time the Brigade returns to the Line. Special attention will also be paid to the training of runners during this period.

5. METHOD OF ATTACK.

Attacking troops will line out on their tapes on Y/Z night, each Battalion on a two-Company Front, and each Company on a two-Platoon Front (See attached Plan).

Movement to be complete by Zero minus 1 hour.

Troops in Support and Reserve will be ready to move on receipt of orders from Brigade Commander, from Zero hour onwards.

At Zero hour the barrage will come down on the RED LINE, where it will remain for 4 minutes - during this time the Infantry will advance such a distance and at such a pace as will ensure the leading line of the assault being within 75 yards of the enemy parapet at Z plus 4. At this hour (Z plus 4 minutes), the barrage will advance and pile up on the BLUE LINE, and the Infantry will assault and Mop up the RED LINE. This will be done by the 2nd wave, the 1st wave carrying straight on behind the barrage, followed by the 3rd, 4th and 5th waves.

At Zero plus 28 minutes, the barrage will lift off the BLUE LINE, and the Infantry will assault and mop up the objective - this will be done by the 1st wave.

The barrage will continue to creep forward until it reaches its final protective position, some 400 yards beyond the GREEN LINE, which is the final objective, except for the Left Flank, where it will pivot about J 31 c 5.9., remaining there until Zero plus 48, when it will advance in conjunction with the 24th Divn.

Waves 3 and 4 will carry straight on from the BLUE LINE and will follow the barrage until it halts, mopping or killing anything it meets.

When the barrage halts, both waves will lie down - the 4th wave at once taking steps to consolidate a line of outposts formed of Strong Points sited -

(a) To get the best possible Cross-fire.

(b) To work as near as possible to our own standing barrage as is compatible with safety.

While this is being done, specially detailed Officers and N.C.O's will go back and site the Strong Points for the GREEN LINE. When this has been done the 3rd wave will pass back through the 4th wave and consolidate the GREEN LINE on the selected sites.

The GREEN LINE will become when completed the Outpost Line, and this should be borne in mind by these Officers, and by C.O's whose duty it is to site it.

The withdrawal of the 4th wave after the consolidation of the GREEN LINE will be left to the discretion of Officers Commanding Battalions.

The 5th wave will halt in the best positions possible between the RED and BLUE Lines, its position being determined by Battalion H.Q.

Waves 2 & 4 carry in addition to mopping or consolidating, No.2 Wave dropping its loads in the RED LINE, No.4 Wave dropping its loads in BLUE LINE, but not halting to do so.

Further details with reference to the barrage will be issued later.

The rate of advance for the creeping barrage will be 100 yards in 4 minutes.

The General Direction of Attack is 127° T.B.

DUTIES OF WAVES.

2nd Wave mop RED LINE.
1st Wave mop BLUE LINE.
3rd Wave mop and consolidate GREEN LINE
4th Wave Outposts.
5th wave - Best positions between RED and BLUE LINES.

Waves 2 and 4 Carry in addition:
Wave 2 dropping in RED LINE,
" 4 " " BLUE LINE.

Wave 2 do Strong Points in RED LINE;
2 Platoons on each Strong Point, except the 23rd Middlesex Regt, who will commence with one, to be joined as soon as possible by another from the Supporting half battalion of their own unit.

Wave 1 do Strong Points on BLUE LINEm
2 Platoons on each, remainder fitting in as desired.

Wave 3 Consolidates GREEN LINE with Strong Points to be joined later or not ~~@2xxxxxxxxx~~ as desired.

Wave 4 - Shell holes.

Wave 5 - Concentrate on Bn. H.Q.

6. STRONG POINTS.

Strong Points will be established as under:-

(a) In Front of the RED LINE.

In vicinity of:-

Railway Embankment, O 6 a 4.4½, by 23rd Middlesex Regt.
Corner of Wood O 6 a 9.7., by 11th Queen's.
I 36 d 20.00, by 10th R.W. Kent Regt.
I 36 d 5.5. by 10th R.W. Kent Regt.

(b) In Front of the BLUE LINE.

In vicinity of:-

O 6 c 80.42, by 23rd Middlesex Regt.
O 6 d 25.80, by 11th Queen's.
O 6 b 50.50, by 11th Queen's.
O 6 b 80.90, by 10th R.W. Kent Regt.
I 36 d 90.50, by 20th Durham L.I.

7. MACHINE GUNS.

There will be a Machine Gun Barrage under arrangements to be made by Corps Machine Gun Officer, for which the following M.G Coys. will be used.

1 Coy. 23rd Division.
1 Coy. 41st Division (124th M.G. Coy.)
1 Coy. 47th Division.
Portions of 4th and 12th Motor M.G. Batteries.

Machine Guns of 123rd M.G. Coy. will be distributed as follows. Those attached to Attacking Battalions advancing with the 5th wave.

(a) For Strong Points mentioned in para.6.

O.C., 11th Queen's	3.	O.C, 23rd Middlesex Regt.	2.
O.C., 10th R.W.Kents.	3.	O.C, 20th Durham L.I.	1.

(b) for Flank Defences.

O.C. 23rd Middlesex Regt. 1.
O.C. 20th Durham L.I. 2.

In Reserve - 4.

It will be seen that each Battalion has 3 Vickers Guns at its disposal. These Guns will be under the orders of the Bn. Commander concerned.

One Vickers Gun will go into each of the Strong Points shown on map.

It is essential that these guns cross with each other. The siting of each Strong Point will therefore be undertaken with this cross as its primary object.

8. STOKES GUNS.

Stokes Guns will be distributed as under. They will be placed in defensive positions, and will advance with the 5th wave.

O.C. 11th Queen's - 1.
O.C. 10th R.W. Kents. 1.
O.C. 23rd Middlesex 1.
O.C. 20th Durham L.I. 1.

In Reserve - 4.

9. SIGNAL COMMUNICATIONS.

The arrangements for Signalling Communications will be issued later.

The Code of Signals as issued with Appendix 1 of 123rd Inf. Bde. Operation Order No.88 of 27-5-17 will be used.

All Units will continually practice the use of this code prior to attack - its usefulness cannot be over-estimated.

10. The following Appendices will be issued later:-

1. Artillery.
2. Employment of R.E. and Pioneers.
3. Contact Aeroplanes.
4. Liaison.
5. Administrative Arrangements.
6. Outline of orders for attack of Brigades on Left and Right.

11. No papers concerning this Offensive will be kept in advance of Brigade Headquarters on returning to the line. Documents may be placed in envelopes, deposited at Brigade Headquarters, and studied when required.

12. ACKNOWLEDGE.

J.S.Bull

for Captain,
Brigade Major,
123rd Infantry Brigade.

Issued to Signals at 6.30am 14.7.17

M Copy No.1 Filed.
M 2 War Diary.
M 3 41st Div. G.
M 4 41st Div. Q.
M 5 11th Queen's.
M 6 10th R.W. Kent Regt.
M 7 23rd Middlesex Regt.
M 8 20th Durham L.I.
M 9 26th R. Fusiliers.
M 10 21st K.R.R.C.
T 11 122nd Inf. Bde.
T 12 124th Bde.
T 13 C.R.A.
T 14 C.R.E.
M 15 123rd L.T.M.B.
M 16 123rd M.G. Coy.
T 17 72nd Inf. Bde.
T 18 O.C. Right Double Group H.A.
T 19 A.D.M.S.
T 20 138th Field Amb.
M 21 233rd Field Coy.
T 22 No.3 Coy. Train.
M 23 Bde. T'Pt. Officer.
M 24 Staff Capt.
M 25 Brigade Signals.

SECRET. WAR DIARY Copy No. 2

Further Administrative Instructions for Forthcoming Operations, reference 123rd.Infantry Brigade Order No.102 of July 12th.1917.

123rd.Inf.Bde.No.A.56/647.

1. BARRAGE RATIONS AND WATER.

The above will be dumped for one day only, namely for consumption on "Z" day.

The rations are actually installed near IMP DUMP grouped in lots of 700 for each of the 6 battalions, but the perishable portions have not been broken and are not divided, and must be divided up evenly.

From the above, the rations for 123rd.Machine Gun Company, 123rd.L.T.M.Battery and Brigade Headquarters will be found as follows:-

123rd.M.G.Company will draw	75	rations from	11th.Queens.
	75	do.	10th.R.W.Kents.
	25	do.	26th.R.Fusiliers.
123rd.T.M.Battery will draw	75	rations from	23rd.Middlesex.
	25	do.	26th.R.Fusiliers.
123rd.Inf.Bde.H.Q.will draw	75	rations from	20th.Durham L.I.
	75	do.	21st.K.R.R.C.
	25	do.	26th.R.Fusiliers.

Regimental Quartermasters and Brigade Quartermaster Sergeant will be responsible that these rations are correctly split up and distributed.

2. WATER.

500 petrol tins have been allotted to the Brigade for the purpose of forming mobile dumps of water as far forward as possible in the trench system.

These will be re-allotted as follows:-

Each Battalion - 95.

Headquarters of Brigade -)
M.G.Coy. -) 30.
T.M.Batty. -)

A dump of reserve patrol tins filled from reserve water carts will be established at NORFOLK LODGE BRIDGE, I 33 d 3.6.

3. AMMUNITION.

5,000 No.3.Red Aeroplane Flares have been allotted to the Brigade. These are re-allotted as follows:-

11th.Queens.	-	1200.
10th.R.W.Kents.	-	1200.
23rd.Middlesex.	-	600.
20th.Durham L.Inf.	-	1200.
21st.K.R.R.Corps.)	receive an allotment	
26th.R.Fusiliers.)	from 124th.Inf.Brigade.	
Brigade Dump.	-	800.
		5000

3. AMMUNITION (cont.).

50 S.O.S. Rockets have been asked for and will be allotted as follows:-

11th.Queens.	-	10.	
10th.R.W.Kents.	-	10.	
23rd.Middlesex.	-	5.	
20th.Durham L.Inf.	-	10.	
Brigade Reserve.	-	15.	50.

(21st.K.R.R.Corps and 26th.R.Fusiliers will obtain an allotment from 124th.Infantry Brigade).

S.A.A., Grenades etc., to equip assaulting troops will be drawn from Divisional Dump under arrangements to be made by Brigade Transport Officer with Transport Officers concerned, at a time and date to be notified later.

4. PRISONERS OF WAR.

The cage will be at N 3 a central, where all prisoners will be sent.

5. MAP.

A revised map showing Tramways, Transport Tracks, Dumps etc. will be issued shortly.

6. ACKNOWLEDGE.

Captain,
Staff Captain,
123rd.Infantry Brigade.

20th.July 1917.

Copy No. 1. Filed.		Copy No.13. C.R.A.		
.. No. 2. War Diary.		.. No.14. CMR.E.		
.. No. 3. 41st.Division G.		.. No.15. 123rd.L.T.M.Battery.		
.. No. 4. 41st.Division Q.		.. No.16. 123rd.M.G.Company.		
.. No. 5. 11th.Queens.		.. No.17. 72nd.Inf.Brigade.		
.. No. 6. 10th.R.W.Kents.		.. No.18. Right Double Group H.A.		
.. No. 7. 23rd.Middlesex.		.. No.19. A.D.M.S.		
.. No. 8. 20th.Durham L.I.		.. No.20. 138th.Field Ambulance.		
.. No. 9. 26th.R.Fusiliers		.. No.21. 233rd.Field Company R.E.		
.. No.10. 21st.K.R.R.C.		.. No.22. No.3.Coy. Div.Train.		
.. No.11. 122nd.Inf.Bde.		.. No.23. Bde.Transport Officer.		
.. No.12. 124th.Inf.Bde.		.. No.24. Brigade Major.		
~~No.13~~		.. No.25. Bde.Signal Officer.		

S E C R E T. Copy No. 2

123rd I.B.
G.387/41.

ADVANCE AGAINST ZANDVOORDE.

(In continuation of 123rd Inf. Bde. Operation Order No.102 dated 12th July 1917.)

---

1. No deliberate attack will be made on ZANDVOORDE on "Z" day.
Should such an attack take place, it will be carried out by 47th Division on a date after "Z" day, properly supported by Artillery, and in conjunction with Corps on either flank.
41st Division would hold the GREEN LINE and assist with covering fire as ordered.

2. The enemy may, however, vacate ZANDVOORDE on "Z" day, especially about the time II Corps reaches TOWER HAMLETS (i.e., about Zero plus 8 hours).
Should this occur 41st Division will occupy ZANDVOORDE under cover of all guns of 41st Divisional Artillery Group which can be brout to bear at the time, together with Howitzers of Xth Corps H.A. engaged on the barrage.
The Reserves of the 41st Division will move forward, occupy and hold the position gained.
The Field Artillery will advance to positions already selected, whence these advanced troops can be adequately covered.
The 141st Infantry Brigade, 47th Division will come under Orders of G.O.C. 41st Division as a reinforcement or reserve.

3. The Divisional Commander considers that the operation outlined in para.2 above may resolve itself into one or other of the following:-

(a) A general and hurried retirement of the enemy from the ZANDVOORDE position.
In this case 123rd Infantry Brigade on orders from Divisional Headquarters will push forward patrols supported by strong fighting detachments to occupy the ZANDVOORDE defences.
This advance will be covered by a creeping barrage of such guns of 41st D.A. Group as are not outranged, and certain Heavy Howrs.
The Divisional Reserve will move forward to occupy and hold the position gained.
Above might take place at any hour after the capture of the GREEN LINE on report from aeroplanes that the enemy is evacuating the ZANDVOORDE position.
In this case serious opposition in gaining the ZANDVOORDE position need not be anticipated, but counter-attack, especially from the N.E. is to be expected.

(b) A retirement from the ZANDVOORDE position probably at the time the II Corps reaches TOWER HAMLETS, i.e. about Zero plus 8 hours.
In this case 41st Division may probably continue the advance in fighting formation. 124th Infantry Brigade (including the 2 Battalions previously under G.O.C. 123rd Infantry Brigade) will pass through 123rd Infantry Brigade and attack the ZANDVOORDE position on a front approximately from J 32 d 9.5. to P 8 a 3.9.
23rd Middlesex Regt. will attack HOLLEBEKE MILL and KORTEWILDE (both in P 13 b).
At the same time a Brigade of the IXth Corps will attack the WARNETON LINE South of the CANAL to about O 18 central.
123rd Infantry Brigade less 23rd Middlesex Regt. and 141 Infantry Brigade, 47th Division becomes Divisional Reserve.

4. Further instructions will be issued concerning para 3(b).

5. ACKNOWLEDGE.

M B Heywood
Captain,
A/Brigade Major,
123rd Infantry Brigade.

July 25th 1917.

Copy No.1 File.
2 War Diary.
3 41st Division. G.
4 11th Queen's.
5 10th R.W. Kent Regt.
6 23rd Middlesex Regt.
7 20th Durham L.I.
8 123rd M.G. Coy.
9 123rd L.T.M. Battery.
10 122nd Infantry Brigade.
11 124th Infantry Brigade.
12 C.R.A.
13 C.R.E.
14 233rd Field Coy. R.E.
15 21st K.R.R.C.
16 26th R. Fusiliers.
17 72nd Infantry Brigade.
18 O.C. Right Double Group H.A.
19 138th Field Ambulance.
20 Brigade Transport Officer.
21 Staff Captain.
22 Brigade Signals.

S E C R E T.   Copy No...2....

123rd Inf. Bde. Operation Order No. 102.

APPENDIX II.

EMPLOYMENT OF R.E. and PIONEERS.

1. Prior to "Y" Day the Technical Troops will occupy present billets and bivouacs, and continue work on preparations for the Offensive, under ordørs of C.E. Xth Corps, and C.R.E. 41st Division, as at present detailed.

2. No Working Parties will be out on "Y" Day or "Y/Z" night, and on "Y" day RME. and Pioneers will concentrate in N 5 a.

3. One Section 233rd Field Coy. R.E. will move forward to a position allocated by G.O.C. 123rd Infantry Brigade.

4. Allotment of Work for "Z" day and "Z/A" Night is shown in attached Table.

ALLOTMENT OF WORK FOR "Z" DAY and "Z/A" NIGHT.

	"Z" DAY.	"Z/A" NIGHT.
233rd Field Coy. R.E. No.1 Section.	(Detached with 123rd (Inf. Bde. to assist (in construction of (S.P's etc.	Return to Field Coy. Bivouac.
No.2 Section. No.3 " No.4 "	(Consolidate and wire positions near RED (LINE N. of CANAL, O.C. Field Coy. to (decide in conjunction with G.O.C. 123rd (Inf. Bde., best time for moving up to (work.	

19th Bn. Middlesex Regt.

"A" Coy.	Continue OAF AVENUE behind BUFFS BANK to BLUE LINE at about O 6 b 4.4.
"C" Coy.	Maintain Tramway System from SHELLEY DUMP to R.A.P's Nos. 1 and 2, and extend line from R.A.P. No.2 to the neighbourhood of TRIANGULAR SPOIL BANK parallel to OAF AVENUE.

SECRET.

123rd Inf. Bde. Operation Order No. 102.

APPENDIX IV.

LIAISON.

The following will be the arrangements for Liaison during the forthcoming operations:-

1. Between 41st Division and neighbouring Division.

(a) 41st and 24th Divisions. An Officer from each will visit Divisional H.Q. alternatively in car, as often as is considered necessary.

(b) 41st and 19th Divisions. In view of the small extent of the intended advance, it is considered that telephone communication should suffice. An Officer at each Divisional H.Q. will be in readiness at a moment's notice in case of necessity.

2. Between 123rd Infantry Brigade and 72nd Infantry Brigade (Left), and 122nd Infantry Brigade (Right).

An Officer and 2 runners will be exchanged with each of the Brigades on the flanks of 123rd Infantry Brigade.

3. Flank Battalions, i.e. 20th Durham L.I., and 23rd Middlesex Regt. will exchange Officers with the Battalions on their Left and Right flanks respectively, and great care must be taken that touch is maintained by flank Companies of Brigades and Battalions, Runners being used.

4. Between Battalions and Brigade. Each Battalion will send an Officer to Brigade Headquarters.

5. ARTILLERY LIAISON.

(a) A Senior Artillery Officer will be detailed for Liaison duty with the Brigade, and will stay at Brigade H.Q. throughout the Operations.

(b) An Officer will be detailed by O.C. Right Double Group H.A., who will be in direct telephone communication with the Right Double Group H.Q., and will also remain with Brigade H.Q. until the completion of the operations.

6. On "Z/A" and subsequent night, the normal Liaison between Divisional Artillery and Battalions (i.e. a F.O.C. at Brigade H.Q. will be maintained.

SECRET. Copy No....2.......

Herewith Appendix 2,"Employment of R.E. and Pioneers", and Appendix IV, "LIAISON", in connection with 123rd Infantry Brigade Operation Order No.102.

Please Acknowledge receipt.

J G Budd

July 19th 1917.

Captain,
for Brigade Major,
123rd Infantry Brigade.

Copy No.3 41st Division. G.
4 41st Division. Q.
5 11th Queen's.
6. 10th R.W. Kent Regt.
7. 23rd Middlesex Regt.
8. 20th Durham L.I.
9. 26th R. Fusiliers.
10. 21st K.R.R.C.
11. 122nd Infantry Brigade.
12 124th Infantry Brigade.
13. C.R.A.
14. C.R.E.
15. 123rd L.T.M. Batty.
16. 123rd M.G. Coy.
17. 72nd Inf. Bde.
18. O.C. Right Double Group H.A.
19. A.D.M.S.
20. 138th Field Amb.
21. 233rd Field Coy.
22. No.3 Coy. Train.
23. Brigade Transport Officer.
24. Staff Captain.
25. Brigade Signals.

PLANS SHOWING WAVES AND LINES ON TAPES.

	"B"		"A"			
1st WAVE. (	1.	2	5	6	x	1st Line.
						2nd "
2nd WAVE.	3		7			3rd "
3rd WAVE. (	9 "D"	10	13 "C"	14		4th "
					100x	5th "
4th WAVE.	11		15			6th "
5th WAVE. (H.Q.)	HEADQUARTERS.				x	7th "

2 ATTACKING COYS.

23rd MIDDLESEX REGT.

	1	"A"	2		
1st WAVE (	1		2	x	1st Line.
					2nd "
2nd WAVE.	3.				3rd "
3rd WAVE (	5	" B "	6		4th Line.
				100x	5th Line.
4th WAVE.	7.				6th "
5th WAVE. (H.Q.)	HEADQUARTERS.			x	7th "

DISTANCES. 10 yds. between Lines.
20 yds. between Waves.

Platoons Nos. 3, 7, 11 and 15 carry for the waves preceding them.

S E C R E T.

123rd Inf. Bde. Operation Order No. 192.

APPENDIX VII(a).

S I G N A L   C O M M U N I C A T I O N S.

1. 11th Queen's & 23rd Middlesex Regt.

(a) Buried Cable direct through Battalion H.Q. to Brigade.
Land line to be laid by Battalion Signallers from Assembly Area to Battalion H.Q. before Zero day, and to be carried forward with attacking Infantry - if possible in duplicate.

(b) Visual - From Enemy Area via about I 36 a 2.5. to O 4 b 4.1. thence by bury to Brigade Headquarters.

(c) Wireless 151 Set to be taken over by 3rd Wave by Brigade Personnel, to be established in enemy lines about boundary dividing the two battalions.
Position to be notified to each C.O. as soon as established.
Messages go via Wireless Station in TRIANGULAR SPOIL BANK to Battalion Headquarters - thence to Brigade by Buried Cable.

(d) Runners -- Posts as follows:-

1. "M Q 1" (1st Relay Post) O 5 a 30.45.
2. "M Q 2" (2nd Relay Post) O 5 b 70.70.
3. "M Q 3" (3rd Relay Post) Wireless station with 3rd Wave.
4. "Q 1" (4th Relay Post) for 11th Queen's only - Forward Visual Station.
5. "M 1" (4th Relay Post) For 23rd Middlesex Regt. only, Forward Visual Station.

Personnel for Runner Posts between original Battalion H.Q. and Brigade H.Q. will be found by Brigade, and those in front of Battalion H.Q. (inclusive) will be found by Battalions.

Personnel for the following will be found by Brigade:-

1. "B A" (1st Relay Post) at 26 R.F. H.Q. I 34 c 25.30.
2. "B B" (2nd Relay Post) Dugout O 4 a.95.95.

(e) Pigeons to Brigade and Battalion H.Q. via Corps Loft.

(d) and (e) only if (a), (b) & (c) absolutely fail.

2. 20th Durham L.I. & 10th R.W. Kent Regt.

(a) Buried Cable to within 300 yards of Battalion H.Q. connection to be made by Overland wire to be maintained by Battalion Personnel. Land Line to be laid to Assembly Area previous to Zero day by Battalion Personnel and carried forward with attacking Infantry if possible in duplicate.

(b) Visual from attacking Infantry via Station about I 36 a 2.5. to Battalion H.Q. or to O 4 b 4.1. - thence from either by bury to Brigade H.Q.

(c) Power Buzzer. Power Buzzers and Amplifiers will be (1) at Battalion H.Q., (2) about I 36 a 6.0. and (3) with third wave of attacking Infantry. Latter to be established as near as possible to boundary dividing Battalions - position when selected to be notified to Commanding Officers concerned.
Personnel for (1) to be found by Brigade, and for (2) and (3) by Battalion concerned.

(d) Runners.

1. "D K 1" (1st Relay Post) I 36 a 6.0.
2. "D K 2" (2nd Relay Post) I 36 d 4.4.
3. "D K 3" (3rd Relay Post) Advanced Power Buzzer Station.
4. "D 1". (4th Relay Post) Forward Visual Station of 20th Durham L.I.
5. "K 1" (4th Relay Post) Forward Visual Station of 10th R.W. Kent Regt.

Personnel for Runner Posts between original Battalion H.Q. and Brigade H.Q. will be found by Brigade, and those in front of Battalion H.Q. (inclusive) will be found by Battalions.

Personnel for the following will be found by Brigade:-

"B.A." (1st Relay Post) at 26 R.F. H.Q. I 34 c 25.30.

(e) Pigeons, to Brigade and Battalion H.Q. via Corps Loft.

(d) and (e) only to be used if (a), (b) and (c) absolutely fail.

3. Lateral Communication.

between - 11th Queen's) and (10th R.W. Kent Regt.
23rd Middlesex Regt.) (20th Durham L.I.
and vice versa,

(a) By Bury.
(b) Runner - Relay Posts.

1. "L A" Dugout I 34 d 40.95.
2. "L B" H.Q. 21st K.R.R.C. I 35 a 55.35.
3. "B B" Dugout O 4 a 95.95.

4. Machine Guns and T.M.B. will use the communications arranged for the Battalions to which they are attached.

5. An additional chain of wireless stations will be prepared to reinforce in case the buried cable is interrupted.

6. A map is attached showing above communications.

7. Present position calls will not be used after Zero hour. A three letter code will be issued and will come into use for "Address to" and "Address from" from that hour.
Later, should normal trench warfare be resumed, fresh position calls will be issued.

SECRET. Copy No. 2

123rd.Inf.Bde.No.A.56/711.

Further Administrative Arrangements for Forthcoming Operations, reference 123rd.Infantry Brigade Order No.102 of July 13th 1917.

SALVAGE.

1. 2nd.Lieut.F.L.DOBBINSON, 20th.Durham L.Inf. has been appointed Brigade Salvage Officer during the Forthcoming Operations.

2. He will organize the salvage of all kinds of material in the Brigade Battle Area.

3. O.C. 26th.Bn. R.Fusiliers will detail a party of 4 reliable N.C.O's. and 16 men to assist him in this work. These men will report to * him at Brigade Headquarters at 9 p.m. on "Y/Z" night, with rations for "Z" day.

4. He will establish Brigade Collecting Dumps at the head of transport tracks on the two main communication routes near the British Front Line, to which all material will be collected.

5. The Brigade Battle Area will be divided into 2 areas, North and South, the dividing line being the boundary of 10th.R.W.Kents and 11th.Queens.

The Battalions in each of these two areas will be responsible for the Salvage of material there.

It must be clearly understood that the Salvage party is formed more with the idea of directing the salvage operations, than of actually collecting.

6. Different forms of salvage to be collected in separate heaps, i.e. Rifles and Equipment, Ammunition, R.E. Stores, should each be dumped apart. Any Very Pistols salved are to be reported to Brigade Headquarters and taken to the Brigade Ammunition Dump and handed to the Officer in charge, They will be re-issued only on authority from Brigade.

7. An N.C.O. is to be put in charge of each of the above dumps, with a small party to help load salvage on to limbers and any other empty transport going back from the line.

8. Transport Officers will be instructed that they are to assist in clearing salvage from the Brigade Dumps to Divisional Dumps, the position of which will be notified later.

9. The balance of the party mentioned above will systematically work over the area, collecting salvage and directing others who have salvage, to the Brigade Dump.

10. Special attention to be paid to the Salvage of Petrol Cans, and Stoppers for same, which will be taken direct to nearest watering point, and ammunition, which when salved, if immediately serviceable is to be returned to Brigade Ammunition Dump. Dirty and damaged ammunition will be returned with other salvage.

It must be borne in mind that if the salving of these two items proceeds satisfactorily, an immense amount of transport work can be saved.

Captain,
Staff Captain,
123rd.Infantry Brigade.

22nd.July 1917.

To
All recipients of O.O. 102, and 2nd.Lt. Dobbinson.

SECRET. 123rd Infantry Brigade No.A.50/583.

ADMINISTRATIVE ARRANGEMENTS FOR FORTHCOMING OPERATIONS

REFERENCE 123rd INFANTRY BRIGADE OPERATION ORDER No. 102 of 12th instant.

---

(1) RATIONS AND WATER.

In order to reduce wheeled traffic on roads and tracks on X and Y days, rations and water as shown below will be dumped at Brigade Headquarters in recesses in the BLUFF TUNNELS.

The dumps will be marked with notice boards as in previous operations, viz :-

MUSCLE
Rations and Water
for "Y" day.

Rations and water for all Units of 123rd Infantry Brigade will be dumped for "Y" and "Z" days and for "Z" day for two battalions of 124th Infantry Brigade (21st K.R.R.C. and 26th Royal Fusiliers) in the same position, calculated at a strength of 700 per Battalion. The amount of water dumped (in petrol tins) will be $^{1}/_{3}$ gallon per man per diem.

Instructions for drawing and dumping will be issued later, but Units will prepare the necessary notice boards without delay.

Rations for "Z" plus 1 day and subsequent days will be delivered by pack transport in the normal way. Commanding Officers will arrange with their Transport Officers the position where transport will meet carriers, but times will be issued from this Office.

(II) WATER.

Details of Water Supply are shown in attached Appendix "A".

A reserve of water carts will be put forward (probably to near bridge O.33.d.3.6) in the event of the breakdown of pipe-line where carriers can exchange empty cans for full petrol tins.

The conserving of petrol cans is of extreme importance and every empty tin found should be returned to nearest water point as soon as possible.

(III) AMMUNITION.

Divisional Dump will be at N.4.a.5.2. Brigade Dump will probably be at I.34.a.5.0. Forward Dumps for Battalions will probably be at O.5.b.5.6 (BUFFS BANK).

The 47th Division will construct and partially fill Brigade and Battalion Dumps.

Amounts of ammunition in each Dump are shown in Appendix "B", which also shows amount of ammunition disposed in the area under the present Defence Scheme.

Second Lieutenant NEWMAN, 23rd Middlesex Regiment will be in charge of Brigade Dump and will ensure that it is kept filled. He will be accommodated at Brigade Headquarters.

A party of 2 Bombers, 1 N.C.O. and 3 other rnaks per Battalion will report to him at Brigade Headquarters at 9 a.m. "Y" day as Dump personnel and carriers.

(IV.) R. E. STORES.

The Divisional R. E. Dump will be at BRASSERIE - N.6.a.1.1.

Advanced R. E. Dump - IMP DUMP - O.4.a.8.8. (old German Crater).

(V.) MEDICAL.

Regimental Aid Posts :-

O.4.B.2.9. = 23rd Middlesex and 11th Queen's.
I.34.d.8.8. = 20th Durham L. I. and 10th R.W.Kents.

The Medical Officers of the 21st K.R.R.C. and 26th Royal Fusiliers will be with their Battalions unless otherwise ordered.

Collecting Post = SPOILBANK, I.33.d.3.2.

Advanced Dressing Station = VOORMEZEELE, I.31.c.4.6.

Collecting Station, Walking wounded, = BRASSERIE, N.6.a.2.2.

Main Dressing Station, Seriously wounded = LA CLYTTE Road, M.6.a.8.6.
Main Dressing Station, Walking wounded = LA CLYTTE, N.7.c.4.5.

(VI.) PRISONERS OF WAR.

Prisoners of War will be escorted by 5 per cent. of their numbers, and should be evacuated direct to Divisional Cage, the position of which will be notified later.
The senior man of each escort should receive a receipt from the Officer i/c Cage.

(VII.) STRAGGLERS.

A line of Divisional Straggler Posts will be established at
O.2.a.4.3 -(BUS HOUSE)
I.32.d.4.4.
I.33.a.2.3.- (BRIDGE).

O.C., 23rd Middlesex Regt. will establish a post at IMP DUMP to be in position not later than 12 midnight, Y/Z night.

O.C., 20th Durham Light Infantry, 10th R. W. Kent Regt. and 11th Queen's Regt. will detail Regimental Police to patrol the line of the old British Front Line from THE BLUFF to I.34.b.9.3.

All Stragglers will be taken to Brigade Dump mentioned above and handed over to the Officer or N.C.O. there for use in carrying up ammunition.

Stragglers arrested by Divisional Posts will be handed over to 1st Line Transport and sent back at first opportunity to rejoin their Units.

(VIII.) REINFORCEMENTS.

There will be no Divisional Reinforcement Camp, but all personnel left behind under S.S.135 will remain in their own Transport Lines, where any drafts which may arrive will also be sent.

Captain A. A. CLARK, 23rd Middlesex Regt. will be in charge of all such personnel and Units will forward to him a Nominal Roll of all Officers and men left in his charge. He will render the return (Appendix C) to Divisional Headquarters, "A" and "Q" Branch, by 4 p.m. daily.

No personnel are to be sent up to join their Units without orders from Divisional Headquarters.

(IX.) PACKS AND SURPLUS KIT.

Packs and surplus kits will be stored in the barn at RENINGHELST at G.35.d.65.80 ; the personnel there now will be maintained and no additional men will be sent by Units.

In order to facilitate rapid issue (should opportunity occur), greatcoats will be rolled in bundles separate from the packs, but men must be warned not to leave private property in the pockets of their greatcoats.

Each bundle will be labelled with number of platoon and roll of owners.

(X.) SALVAGE.

An Officer will be detailed by Brigade to organize Salvage Parties and detailed instructions will be issued to him direct.

Please acknowledge.

J.S. Budd

Captain,
Staff Captain,
123rd Infantry Brigade.

16th July 1917.

Copy No.1 Filed.
2 War Diary.
3 41st Div. G.
4 41st Div. Q.
5 11th Queen's Rgt.
6 10th R.W.Kent Rgt.
7 23rd Middlesex Rgt.
8 20th Durham L.Infy.
9 26th Royal Fusiliers.
10 21st K.R.R.C.
11 122nd Inf. Bde.
12 124th Inf. Bde.
13 C.R.A.
14 C.R.E.
15 123rd L.T.M.Battery.
16 123rd M.G.Company,
17 72nd Inf. Bde.
18 O.C., Right Double Group H.A.
19 A.D.M.S.
20 138th Field Ambulance.
21 233rd Field Company, R.E.
22 No. 3 Company, Div. Train.
23 Brigade Transport Officer.
24 Brigade Major.
25 Brigade Signals.

APPENDIX "A".

1. Water Cart refilling point - I.31.d.2.4.
2. Water Tanks and Stand Pipes - N.8.a.10.10.
   N.5.a.90.95.
   N.5.b.30.80
   I.31.d.20.40.
   ~~I.31.d.33.75.~~
   I.31.d.80.85.
   O.1.d.35.75.
   O.8.a.65.90.
   O.9.a.70.20.
   I.33.a.50.10. *
   I.33.c.80.70. *
   I.33.c.50.45. *
   I.33.d.30.50. *
   O.4.a.75.60. *

Tanks **marked** * mean supply unreliable.

3. Stand Pipes **only** - N.6.a.2.9.
   N.6.b.4.9.

4. Wells.

I.31.c.40.60.	Notice Boards erected showing amount of chlorination required.
I.31.c.60.40.	
O.2.a.60.70.	
O.3.c.95.10.	
I.33.c.80.85.	
I.32.d.85.20.	
O.10.b.10.40.	
O.9.d.35.25.	

APPENDIX "B".

	Brigade Dump.	Forward Dump (Total)
S.A.A.	125,000.	125,000.
No.5 Mills Grenade.	2,500.	2,500.
Rifle Grenades and blank.	1,000.	1,000.
Stokes shells with cartridges.	500. ~~(Pipe charges)~~	500.
Very Lights 1"	500.	500.
-do- -do- 1½"	250.	250.
Webley Pistol and S.A.A.	250.	250.
P. Grenades	250.	250.
S. O. S. / Flares. / Rockets. / Coloured Very Lts. / Smoke Candles.	50% of allotment when available.	50% of allotment when available.

This does not include the ammunition for equipping assaulting troops, which must be drawn before going in the line.

Existing in Area at present :-

	CORD LANE.	HEDGE ROW.	KINGSWAY.
S.A.A.	50,000	50,000	50,000.
Mills No.5.	2,000	2,000	2,000.
Rifle Grenades.	1,500	1,500	500.
Stokes Shells.	1,500	1,500	500.
Very Lights 1"	700	700	900.
-do- -do- 1½"	300	300	260.

	Right Battn. Sector.	Left Battn. Sector.	Support Battn. Sector.
S.A.A.	100,000	50,000	20,000
MILLS No. 5.	2,000	2,000	1,000
Rifle Grenades.	400	200	70
Very Lights 1".	1,000	1,000	150

APPENDIX "C"

RETURN OF PERSONNEL .... INFANTRY BRIGADE.

Battalion.	Details left behind by Brigades.		Reinforcements who have not been out before.		Reinforcements who have been out before.		Sent up to join Units.		Remarks.
	Offrs.	O.Rks.	Offrs.	O.Rks.	Offrs.	O.Rks.	Offrs.	O.Rks.	

Date....................

i/c Personnel .... Inf. Brigade.

10th Royal West Kent Regt. — **WAR DIARY** or **INTELLIGENCE SUMMARY** (*Erase heading not required.*) — August 1917 Sheet I — Army Form C. 2118.

Instructions regarding War Diaries and Intelligence Summaries are contained in F. S. Regs., Part II. and the Staff Manual respectively. Title Pages will be prepared in manuscript.

Vol 16

Place	Date	Hour	Summary of Events and Information	Remarks and references to Appendices
KLEIN ZILLEBEKE RED & BLUE LINE	1/8/17		Objectives gained in Mud field and consolidated. Enemy heavily shelled position and Snipers active throughout day and night. Weather conditions extremely unfavourable, Men in some places up to waist in mud and water. Communication very difficult, forward companies relying on visual signalling. Strength Offs. 22. O.R. 729.	
"	2/8/17	10 P.M.	Similar conditions of previous day. At 10 P.M. the Battalion was relieved by the 26th Bn Royal Fusiliers and withdrawn to Reserve position at RAVINE WOOD. Bn H.Q. at IMPACT SUPPORT TRENCH. Strength Offs 22 O.R. 729	
RAVINE WOOD	3/8/17	5 P.M.	Situation normal. 4 P.M. Battalion relieved by 32nd Royal Fusiliers and withdrawn to ELZENWALLE CHATEAU, this operation was carried out successfully. Total casualties during operations July 25th to Aug 3rd Officers Killed:- 2Lt Driffield, 2Lt Dillon 2Lt Godfrey. Wounded:- Lt Green 2Lt Lodder, 2Lt Grey, Missing:- 2Lt Costin, 2Lt Woodroffe. Other Ranks:- Killed 33 Wounded:- 150 Missing:- 56. Strength Offs 22. O.R. 729.	
ELZENWALLE CHATEAU	4/8/17		Situation normal. In Reserve, reorganization. 5 Officers joined 2Lts. L. Churchward, B. May, R.H. Chandler F.J. Cooper, A.E. Ashman. Strength Offs 25 O.R. 729.	
"	5/8/17		Situation normal. In Reserve Strength Offs 28 O.R. 729	
"	6/8/17		" " Strength Offs 28 O.R. 729	
"	7/8/17	7 P.M.	Situation normal, 7 P.M. The Battalion moved forward to take up position in FRONT LINE KLEIN ZILLEBEKE relieving 32nd Bn Royal Fusiliers, this operation was carried out successfully. Strength Offs 28 O.R. 729.	
FRONT LINE KLEIN ZILLEBEKE	8/8/17		Situation normal, Enemy's Artillery quiet in comparison with previous occupation of line, 2Lt Churchward wounded Strength Offs 28 O.R. 721	
"	9/8/17		Situation normal. Quiet both Day and night Strength Offs 27. O.R. 703	
"	10/8/17	3.30 A.M.	Situation normal. About 3.30 A.M. A Party consisting of 15 O.R. was organized to clear M.G. Emplacements in Enemys Lines. A successful clearance was made of two M.G. Emplacements and about 40 prisoners taken, on Return the Party came under Enemys fire and only 16 prisoners reached our lines. Our casualties 1 O.R. wounded A very successful Raid.	
		8.30 P.M.	Battalion relieved by the 32nd Royal Fusiliers and withdrawn to RIDGE WOOD H.35.c.5.3. this operation was carried out successfully. Total casualties from 7th to 10th incl Killed O.R. 4. Wounded O.R. 10 Strength Offs 27. O.R. 714.	
RIDGE WOOD H.35.c.5.3.	11/8/17	9 AM	Situation normal. The Battalion withdrawn to HALLEBAST and proceeded from there by Bus and Lorry to BERTHEN AREA (METERIN X.10.a.4.9.), this Operation was carried out successfully. Strength Offs 27. O.R. 714	
METERIN X.10.a.4.9.	12/8/17		Situation normal. Rest & Re-equipping Strength Offs 27. O.R. 714	
"	13/8/17		" " Strength Offs 27. O.R. 714	
"	14/8/17		" " " Strength Offs 27. O.R. 729	
"	15/8/17		" " " Strength Offs 27. O.R. 729	
"	16/8/17		" " 2Lt Ozzens transferred to Tank Corps Strength Offs 26 O.R. 729	
	17/8/17		" " 12 O.R. awarded Military Medal. Strength Offs 26 O.R. 729	

10th Bn Royal West Kent Regt

Instructions regarding War Diaries and Intelligence Summaries are contained in F. S. Regs., Part II. and the Staff Manual respectively. Title Pages will be prepared in manuscript.

WAR DIARY or INTELLIGENCE SUMMARY

(Erase heading not required.)

August 1917 Sheet II

Army Form C. 2118.

Place	Date	Hour	Summary of Events and Information	Remarks and references to Appendices
METERIN X10.a.4.9.	18/8/17		Situation normal, Rest, Officers joined :- 2Lts F. R. Brown, H. Robinson, J. E. Hudson, E. F. Weston, S. J. Thomas. Evacuated Sick O.R. 21. Strength Offs 32. O.R. 708	
"	19/8/17		" " " During period from 13th to 19th inst. Re-organization and re-equipment of Battn. Games and recreation inter-Platoon and Company Football. Reinforcements O.R. 14 Strength Off 32 O.R. 722	
"	20/8/17	6.30AM	Situation normal. The Battalion proceeded by Route-march to STABLE AREA O.29.b.0.8. en-route for SOUTH TILQUES arriving about 1PM. Strength Off 32. O.R. 722	OPR. ORDER No 101 APPX.
STABLE O.29.b.0.8.	21/8/17	8.30AM	Situation normal, March resumed arriving at QUELMES W.13.b.8.0. about 6PM. Close billets in village. Strength Off 32. O.R. 722	OPR. ORDER No 102 APPX.
QUELMES W.13.b.0.8.	22/8/17		Situation normal Rest & Training Officers joined 2Lts F. D. Lyons, W. F. Robinson, G. H. Ballington. Strength Off 35. OR 719	
	23/8/17		" " " " 3. O.R. awarded Military Medal. Strength Off 35. OR 722	
	24/8/17		" " " " 2Lt Pickett sick to England. Strength Off 34. OR 722	
	25/8/17		" " " " Strength Off 34 OR 722	
	26/8/17		" " " " 2Lt Percival sick to England Strength Off 33 OR 722	
	27/8/17		Strength Off 33 OR 722	
	28/8/17		" " " " Reinforcement O.R. 10 Strength Off 33 OR 729	
	29/8/17		" " " Strength Off 33 OR 739	
			Capt. Vernon Holden & 2Lt A. Donaldson awarded Military Cross.	
	30/8/17		" " " " Strength Off 33 OR 739	
	31/8/17		" " " " Reinforcement O.R. 2 Strength Off 33 OR 741	

S. H. Beattie Lt Col.
Comm'g. 10th Royal West Kent Regt

2449 Wt. W14957/M90 750,000 1/16 J.B.C. & A. Forms/C.2118/12.

APPENDIX "A".

LIAISON. 2/LIEUT. A.J. DONALDSON will report to Brigade Headquarters when the Battalion has completed assembling on the tapes., and remain with Brigade Headquarters as Liaison Officer. He will take 2 runners with him.

O.C. "A" Coy. will detail 1 Sergeant to report to the 20th. DURHAM LIGHT INFANTRY., on "Y" day.

O.C. "C" Coy. will detail 1 Sergeant to report to the 11th. QUEENS Regt on "Y" day

Each of these N.C.O.s will take 2 runners with him.

CONTACT AEROPLANES. 1 contact aeroplane will be up from zero to Zero plus 3 hours.
The leading Companies will light flares approximately at Zero plus 60 minutes, and by "D" company at Zero plus 125 minutes.
It must be ensured that the aeroplane is calling for flares before these are lighted.
The 4th. Wave which is pushed forward to cover consolidation will not light flares.

SECRET Copy. No. 14

IOTH. BN. ROYAL WEST KENT REGT. OPERATION ORDER NO.96.

Reference Map - Sheet 28.

1. INTENTION . The 123rd. Infantry Brigade will attack on a date to be notified later North of the YPRES-COMINES canal, in conjunction with the 72nd. Brigade (24th. Division) on the Left and the 122nd. Brigade (South of the Canal) on the Right.

2. DISPOSITION of BRIGADE. On the Left 20th. Durham L.Inf. H.Q. I.35.b.45.55.
On the Centre.10th.R.W.Kent Regt. H.Q. ~~I.35.b.35.55~~ I.35.b.35.55.
On the Right. 11th. Queens Regt. H.Q. O.5.a.9.5.
2 Companies 23rd. Middlesex Regt. will be on the Right of the 11th. Queens, with 2 Companies in support at about O.5.a.2.5.
In Support --- 21st. Kings R.R.C.
In Reserve --- 26th. R.Fusiliers.

3. BATTALION BATTLE ORDER. The Battalion will attack on a 2 Company front each Company having 2 Platoons in its leading wave and 1 Platoon in the next wave in 1 line only covering the whole of the 2 Platoons in front.
"A" Coy. on the Left. Supported by "D" Coy.
"C" " on the Right Supported by "B" "
Distance of 10 yards between lines in waves 1 & 3.
Distance of 20 yards between waves.

Battalion H.Q. will form a 5th. wave.

4. BATTALION BOUNDARIES. On the Left - I.36.a.7.1.- I.36.d.0.8. - J.31.c.4.0
On the Right - I.36.c.4.6.- I.36.d.1.1. - O.8.b.9.3.
As shewn on attached Map.

5. PREVIOUS TO ASSAULT. The Battalion will take over the trenches on its battle front echeloned in depth.
Company Commanders, Guides and markers will reconnoitre the assembly area very carefully each night until "Z" day from the time the Brigade returns to the Line, special attention being paid to the training of runners during this period.

6. METHOD OF ATTACK. The Battalion will line out on its assembly tapes on Y/Z night and be in position by zero minus 1 hour.
At zero hour the barrage will come down on the RED LINE where it will remain for 4 minutes.
During this time the Battalion will advance at such a pace to ensure the leading wave being within 75 yards of the enemy trench at zero plus 4.

Zero plus 4. At this moment the barrage will lift and pile up on the BLUE LINE and the Battalion will assault and mop up the RED LINE.
The 1st wave will continue straight on behind the barrage.
The 2nd wave will mop up the ReD LINE.
The 3rd. 4th and 5th. waves will follow on behind the 1st. wave.

Sheet No. 2.

Zero plus 28. At Zero plus 28 minutes, barrage will lift off the BLUE Line and the Battalion will assault and mop up this objective.
The mopping up will be done by the 1st. Wave.
The 3rd. and 4th. Waves will carry straight on behind the barrage which will continue to creep forward to the line of the final objective. (GREEN LINE).

Zero plus 40. At zero plus 40, the barrage will halt for 5 minutes in front of the GREEN LINE where the 3rd. Wave will remain and consolidate.

Zero plus 45. After the 5 minutes halt the barrage will creep forward to its final protective position followed closely by the 4th. wave. When the barrage finally halts, the 4th. wave will form a protective line of outposts formed of strong points to:-

(a) Get best possible cross fire.
(b) Work as near as possible compatible with safety to the standing barrage

The Green Line will be consolidated by a carefully selected line of Strong Points- Specially selected Officers and N.C.O.s will be detailed by "B" and "D" Coys. to site these.
The best possible position near the line indicated by the 5 minutes pause in the barrage should be chosen with due regard to observation over ground in immediate front.

"B" and "D" Coys. will each construct 1 S.P. on GREEN LINE.

It should be borne in mind that the GREEN LINE will eventually become the FRONT LINE, and when completed the 4th. Wave will be withdrawn to rhis line but definite instructions from Battalion H.Q. must be awaited before this is done.

The 5th. Wave will remain in the best possible position between the RED and Blue LInes and consolidate there.
No. 2 Wave will carry in addition to consolidating the RED Line, and deposit on that Line.
No.4 Wave will carry and deposit on the BLUE Line but not halting to do so.
The following will be carried by each Platoon in these waves.

1. Bandolier S.A.A. by every man.
6. Tins water
6. Panniers Lewis Gun magazines (Reserve)
8. Coils Barbed wire.
16. Screw pickets.

7. STRONG POINTS. No.2. Wave will construct the following S.P.s
(a) I.36.d.20.00 - - ("C" Coy.)
(b) I.36.d.5.5. - - ("A" ")
NO. 1. Wave will construct the following ~~the~~ S.P.s in front of the BLUE LINE.
(a)0.6.b.80.90. - - (A" Coy.)
(b)To be sited by O.C. ("C" ")
2 Platoons to work on each S.P.

8. MACHINE GUNS. 3 Vickers Guns will be allotted to the Battalion- These will proceed with Battalion H.Q. with the 5th. wave. 2 will remain at the RED LINE (1each with "A" and "C" Coys) and the 3rd. at the BLUE LINE (with "A" Coy.) and take up the most suitable position obtainable adjacent to the new S.P.s which when constructed will be manned by these guns.

9. STOKES GUNS. 1. 1 Stokes Gun will proceed with Battalion H.Q. in the 5th. Wave to be available as required.

Sheet No. 3.

10. RATIONS & WATER — Rations for "Z" day will be dumped at IMP DUMP O.4.a.8.8.
Water — Water cart refilling point I.31.d.2.4. (VOORMEZEELE SWITCH)
Stand pipe and tank. I.31.d.80.85. (VOORMEZEELE SWITCH & CONVENT LANE)
SPOIL BANK. O.4.a.75.60.

11. AMMUNITION. Brigade Dump at I.34.c.5.0.
Battalion forward dump. Approx. I.35.b.35.55.

Ammunition for arming the troops (as laid down for previous operations) and materials for carrying waves will be drawn from separate dump near Bn.H.Qrs.

Picks and shovels (1 for every other man) and sand bags (3 per man) will be also drawn from this dump.

12. R.E. STORES. IMP DUMP O.4.a.8.8.(Old German Crater).

13. MEDICAL
Regimental Aid Post I.34.d.8.8.
Collecting Post. SPOIL BANK I.33.d.3.2.
Advanced Dressing Station VOORMEZEELE I.31.c.4.6.

14. PRISONERS OF WAR To be escorted by 5% of their numbers and evacuated direct to the Divisional Cage (position to be notified later) Senior man of escort to obtain receipt from Officer i/c Cage.

15. DETAILS . Personnel to remain behind Vide S.S. 135, will be accommodated at Battalion Transport Lines.

16. PACKS & SURPLUS KITS. Stored in barn at RENINGHELST G.35.d.65.80. Great coats to be rolled separately in bundles by Platoons. Each bundle to be labelled and a nominal roll of owners attached. Men should be warned that nothing should be left in the pockets of these great coats.

D. V. Piggott.
2/Lieut.
A/Adjt.
For. Officer Commanding.

To.
O.C. "A" Coy.
"B" "
"C" "
"D" "
C.O.
War Diary.

Transport Offr.& Q.M.
20th. D.L.I.
11th. Queens Regt
123rd. M.Gun Coy.
123rd. L.T.M.B.
123rd. Inf. Bde.

SECRET. Copy No APPX 4

10th R W Kent Regt

Operation Order No. 103.

1. The Brigade will continue its march to the forward area tomorrow 15th inst.

2. Nos 2 and 3a of Operation Order No 102 will apply.

3. Starting Point for Battalion will be U.3.d.5.0 Sheet 27 BELGIUM FRAN road junction.

4. Companies will pass Starting Point in column of route facing EAST at the following times

"D"	Coy.	11.15 am
"C"	"	11.15½ "
"A"	"	11.16 "
"B"	"	11.16½ "

Transport will proceed in rear of Battalion.

Headquarters, Signallers & Runners will be in front of Battalion remainder in rear.

5. Officers Valises and packs of men excused marching by Medical Officer will be dumped outside their Coy Billets by 9.30 am. Mess Boxes will be ready by 9.30 am. Lieut A.A. Willoughby will supervise loading and unloading of lorries.

6. [illegible] [illegible] to be dumped at Q M Stores by 8 am. Mess boxes to be ready by 6.45 am.

7. O R excused marching by the Medical Officer will report to Lieut A A Willoughby at Q M Stores at 6.30 AM [illegible] full Marching Order.

8. Watches will be synchronized by the Adjt at the Orderly Room at 8.45 am.

15/9/17

Capt & Adjt
10th R W Kent Regt

To (1) 123rd Inf Brigade
(2) C O
(3) O C A Coy
(4) " B "
(5) " C "
(6) " D "
(7) File

No 104. Copy No

APPX III

Operation Order
by Lt Col S H. Beattie M.C.

1 The 123rd Infantry Brigade will continue the march to the Forward Area to morrow 16th inst.

2. Distances will be 880x between Bns
50x between Coys.
50x between Bns & their Transport.

3. Normal Halts will be observed.

4. Bn Starting Point will be at Cross Roads LES FILS AYMON at X.4. c. 3.4. Coys will reach this starting point at the following times.

C Coy	9.50 AM
B "	9.50½ "
A "	9.51 "
D "	9.51½ "

Hdqs Signallers & Runners in front, the remainder of Hdqs in rear

DRESS Marching Order.

APPX I

9

SECRET. Copy No......

10TH. BN. R.W. KENT REGT.

OPERATION ORDER NO. 102.

1. INTENTION. The 123rd. Infantry Brigade Group will concentrate in the Forward Area tomorrow 14th. September.

2. DISTANCES. The distances between units will be:-
   - 100 Yards between Battalions.
   - 50 Yards between other units.
   - 50 Yards between each unit and its Transport.

3. HALTS. (a) The normal halts will be observed, each unit halting automatically at 10 minutes to every clock hour and resuming the march at every clock hour.
   (b) There will be a long halt at about 12.30. Units will be notified of this halt on the march.

4. STARTING POINT. The Starting Point for the Battalion will be Cross Roads W.14.c.3.6.
   Companies will pass the starting Point, facing S.E. at the following hours.

"A"	Coy.	7.35 a.m.
"B"	"	7.35½ a.m.
"C"	"	7.36 a.m.
"D"	"	7.36½ a.m.

   Transport in rear of the Battalion.
   Headquarters Signallers and Runners in front of the Battalion, remainder in rear.

5. VALISES & PACKS. Officers' valises and mens' packs will be dumped outside their Company billets by 6.30 a.m. and a guard placed over them to consist of men unable to march. This guard must be reduced to a minimum and should not exceed 4 per Company.
   Headquarter Officers' valises and mens' packs will be dumped outside Battalion H.Qrs. at 6.30 a.m.
   Mess boxes to be ready by 7.0 a.m. Lieut. A.A. Willoughby will superintend the loading and unloading of lorries.

6. REAR GUARD. O.C. "D" Coy. will detail 1 N.C.O. and 3 men to march behind the Transport to deal with stragglers.

7. SYNCHRONIZATION OF WATCHES. Watches will be synchronised by the Adjutant at Battalion Orderly Room at 6.30 a.m.

8. DRESS. Fighting order.

9. BRIGADE STARTING POINT. The Brigade Starting Point for the Battalion is W.11.b.6.9. Time at which head of Battalion will reach this point - 9.0½ a.m.

(Signed) [illegible]

Capt. & Adjt.

13.9.17. 10th. R.W. Kent Regt.

No. 1 C.O.
2. O.C. "A" Coy.
3. O.C. "B"
4 O.C. "C"
5. O.C. "D"
6. Transport Officer.
7. Quarter Master.
8. War diary.
9. File.

APPX. IV

SECRET. OPERATION ORDERS NO.105 Copy. No...7.....

By,

LIEUT. COL. S.H. BEATTIE M.C. COMMDG. 10TH. BN. R.W. KENT REGT

---

1. INTENTION

The 123rd. Infantry Brigade will concentrate in the RIDGE WOOD area, today 18th. September.

2. DISTANCES.

All Units moving before 7.45 p.m. will maintain a distance of ¼ mile between Platoons.

3. STARTING POINT.

The Starting Point for the Battalion will be Junction Road and Track M.6.a.9.7. Time for head of the Battalion to pass starting point -- 5.40 p.m. Distance of ¼ mile to be kept between Platoon.s. Companies will move in the following order "A". "B" "C" and "D". Headquarters

4. ROUTE.

Route to be taken - Via LA CLYTTE and HALLEBAST CORNER.

5. COOKERS.

2 Cookers will proceed with the Battalion to RIDGE WOOD, under arrangements of the Transport Officer.

6. DRESS.

Dress and equipment to be worn by all ranks will be as laid down for the operations of June 7th. except that bombers will carry 100 rounds S.A.A. and only 5 Bombs. Extra S.A.A. Grenades, Tools, Flares etc. will be issued to men at RIDGE WOOD so as to avoid unnecessary movement in the forward area.

7. DETAILS.

Orders for details not going into action will follow.

(Signed) F.W. WAYDELIN.

Capt. & Adjt.

10th. R. W. Kent Regiment.

18.9.17.

Copy. No. 1. C.O.
2. O.C. "A" Coy.
3 "B"
4 "C"
5 "D"
6. Transport Officer & Q.M.
7. War Diary.

APPX 56

SECRET.

Copy. No.........

ORDER NO. 106.

10th. BN. R. W. KENT REGT.

26th. Septr. 1917.

ROUTINE.

Reveille.-----4.30 a.m.
Breakfasts.--5.15 a.m.

The Battalion will relieve the 2/6th. LANCASHIRE FUSILIERS in the ZUYDCOOTE COAST Defence Area, tomorrow the 27th. Inst.

Relief to be complete by 10.0 a.m.

Headquarters will pass starting point I.9.d.0.5. at 6.47 a.m. followed by "A" Coy. 6.47½ --- "B" 6.48 "C".--6.48½. "D".--6.49 a.m., facing North East.

The normal halts will be observed.

Dress.-- Marching Order.

Officers' Valises, Mess boxes to be dumped outside Quarter Masters Stores by 6.0 a.m.

(signed) F.W. WAYMELIN.
Capt. & Adjt.
10th. R.W. Kent Regiment.

Copy No. 1 O.C."A" Coy.
2. "B" "
3. "C"
4 "D"
5. Qr. Master & Transport Officer.
6. File War Diary.

41

10th Bn Royal West Kent Regt — Sheet I — September 1917

Army Form C. 2118.

WAR DIARY
or
INTELLIGENCE SUMMARY.
(Erase heading not required.)

Instructions regarding War Diaries and Intelligence Summaries are contained in F. S. Regs., Part II. and the Staff Manual respectively. Title pages will be prepared in manuscript.

14

Vol 17

Place	Date	Hour	Summary of Events and Information	Remarks and references to Appendices
QUELMES M.F. FRANCE 27 S.E. W 13 b. 5.0.	1/9/17		Situation normal Rest and Training Strength Off 36 OR 750	
	2/9/17		" " " " " " 36 OR 750	
	3/9/17		" " " " " " 36 OR 750	
— —	4/9/17		" " " " " " 36 OR 750	
— —	5/9/17		" " " " " " 36 OR 750	
— —	6/9/17		" " " " " Officers joined 2/Lts Edmett, Peters, Preston, Pentrec, Strength Off 36 OR 750	
— —	7/9/17		" " " " " Evacuated Sick OR 6 Strength Off 40 OR 744	
— —	8/9/17		" " " " " " " 40 " 744	
— —	9/9/17		" " " " " " " 40 " 744	
— —	10/9/17		" " " " " " " 40 " 744	
— —	11/9/17		" " " " " " " 40 " 744	
— —	12/9/17		" " " " " Reinforcements OR 32 " " 40 " 744	
— —	13/9/17		" " During above period of Training the Battalion was exercised for Open Warfare. Inter-Platoon and Company matches arranged and Sports held. Reinforcements OR 19 Strength Off 40. OR 776	

A6945 Wt. W11422/M1160 350,000 12/16 D. D. & L. Forms/C./2118/14.

10th Bn Royal West Kent Regt — Sheet 11 — September 1917

Army Form C. 2118.

WAR DIARY
or
INTELLIGENCE SUMMARY.
(Erase heading not required.)

Instructions regarding War Diaries and Intelligence Summaries are contained in F. S. Regs., Part II, and the Staff Manual respectively. Title pages will be prepared in manuscript.

Place	Date	Hour	Summary of Events and Information	Remarks and references to Appendices
QUELMES	14/9/17	7.30AM	The Battalion proceeded by Route march to STAPLES U.3.c.5.2. en route for RENINGHELST	OP.ORD.102
W.12.b.8.0			arriving at STAPLES about 6 PM. Strength Offs 40. O.R. 795	APPX I
STAPLES	15/9/17	11AM	Situation normal. The Battalion continued the march arriving at METEREN X.10.c.1½.4.	OP.ORD.103
U.3.c.5.2			about 5 PM. 2/Lt Kill joined. Strength Off 40. O.R. 795	APPX II
SHEET 27 BELGIUM METEREN X.10.c.1½.4	16/9/17	9.30AM	Situation normal. The battalion continued march arriving at ONTARIO CAMP M.5.a.2.8	OP.ORD.104
			about 1 PM. Strength Off 41. O.R. 795	APPX III
ONTARIO CAMP	17/9/17		Situation normal. Rest. Reinforcements 132 O.R. Strength Off 41. O.R. 795	
M.5.a.2.8	18/9/17	8PM	Situation normal. The battalion moved forward to RIDGE WOOD area arriving about	OPR ORD 105 APPX IV
			12 MN encamped for the night. Reinforcements 5 Offs from 21st [illegible] Capt Cotsworth,	
			2/Lts Oldham, Gifford, Melville, Rotham. O.R. 71 Strength Off 46 O.R. 914	
RIDGE WOOD	19/9/17	5PM	Situation normal. The Battalion moved forward to Assembly Area to take up position	
			with 123rd Brigade in Reserve. Bn HQrs HEDGE STREET TUNNELS. The operation was carried	
			out successfully. Strength Off 46 O.R. 982	
[illegible]	20/9/17	5.40 AM	Attack commenced. 10 AM The battalion moved forward to Old BRITISH FRONT LINE during	
			the Evening the battalion received orders to reinforce but later order cancelled.	
			Strength Off 46 O.R. 982	

A6945 Wt. W11422/M1160 350,000 12/16 D. D. & L. Forms/C./2118/14.

10th Bn Royal West Kent Reg   Sheet III   September 1917

WAR DIARY
or
INTELLIGENCE SUMMARY.
(Erase heading not required.)

Army Form C. 2118.

Instructions regarding War Diaries and Intelligence Summaries are contained in F. S. Regs., Part II, and the Staff Manual respectively. Title pages will be prepared in manuscript.

Place	Date	Hour	Summary of Events and Information	Remarks and references to Appendices
Supports to	21/9/17			
122 & 124 Brigade		9.45 PM	The Battalion moved forward to attack captured 1st objective and consolidated held up	
			from further advance. During occupation two counter attacks made by the enemy were repulsed	
			In the evening a further counter attack attempted by enemy but this melted away under our	
			Artillery barrage. Evacuated Sick 6 Strength Off 46 OR 976	
1st Objective	22/9/17		Situation normal. The Battalion still holding ground gained and consolidating. Casualties	
			during operations, Officers Captain Roberts, 2Lt Thomas & Lt Robinson killed.	
			Capt Richmond, 2Lt Edmett, Maj. F.P. Brown wounded. O.R. Killed 29 Wounded 107	
			Missing 24. Evacuated Sick 1 Strength Off 46 OR 975	
"	23/9/17	12 MN	Situation normal. Battalion relieved during the night by a Battalion of Essex Regt and	
		4 PM	withdrawn to MICMAC CAMP. At 4 PM. The Bn entrained for CAESTRE AREA. These operations	
			were carried out successfully. Strength Off: 39 OR 820	
CAESTRE	24/9/17		Rest Strength Off 39 OR 820	
AREA	25/9/17		Rest Strength Off 39 OR 820	
P30.a.95.35	26/9/17	6.45 AM	Situation normal. The Battalion proceeded by motor bus to TETEGHEM Sheet 19 B&F, I 15 central	
			en route for Coast Defence Area arriving about 1 PM. The Transport proceeded by road the previous	
			day. Strength Off 39 OR 820	

A6945 Wt. W11422/M1160 350,000 12/16 D. D. & L. Forms/C./2118/14.

10th Bn Royal West Kent Regt — Sheet IV — September 1917

Army Form C. 2118.

WAR DIARY
or
INTELLIGENCE SUMMARY.
(Erase heading not required.)

Instructions regarding War Diaries and Intelligence Summaries are contained in F. S. Regs., Part II. and the Staff Manual respectively. Title pages will be prepared in manuscript.

Place	Date	Hour	Summary of Events and Information	Remarks and references to Appendices
TETEGHEM Sheet 19 SE F I 15 Central	27/9/17	6.30 AM	Situation Normal. The Battalion proceeded by route march to BRAY DUNES, Coast Defence area. DQ.6.99 arriving about 10 a.m. relieving 2/6 Lancashire Fusiliers. This Operation was carried out successfully. Strength Offs 39. OR. 820	OP. ORD. No. 106 APPX V
BRAY DUNES DQ.6.99.	28/9/17		Situation Normal. 2/Lt Spillett sick to England " " 38 " 820	
	29/9/17		" Training " " 38 " 820	
	30/9/17		" " " 38 " 820	

S. H. Beattie Lt Col.

Commdg 10th Bn Royal West Kent Regt

A6945 Wt. W11422/M1160 350,000 12/16 D. D. & L. Forms/C./2118/14.

10th (S) Bn Royal West Kent Rgt. **WAR DIARY** or ~~INTELLIGENCE SUMMARY.~~ (Erase heading not required.)

Army Form C. 2118.

Instructions regarding War Diaries and Intelligence Summaries are contained in F. S. Regs., Part II, and the Staff Manual respectively. Title pages will be prepared in manuscript.

Sheet No 1

Vol 18

Place	Date	Hour	Summary of Events and Information	O.	OR.	Remarks and references to Appendices
BRAY. DUNES M.R. D.9 & 9.9.	1/10/17		Situation normal. Battalion training + Coast defence. Strength	38.	819.	
"	2/10/17		" " reinforcements 106 OR. "	38.	819.	
"	3/10/17		" " "	38	925.	
"	4/10/17		" " Major. L.A WALLIS. to England on Senior Officers Course			
			Capt COATSWORTH. 21st LANCERS (attached.) to 23rd MDLX. Rgt. as 2nd i/c. Strength	38.	925	
"	5/10/17	12 Noon	Situation normal. Battn moved forward to camp at ST. IDESBALDE M.R. W.11.C.4.6.			
			3 platoons of C Coy attached 2nd Aus. Tun. Coy for fatigue. Strength	36.	925.	
St. IDESBALDE M.R. W.11.C.4.6.	6/10/17	5.15 pm	Situation normal. Battn moved forward to take over NIEUPORT-BAINS sector Right sub sector from 1/5 MANCHESTER RGT.			
			2 Coys in the line D Coy to YORKSHIRE CAMP. X.3.a.9.1 for working parties.			
			Operation successfully carried out platoons at 500 yds. Evacuated OR. 3 to Cadet school. U.K.	36.	925	
Right SUB SECTOR.	7/10/17		Situation normal. 2Lt. A.P. LEDGER rejoined Strength	36	922	
	8/10/17		" Wiring + working parties by night. Evac sick OR. 1	37	922	
	9/10/17		" " " " " Strength.	37	921.	
			reinforcements OR. 4. Evacuated sick. Off. 1. 2Lt F.D. LYONS.			
	10/10/17		Situation normal. enemy artillery active on back area but not much effect. Strength	36.	925	

S.H. Beattie Lt. Col.
10th R. W. Kent Regt.

A6945 Wt. W11422/M1160 350,000 12/16 D. D. & L. Forms/C./2118/14.

10th (S) Bn R West Kent Regt

Instructions regarding War Diaries and Intelligence Summaries are contained in F. S. Regs., Part II. and the Staff Manual respectively. Title pages will be prepared in manuscript.

Sheet No 2

WAR DIARY
or
~~INTELLIGENCE SUMMARY~~.
(Erase heading not required.)

Army Form C. 2118.

Place	Date	Hour	Summary of Events and Information	Remarks and references to Appendices
Right Sub Sector	11/10/17	6 pm.	Situation normal. The Bn was relieved by 11th Bn QUEENS (RWS) Regt & returned by	
"			platoons to YORKSHIRE CAMP MR. X 3a 9.1. as support Batt. Strength O 36 . OR. 925.	
YORKSHIRE CAMP X 3a. 9.1. 115E	12/10/17		Situation normal. Working parties daily with R.E. in support lines. " 36 . 925	
" "	13/10/17		" " " " " " " " " 36 . 925.	
			reinforcements 1 OFF. LT. G.C. SPARKS.	
" "	14/10/17		" " working parties strength 37 . 925	
" "	15/10/17	2.45 PM	" " The Battalion was relieved by 11th QUEENS (RWS) Regt & returned less 'C' Coy. 3 platoons	APPX. No I
			to BRAY DUNES. this operation was successfully carried out. strength. 37. 925	OO 112.
BRAY DUNES. MR. D.3 C.0.	16/10/17		Situation normal. Training in open warfare. reinforcements OR. 4. evac sick OR. 1.	
"			1 NCO. (Sgt Warner) awarded D.C.M. for gallantry. strength 37 925	
"	17/10/17		" " Training. reinforcements 1 O 3 OR strength 37. 928.	
"	18/10/17		" " " " 1 OFF. Capt. C.H. WILD rejoined. 38. 931	
"	19/10/17		" " " " 2 OFF. 2nd LT. P.A. PERCY & 2LT. F. HENSTOCK. strength 39. 931	
"	20/10/17		" " " strength 41. 931	
"	21/10/17		" " evac. sick OR. 4 " 41. 931	
"	22/10/17		" " " 3 " 41 927.	

S.H. Beattie Lt Col
10th R W K Regt

A6945 Wt. W11422/M1160 350,000 12/16 D. D. & L. Forms/C./2118/14.

10th (S) Bn. R West Kent Rgt.

Army Form C. 2118.

WAR DIARY
or
~~INTELLIGENCE SUMMARY~~.
(Erase heading not required.)

Instructions regarding War Diaries and Intelligence Summaries are contained in F. S. Regs., Part II. and the Staff Manual respectively. Title pages will be prepared in manuscript. Sheet No. 3.

Place	Date	Hour	Summary of Events and Information	Remarks and references to Appendices
BRAY DUNES MR. D.3.C.1.1.	23/10/17		Situation normal. Training for open warfare & special training under R.E. supervision Strength O. 41. O.R. 924.	
"	24/10/17		" " " " " " " 41. 924.	
"	25/10/17		" " " " " " " 41. 924.	
"	26/10/17		" " " " " " " 41. 924	
"	27/10/17		" " " " " " "	
"			reinforcements O.R. 11 Lt. A.J. DONALDSON Transferred for training U.S.A. troops " 41. 924	
"	28/10/17		" " Training evac. sick O.R. 2. Strength 40. 935	
"	29/10/17		" " " reinforcements O.R. 45. " 40. 933	
"	30/10/17		" " " " 40. 975.	

S.H. Beattie Lt. Col.
Cmdg. 10th (S) Bn. Royal West Kent Rgt.

A6945 Wt. W11422/M1160 350,000 12/16 D. D. & L. Forms/C./2118/14.

WO 95/2638 (2)

10/Queen's Own (RW Kents)

Mar '18 – Feb '19

123rd Inf.Bde.
41st Div.

Battn. with Bde. returned to France from Italy 2/7.3.18.

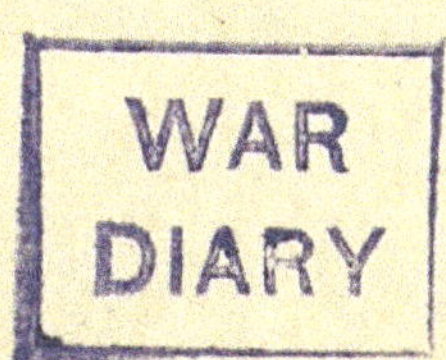

10th BATTN. THE QUEEN'S OWN ROYAL WEST KENT REGIMENT.

M A R C H

1 9 1 8

Attached:-

Report on Operations near BEUGNY.

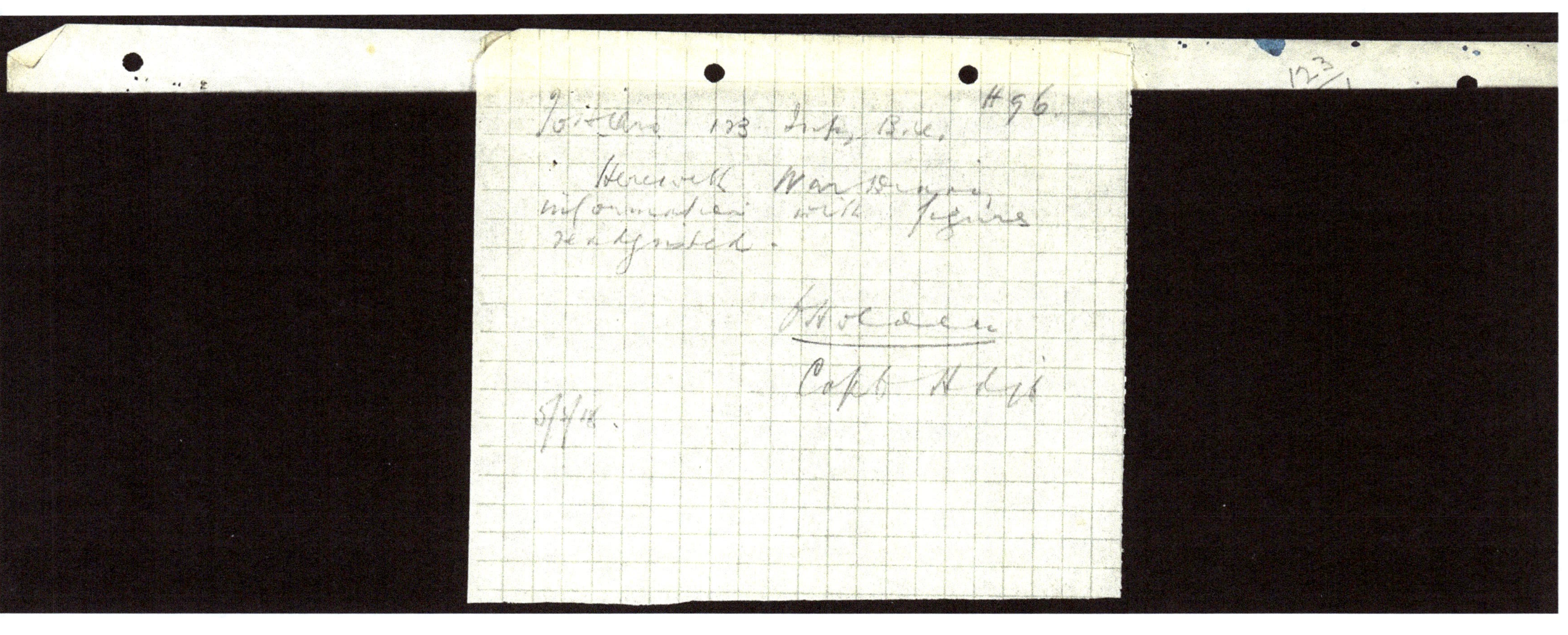

To:– Adm 123 Inf. Bde. #96.

Herewith War Diary information with figures as requested.

[illegible]

Capt. Adjt.

5/7/18.

Instructions regarding War Diaries and Intelligence Summaries are contained in F. S. Regs., Part II.

Army Form C. 2118.

123/41

ROYAL WEST KENT REGT

To [illegible] 123 Infy Bde   N 96.

The numbers of men taken into action on 23/3/18 at BEUGNY were 18 Off. + 580 OR

We arrived at GOMMECOURT first with 3 off + 70 OR + when we again went up we mustered 5 off + 170 OR (50 being collected from transport lines (Specialists left behind)

[illegible]

Capt [illegible]

5/5/18

123/41

Army Form C. 2118.

Instructions regarding War Diaries and Intelligence Summaries are contained in F. S. Regs., Part II. and the Staff Manual respectively. Title pages will be prepared in manuscript.

ROYAL WEST KENT REGT
MARCH 1918.

~~INTELLIGENCE SUMMARY~~.

(*Erase heading not required.*)

Vol 23.

Place	Date	Hour	Summary of Events and Information	Remarks and references to Appendices
			Battalion Strength: Officers 46, O. Ranks 846	
S GEORGIO	1/3/18		Situation normal	
della PERTICHE	2/3/18	4 AM	"A" and "B" Coys & one-half Battalion Transport proceeded by bus to PADOVA and entrained for FRANCE. Time of Entrainment 8.30 am. The remainder of	
"		8.30 AM	Battalion embussed at 8.30 am and entrained at PADOVA at 1.30 pm	
	3/3/18		Situation normal. Strength Officers 46 OR 842	
	4/3/18			
	5/3/18			
	6/3/18			
	7/3/18	2 AM	First half Battalion arrived at DOULLENS (Map Ref LENS 11 FRANCE) detrained and proceeded by march route to BEAUDRICOURT	
		12 noon	Second half Battalion detrained at MONDICOURT and proceeded by march route to BEAUDRICOURT.	
			Capt G.W. HINDLE Awarded M.C. for Gallantry whilst in charge of a Patrol across the R. PIAVA on 19/2/18. 21222 Pte H WAITE and 19795 Pte W. STONE awarded M. M. for gallantry whilst on Patrol with Capt HINDLE across the R. PIAVA.	

A6945 Wt. W11422/M1160 350,000 12/16 D. D. & L. Forms/C./2118/14.

Army Form C. 2118.

Instructions regarding War Diaries and Intelligence Summaries are contained in F. S. Regs., Part II. and the Staff Manual respectively. Title pages will be prepared in manuscript.

WAR DIARY
or
INTELLIGENCE SUMMARY.
(*Erase heading not required.*)

Place	Date	Hour	Summary of Events and Information	Remarks and references to Appendices
BEAUDRICOURT. Map ref LENS SHEET 11.	8/3/18 to 15/3/18		Situation Normal. Strength Offrs 46 Othr Ranks 840	
	16/3/18		Reorganisation of 123rd Inf Bde carried out under new Army Order. This necessitated 11th BN R. W. KENT REGT being disbanded and the following Officers and 250 Other Ranks of that Battalion were taken on strength as from today. LIEUT COL A C CORFE DSO, MAJOR A J JIMENEZ MC, CAPT R KERR MC, CAPT C F HALL, LIEUT LE HALE. LIEUT COL A.C. CORFE took over command of the Battalion from today.	
			The 20th Durham Light Infantry is transferred from 123rd to 124th Brigade	
	17/3/18 to 20/3/18		Situation Normal. Strength Offrs 51 Othr Ranks 1040.	
			During period 9th to 20th inclusive the Division was in G. H. Q. Reserve and the Battalion carried on training, special attention being paid to the various Methods of Attack and Defence for Open Warfare	
ACHIET LE GRAND Ref Map LENS 11 1/100,000	21/3/18		The Battalion proceeded by March Route to MONDICOURT and entrained for ACHIET LE GRAND, arriving there at 10 15 pm, and spending the night at RITZ CAMP.	

A6945 Wt. W11422/M1160 350,000 12/16 D. D. & L. Forms/C./2118/14.

Instructions regarding War Diaries and Intelligence Summaries are contained in F. S. Regs., Part II, and the Staff Manual respectively. Title pages will be prepared in manuscript.

WAR DIARY
or
INTELLIGENCE SUMMARY.
(*Erase heading not required.*)

Army Form C. 2118.

Place	Date	Hour	Summary of Events and Information	Remarks and references to Appendices
			Strength Offrs 50 O.RANKS 1070	
FREMICOURT and MORCHIES	22/3/18	1.30pm	The Battalion moved forward to FREMICOURT preparatory to taking up position for Battalion Action. Fighting strength being 18 Officers 580 other Ranks. On night of 22nd Battalion proceeded to relieve the 18th Brigade, 6th Division, occupying the Front immediately west of MORCHIES facing North, relief being	
	23/3/18	12 noon	completed by about 3 am 23/3/18. At about 12 noon a Mass of Germans (estimated at about 700) advanced round ridge on our left flank, full particulars of Attack being attached (Appendix 1). Casualties Officers Missing:- LIEUT COL A C CORFE DSO, MAJOR A J JIMENEZ, MC. CAPT F W WAYDELIN CAPT C.F. HALL. LIEUT L A PANCHAUD, LIEUT L E HALE, 2/LT J R PHILLIPS, 2/LIEUT F.C RENNELLS, 2/LIEUT F.C VASS, 2/LT R.H. CHANDLER, 2/LIEUT K THOMPSON SMITH, CAPT A. J. CHILLINGWORTH (RAMC). Wounded & Missing 2/LIEUT B E LONG. Wounded 2/LIEUT P A PERCY, 2/LIEUT F W COOPER Other Ranks Killed 14 Wounded 31. Wounded & Missing 15, Missing 391. On the evening of the 23rd March, the remainder of the Battalion	
ACHIET LE PETIT	23/3/18		(approximately 120) proceeded from ACHIET-LE-PETIT and took up a line	
BIHUCOURT	24/3/18		just behind BIHUCOURT. There was heavy fighting in front of this	

A6945 Wt. W11422/M1160 350,000 12/16 D. D. & L. Forms/C./2118/14.

Instructions regarding War Diaries and Intelligence Summaries are contained in F. S. Regs., Part II. and the Staff Manual respectively. Title pages will be prepared in manuscript.

WAR DIARY
or
~~INTELLIGENCE~~ SUMMARY.
(Erase heading not required.)

Army Form C. 2118.

Place	Date	Hour	Summary of Events and Information	Remarks and references to Appendices
BIHUCOURT	24/3/18		village on the 24th and the front line withdrew on us ~~on the~~ by Mid-day. We held that line all the evening and then received orders to withdraw because the right flank had gone. This we did and were clear by	
GOMMECOURT ↓ FONQUEVILLERS.	25/3/18		2.15 am 25/3/18, and marching all night arrived at GOMMECOURT about 9 am. The enemy was still advancing and we had to take up a defensive flank between GOMMECOURT and FONQUEVILLERS	
	25/3/18	11 pm	At 11 pm we went back to BIENVILLERS and bivouaced for the night.	
GOMMECOURT	26/3/18	12 noon	At 12 noon 26/3/18 we proceeded to GOMMECOURT in reserve to 41st Division and at 12 midnight we moved to left flank to ESSARTS and became reserve to 42nd Division.	
ABLAINZEVELLI	29/3/18		On the 29th we proceeded and relieved the 1/8th Manchesters in front line at ABLAINZEVELLI.	
	28/3/18		Situation normal.	
	29/3/18		"	
	30/3/18		"	
	31/3/18		"	

* (Fighting Strength 18 Off. 204 OR)

Battalion Strength O 36 OR 629 *
5

C. F. Stallard Major
Cmdg. 10th R W Kent Regt.

A6945 Wt. W11422/M1160 350,000 12/16 D. D. & L. Forms/C./2118/14.

A P P E N D I X N o . 1.

Report on Operations near BEUGNY.

APENDIX No 1

10th Bn. Royal West Kent Regt.

Report on Operations near BEUGNY.

On the night of 22nd March 1918, we received orders at VRAUCOURT to proceed to relieve the 18th Brigade, 6th Division, who were occupying the front immediately West of MORCHIES, facing NORTH.

This was completed about 3 a.m. 23/3/18., and we dug three lines of trenches before daybreak, front, support and reserve, "D" Coy. on left, "C", "B", & "A" Coys. on right.

We occupied the valley with some Royal Welsh Fusiliers and Queens on right and 124 Brigade on left. During the morning 23/3/18. there was little shelling and machine gun fire from the enemy.

About 12 noon a mass of Boche (estimated 700) advanced round ridge on our left flank. We opened fire on them and our Lewis Guns accounted for a good number until they were out of sight round ridge.

As no rifle or machine gun fire was heard from the left presumed that there was a large gap between our Battalion left flank and the right Battalion 124 Brigade, through which the Boche proceeded. The enemy advanced on right flank but we could not see him.

At 2.30 p.m. the Queens, under orders, withdrew on right behind BEUGNY, which left both our flanks in the air. "C" Coy. shortly afterwards withdrew over ridge on left and are presumed to have been all captured by the mass of Boche we saw going round the left flank.

During this time we were shelled heavily by enemy artillery and enemy machine guns were extraordinary active from front and left flank.

About 5 p.m. the Boche advanced on our position from our right front. Our Lewis Guns caused the enemy casualties at 600 yards, then our position being completely hopeless, enemy fire coming from front, left and right flank and right rear, we withdrew to behind BEUGNY.

During the withdrawal we were barraged with enemy artillery and terrific Machine Gun fire from right and left flank and right rear.

About 70 succeeded in reaching the GREEN LINE behind BEUGNY, unwounded, about 6 p.m. Here the Boche was held all that night.

Vernon Holden

Capt.

10th Bn. Royal West Kent Regt.

5th April 1918.

41st Division.
123rd Infantry Brigade

WAR DIARY

10th BATTALION

THE ROYAL WEST KENT REGIMENT

APRIL 1 9 1 8

1

Instructions regarding War Diaries and Intelligence Summaries are contained in F. S. Regs., Part II. and the Staff Manual respectively. Title pages will be prepared in manuscript.

WAR DIARY
or
INTELLIGENCE SUMMARY.
(Erase heading not required.)

APRIL 1918. Army Form C. 2118.

10th R.W. Kent

Vol 24

Place	Date APRIL	Hour	Summary of Events and Information	Remarks and references to Appendices
ABLAINZEVILLE	1st		Battalion in Front line trenches.	
	2nd		Battalion relieved on night of 1/2nd. by 1/5th BN E. LANCS REGT, and proceeded to THIEVRES.	
THIEVRES	3rd		Battalion embussed and proceeded to BONNIERES.	O.O. 20
BONNIERES.	4th		Battalion entrained FREVANT at 7 am for POPERINGHE, thence proceeded by bus to billets at EECKE.	
EECKE	5th		Reorganising. Lt. E.M. GODFRAY, 2/LTS. T.W.E. HALL & S.C. HARRIS, joined Battalion for duty. LT. H.L. BEESTON, Evac. Sick to ENGLAND 25-3-18. Struck off Strength of Battalion. Draft of 700 Other Ranks joined Battalion.	
	6th		Battalion inspected by SIR HUNTER WESTON, G.O.C. VIIIth CORPS.	
	7th		Re-organising. CAPT. T. ROONEY M.C. JOINED BN. & posted as O.C. C Coy.	
ST JEAN	8th		Battalion proceeded by rail to ST. JEAN, and camped at IRISH FARM. MAJOR C.F. STALLARD, M.C. joined Bn. and assumed duties of Second in Command.	O.O. 21
	9th		Battalion, 540 strong, relieved 1st NEWFOUNDLAND REGT in front line WEST of PASCHAENDAEL. Disposition = 3 Coys Front line, 1 Coy in GOUDBERGH SPUR. Remainder of Battalion proceeded to DIRTY BUCKET CAMP. under MAJOR C.F. STALLARD. M.C.	O.O. 22
	10th		Holding position. } Details in Training under R.S.M. & Specialist N.C.O's	
	11th		— do —	

continued —

D. D. & L., London, E.C.
(A10266) Wt W5300/P713 750,000 2/18 Sch. 52 Forms/C2118/16.

APRIL 1918. CONTINUED

Army Form C. 2118.

SHEET 2.

WAR DIARY
or
INTELLIGENCE SUMMARY.

(Erase heading not required.)

Instructions regarding War Diaries and Intelligence Summaries are contained in F. S. Regs., Part II. and the Staff Manual respectively. Title pages will be prepared in manuscript.

Place	Date APRIL	Hour	Summary of Events and Information	Remarks and references to Appendices
	12th		The 23rd BN. MIDDLESEX REGT. on left withdrew to Battle Line, and this Battalion took over the whole of the Brigade Front holding same as OUTPOST LINE. B & C Coys. in Original Front Line, with A & D " in Support & Reserve.	O.O. 23
			Battalion came under the orders of G.O.C. 124 INFANTRY BRIGADE, who was appointed O.C. CORPS OUTPOST LINE.	
	13th		Battalion remained in OUTPOST LINE.	
	14th		" " " " "	
	15th		" " " " "	
	16th		At 9 pm 15th A & D Coys withdrew to LA BRIQUE CAMP. At 2 am 16th B & C Coys commenced to withdraw from the front line, leaving party of 6 per Company till 3.30 am, & finally reached LA BRIQUE at 8 am.	Report attached.
			Battalion resting and 2 Companies working on YPRES Defences.	
			Headquarters moved to CANAL BANK.	
	17th		Battalion working on YPRES DEFENCES.	
	18th		LIEUT PERCIVAL and 100 Other Ranks joined Battalion from Details Camp	
	19th		Battalion working on YPRES DEFENCES	
	20th		——— do ———	
	21st		——— do ———	
	22nd		——— do ———	
	23rd		——— do ——— LT T.E. TATHAM posted to Bn. & joined 41st DIVL. WING	
	24th		——— do ———	
	25th		——— do ——— LT R. BARTHOLOMEW, & 2nd LT. W.C. RHODES JND FOR DUTY	
	26th		——— do ——— Nearly 200 Casualties sustained, by enemy Gas Shelling	
			CAPT. G.J. BROWN, LT H.T. JOHNSON, LT F.E.E. NORRIS, 2ND LT. A.H. SMITH Joined for Duty	

D. D. & L., London, E.C.
(A10206) Wt W5300/P713 750,000 2/18 Sch. 52 Forms/C2118/16.

Instructions regarding War Diaries and Intelligence Summaries are contained in F. S. Regs., Part II. and the Staff Manual respectively. Title pages will be prepared in manuscript.

WAR DIARY
or
INTELLIGENCE SUMMARY.
(Erase heading not required.)

APRIL 1918 Continued

SHEET 3.

Army Form C. 2118.

Place	Date	Hour	Summary of Events and Information	Remarks and references to Appendices
	26/27		Battalion relieved by 20th BN. DURHAM LIGHT INFANTRY, and marched to V.3 on the BRIELEN LINE	
	27th		Battalion working on V3 LINE. A serious explosion occurred behind the Detail Camp, at G6, a 2.3. Sheet 28 N.W. BELGIUM about 12.30 pm caused by a H.V. enemy shell striking an Ammunition and Guncotton Dump. The Camp was wrecked and numerous huts set on fire by the explosion. Rescue parties at once set to work to assist in recovering the numerous casualties from the debris, and extinguish the fires, in face of great danger from recurring explosion from the dump. Casualties suffered by the Battalion totalled:- KILLED - LIEUT D.F. ANDERSON, Other Ranks 17, WOUNDED - Other Ranks 28. MISSING - Other Ranks 1. Most of the Battalion Records were lost in this explosion.	
	28th		Battalion working on V3 LINE. Capt R. KERR. MC. appointed Staff Captain 122 Bde. Capt. V. HOLDEN, appointed Adjutant, vice Capt. KERR. The undermentioned awards were notified:- No 205401 PTE F. WHAITES, - BAR TO MILITARY MEDAL. No 19814 PTE. A.B. BRAGGS. - MILITARY MEDAL.	
	29th		2/LT LEDGER, transferred to ROYAL AIR FORCE, d/29.4.18 and struck off strength. T/CAPT. A.S. RICHMOND, WOUNDED 21-9-17, removed from EST. of BATTN with effect from 17/3/18.	
	29th 30th		Battalion working on V3 LINE. Strength of BN. OFFICERS 39 OTHER RANKS 1042.	

[signature]
Lt Colonel
Comdg. 10th Bn Royal West Kent Regt.

D. D. & L., London, E.C.
(A10266) Wt W5300/P713 750,000 2/18 Sch. 52 Forms/C2118/16.

Instructions regarding War Diaries and Intelligence Summaries are contained in F. S. Regs., Part II. and the Staff Manual respectively. Title pages will be prepared in manuscript.

WAR DIARY
or
INTELLIGENCE SUMMARY.
(Erase heading not required.)

MAY 1918

10 R W Kent Rg

Army Form C. 2118.

V8 25

Place	Date	Hour	Summary of Events and Information	Remarks and references to Appendices
ST. JEAN	1st.		Battn. relieved 11th "Queen's" Regt. in left Sub. Sector Outpost Line. Mapref 28 N.W. (1.3.a, 6.7.)	
	2nd		" in the line.	
	3rd		Battn. relieved by 23rd Bn. Middlesex Regt, and moved back into Reserve.	
	4th		In Reserve trenches. 2/Lt. E.C.H. SALMON, M.C. posted to Battn (from 11th Bn) and retained on Divisional Hd. Qrs as Observation Officer. Strength of Battn. OFFICERS. 40. OTHER RANKS. 1077.	
	5th 6th 7th		In Reserve trenches.	
SIEGE CAMP.	8th.		Half Battalion (A & C Coys) moved back to SIEGE CAMP. B & D Coys. remaining in Reserve Trenches.	
	9th		B & D Coys relieved A & C Coys. in Reserve trenches.	
	10th		LT. COL. the Hon. E.R. THESIGER joined Battn. & took over Command. MAJOR. C.F. STALLARD. M.C. left Battn. to take over Second in Command of 23rd BN MIDDLESEX REGT.	
FOSTER CAMP.	11th		Battn. moved back to FOSTER CAMP and 'B' CAMP. The following Officers struck off Strength:- 2/LIEUTS. W.H. PETERS and W.F. ROBINSON. SICK TO ENG. 11-5-18. CAPT. I.A.V. STANLEY. transf to 3RD. ARMY. CAVALRY DEPOT.	
	12th		Battn. Cleaning up and resting. Strength of Bn. OFFICERS 40. OTHER RANKS 928	
	13th		Bathing & Training under Company arrangements. Specialists under Specialist Officers & N.C.O's	
	14th		~~Training~~. LT. J. LINDSAY M.C., from 6 mos tour of duty in Eng. Joined Bn. (from 11th Bn) Battn. working under R.E's on GREEN LINE.	[signature]

D. D. & L., London, E.C. (A10266) Wt W5300/P713 750,000 2/18 Sch. 52 Forms/C2118/16.

Instructions regarding War Diaries and Intelligence Summaries are contained in F. S. Regs., Part II. and the Staff Manual respectively. Title pages will be prepared in manuscript.

WAR DIARY
or
INTELLIGENCE SUMMARY. MAY 1918. Continued:-
(Erase heading not required.)

Army Form C. 2118.

Place	Date	Hour	Summary of Events and Information	Remarks and references to Appendices
FOSTER & "B" CAMPS.	14th		2/LT. H. ALDERTON. evacuated Sick to ENGLAND, and Struck off Strength of Battn.	
	15th		Battn. working on GREEN LINE.	
	16th		" " " . MAJOR. F. A. WALLIS. M.C. proceeded on leave to ENGLAND	
			The following Honours & Awards notified.	
			CAPT. V HOLDEN M.C. — "THE DISTINGUISHED SERVICE ORDER."	
			2/LT. E. S. CHEEL. — "THE MILITARY CROSS"	
			No 6884 C.S.M. COOPER. D.C.M — "BAR TO D.C.M."	
			No 19762 L/SGT WHITE. J. — "THE DISTINGUISHED CONDUCT MEDAL"	
			No 4883 SGT. DEWING. W. / No 6942 L/CPL. LAING. F. / No 8565 PTE. RUSSELL. H / No 11647 " TAYLOR. W. — "THE MILITARY MEDAL."	
EAST OF YPRES.	17th		Battn. relieved 15th HAMPSHIRE REGT (122 Bde) in left Sub. Sector.	
			Details moved back to BRAKE CAMP.	
			CAPT. V. HOLDEN. D.S.O., M.C., appointed Adjutant with effect from 27-4-18. (Authy:- 2ND CORPS. "A" D.F./2672 d/17.5.18.)	
			Strength of Battn. Officers. 40. Other Rank 1000.	
	18th		Battn. in the line	
	19th		— do —	
	20th		— do —	
	21st		MAJOR C.F. STALLARD, M.C. returned to Battn, to temp. Command, vice LT. COL. the Hon. E.R. THESIGER evacuated to F.A.	
			2/LTS, BARCLAY, FLINT & SHAWE, 23rd Middlesex Regt. attached to Battn. (temporary) replacing Officers evacuated Sick from the line.	E. R. Thesiger

D. D. & L., London, E.C.
(A10266) Wt W5300/P713 750,000 2/18 Sch. 52 Forms/C2118/16.

Instructions regarding War Diaries and Intelligence Summaries are contained in F. S. Regs., Part II. and the Staff Manual respectively. Title pages will be prepared in manuscript.

WAR DIARY
or
INTELLIGENCE SUMMARY. MAY 1918 continued:
(Erase heading not required.)

Army Form C. 2118.

Place	Date	Hour	Summary of Events and Information	Remarks and references to Appendices
EAST OF YPRES.	22nd		Battn in the line.	
			CAPT. V. HOLDEN. D.S.O., M.C., appointed to Command of 41st DIVISIONAL WING.	
			LIEUT. R. C. RUSSELL M.C., assumes duties of Acting Adjutant.	
	23rd		Battn in the line. LIEUT. A. A. WILLOUGHBY, Wounded in action.	
	24th		" " " " 2/LT. F. P. BROWN. Wounded 24th & DIED of WOUNDS same day.	
			LIEUT. A. S. K. PERCIVAL, assumes duties of Assistant Adjutant.	
	25th		Battn in the line.	
	26th		Battn relieved in front line by 23rd Bn. MIDDLESEX REGT. Bn. H.Q. in RAMPARTS YPRES. STRENGTH OF BATTN. OFFICERS 36. OTHER RANKS 1007	
	27th		Battalion in support.	
	28th		" " "	
	29th		" " "	
	30th		" " "	
	31st		18th to 31st. Details training under R.S.M. and Specialist N.C.O.s.	
			CASUALTIES FOR MONTH OFFICERS DIED OF WOUNDS 1 WOUNDED 1	
			OTHER RANKS. KILLED & D/W 9, WOUNDED 30, GASSED 224.	

[signature] Lt-Colonel
Comdg. 10th Bn. R. WEST KENT REGT.

D. D. & L., London, E.C.
(A10266) Wt W5300/P713 750,000 2/18 Sch. 52 Forms/C2118/16.

SECRET Copy No. 1.

16th Battn R W Kent Regt.

Operation Order No. 2

1/ The 23rd Middx Regt will take over the left sub-sector Outpost line tomorrow night.

2/ "B" Coy Middx will be relieved by "A" Coy Middx.
"C" Coy Middx will be relieved by "D" Coy Middx.

3/ On completion of the "B" Coy Middx will relieve C + D Coys RWKents,
3 platoons "C" Coy Middx + No 14 platoon Middx, will relieve A + B Coys RWKents
No 12 platoon Middx will remain in its present position + the right platoon of A + B RWKents, will be relieved by No 14 Middx

4/ On completion of relief, A + B + C + D Coys RW Kents will proceed to V.H. movement platoons 100x interval
2 guides per Coy will meet Coys at X Roads H 5 d 8.4 (Sheet 28 N.W.)

5. Middlesex guides will return to their companies at dusk to guide same up to front line when relieved in SUPPORT & RESERVE

6 There will be limbers for Lewis Guns at Battn H.Qrs. O/C Coys R W Kents will each detail one L. Gun N.C.O to remain & return with limbers to new line

6A All Trench Stores, defence schemes, etc to be handed over.

7 All empty petrol tins will be brought away from front line & dumped at Battn H.Qrs.

8 Completion of relief will be notified by wiring code word ENGLAND. Company Comdrs R W Kents to report personally to Bttn H.Qrs.

9 ACKNOWLEGE.

No 1 O.C. Outposts
2 O.C. 23rd Middx Regt
3 C.O.
4 O/C "A" & "B"
5 O/C "C" & "D"
6 O/C "B" Coy Middx
7 O/C "C" " "
8 War Diary

[illegible signature]

2/5/18

Capt & a/Adjt
10th R.W. Kent Regt.

6

-1-

10 RW Kent Regt
JUNE 1918
Vol 26

Army Form C. 2118.

Instructions regarding War Diaries and Intelligence Summaries are contained in F. S. Regs., Part II. and the Staff Manual respectively. Title pages will be prepared in manuscript.

WAR DIARY
or
INTELLIGENCE SUMMARY.

(Erase heading not required.)

Place	Date	Hour	Summary of Events and Information	Remarks and references to Appendices
RAMPARTS YPRES (SHEET 28 N.W)	1st		Battalion holding Line. Strength of Bn. Officers 36, Other Ranks 1047. Details at Transport Lines. Specialist Classes carried on under Specialist N.C.O's and R.S.M.	
	2nd	12:30 AM	On night of 1st/2nd a raiding party consisting of Lieut. Tatham, made a raid on "Rifle Farm" and enemy trenches. Unfortunately no enemy could be found in either place, and party returned after a careful search. Our Casualties were - 2 Other Ranks Missing. Congratulatory messages were received from the Divisional Commander and Brigade Commander, on the manner in which the raid was organised and carried out.	
PROVEN (HAZEBROUCK) 5A	3rd		Battalion was relieved on night 2nd/3rd by the 4th Bn. Yorks & Lancs. Regt and proceeded by train to "N" Camp on Proven - Poperinghe Road, arriving in Camp about 6 am 3rd. Details and transport proceeded by March Route on afternoon of 2nd inst. Major F. A. Wallis, M.C., rejoined Bn from leave to England, and took over Temp. Command vice Major C. F. Stallard, M.C. who returned to 23rd Bn. Middlesex Regt. as Second-in-Command.	O.O. No 9
ST. MOMELIN (HAZEBROUCK) 5A	4th		Battn. marched to Railway Siding, PROVEN, and entrained at 3 A.M. for the ST. MOMELIN AREA, detraining at WATTEN about 6.30 AM. Part of Transport accompanied Battn. on train, remainder proceeded by road, Brigaded. Battalion arrived in Billets about 10 A.M.	O.O. No 10
	5th		Training under Coy. arrangements. Capt. F.H. Solomon, attached from 23rd Bn. Middlesex Regt. for duty.	

D. D. & L., London, E.C.
(A10266) Wt W5300/P713 750,000 2/18 Sch. 52 Forms/C2118/16.

[illegible] WO

Instructions regarding War Diaries and Intelligence Summaries are contained in F. S. Regs., Part II. and the Staff Manual respectively. Title pages will be prepared in manuscript.

WAR DIARY
or
INTELLIGENCE SUMMARY.
(Erase heading not required.)

JUNE 1918
CONT:-

Army Form C. 2118.

Place	Date	Hour	Summary of Events and Information	Remarks and references to Appendices
ST. MOMELIN	6th		Battn. bathing and Training. notification received of Lieut. G. C. L. Sparks' evacuation Sick to ENGLAND d/22.5.18	
	7th		Training continued. The following Honours & Awards were published. For Gallantry in the Field. 2/Lt. H. L. Shrimpton awarded "The Military Cross" 205807 C.S.M. (A/R.S.M.) BYRNE W.J. "The Distinguished Conduct Medal"	
	8th		Bathing and training.	
	9th		Sunday. Day of Rest. Divine Service. The Battn. Concert Party "THE LIVE ROUNDS" gave an open-air Concert at 7 pm. 2/Lieut. J. T. Thornton, joined Bn. for duty from East Surrey Regt. Strength of Battalion. Officers 36. Other Rank 1055. The following Honours & Awards were published in THE TIMES d/7.6.18. Capt. T. J. Guest – Military Cross. T/Capt. F. W. WAYDELIN – Military Cross. 11523 L/Sgt. Gibson A.D. M.S.M. 6958 Pte. Farmer, A. M.S.M. 767 Sgt. Carter W. D.C.M.	
	10th		Training	
CORMETTE	11th		Battn. moved to TATEGHEM AREA by March Route. Battn. H.Q. being in billets at CORMETTE. Coys in neighbouring Villages.	O.O. No 11.
QUELMES	12th		Owing to Sanitary Condition of Coys Billets, Battalion moved to QUELMES.	
	13th		Bathing and Training. A.R.A. platoon Competition fired on "A" Range by Half Battn.	
	14th		Training on Battalion Training Area.	
	15th		Bathing and Training. A.R.A. platoon Competition fired on A Range by remaining Coys. Strength of Battalion Officers 37 Other Rank 1080.	[illegible signature]

D. D. & L., London, E.C. (A10266) Wt W5300/P713 750,000 2/18 Sch. 52 Forms/C2118/16.

Army Form C. 2118.

Instructions regarding War Diaries and Intelligence Summaries are contained in F. S. Regs., Part II. and the Staff Manual respectively. Title pages will be prepared in manuscript.

WAR DIARY
or
INTELLIGENCE SUMMARY.
(Erase heading not required.)

JUNE 1918
CONTINUED.

Place	Date	Hour	Summary of Events and Information	Remarks and references to Appendices
QUELMES (HAZEBROUCK) 5.A	16th		Sunday. Day of Rest. Divine Service. Regimental Sports held from 2 pm to dusk.	
	17th		60 Other Ranks proceeded to 41st Divisional Reception Camp, being number over strength allowed with Unit. Bathing and Training.	
	18th		Battalion took part in Brigade Scheme vide O.O. No 12 attached. 2/Lt. J.W.E. Hall, notified as Evacuated Sick to England d/4. 6. 18.	O.O. No 12
	19th		Training continued.	
	20th		Training continued. Drill Competition. Battalion congratulated by General Commanding 123 Brigade on their turn out and Drill. Divisional Boxing Competition. No. 19779. L/C Schofield winning Silver Medal. Divisional Horse Show. Battalion Transport entered and were awarded. - Aggregate Prize, 2 First prizes and 2 Second Prize. Major V. Holden. D.S.O., M.C., taken on Est. of 41st DIV. Reception Camp.	
	21st		Training Continued.	
	22nd		-do- Lt. G.N. Bunyard. - Absorbed into Est. of Central Sch. G.H.Q. Italy d/17-6-18 Hon. Lt. & Q.M. Jarrett. Evac. Sick to England 12.6.18	
	23rd		Training	
	24th		-do-	[signature] Lt Col

D. D. & L., London, E.C.
(A10266) Wt W5300/P713 750,000 2/18 Sch. 52 Forms/C2118/16.

Instructions regarding War Diaries and Intelligence Summaries are contained in F. S. Regs., Part II. and the Staff Manual respectively. Title pages will be prepared in manuscript.

WAR DIARY or INTELLIGENCE SUMMARY.

(Erase heading not required.)

JUNE 1918. CONTINUED

Army Form C. 2118.

Place	Date	Hour	Summary of Events and Information	Remarks and references to Appendices
QUELMES. (HAZEBROUCK) 5A.	24th		During the period June 11–24th, a large number of men reported sick with Influenza. Owing to the immediate action and Isolation of these cases, taken by the Medical Officer, Capt. Montgomery, a very small percentage only were evacuated to Field Ambulance.	
ST. MOMELIN.	25th		Battalion moved back to Billets in the ST. MOMELIN AREA, proceeding by March Route.	O.O. No 14
LEDRINGHEM. (HAZEBROUCK) 5A.	26th		Battalion proceeded by March Route to billets at LEDRINGHEM.	O.O. No 15
	27th		Training continued under Coy Arrangements	
	28th		" " "	
	29th		Bathing at ARNEKE. & Training. Battalion Concert Party "The Live Rounds" gave Grand Concert. 7 pm.	
	30th		Sunday. Divine Service.	
		12.30 pm	Battalion proceeded by March Route to billets at ABEELE AERODROME arriving about 10. pm. Strength of Battalion Officers 36. Other Ranks 1036.	O.O. No 16

Lt Colonel
Comdg 10th Bn R West Kent Regt.

D. D. & L., London, E.C. (A10266) Wt W5300/P713 750,000 2/18 Sch. 52 Forms/C2118/16.

SECRET — — Copy No. 10

Operation Orders No 9
by Major C F STALLARD, M.C
Comdg 10th Bn R. W. Kent Regt

Ref: Sheet 28. N W 1/10,000 — June 1st 1918
" 27 1/40,000

1 The Battalion will be relieved on the night 2/3rd June 1918 by the 4th Bn Yorks + Lancs Regt

2 Coys. will be relieved as follows:-

"A" Coy KENTS	by "A" Coy. YORKS + LANCS.			
"B" "	"	by "B" "	"	"
"C" "	"	by "C" "	"	"
"D" "	"	by "D" "	"	"

3 Each Coy. will detail 1 Guide per platoon to be at "B" Co. H.Q. at 10/15 pm to meet the corresponding platoon of the incoming Battn., who will arrive in the following order:-
H.Q., B, C, A, D. Head of column will arrive at "B" Coy. H.Q. about 10/30 pm. O/C "B" Coy. will detail an Officer to see that guides get their right Platoons and carry on with them as quickly as possible.

(Continued)

4. All maps 1/10,000 and all maps 1/20,000. (with the exception of one per Coy.) Aeroplane photos, defence schemes and Trench Stores will be handed over and receipts forwarded to this Office as soon as possible after arrival in Billets.

5. All A.A. Lewis Gun positions will be handed over.

6. Each Coy. will leave behind 1 officer for 24 hours after relief or until their services are dispensed with by the relieving Coy.

Transport arrangements for these officers will be notified when known.

7. On Relief the Battn. will move to "N" Camp (Sheet 27. F.27.d.) by train. Details of Train arrangements will be notified later. As far as at present known there will be two trains for the Battalion, which will entrain at FORWARD SIDING. H.6.c 3.4 on plank road.

(continued)

8. Any surplus Kit, Officers Trench bundles or Officers Mess boxes which were not sent down tonight should be sent tomorrow, as soon as it is dark enough, to FORWARD SIDING.

9. Any Petrol Tins remaining with Coys. should be handed over on relief, and tins should be left in the cookhouses. Company Commanders are responsible also that the Trenches are handed over thoroughly and in as clean a condition as possible.

10. Completion of Relief will be notified by Wire, as follows:- "In reply to your R.X 12 - 2 please"

11. ACKNOWLEDGE.

(Sd) R.D. RUSSELL for 1A/Adjt
10th Royal West Kent Regt

Copy No. 1.	C.O.	No. 6	O/C 4th Y + L. Regt
2	O/C. A	7	O/C 12th E Surreys.
3	O/C. B	8	T.O. + Q M.
4	O/C. C	9	War Diary
5	O/C. D	10	File.

Operation Order No 10
by Major F A. WALLIS
Comdg 10th Bn. R WEST KENT REGT
3 - 6 - 18

Ref Map. Sheet 27 NE . HAZEBROUCK 5A.

1/ The Battalion will entrain tomorrow morning with truck at PROVEN, for the 2nd Army Training Area. Part of transport will also entrain, the remainder will proceed Brigaded.
Personnel of the Battalion will entrain at 3am. Transport & personnel will entrain at 8am. Duration of journey about $3\frac{1}{2}$ hours.
No baggage except that which is carried on the person will be allowed on the 1st train.

2 PARADE Coys & Headqrs will parade in full marching order on their respective parade ground ready to move off at 12-15 am. They will be told off into parties of 40 each under the senior NCO who will travel in the truck with his party. Owing to shortage of accommodation each party of 40 must be got into one truck. The NCO i/c truck is held responsible that no man leaves the truck without orders once the Battalion is entrained. Entrainment must be effected quickly.
The Battalion will move off in parties of 40 with 50 yards interval between each, in the following order - H.Q., A, B, C, D Coys.
The Transport will move off in time to arrive at PROVEN 3 hours before departure of train. Loading party will be found by RE Field Coy.

3 The following is a list of transport & personnel proceeding on Second train :-

		Personnel	Axles	Horses
4	G.S. Limbered Wagons	4	8	8
1	Water Cart	4	1	2
1	Mess Cart	1	1	1
2	Travelling Kitchen	2	4	4
1	Maltese Cart	1	1	1
11	Riding horses and 6 pack	17	-	17

The extra baggage will be taken by the transport train and must be off-loaded and a guard placed over it immediately on arrival at destination

4 Lt. TATHAM and the Intelligence Sergt will proceed to PROVEN ahead of the Battn in order that entrainment may be facilitated.

5 The Bn will detrain at WATTEN and proceed by march route to Billets in the ST. MOMELIN AREA.

6 Officers Mess boxes will be dumped outside HQ mess by 9pm tonight. No other baggage can be taken on Mess Cart.

7 Coys & HQ must arrange for tea for their men immediately before leaving camp as there will be no facilities at either entraining or detraining Station owing to the fact that the whole Brigade is proceeding by the one train

8 On arrival in Billets Coys will immediately inform HQ. of the location of their HQ.

9 Acknowledge.

Water bottles must be filled before moving off

(sgd) R.O. RUSSELL LT: A/A
10th BN R. WEST KENT RGT

Operation Order No 16
by Lt. Col. THE HON. E.R. THESIGER
Comdg 10th Bn. Royal West Kent Regt

1 The Bn. will move to the Tategham Area.

2 The Bn. will form up in columns of 3s facing St. Momelin, head of column at Bn. H.Q. in the following order. A, H.Q., Band, D, C, & B. with 100yds interval between Coys. at 2.45 p.m. Dress – full marching order.

3 Route St. Momelin – northern outskirts of St. Omer, – St. Martin-au-Laert. Usual clock hour halts will be observed.

4 Transport will move in rear of Bn. as far as St. Momelin, and then proceed via. Saques – Moulle.

5 Officers Valises to be stacked outside Coy. Billets by 1. am.
Mess Boxes " " by 2. p.m.

6 All Tents and any other Area Stores must be ready to be picked up by Transport at 11. am

7 Coy. Comdrs. will report that all Billets etc are left scrupulously clean. Certs. to this effect will be rendered to the Adjutant on Parade.

8 Any Officers Kits not collected by Transport at 11. am. will be dumped at Battn. H.Q. and a guard left over it.

9 Coys will carry out foot Inspection on arrival in new Billets and report made of all cases of sore feet.

10 ACKNOWLEDGE

(SGD) F.A. Wallis Major.
10th Bn Royal West Kent Regt

10. 6. 18

10th. BN ROYAL WEST KENT REGT.   COPY No

OPERATION ORDER No. 12.

18th JUNE 1918

MAP REF H.5A.

INFORMATION. A German force is advancing from the direction of DUNKERQUE on ST. OMER.

A German detachment estimated at one Regiment (2 Battns) passed through ST. TO[illegible]UIN yesterday and halted about POLINCOVE [illegible]night.

INTENTION. The 123 BRIGADE will move from assembly position to establish itself on high ground between GRAND DIFQUES and MORINGHEM.

BRIGADE DETAIL. 23rd MIDDLESEX will move VIA ETREHEM – LEULINE and CORMETTE to a line about [illegible] – Q 26, c.q.5.

11th QUEEN'S VIA CROSS ROADS W 29. b. 0.9. – LEULINGHEM – ZUDAUSQUES to a line Q 26. c.9.5. to about Q 25 a. 3.0.

REGTL. DETAIL.

1. 10th R.W.KENTS less 1 Coy BRIGADE RESERVE, will march ~~[illegible]~~ [illegible] same road as 23rd MIDDLESEX. STARTING POINT X ROADS W[illegible]
2. TIME. 7·45 am.
3. ORDER OF MARCH, H.Q., A. [illegible] D. TRANSPORT.
4. BATTN. less 1 Coy, less Transport march to High Ground approx. W.16, a. for Educational Purposes.
5. TRANSPORT march to TATINGHEM, to halt when head reaches X ROADS. X7. a, 2.9.
6. LIAISON O.C. A. will keep touch with 23 Middlesex
   Officer Patrols O.C. C " " " " 11 Queens
   during operations.
7. S.A.A. Ammunition pack animals under Regt. Sergt. Major will march in rear of Battalion.
8. MEDICAL. Doctor & Stretcher Bearers in rear of ammunition.
9. TRANSPORT. B Echelon will assemble under LT. HICKMAN, 11. Queens on road from X 8 a, 0.8. – X 2, c. 1. 2. facing S. and will [illegible] in [illegible] by 9·30 a.m.
10. REPORTS to head of Battalion.

Copies to. BRIGADE.
A
B
C
D
TRANSPORT
Q.M.
H.Q. & Doc. Regt.

(SGD) B. T. COMINS [illegible]
10th Bn. ROYAL WEST KENT REGT.

10th Bn. ROYAL WEST KENT REGT

OPERATION ORDERS No 13

Ref Map Sheet 27A S.E. and
HAZEBROUCK 5A

INFORMATION

A Blue force, which has advanced from the Eastward is holding the line of the R.Aa and the Aa Canal, from WATTEN to ARQUES. A detachment is covering the Bridge at ST OMER.

A Red force is advancing from the Westward with the object of seizing the Bridge at ST. OMER, prior to attacking the Blue force.

INTENTION

The 123rd Infantry Bde. less one Battn. (part of Red Force) has been ordered to drive in the Blue protective troops & compel the enemy to disclose the position of the defences of the Bridge Head north of the road running through TATINGHEM to ST MARTIN-AU-LAERT.

BRIGADE
DETAIL

The 123rd Infy. Bde. less 23rd Middx. 139th F.A. and 2 Section M.G.C. under command of Lt. Col. The Hon E.R. THESIGER will rendezvous

-2-

at QUELMES VILLAGE West of a North and South Road through W. 14. Central. No one of the Red force will be East of that line between 9-45 a.m. and 10-15 a.m.

Operations commence at 10-15 a.m.

REGIMENTAL DETAIL

(1) 10th R. W. Kent Regt. Starting Point Parade in Football Field.

(2) TIME. 9-30 AM

(3) TRANSPORT B Echelon on Road from W. 13 & 7. 4 – W. 13. b. 3. 4. Under Lieut HICKMAN.

(4) Bde. Ammunition & Tool Reserve of 1 S.A.A. & 1 Tool Limber will concentrate at W. 14. c. 5. 3 at 10 a.m. under Sgt PEIRCE, Bde H.Q.

(5) 'A' Echelon. In QUELMES SQUARE. Head of column facing School.

(6) MEDICAL. Doctor & Stretcher Bearers in rear of ammunition.

(Sd) B.T. COMINS.

Lt & A/Adjt

10th Bn. R. W. Kent Regt

24/1/18

Operation Orders No 14
10th Bn Royal West Kent Regt

24/6/18

Map Ref 27A. SE + NE.

1/ The Brigade will move to the ST MOMELIN area tomorrow.
The Battn will take over same billets as previously occupied.

2/. Battn will parade at 8.45 am in the following order.
HQ. Band. B. C. D. A. head of column at Crossroads W14 a 6.5 at 9 am

3/ Advance party 1 NCO per Coy + HQ to report to area Comdt. ST. MOMELIN at 10 am
Report Bn Orderly Room 8.30 am

4/ all tents + area Stores, including Sanitary Stores, to be handed over to Billet Warden (at A Coy Billet QUELMES) by 7.30 am and receipt obtained which must be handed in to Orderly Room at once.

5/ Band Packs must be stacked outside the Canteen by 8 am
Officers Valises to be outside Battn HQ. (Orderly Room) by 7.30 am. Officers Mess Boxes to be outside Coy HQ by 7.30 am

6 Billets to be left clean and a certificate obtained that no damage has been done to property.
These to be rendered to Orderly Room.

Contd.

Contd

7/ Reveille — 5 am.
Breakfast — 6 am.
Sick Parade — 6 am.

(Sgd) B.T. COMINS
Lt + A/Adj
10th Bn Royal West Kent Regt.

Copies to
CO.
Adj
War Diary
OC A
B
C
D
TO + QM

10th BN R. WEST KENT REGT
OPERATION ORDER No 15

25th June 1918

1 The Battalion will continue move tomorrow, and will proceed to the ARNEEKE AREA.

2 Batn will parade in the following order – H.Q. Band, D. A. C. B.
Head of column to be at road junction M.2. d. [illegible] at 10 am.

3 Officers Valises. Mess Boxes [illegible] will be dumped outside Coy. H.Qrs by 8 30 am

4 Billeting N.C.O's from each Coy and Headqrs will report at Bn. H.Q. at 6 15 am.

5 Reveille – 7 AM.
Breakfasts – 8 AM
Sick Parade 7 AM

6 Present billets will be left clean and certificate rendered to the effect.

7. Notes 1 The Commanding Officer wishes to congratulate the Battalion on the way it marched today.
2 No man will drink

(Contd).

8. List of trench stores taken over to be rendered to Bn H.Q. by 6am 7th inst.

9. Completion of Relief to be reported to Battn H.Q. by runner.

?. Acknowledge.

Note. No Sick Parade tonight. Any man unfit to march must parade at Battn H.Q. at 9 pm.

As many tools as possible to be carried to new line on the man.

Copies to. ?O ?

[illegible]
Commanding
M.O.

1918.

[illegible]
Clay

Instructions regarding War Diaries and Intelligence Summaries are contained in F. S. Regs., Part II. and the Staff Manual respectively. Title pages will be prepared in manuscript.

WAR DIARY
or
INTELLIGENCE SUMMARY.
(Erase heading not required.)

JULY, 1918.

Army Form C. 2118.

Place	Date	Hour	Summary of Events and Information	Remarks and references to Appendices
ABEELE Sheet 27	1/7/18		Battn. resting & preparing for trenches.	
		10pm	Battn. proceeded to relieve the POIGNY BN. of the 104th French Infantry Brigade in the Reserve Line, near RENINGHELST Vide O.O. 17.	O.O. 17
RENINGHELST SHEET 28 NW	2nd		Situation normal. Details moved from ABEELE AERODROME to BEAUVOORDE WOOD.	
	3rd		Situation normal	
	4th		– do –. A/Capt. N.G. Kill, evac. Sick to Eng. 26-6-18. The following Officers joined Battn for duty. 2/Lt. A. J. STUBBS., 2/Lt. SQUIBB. L.E. 2/Lt ROGERS E, 2/LT. MEATES. G.M. Hon Lt & Qmr. W.G. RICE.	
	5th		Battn. in Divisional Reserve in RENINGHELST. STRENGTH. OFF. 39. O.R.s 1009.	
LA CLYTTE.	6th		Battn. relieved 11th Bn "QUEENS" R. WEST SURREY REGT., in support line on LA-CLYTTE – LOCRE ROAD. 23rd MIDDLESEX REGT. took over Divisional Reserve. Relief completed without incident.	O.O. 18
	7th		Situation normal	
	8th		-do-	
	9th		-do-	
	10th		-do-	
	11th		Battn. relieved 11th Bn "QUEENS" in Front Line. "B" & "D" Coys. took over Outpost Line on BRULOOZE ROAD. A Coy in Strong Point at FERMOY FARM. "C" Coy in support on LA CLYTTE – LA LOCRE ROAD.	O.O. 19
	12th		Situation normal. 4 Officers and 18 N.C.O.s from 107th Regt. American Army attached for instruction. They created a most favourable impression in every way.	[illegible]

D. D. & L., London, E.C.
(A10266) Wt W5300/P713 750,000 2/18 Sch. 52 Forms/C2118/16.

Secret

Operation Order No 16

10th Bn Royal West Kent Regiment

Ref. Sheet 27 1/40000

I The Battalion will move by March route tomorrow 30th inst. to ABEELE AERODROME L 31 a prior to relieving a Battalion of the 94th French Infantry Brigade.

II Route —— ZERMEZEELE — HADIFORT — RWELD — STEENVOORDE.

III Order of March —— H.Q. B, A, C, D Coys, Transport. Normal distances will be observed and strict march discipline enforced.
Attention is called to Btn. R.O. No 394 of 27.6.18.

IV Dress —— Dress will be notified later. It is hoped to get lorries to convey packs.

V Parades —— Companies & H.Q. will rendezvous with head of Battalion at Road Junction I 8 a 6.8 at 12.45 p.m. and the Battalion will move at 1.4 p.m. There will be a long halt at about 4 p.m. so that Battalion does not reach bivouacs before 9.30 p.m.

VI —————— The Band will accompany "B" Coy. to Starting Point and play until the Battn has passed. They will remain for the night in present billets and proceed to Divl Reception Camp on the morning of 1st July under instructions [illegible].

VII Officers Valises, Mess Kit, and O.R. Boxes will be stacked outside respective H.Qrs by 10.30 a.m. T.O. & Q.Ms will arrange to collect them.

VIII All waterbottles must be filled before departure.

IX Billets must be left clean and latrines filled in.

X On a visit in the neighbourhood of Bivouacs and forward of these, the greatest care must be taken to conceal all movement and signs of [illegible].

XI Acknowledge ——

(Sgd) R. O. Russell
Lt. & Adjt.
10th Bn Royal West Kent Regt.

29.6.18

Instructions regarding War Diaries and Intelligence Summaries are contained in F. S. Regs., Part II. and the Staff Manual respectively. Title pages will be prepared in manuscript.

WAR DIARY
or
INTELLIGENCE SUMMARY.
(Erase heading not required.)

JULY 1918. Cont:

Army Form C. 2118.

Place	Date	Hour	Summary of Events and Information	Remarks and references to Appendices
LA CLYTTE (Sheet 28 S.W.1 - KEMMEL)	12th	Cont:-	Three front Companies engaged upon improving & strengthening their lines by night. Patrols active. "C" Coy carried all rations from Dump to line.	
			Strength OFF. 38. O.R.s 1009.	
			Men surplus to Establishment (about 60) sent to "J" Depot. Etaples, from Battalion and Divisional Reception Camp.	
	13th		Situation normal.	
	14th		- do -	
			Hostile Shelling above normal on account of a raid carried out by 124th Infantry Brigade on night of 14th.	
	15th		Situation normal.	
	16th		Lieut. H.P. JOHNSON. Wounded. re-evacuated. (Slight wound)	
			Officers & men of the American Army left.	
			Battalion relieved 23rd Middlesex Regt. in Support. Relief completed without incident. "A" Coy less 1 Platoon, and "C" Coy on main line of resistance in front of LA CLYTTE-LOCRE ROAD. One Platoon of "A" Coy in Strong Point, KIMBERLEY CAMP.	O.O.20
			"B" & "D" Counter attack companies in rear near Brigade H.Q.	
	17th		Situation normal. Special vigilance by night.	
	18th		- do -	
	19th		- do - Strength. OFF. 38. O.R.s 936.	
	20th		Situation normal. Battalion engaged upon wiring and strengthening Main Line of Resistance by night. Heavy Rain caused some damage to trenches.	
	21st		Situation normal. Special Vigilance.	[signature]

D. D. & L., London, E.C.
(A10266) Wt W5300/P713 750,000 2/18 Sch. 52 Forms/C2118/16.

4

Instructions regarding War Diaries and Intelligence Summaries are contained in F. S. Regs., Part II. and the Staff Manual respectively. Title pages will be prepared in manuscript.

WAR DIARY or INTELLIGENCE SUMMARY.

(Erase heading not required.)

10 R W Kent

JULY 1918 cont.

Army Form C. 2118.

WO 27

Place	Date	Hour	Summary of Events and Information	Remarks and references to Appendices
LA CLYTTE	22nd		Situation normal.	
(Sheet 28.S.W. - KEMMEL	23rd		" "	
	24th		" " Two Company Commanders from U.S. army arrived. Attached for instruction.	
	25th		Situation normal. Hostile Shelling heavier than usual. U.S. Officers left.	
	26th		Situation Normal. "K" Coy and "L" Coy. 3rd Bn 106th American Regt, also M.O., I.O., and 12 O.Rs joined Bn. for Instruction. Two platoon to each Coy. M.O., I.O., and 12 O.R.s to Headquarters. STRENGTH OF BN. OFF. 39. O.R.s 909.	O.O. 21 O.O. 22
	27th		Situation Normal.	
	28th		- do - Battalion with attached American personnel, relieved 11th Bn "Queens" in Front line.	O.O. 23
	29th		Situation normal. Readjustment of English & American troops in Front Line.	O.O. 24 para 1 (cancelled)
	30th		- do - American Infantry 3rd Bn. 106th Regiment relieve the English	O.O. 25
	31st		Coys in Front Line; the latter moving back into supports. Strength of Battalion Officers 42. Other Rank 919. Casualties for period 1-31st July. Officers. Wounded 1 Gassed 1 Other Rank " 39	

Eric Thesiger Lt Colonel
Comdg Royal West Kent

D. D. & L., London, E.C. (A10266) Wt W5300/P713 750,000 2/18 Sch. 52 Forms/C2118/16.

Office Copy

Reference Operation Order No 17 dated 1st July 1918

Para 3. For <u>9.30 pm</u> read <u>11.20 pm</u>

R G Russell
Lieut A/Adjt
11 Bn Royal West Kent Regt

1/7/18

SECRET

10th Bn. ROYAL WEST KENT REGT

OPERATION ORDER. No 17.

Maps Sheets 27 & 28 1st July 1918

1. The Battn. will relieve the POIGNY Bn of the 104th French Inf. Bde. in the Reserve Line near RENINGHELST to-night.

2. Coys. will take over in the following order:-

A. Coy on RIGHT. B. Coy. RIGHT CENTRE.

C " LEFT CENTRE. D. " LEFT.

Location of H.Q. will be at Sheet 28. M.5. a. 25.50.

3. The Bn. will move in the following order:-

A. B. C. D. Coys. and Headqrs. with platoons at 100 yds. distance. Care must be taken that touch is not lost, leading platoon of 'A' Coy will pass point on Main Road L 31 central at 9-30pm.

DRESS.- Fighting Order, less greatcoats. Box Respirators at the Alert.

4. Coys. will take up 7 Lewis Guns per Coy. These will be carried on the man. H.Q. will take the 4. A.A. Guns. Two of these at least must be mounted before morning. The advance Party sent forward this morning will meet their respective platoons at the junction of the RENINGHELST ABEEL and the RENINGHELST-WESTOUTRE Road. Sheet 28. G. 34. d. 0. 6.

5. WATER. Owing to contamination, no water except what is brought up from the Transport Lines may be consumed. Transport will bring up to-night about 20 tins per Coy & in addition 1 Water Cart will proceed to Battn. H.Q. ALL water bottles MUST be filled before leaving present billets.

6. S.A.A. - 50 Boxes S.A.A. will be taken up to-night by Transport. These will be dumped at Battn. H.Q. whence Coys. will draw 6 boxes each as soon as relief is complete.

7. Coys. and Lt. PERCIVAL for H.Q. will render a Marching Out State by 7 pm to-night.

8. All men for Battn. Classes and other personnel for Transport Lines will parade under the R.S.M. at 5-30pm. in Full Marching Order.

9. Packs of men proceeding to the line will be dumped in same position as last night by 8-30 pm. These must be clearly marked. The Q.M. will arrange that these packs are carefully guarded the whole time they are in his charge.

10. Officers valises must be dumped at Q.M. Stores by 2-30 pm. Officers Trench Bundles & Mess Kit at the same place at 8-30pm

11. The French Battn. is leaving 1 Officer per Coy. and 1 at Battn H.Q. for 24 hours after Relief.

12. Completion of Relief will be notified by runner.

13 Acknowledge

(Sd) R.O. RUSSELL. Lt & A/Adjt
10th Bn R. W. Kent Regt

War Diary

10th Battn. Royal West Kent Regt.
Operation Orders No. 18.

SECRET.

6th July 1918.

1/ The Battn will relieve the 11th Queens in Support tonight.

2/ Battn will move in the following order at times stated below.

H.Q.	10. pm
A	10.30 pm
C	10.30 pm
B	11.0 pm
D	11.0 pm

The usual intervals between Platoons will be observed.

The N.C.Os who reconnoitred the line yesterday will act as guides for their platoons

All Trench Maps and Stores to be handed over and receipt obtained

All Empty Petrol tins and Dixies etc will be dumped at B.H.Q. Orderly Room by 9.30. pm

Extra Lewis Gun Panniers will be distributed among the Platoons to be carried on the man

Ration parties to be sent to Ration DUMP – M12. B.0.4 as soon as Relief is complete.

Capt.

from his waterbottle whilst on the march without orders from his platoon Commander.

(sgd) B. T. Cumins

Lieut & A/Adj

10th R.W. Kent Regt

SECRET. 10th Battn Royal West Kent Regt.

File:- Operation Orders No 19

11th July 1918.

Ref sheet 28 S W 1/10000.

1/ The Battn will relieve the 11th Queens Regt in the Front Line (Centre Section) on the night of the 11/12th July.

The 23rd Middlesex Regt will take over the trenches at present occupied by the Battn.

2/ The Coys will take over as follows:-

D. Coy	Kents from	A Coy	Queens	(Left front line)
B	"	B	"	(Right front line)
A	"	C	"	(FERMOY FARM)
C	"	D	"	(RESERVE)

3/. Advance parties will be exchanged as already ordered.

4/. Companies will move in the following order under the guidance of the Queens men already with them.

D. B. A. C.

OC D and B Coys will arrange to pick up rations at DUMP as soon as they arrive, and move off immediately.

(Cont.)

5. All Defence Schemes, programmes of Work, Trench maps + stores and all information re Patrols, Wire, work etc will be handed over on relief.

6. No movement will take place before dark and relief must be carried out as quickly and as quietly as possible, no smoking under any circumstances will be allowed.

7. Empty Petrol tins will be brought down and rations will be drawn on completion of relief.

8. Trenches, Dugouts, will be left clean and Sanitary.

9. Completion of Relief to be reported by runner.

10. ACKNOWLEDGE.

15/7/1918. (Sgd) R. C. RUSSELL
Lieut + A/Adjt

10th Bn Royal West Kent Regt

SECRET 7th Royal West. Kent Regt.

Operation Orders No. 20.

Ref sheet 28 S.W. 1 KEMMEL.

1/ The Battn. will be relieved in the front line on the night of 16/17th July by the 23rd Middlesex Regt. as under:-

D Coy KENTS will be relieved by D Coy Middlesex.
B " " " " C " "
A " " " " B " "
C " " " " A " "

Order of march D. C. B. A.

On completion of relief Coys will take over the trenches in SUPPORT vacated by the Middlesex Regt. occupying same positions as before namely:-

*C Coy. FRONT LINE of RESISTANCE at present occupied by B Coy Middlesex.

A Coy. LINE OF RESISTANCE - do - by A Middlesex Coy.

B Coy. RIGHT RESERVE - do - by C Coy Middlesex.

D Coy. LEFT RESERVE - do - by D Coy Middlesex.

* C. Coy KENTS will relieve B Coy MIDDLESEX before the latter proceeds to the LINE.

[illegible]

2/ GUIDES.

Guides as under will report to Bn H.Q at 1.30 AM 16th inst. They will bring rations and stay during the day with the relieving Coy. of the MIDDLESEX. and at night will guide them to their respective positions in the Line.

A & C Coys — 1 N.C.O. per platoon
B & D " — 1 N.C.O. per section = 4 per platoon
1 intelligent man per front line section = 9
Total per Coy = 13.

3/ ADVANCE PARTIES

(a) 1 Senior NCO per Coy. will report at Bn H.Q at 1.30 am 16th inst. and they will be despatched to Middlesex Regt to take over work etc in SUPPORT LINE.

(b) 1 Officer per Coy and 1 NCO per platoon of Middlesex Regt will be sent up to Coys tonight 15/16th inst, the Officers will remain in the Line, the NCOs will return to their Unit.

Every assistance must be given to this advance party in learning all there is to know.

4. 1 Officer per Coy, 1 NCO per platoon will remain in the line for 24 hours after relief to hand over work etc in hand.

— Contd —

4/ Continued –
OC "A" Coy will arrange to leave two guides to take the platoon of the 23rd Middlesex Regt to "KIMBERLEY TRENCH" and 1 platoon to take up his rations.
OC "C" Coy will not move until relieved by "B" Coy of the 23rd Middlesex Regt, he will fetch rations under his own arrangements, he will also be required to work on the night of the line of resistance under the R.E. Officer.

5/ All movement will be by platoons, no movement to take place till dusk.

6/ Advance parties will meet their Sections and Platoons as under: –
Section Guides at Platoon Headquarters
Platoon " " Company "

7. Headquarter Lewis Gunners will report back to their Companies at 7 pm and will be taken into the line with them.

8/. All Defence Schemes, Programmes of Work, Trench Maps and Stores, Patrols etc, will be carefully taken over.

Contd –

Continued —

9/. The greatest possible care must be taken to prevent noise etc during relief.

10/. Completion of relief to be notified by wiring the words "Ref your R.O.101 — NIL".

11/. Acknowledge

Copies to { C.O.
{ Adj
OC A
" B
" C
" D
. File
11th Queens.

(Sgd) R.O. Russell
Lt A/Adj
10th Bn R.W. Kent Regt.

ADDENDUM to
O.O No 21.

July 26th 1918.

1. Reference Para 4 of Above.
The 3 Platoons of "B" and 4 Platoons of "D" will proceed to Huts and Bivouacs at Sheet 27 L.28.d. and L.29.c. near Brigade Rear H.Q. instead of to the WESTOUTRE LINE.

They will take with them a proportion of Signallers & Runners and the 7 Platoons will be under the Command of the Senior Officer, who will establish his Headquarters at Bde Rear H.Q. L.29.c.7.2., from which point he is in telephonic communication with Brigade H.Q.

One Officer of each Coy. has been sent to reconnoitre these positions, and they will return and guide their Coy. down to-night.

2. As soon as possible after the arrival of the Americans, each Coy. Commander will

O/C 'A' Coy. until further notice.
O/C 'C' Coy. will arrange to send One Officer and Nos. 9 & 11 platoons at dusk to report to O/C "D" Coy, under whose command they will come until further notice.
O/C "A" Coy will send One Officer and Nos. 1 & 3. platoons at dusk to report to O/C 'B' Coy. under whose command they will come until further notice.

A residue of the H.Q. personnel of "B" and 'D' Coys. may be kept back to assist in the running of the new Composite Coys.

5. Completion of No 4. (above) will be reported to this Office by Runner.

6. On the arrival of the Americans they will be guided into the platoon fronts thus vacated, where they will remain until daylight.

At daylight they will be split up man for man, amongst the English personnel, and composite Coys. thus formed.

Completion of this latter move to be notified to this Office by Runner.

7. No Trench Stores will be moved. Coys. are responsible that before

the reorganization takes place, all Trench Stores, such as Gum Boots &c are collected in convenient dumps and kept under supervision.

8/. All English personnel must do their utmost to assist the American personnel in learning Trench routine &c.

9. During this individual attachment of American personnel, the latter will come under the command of the English personnel. Once the Americans are reformed into platoons or companies, they will come under the command of their own officers.

10/. O.C. "A" & "D" Coys. will arrange that the composite Coys. under their command carry on the existing Tunnelling Fatigues found by their Coys.

11. ACKNOWLEDGE.

(Sd) R.O. RUSSELL

Lt & A/Adjt.

10th R. W. Kent Regt.

SECRET

10th Bn Royal West Kent Regt
Operation Order No 21.

JULY 26th 1918

Ref. Sheet 28 S.W.1. – KEMMEL.

1. Two Coys. of the 3rd Bn. 106th Inf. Regt U.S.A will arrive to-night for attachment the Bn.

2. They will be attached as follows:-

2 Platoons of	"L" Coy	106 Regt. U.S.A.	to	"A" Coy.
2 "	" L	" "	to	"B" "
2 "	" K	" "	to	C "
2 "	" K.	" "	to	D "

3. GUIDES. Guides as already detailed, viz:- 2/Lieut. ROGERS, 16 Guides and 2 H.Q. Runners, will meet these 2 Coys. at Sheet 28. G. 32. C. 1. 8. at 9-30 pm. to-night and will guide them to the Coy. H.Q. of the Coy. to which they will be attached. One guide will bring each ½ platoon which will move at 50 yards distance

4. At dusk O/C "B" Coy. will arrange to send 3 Platoons, and O/C "D" Coy 4 platoons of his Coy. to the WESTOUTRE LINE to positions previously reconnoitred.

The fourth platoon of "B" Coy. will proceed to "A" Coy H.Q. and will come under the command of forward to this Office a Trench Strength of his Composite Coy. Shewing:-

(a) English personnel

(b) American do-

In addition O's.C. B + D. Coys will forward exact numbers sent down to Reserve Positions

(Sd) R.O. RUSSELL

Lieut & A/Adjt

10th Bn. R. W Kent Regt

SECRET

10th Bn R. W. Kent Regt
Operation Order No 22

Ref Sheet 28 S.W.1 - KEMMEL

1. The Brigade Northern Boundary has been adjusted and now runs N.W. from Front-Line to N.7.d. 55.20 to M.12.B.5.6

2. The dispositions of the Battn. in Support are therefore altered accordingly.

3. O.C. "A" Coy will take over to-night portion of the Line of Resistance from old Brigade Boundary to N.7.d.2.5. from a Platoon of 18th K.R.R.C. and will make arrangements with O.C Reserve Coy 18th K.R.R.C to take over the Coy. Headquarters at present occupied by the latter. All arrangement for this Relief will be made by O's. C. Companies concerned.

4. O.C. "B" Coy. will send one platoon to O.C "A" Coy. at dusk This platoon will come under orders of O.C. "A" Coy. until

further orders.

5. Dispositions of "A" Coy. on completion of re-adjustment will be as follows:-

1. Platoon in KIMBERLEY TRENCH

2. Platoons in Line of Resistance from Divl O.P. to Northern Bde. Boundary.

1. Platoon in camouflaged trench in rear of DEVON CAMP.

1. Platoon in present line until trench running N.E. from Battn H.Q. is deep enough to live in. Company H.Q. in present Reserve Coy's HQ of Bn on left.

6. O.C. "C" Coy. will take over the positions vacated by "A" Coy. in the BOYAU. MORENTON. C.T. with One Platoon from his support line.

7. Completion of Adjustment to be reported to this Office by Runner

8. ACKNOWLEDGE.

(Sd) R.O. RUSSELL
Lt + A/Adjt
10th R.W. Kent Regt

26/1/18.

SECRET.

10th Bn R.W. Kent Regt
Operation Order No 23.

July 27th 18

Ref Sheet 28 S.W.1 - KEMMEL

1. The Battn. with attached American personnel, will relieve 11th Queens in the front line tomorrow night 28/29th July 1918.

2. Coys. will take over in the following order:-

"C" Coy Kents from "B" Coy Queens R. front line
"A" " " " "D" " " L. " "
"B" " " " "C" " " FERMOY FARM
"D" " " " "A" " " Reserve.

Positions in Support will be taken over by 11th Queens as follows:

"A" Co. Line of Resistance (Left) by "I" Coy 3rd Bn 106 Regt U.S.A.
"C" " " " (Right) " "A" Coy. Queens.
"D" " Bde Reserve Line (Left) " "M" Coy 3rd Bn 106 Regt U.S.A.
"B" " " " (Right) " "C" Coy. Queens.

O/C "C" Coy. will not move from present position until relieved by "A" Coy. Queens.

O/C "A" Coy. will not move until his 2 Platoons in Line of Resistance are relieved. Relief will commence about 10. p.m.

Contd.

3. Advanced parties of 11th Queens consisting of 1 N.C.O. per platoon (17 Platoons) will report at Bn H.Q. at 12-15 am. 28th, when they will be despatched to respective Coys. In addition One Officer per Coy. will report during the course of tomorrow 28th.

4. GUIDES. (a) Each Coy. will detail 1 N.C.O. per Platoon (17 Platoons) to Report at B.H.Q at 8-15 pm tomorrow, 28th. These guides will meet their respective Platoons at 11th Queens H.Q. and guide them to the positions in the Support Line. On completion of their duties, they will report back to their Coys.

(b) No guides will be furnished by 11th Queens to take Battn. into the Line. Guides, however, will be furnished from the surplus personnel of B. and D. Coys. as already arranged, to take A & C. Coys. to their respective positions in the front line.

(c) O/C "A" Coy. will send 1 Guide per Platoon to O/C "B" Coy tomorrow

(Contd)

afternoon to act as guides to FERMOY FARM.

(D.) O/C "D" Coy. will arrange to reconnoitre the Reserve Coy. line so that he will need no guide.

~~4. RATIONS. Rations for 2 days will be drawn to-night (27th)~~

5 ~~4~~. TRENCH STORES. The greatest possible care will be taken in handing over and taking over all Trench Stores and Reserve Rations &c. Dumps must be checked. Receipts in duplicate will be given or taken and a copy forwarded to this office before day break 29th

SOS. ROCKETS. Especial care must be taken to see that the proper number of S.O.S. Rockets are handed or taken over and that they are complete and in working order.

6 ~~7~~. Completion of Relief will be reported by wiring the words "Ref. K. 20. Nil required"

7 ~~8~~. ACKNOWLEDGE.

(Sd) R.O. RUSSELL
Lieut & A/Adjt
10th R. W. Kent Regt.

SECRET.

10th Bn Royal West Kent Regt
Operation Order No 24

July 28th 1918.

Ref Sheet 28 SW 1. – KEMMEL
and Sheet 27

1 The following re-adjustments of personnel will take place during the tour in the front line.

(a) Night of 29/30th July Each Coy will arrange to reform with Platoons of English and Americans respectively. On completion Platoons will be disposed as under :-

1 Platoon American	1 Platoon English	1 Platoon American		1 Platoon American	1 Platoon English	1 Platoon American
	1 Platoon English				1 Platoon English	

No alteration will be made as to the disposition of the Lewis Gun posts, that is, Lewis Guns whether manned by English or Americans will be located in the same positions as usual

(b) (1) Night of 30/31st July. The 2 English platoons of the left front Coy will be relieved by 2 Platoons Americans from FERMOY FARM, thus making a complete Coy (Coy "L") of Americans under their own Company Commander. On Relief the 2 English platoons will proceed to FERMOY FARM and come under Command of Capt RUTHVEN who will then have the four platoons of 'A' Coy under his Command

(b)(2) The 2 American platoons of "K" Coy. attached to Right front Coy. will be relieved by 2 English platoons from the Reserve Coy, who will bring with them the rations for the Right front Coy. Capt. Solomon will therefore have under his Command 4 platoons of "C" Coy. The 2 American platoons thus relieved from the Right front will come back into Reserve and form complete American Coy (Coy K) under Command of their own Company Commander.

(b. 3.) On completion of above Relief, O/C Right front Coy. will send down to Battn. H.Q. 1 guide per Section for the 3 Platoons in front line = 9, plus 1 guide for each Platoon H.Q. = 4, plus 1 N.C.O. for Coy. H.Q. = 1 (Total 14) to guide up the American Company coming in next night.

(b)(4) Commander of FERMOY will

Similarly send down 1 guide per platoon and 1 N.C.O. for Coy H.Q. (Total 5)

(C) Night of July 31st/1st Aug.

One Coy of Americans at present attached to 11th Queens, will relieve FERMOY FARM and One Coy Americans will relieve the Right front Coy. On relief the 2 English Coys. will proceed to Huts and Bivouacs in L.28.a & 29.c. Sheet 27 where they will remain until 23rd Middx Regt. have vacated Reserve Battn. Position near WIPPENHOEK on the evening of Aug 2nd.

2/Lt COOPER will arrange to have Twelve intelligent men at Battalion H.Q. at 10. pm on 31st July to guide platoons of "A" & "C" Coys to L.28.d. area on Relief.

2. Completion of each of above adjustments will in all cases be reported by Coys. to Battn H.Q. by wiring " All well at Home "

3 Coy Commanders will remain themselves, and retain any English personnel they think necessary, for 24 hours after the American Coy Commanders have taken

over, or longer if the latter so wish.

4 Every assistance will be given to the American Officers & men by all ranks.

English Coy. Commanders must carefully instruct the American Coy. Commanders who relieve them, as to the nature and times of all the usual trench Routine Returns.

5 Acknowledge

(Sd) R.O. RUSSELL

Lt A/Adjt.

10th Bn R. W. Kent Regt.

SECRET. Copy No.

10th Bn R. W. Kent Regt

OO No. 25

Ref sheet 28 SW1 - KEMMEL 30.7.18

(a) On the night of July 31st/1st Aug "I" and "M" 3rd Bn. 106 Regt U.S.A will relieve the English Coys in the right front line and FERMOY FARM and the command of the Sector will pass to O.C 3rd Battn. 106 Regt U.S.A.

(b) On relief of these 2 Coys and Battn HQ the Battn will move into Support in relief of the 11th "Queens"

2. (a) "C" Coy in Right front will be relieved by "I" Coy Americans. FERMOY FARM will be relieved by "M" Coy Americans.

(b) Support positions will be taken over as follows:-

"D" Kents with one platoon "A" will relieve "I" Coy Americans in Line of Resistance left.

"B" Coy Kents will relieve "A" Queens in Line of Resistance ~~[illegible]~~ right.

On relief "A" Coy Kents, less one platoon (at present in FERMOY) will proceed to RIGHT RESERVE (DE STER CABARET) at present occupied by "C" Coy Queens.

On relief "C" Coy Right front will proceed to Left Reserve, at present occupied by Coy "M" Americans.

RELIEF WILL COMMENCE AT DUSK

3. (a) Advance Parties & Guides

16 O R's (one per Section) of "I" Coy Americans will report to O/C "C" Coy Kents. Right front tonight.

5 Guides from Coy "M" Americans, will report to O/C FERMOY FARM to-night.

These will all remain in the line during the day and at dusk tomorrow (31st) will come down to Battn H.Q to guide in their respective Sections and Platoons.

This advance party must be given as much information as possible. Work in hand, dispositions, wire, duties & etc. must all be carefully explained.

(b) O/C FERMOY FARM will arrange to send down tonight to Battn H.Q, 1 N.C.O. from each "A" Coy Platoon under his Command and 1 for Coy. H.Q (TOTAL 5)

These will report at Battn H.Q at 1.30 a.m. 31st

O/C "C" Coy will similarly send down 1 N.C.O per Platoon and 1 for Coy HQ (all "C" Coy men)

These also will report at Battn H.Q at 1.30 A.M. 31st

These 10 guides will be despatched

to the positions which their Coys will occupy in Support. They will take over all Trench Stores, Reserve Rations, Work in hand etc and will report back to Battn H.Q. at 10.30 p.m July 31st

There they will pick up their respective Platoons & guide them to their positions

(c) 2/Lt F.S. COOPER will arrange to send up to Battn HQ tonight the following:-

One N.C.O per platoon and 1 per Coy H.Q (TOTAL 10) to take over the positions in Line of Resistance to be occupied by 'B' and 'D' Coys. These will report here at Battn H.Q at 1.30AM (31st)

They will then be sent to take over the Trench stores work etc in their new positions

Tomorrow night (31st) they will report back here at Battn HQ at 10.30 pm where they will pick up their Platoons and guide them to their respective positions

Every guide will receive a slip stating position he is to go to and he must keep this slip until the whole relief is complete.

4 Rear Parties

Capt BARTHOLOMEW will leave with L Coy Americans the following:-

One good officer and the senior N.C.O.

and 1 Junior N.C.O. per platoon (TOTAL 1 officer and 8 N.C.O's) [4 written above]

O/C "D" Coy will similarly leave one officer and 8 N.C.O's with Coy "K" American.

These Officers and N.C.O's are merely advisors and will give every possible assistance to the Coy with which they are left.

On relief of the American Battalion by the 23rd MIDDLESEX Regt on the night of 2/3rd August they will rejoin their own Battn.

(b) SIGNALS. Signal communications will be maintained by our own Battn Signallers during the tour of the American Battn in the line. The Signal Sergt will arrange all details.

Apart from above Rear Parties no other West Kent personnel will remain in the line.

5. RATIONS for Aug 1st.

The Quartermaster will arrange to bring these up to the usual Ration Dump, whence Coys will draw their own rations.

6. All defence schemes, Maps of dispositions, information re W.E. Patrols, Enemy Dispositions, habits etc — must be carefully handed over and receipts taken.

One copy to be forwarded to this office.

All Trench stores will be carefully

5/

[...]ted in Dumps, checked and handed over every detail - receipts will be obtained duplicate and one copy forwarded to [thi]s office by 9 a.m. (1st.)
Similarly lists of Trench Stores taken [...]y in support will be forwarded to this [of]fice by 9 a.m.
<u>PETROL TINS</u> All empty Petrol Tins must [b]e brought out of the Line by Coys on relief. [C]ompletion of relief in the Line of Right [F]ront + FERMOY FARM Coys will be [n]otified to this office by Runner.
All Coys will inform this Office as [s]oon as they are in position in Support Line.
Acknowledge.

(S.) R.O. RUSSELL
Lt. + a/Adj
7 O.J.[?]

Reference O.O. No 24

Para 1 (c) is hereby cancelled.
O.O. 25 will deal with this relief

[signature]

Lt a/Adjt
30-7-18. 10 J V

Instructions regarding War Diaries and Intelligence Summaries are contained in F. S. Regs., Part II. and the Staff Manual respectively. Title Pages will be prepared in manuscript.

WAR DIARY
or
~~INTELLIGENCE SUMMARY~~
(Erase heading not required.)

Army Form C. 2118.

10 R W Kent Regt
Vol 28

Place	Date 1918	Hour	Summary of Events and Information	Remarks and references to Appendices
KEMMEL	AUG. 1st		Battn. in support line just behind MONT KEMMEL. Situation fairly quiet. The whole Battn. was engaged upon digging of various kinds, making saps &c., and generally improving the Trenches occupied.	
	2nd		The Battn. was relieved by a "Composite" Battn. composed of half 23rd Bn. Middx. Regt. and half 2nd Bn. 108 Regt U.S.A., and moved back to DALLINGTON CAMP (L. 29. c. 8. 2. Sheet 27). not far from POPERINGHE. About 11. pm the enemy shelled our ration dump causing 1 Officer (2/Lt C.H. PERTWEE) and 4 men to be wounded. One man (L/C. LAING M.M.) although badly wounded in the back with shrapnel, carried out his duties, reporting to Battn. Headquarters in place of his Officer, and it was not until he got back to the CAMP - some five hours later - that he would have his wounds dressed. For his devotion to duty and utter disregard for personal safety he was awarded a bar to his Military Medal. Strength of Battalion 42 Officers. 919 Other Rank.	O.O. 26.
DALLINGTON CAMP	3rd		No work was done to-day. The Battn. rested and bathed.	
	4th		Sunday. A Church Parade service was conducted by The Revd F. BARNETT. The Commanding Officer (Lt Col. The Hon E.R. THESIGER) congratulated the Battn. upon its good work in the line, in the following terms:-	

2449 Wt. W14957/M90 750,000 1/16 J.B.C. & A. Forms/C.2118/12.

Instructions regarding War Diaries and Intelligence Summaries are contained in F. S. Regs., Part II. and the Staff Manual respectively. Title Pages will be prepared in manuscript.

WAR DIARY
or
~~INTELLIGENCE SUMMARY~~
(Erase heading not required.)

Army Form C. 2118.

Place	Date 1918	Hour	Summary of Events and Information	Remarks and references to Appendices
	Aug		"I wish to congratulate the Regt. upon their behaviour and "work during their long period of service in the Front "Line. I have received a most gratifying Report on "the Regiment from an American visitor, which I know "was their genuine opinion. I feel sure that in the "future the Regt. will compete against any Battn. in the "Division or amongst the Allied Troops in proving that "they have the true "offensive spirit."	
	5-7		The Battalion carried out general Infantry training. Lieut. G. Gordon-Smith joined the Battalion for duty. Capt. J. N. Ruthven left the Battn. to proceed to England for 6 mos. tour of duty.	
ZEVECOTEN	8		The Battalion relieved the 15th Bn. Hampshire Regt. in the Reserve Line of the ZEVECOTEN AREA Situation quiet.	OO 27
	9		Battn. in the Line. Situation Normal. Minor operation successfully carried out by Left Brigade. Strength of Battalion 39 Officers 901 other Ranks.	
	10		Battn. in the Line. Situation Normal. Capt. R. Bartholomew left the Bn. to join the 6th Bn. R.W. Kent Regt. 2/Lieut. E. Rogers joined the Bn. for duty.	

Instructions regarding War Diaries and Intelligence Summaries are contained in F. S. Regs., Part II. and the Staff Manual respectively. Title Pages will be prepared in manuscript.

WAR DIARY
or
~~INTELLIGENCE SUMMARY~~
(Erase heading not required.)

Army Form C. 2118.

Page 3.

Place	Date 1918	Hour	Summary of Events and Information	Remarks and references to Appendices
Near MORRUMBRIDGEE	AUG. 11th		Battalion in the line. At dawn the enemy counter-attacked. The Battn. "Stood to" in the Reserve positions. At night we moved up to the support line and relieved the 12th Bn. E. Surrey Regt. Our "A" Coy was attached to 12th E. Surrey Regt in front line.	OO. 28.
	12		Battn. in the line. Situation normal. A Barrage was put down at 3.15 AM in reply to our counter preparation "Shoot"	
	13		Battn in the line. Situation unchanged.	
	14		— " — A Barrage was put down by the enemy at 10/30. p.m. Otherwise the situation remained normal.	
	15		Battn. in the line. During the afternoon Battn. Head quarters was shelled by 21. c.m Howitzer and in the evening by Gas shells, causing a few casualties. The situation in the other part of the line remained unchanged.	
	16		Battn. in the line. A very quiet day. Strength of Battn. 42 Officers 916 Other Ranks.	
	17		Battn. in the line. The enemy Artillery was very active, especially on our communications. Otherwise situation normal.	

Instructions regarding War Diaries and Intelligence Summaries are contained in F. S. Regs., Part II. and the Staff Manual respectively. Title pages will be prepared in manuscript.

WAR DIARY
or
~~INTELLIGENCE SUMMARY.~~
(Erase heading not required.)

Army Form C. 2118.

Page 4.

Place	Date	Hour	Summary of Events and Information	Remarks and references to Appendices
	1918 AUG. 18th		Battn. in the Line. About 10/30 pm. the enemy endeavoured to "rush" our Outpost Line, but were successfully repulsed. The following Officers joined the Battn. for duty:- Capt L Doubleday. Lieut E Combley 2/Lt. W.H. Luck.	
	19-20		Battn. in the Line. Situation Normal	
ZEVECOTEN	21		The Battn. relieved the 12th Bn. E. Surrey Regt. in the Divisional Reserve Area at ZEVECOTEN, the relief was carried out successfully.	O.O. 29.
	22		Battn. in Reserve Line. Situation Normal.	
	23		—— do —— Strength of Battn. 41 Officers. 904 Other Ranks.	
	24-25		Situation Normal. Nothing of importance took place during this period	
SCHERPENBERG -DICKEBUSCH	26		The Battn. relieved the 18th Bn. Kings Royal Rifle Corps in the SCHERPENBERG -DICKENBUSCH LINE.	O.O. 31
	27-28		Battn. in front Line. Situation Normal.	
	29		The Battn. was relieved by the 2nd Bn. Loyal North Lancs. Regt. and proceed to LOYE Siding and entrained the following morning for ST MOMELIN.	O.O. 32.

D. D. & L., London, E.C.
(A10266) Wt W5300/P713 750,000 2/18 Sch. 52 Forms/C2118/16.

Instructions regarding War Diaries and Intelligence Summaries are contained in F. S. Regs., Part II. and the Staff Manual respectively. Title pages will be prepared in manuscript.

WAR DIARY
or
~~INTELLIGENCE SUMMARY.~~
(Erase heading not required.)

Army Form C. 2118.

Page 5.

Place	Date 1918	Hour	Summary of Events and Information	Remarks and references to Appendices
WIZERNES	AUG 30		The Battn arrived at ST MOMILIN and after a short 'Halt' for Tea, proceeded by march route to Billets in WIZERNES arriving there about 8 30 pm. Strength of Battn. 42 Officers 907 Other Ranks.	
	31		Battn at Rest. The day was spent in cleaning up and bathing. The following Officers joined the Battn for duty 2/Lieut. R. J. Metherell " W. B. Hobb " F. Hobbs J.G.H.S. Russell H.W.H. George	

B Morris Lt/Col Major
Comdg. 10th Bn. R. W. Kent Regt

D. D. & L., London, E.C.
(A10266) Wt W5300/P713 750,000 2/18 Sch. 52 Forms/C2118/16.

SECRET

Copy No

10th Bn. R.W. Kent Regt

Operation Order No. 26

Aug 1st 1918

Ref. Sheet 28 SW 1 - KEMMEL
& Sheet 27.

1. The Battn. will be relieved on the night of the 2/3rd Aug. by "Y" Composite Bn. (½ 23rd Middx Regt. and ½ 2nd. Bn. 108 Regt. U.S.A.) Companies will be relieved as under :-

D. Coy KENTS (L. Front) (+ attached A Coy Platoon) } by B. Coy "Y" Bn & 1 Platoon C. Coy Y Bn

B. Coy KENTS - by A Coy Y. Bn

C. " " - by D " Y. Bn

A. (less 1 Platoon) - by C " Y. Bn (less 1 Platoon)

2. Advance Party. The advance Party of Y Bn. already present will not stay in line merely take over and return to their Unit.

One N.C.O. per Coy of the KENTS ~~will~~ and 1 man per Platoon, will report at Bn. H.Qr. at 5 AM tomorrow (2nd) bringing rations for 2nd. They will be despatched to take over the accomodation in L. 29. area, vacated by the 23rd Middx. Regt.

3. The Battn., on Relief, will move by Platoons to the L. 29. Area. The guides detailed in para 2. will meet their respective Platoons at LOYE Cross Rds. L. 35. d. 1. 5. (Sheet 27) and guide them to their accommodation.

4. Attachment. Capt HINDLE (MC) and 1 officer each from A, B, C Coys. and 5 N.C.Os per Coy. will report to O/C. 23rd Middx Regt at (Sheet 27) ~~[illegible]~~ L. 29. c. 8. 2. at 12 noon tomorrow 2nd.inst. They will be attached to "Y" Composite Bn. for an indefinite period. They will be able to act as guides to "Y" Bn, coming in. The Quartermaster will arrange with the Middx Q.M for their Rationing while attached.

5. On relief all Trench Stores, Defence Schemes, Program of Work Reports, and sketches & Programmes of Work, permanent Working Parties & all information regarding dispositions will be carefully handed. Receipts for

Trench Stores must be obtained in duplicate and one copy MUST REACH THIS OFFICE BY TWELVE NOON 3RD INST.

6 Rations. The Q.M. will arrange for rations for 3rd to be delivered at new area (L. 29.)

7. Petrol Tins. The T.O. will arrange to have 1 Limbers at usual ration dump (near Brigade H.Qrs.) at 11-p.m. Companies and Headquarters will arrange to have ALL Petrol Tins at the Ration dump by this time. L/Cpl Munday will see that all ~~cans~~ cans are put on the limbers and will not allow the limber to depart until all Tins are on. He will proceed to Transport Lines with the limber.

8. All mess Kit, Officers Trench bundles & Medical Stores will be dumped at the ration dump at 11-p.m.

The Transport Officer will arrange for a limber to be at the ration dump to convey these to the new Area.

9. Lewis Guns. The T.O. will arrange to have the L.G. limbers at the Ration Dump at 11-pm to take Lewis Guns to new area. Each Coy. will send one Lewis Gunner down in charge of the limber. NOTE. In case of shelling of ration Dump, horses will be unhooked and taken to a safe distance. The limbers will not be moved until their load is complete.

10. Coys. will notify completion of Relief in Support Line by Runner & will similarly report arrival in billets in new area

11 Acknowledge

(Sd) R O RUSSELL
Lt & A/Adjt.
10th R.W. Kent Regt

Copies to:-

1	C.O.	5	O/C A	9	Bde. H.Q.	13	23rd Middx
2	Adjt	6	" B	10	TO & QM	14	RSM
3	Office	7	" C	11	O/C Details		O/C Y. Bn
4	W Dy	8	" D	12	HQ Officers		O/C KIKI.

SECRET.

10th Battn Royal West Kent Regt. Copy No. 5.

Operation Order No 27.

Maps: Sheets 27 & 28. Aug 8th 1918.

1. The Battalion will relieve the 15th Bn. Hampshire Regt. in the Reserve Line in the ZEVECOTEN area tonight.

2. Companies will take over as follows:—

D on the Right
A. in the Centre
C. on the Left
B in the Rear.

B.H.Q. will be at M 35. C. 35. 40.

3. The Battalion will move as follows.

H.Q. A. B. C. D Companies. An interval of 100 yards will be maintained between platoons. H.Q. will be ready to move from billets at 8. PM. followed by the leading platoon of "A" Company. Remaining companies will take up their positions in the line of march as specified above.

DRESS. Fighting order less greatcoat. S.B.Rs at alert. ~~Housewifes~~ will be carried.

4. Companies will take their 8 Lewis Guns. These will be carried on the man. A.A. Guns will be mounted before daybreak.

5. WATER. All water bottles will be filled before leaving billets. When in the ZEVECOTEN area, no water except that brought up by the Transport may be consumed. Transport will bring up 17 Tins per company, and 12 for B.H.Q.

6. RATIONS. for the 9th inst will be carried on the man.

7. All men for Courses commencing on or before 10th inst and other personnel for the Transport Lines will parade under the R.S.M. at 5 pm in full marching order at B.H.Q. They will proceed to Transport Lines under the command of the Senior N.C.O.

8. Companies and Lieut Percival for H.Q. will render a marching out state by 7. p.m tonight.

9. Packs of men proceeding to the line will be dumped by companies at B.H.Q. by 2 pm.
O.C. Companies will ensure that every pack is clearly marked with the owners Company, name and Regtl number.
All soft caps will be left in mens packs.

10. Officers Valises will be dumped at B.H.Q. by 2. p.m.
Officers Trench Bundles will be dumped at B.H.Q by 8.30 pm.

12. Completion of Relief will be notified to H.Q by runner.

13. Acknowledge.

(Sgd) T. E. Tatham.
Lt + A/Adj
10th Bn R.W. Kent Regt.

P.T.O

SECRET. Copy No. 3.

10th Bn. ROYAL WEST KENT REGT.

OPERATION ORDER No.28
****

Ref:- Map Sheet 28 S.W.1. 11th August 18

1.- The Battalion will relieve the 12th Bn. East Surrey Regt. in Support to-night.

2.- Companies will take over from their opposite numbers -

Dispositions.- "A" Coy. in Front Line under Command of O.C. 12th East Surrey Regt.
"B" Coy. Left Front Support N 1 c and d area.
"C" Coy. Left Reserve N 6 b area, with 2 Platoons in Strong Point at N 6 a 80.80.
"D" Coy. Right Front Support in MURRUMBIDGEE CAMP.

"D" Coy. and 2 Platoons of "C" Coy. will be held in reserve.

3.- GUIDES and ADVANCE PARTY.

"A" Coy. will detail 1 Officer and 1 N.C.O. who will be taken to the position the Company is to occupy by Guides from the 12th E.Surrey Regt. and 18th K.R.R.C. They will reconnoitre the position, take over stores etc., and remain in the position until the Company arrives.

The Company will be conducted to the line by Guides from the 18th K.R.R.C.

"B" and "D" Companies will detail 1 Officer and 1 N.C.O. who will reconnoitre their positions, take over stores etc., and return to N 6 d 75.80. where they will meet their Companies and guide them in.

"C" Company will detail the C.S.M. and 2 Other Ranks who will act similarly. One N.C.O. will reconnoitre and take over the Strong Point at N 6 a 80.80.

All Guides will report at B.H.Q. at G.36.c.80.35 at 7.15 p.m. to-day 11th inst.

Guides from 18th K.R.R.C. will meet "A" Coy. at N 1 c 8.1. and take the company right in.

4.- RATIONS.

"A" Coy. will issue rations to the men before leaving their present position.

Limber will be up by 9.15 p.m.

B, C, and D Coys. rations will be dumped at N 6 d 75.80 where ration parties will report as soon as possible after relief is complete.

5.- WATER. "A" Coy's will be dumped at N 6 d 75.80 and will be carried up by the company.

6.- Relief complete will be notified to H.Q. by runner.
"A" Coy. will also notify 12th East Surrey Regt.

7.- No movement will take place before 8.45 p.m.
Times will be notified later.

8.- Lists of Trench Stores etc, Defence Schemes and Maps taken over will be sent to B.H.Q. by 4 p.m. 12th inst.

9.- Acknowledge.

(sd) Trevor E. Tatham
Lieut.A/Adjt.
10th Bn.Royal West Kent Rgt.

Copies to:-
No. 1 C.O.
2 Adjt.
3 War Diary.
4 O.C. A Coy.
No. 5 O.C. B Coy.
6 O.C. C Coy.
7 O.C. D Coy.
8 122 Bde.
No. 9 123rd Bde.
10 Office.
11 T.O. & Q.M.
12 12th E.Surreys
No.13 18th K.R.R.C.

Copies to:- No.- 1 Commanding Officer.
2 Second-in-Command.
3 Adjutant.
4 War Diary.
5 Office copy.
6 O.C., 'A' Coy.
7 " 'B' "
8 " 'C' "
9 " 'D' "
10 Lewis Gun Officer.
11 Transport Officer.
12 Medical Officer.
13 Quartermaster.
14 R. S. M.
15 15th Hampshire Regt.
16 123rd Infantry Brigade.

S E C R E T.   Copy No. 3

10th Bn. ROYAL WEST KENT REGT.

OPERATION ORDER No. 31.

Ref. Sheet 28 S.W.1.   25th August 1918.

1.- The Battalion will relieve the 18th Bn. King's Royal Rifle Corps in the Line on the night of 26th/27th August 1918.

2.- DISPOSITIONS. B.H.Q. N 1 c 5.0.
'D' Coy. OUTPOST LINE.
One Platoon of 'A' Coy. in Support of Outpost Line on the Left.
One Platoon of 'C' Coy. -do- -do- -do- on the right.
'B' Coy. Left Company SCHERPENBERG - DICKEBUSCH LINE.
'A' Coy. Centre Company -do- -do- -do- -do-
'C' Coy. Right Company -do- -do- -do- -do-

3.- GUIDES. 18th K.R.R.C. send to 10th R.W.Kent Regt.

1 Guide per Post from the Outpost Company	= 8
1 Guide from each of Support Platoons of Outpost Coy.	= 2
1 Guide from Outpost Company H.Q.	= 1
1 Guide per Platoon & 1 per Coy.H.Q.from Left Coy.	= 5
1 Guide per Platoon & 1 per Coy.H.Q. from Centre Coy.	= 4
1 Guide per Platoon, 1 from isolated L.G.Section and 1 from Coy.H.Q. Right Coy.	= 6

All these guides will be at H.Q. 18th K.R.R.C. N 1 c 5.0. at 9.45 p.m. 26th inst.

4.- ADVANCE PARTY. 10th R.W.Kent Regt. send to 18th K.R.R.C. an exactly similar party to above.
This party will report at H.Q. N 1 c 5.0. at 12 m.n.tonight 25th inst.

5.- RATIONS and WATER. A double issue of rations and water will be made on the night of the 25th inst. These rations will be carried to the line by Companies.
Empty water tins will be dumped at B.H.Q. G 35 c 4.4. at 8.30 p.m. 26th inst. together with Company mess boxes.
The Transport Officer will detail a limber to be at G 35 c 4.4. at 9.15 p.m. 26th inst to take mess boxes etc. to new H.Q. at N 1 c 5.0.
This limber will load empty water tins at G 35 c 4.4. on its return and will convey same to transport lines.

6.- 'D' Company will move at 9.30 p.m. followed by 'C' 'B' and 'A' Companies in that order.
All movement will be by Platoons at 100 yards interval.

7.- Relief complete will be notified to B.H.Q. either by runner or by wiring name of O.C. Company.

8.- Acknowledge.

(sd) Trevor E.Tatham Lt.A/Adjt.
10th Bn.Royal West Kent Regt.

Issued to.-

No. 1 C.O.	No. 8 18th K.R.R.C.
2 Adjt.	9 122nd Inf.Bde.
3 War Diary.	10 123rd Inf.Bde.
4 O.C. 'A' Coy.	11 T.O. & Q.M.
5 O.C. 'B' Coy.	12 Office.
6 O.C. 'C' Coy.	13 M.O.
7 O.C. 'D' Coy.	14 15th Hants.Regt.

S E C R E T 10th Bn. ROYAL WEST KENT REGT. Copy No. 1

OPERATION ORDER No.32

****

Ref.Sheet 28 S.W.1. 28th August 1918

1.- The Battalion will be relieved on the night of 29th/30th August 1918 by the 2nd Loyal North Lancashire Regt. and will move to 'A' Area. WIZERNES

2.- Companies will detail one N.C.O. each as Advance Party. They will report to B.H.Q. as soon as practicable to-night and will proceed to K 24 c 9.8 whence they will proceed by lorry to ST. MARTIN AU LAERT. Lorries will leave Embussing Point K 24 c 9.3. at 6 a.m. 29th inst. Rev.R.F.BURNETT C.F. will be in charge of this party. On arrival at ST MARTIN AU LAERT he will report to the Staff Captain or his representative at the Area Commandant's Office at 11 a.m.

3.- On relief Companies will proceed by Platoons to LOYE CROSS ROADS where they will close up. Two guides per Company will be met at this point to conduct Companies to the Entraining Point.
One Officer per Company and one N.C.O. per Platoon will remain with the relieving unit for 24 hours after relief. At the end of this period the party will reportto Captain Sir W.A. BLOUNT.Bart. who will remain at H.Q.

4.- Lewis Gun limbers will be at M 6 d 80.80 at 11.30 p.m. 29th inst. Companies will instruct their Lewis Gun N.C.O's to be as this point at 11.30 p.m. to superintend the packing of the guns and ammunition. They will remain until all their guns and ammunition are packed.
Platoons will dump their guns and ammunition at their own limber as they come out.

5.- Two day's rations will be issued tonight for consumption 29th - 30th August. Those for 30th will be dumped at the entraining point LOYE and will be distributed on arrival of Companies.

6.- Empty water tins which are in the line on the night of 29th/30th will be handed over to the incoming unit together with all ammunition, gum boots, trench stores, defence schemes, dispositions, progress of work reports, and all information obtained from Patrols etc.
Receipts will be obtained and forwarded to H.Q. on arrival at the entraining Point.

7.- Only light trench bundles can be taken on the trains. All possible surplus kit, mess boxes etc. must be sent to the Transport Lines tonight 28th inst.

8.- Arrangements are being made to supply the troops with tea on arrival at the entraining point, if possible.

9.- Relief complete to be reported to these H.Q. personally by Company Commanders.

10.Acknowledge.

(sd) Trevor E.Tatham
Lieut.A/Adjt.
10th Bn.Royal West Kent Rgt.

Issued to:-

Copy No.		No.	
1	C.O.	7	O.C. 'D' Coy.
2	Ajt.	8	123rd Inf.Bde.
3	War Diary.	9	2nd L.N.Lancs.
4	O.C. 'A' Coy.	10	Office.
5	O.C. 'B' Coy.	11	T.O. & Q.M.
6	O.C. 'C' Coy.	12	M.O.

123/41

Instructions regarding War Diaries and Intelligence Summaries are contained in F. S. Regs., Part II. and the Staff Manual respectively. Title pages will be prepared in manuscript.

WAR DIARY
or
INTELLIGENCE SUMMARY.
(Erase heading not required.)

September 1918 Army Form C. 2118.

10 R W Kent Rgt

WO 29

Place	Date	Hour	Summary of Events and Information	Remarks and references to Appendices
WIZERNES	1st		Battalion at WIZERNES. The day occupied by Bathing and issue of new clothing. Preparing for move.	O.O 33
	2nd	9am	Battn. entrained at WIZERNES and detrained at ABEELE, thence proceeded by Route March to REMY.	
		10pm	Relieved 10th Bn "Queen's" R.W. Surrey Regt in Divisional Reserve Area	O.O 35
Sheet 28. S.F G.04.b.7.6	3rd		Battn. in Div. Reserve Area.	
	4th	5am	Battn. Stood to ready to move in support of attacking troops	
DICKEBUSCH AREA	5th		Battn. in Brigade Reserve, relieved 10th "Queen's" in support to LEFT BATTN.	
			Battn. moved to DICKEBUSCH LAKE AREA Bn H.Q at H 28. d, 5.2. (near Lake)	O.O 36
			Transport Lines moved to BUSSEBOOM Sheet 28 G21. b. 2.7.	
			Capt. J. LINDSAY rejoined Battn from Sick Leave to U.K.	
			Strength of Battalion Officers 46 Other Ranks 915.	
	6th		Battn in DICKEBUSCH AREA. Lt. Col. the Hon. G.R. Thesiger, rejoined from Leave and took over Command of Battn. in the line.	
			Battalion Headquarters heavily shelled.	
	7th		Enemy attacked Middlesex Regt on our right with strong raiding party. No change in situation.	
	7/8th		A re-adjustment of the disposition of Companies took place during the night.	O.O 37
	8th		Battalion relieved 26th Bn Royal Fusiliers in Front Line	
			Bn H.Q. at N.4 central.	O.O 38
	9th } 10th }		Situation unchanged.	

G.R. Thesiger

D. D. & L., London, E.C.
(A10206) Wt W5300/P713 750,000 2/18 Sch. 52 Forms/C2118/16.

Page II

September 1918

Continued:-

Army Form C. 2118.

Instructions regarding War Diaries and Intelligence Summaries are contained in F. S. Regs., Part II. and the Staff Manual respectively. Title pages will be prepared in manuscript.

WAR DIARY
or
INTELLIGENCE SUMMARY.
(Erase heading not required.)

Place	Date	Hour	Summary of Events and Information	Remarks and references to Appendices
DICKEBUSCH AREA	11th		Adjustment of Companies to enable the Front Line to be held by 2 Coys.	O.O. 39
			Battn. relieved by 23rd Middlesex Regt. & moved to Right Support Area	O.O. 40
	12th		Lieut. H. P. Johnson rejoined from Wounded.	
			Lieut. F E E. NORRIS, returned from Duty at 41st Div. Reception Camp.	
			Strength of Battalion Officers 46 Other Ranks 897	
	13th		Enemy Artillery very active on Company positions.	
	14th		Battn. relieved by 15th Bn. Hampshire Regt. & proceeded to the Support Area, Left sub. sector, relieving the 10th Bn. "Queen's" Regt.	O.O. 41
	15/17		Enemy shelled support Area at intervals, otherwise Situation unchanged.	
	18/19		Battn. ~~vacated~~ support Area and entrained at HALLEBAST SIDING at 5 am for DALLINGTON CAMP. LAPPE AREA.	O.O. 42
LAPPE AREA SHEET 27. L.29.	19th		Battn. detrained at REMY NORTH, and moved to billets in LAPPE AREA.	
			BN. H.Q. at L.29. c.8.2.	
			Strength of Battalion - Officers 46 Other Ranks 853. Casualties for period 2-18th KILLED & DIED of W'DS. 3. WOUNDED 22.	
	20		Battn. resting & cleaning up.	
	21/22		Bathing & refitting Coys. with new Clothing etc.	
			During the afternoon of the 21st the enemy shelled Billets with long range gun. Three shells hit Farm occupied by 'A' Company causing several Casualties. Stretcher bearing parties were quickly organised and the Wounded removed to REMY C.C.S.	
			Total Casualties incurred:- Killed & Died of Wounds 3. Wounded 9. Wounded, at Duty 6.	[signature]

D. D. & L., London, E.C.
(A10266) Wt W5300/P713 750,000 2/18 Sch. 52 Forms/C2118/16.

Instructions regarding War Diaries and Intelligence Summaries are contained in F. S. Regs., Part II. and the Staff Manual respectively. Title pages will be prepared in manuscript.

WAR DIARY or INTELLIGENCE SUMMARY.

(Erase heading not required.)

Page 111

September 1918

Continued

Army Form C. 2118.

Place	Date	Hour	Summary of Events and Information	Remarks and references to Appendices
LAPPE AREA (CONT)	23/26		Battalion Training. Bathing etc during this period	
DOMINION CAMP Sheet 28 (3)	27th		Battalion left Dallington Camp, and proceeded by Route March to Dominion Camp and billetted there for the night. Strength of Battn. OFFICERS 45 OTHER RANKS 843	O.O. 43
G17.a - G11.c	28th		Battalion paraded at 7.30 am, and marched to LEICESTER FARM, resting here for 4 hours, then proceeded to RAVINE WOOD. At dusk Battn. proceeded to E. Side of YPRES-COMINES CANAL, in vicinity of Lock No 6.	
(Detailed account below)	29th		At Daybreak Battn. assembled on E. Side of Lock No 6 and attacked, reaching line E. of HOUTHEM. Battn. relieved at night by 10th QUEENS	
HOUTHEM.	30th		Battn. marched to HOUTHEM and rested.	
			Casualties for period 29-30th Sept were as follows:-	
			Officers. Died of Wounds 2/Lt. J.G.H.S. RUSSELL. 29th.	
			WOUNDED:- CAPT. G.W. HINDLE, M.C. CAPT. L. DOUBLEDAY.	
			✱ since Died of Wounds. ✱ 2/LT. S.R. HICKMOTT 2/LT. H.W.H. GEORGE.	
			" S.R. LAWRENCE. " J.C. HUDSON	
			✱ LIEUT. F.E.E. NORRIS	
			Other Ranks:- KILLED (Died of wds) 35 WOUNDED. 90 MISSING 20	
2 right 2 left	29th	Continued	At 5.35 am the Battalion formed up to attack down the Eastern sides of the YPRES-COMINES CANAL, final objective being E. of HOUTHEM and 500 yards north of COMINES Railway Station. The 23rd Bn. Middlesex Regt. had their left on the Canal, and their Right 600 yards EAST. The 10th Kents attacked on a 1200 yard front on the Middlesex Left. Both Battalions passed through the Outpost line of the 124 Brigade at KORTWILD	[illegible signature]

D. D. & L., London, E.C. (A10266) Wt W5300/P713 750,000 2/18 Sch. 52 Forms/C2118/16.

Instructions regarding War Diaries and Intelligence Summaries are contained in F. S. Regs., Part II. and the Staff Manual respectively. Title pages will be prepared in manuscript.

WAR DIARY or INTELLIGENCE SUMMARY.

(Erase heading not required.)

SEPTEMBER 1918. Continued.

Army Form C. 2118.

Place	Date	Hour	Summary of Events and Information	Remarks and references to Appendices
	29th Continued.		The morning was fine but a ground fog hid the attack from the enemy. Several M.G. Posts were surprised and outflanked with little loss. Four Howitzers, a Battery of 4·2 taken at breakfast. Three 7.7cm captured, 40 Prisoners, 5 Machine Guns, and at 9.15 am the Battalion was on the COMINES. Railway Line, and the 23rd Bn. Middlesex Regt. had sent out Patrols to get in touch with the XVth Corps coming up from WARNETON. Casualties up to time of reaching objective 6.	
			Enemy seen flying in Motor Cars from COMINES, and from MESSINES in Motor Lorries.	
			Owing to the Brigade on the left not coming up and the XV Corps not gaining their objectives the 123 Brigade had made a salient of 4500 yards X 1800 yards. Both flanks of the 10th Kents were exposed and the enemy pushed out Machine Guns and enfiladed both flanks. 7.7 cm guns fired from other side of Canal into their backs over open sights.	
			The 10th Kents. Middlesex were compelled to withdraw to HOUTHEM. 2/Lt. E.F. WESTON, in Command of "B" Coy, and 3 Machine Guns covering the left flank. The enemy counter-attacked twice trying to recover his guns and lost heavily from Rifle Fire, Machine Guns and our Artillery Barrage leaving many dead in front of COMINES. That night the 10th QUEENS' relieved the 10th KENTS in the HOUTHEM LINE.	Pinstripe [signature]

D. D. & L., London, E.C. (A6036) Wt W5300/P713 750,000 2/18 Sch. 52 Forms/C2118/16.

Army Form C. 2118.

Instructions regarding War Diaries and Intelligence Summaries are contained in F. S. Regs., Part II. and the Staff Manual respectively. Title pages will be prepared in manuscript.

WAR DIARY
or
INTELLIGENCE SUMMARY.
(Erase heading not required.)

SEPTEMBER 1918
continued:

Place	Date	Hour	Summary of Events and Information	Remarks and references to Appendices
	29th continued		This was the Battalion's first experience this year in open warfare, and the men had thoroughly learnt the lessons of encircling machine Guns and keeping their extension. The losses up to the final objective being only 6 proving this, as they worked at times under very heavy machine Gun fire from front and both flanks. The leading and direction in a thick ground fog was excellent Total Casualties for the day. Officers Wounded. 7. Other Ranks Killed & Died of Wds. 35. WOUNDED 90. MISSING 20.	

[signature]
Lt Colonel
Comdg 10th Bn R West Kent Regt

D. D. & L., London, E.C.
(A10206) Wt W5300/P713 750,000 2/18 Sch. 52 Forms/C2118/16.

SECRET. OPERATION ORDER NO: 33 1st Sept 1918

1. The battalion will move to the ABEELE area tomorrow 2nd inst.

2. The battalion will entrain at WISERNES.
Companies will proceed to the station in the following order "A" "B" "C" "D".
"A" Company will arrive at the station at 8·15 A.M. the remaining companies will follow independently.

3. Rations and water for the day will be carried on the man.
Camp kettles will be taken.

4. On arrival at the station Os C. companies will hand in a return shewing their entraining strength to H.Q.

5. One motor lorry will report to Qr: Mr: Stores at 8·30 AM for surplus kit and when loaded, will proceed to ABEELE aerodrome and await orders before off loading.
The Qr: Mr: will detail a small advance party to accompany this lorry.

6. On night 2nd – 3rd 123rd Infantry Brigade will relieve the 124th Infantry Brigade in the 27th American Division Reserve area.

7. Acknowledge.

1.9.18

Trevor E. Tatham
Lt. A/Adjt

SECRET

10th Bn. ROYAL WEST KENT REGT.

OPERATION ORDER No.35.
****

Ref.Sheet 28 S.W. 1/20,000 3rd September 1918.

1.- The advance will be resumed tomorrow morning 4th September 1918 to the 2nd Objective, i.e. the line KRUISSTRAAT Cab.- PECKHAM - E.edge of PETIT BOIS - Cross Roads O 13 c 4.7. thence N. along road to Cross Roads O 1 a 12.38.
Should resistance met with be slight the advance from this line will be continued to the line MESSINES - ST.ELOI Road, which when taken, will be consolidated and have outposts pushed out in front of it.

2.- The Division will be disposed as follows:-
122nd Infantry Brigade and 1 Coy. 41st Bn.M.G.C. on the Right.
124th Inf.Bde. and 1 Coy.41st Bn.M.G.C. on the Left.
Dividing Line between Brigades, a line running from N 11 d (central) through Pts.O 7 c 9.7. and O 8 a 7.2.

3.- The 123rd Inf.Bde. and 1 Coy.41st Bn.M.G.C. will be in Reserve and will stand to in their present positions ready to move at 1 hour's notice.

4.- Zero Hour will probably be at 5.30 a.m. on the 4th September.

5.- The following Boundaries are laid down as a guide to the direction which the Division would take in following up and pressing the enemy in his retirement:-

Southern Boundary

N 22 a 7.2.
Road to N 24 a 0.6. (inclusive to Right Division.)
Southern corner of GRAND BOIS (O 13 c 8.7.)
MARTENS FARM (O 8.d.)

NORTHERN BOUNDARY.

MOATED GRANGE.
O 4. central.
ZANDVOORDE.

6.- In accordance with these Orders Companies will Stand to in their billet positions at 5.30 a.m. and will be ready to move at 6.30 a.m. if necessary.
The Commanding Officer will see all Company Commanders at 'D' Coy.H.Q. at 6 a.m. tomorrow, 4th inst.

(sd) Trevor E.Tatham.
Lieut.A/Adjt.
10th Bn.Royal West Kent Regt.

Issued to A, B, C, and D Coy .

SECRET Copy No. 3

10th Bn. ROYAL WEST KENT REGT.

OPERATION ORDER No.88

Ref. Sheet 28. 8th September 1918.

1.- The Battalion will relieve the 26th Bn. Royal Fusiliers in the Line to-night.

2.- Companies will be disposed as follows in accordance with the reconnaissance carried out last night:-

Battalion H.Q.	N 4 central dugouts.
'A' Company.	Left Front Company.
'B' Company.	Centre Front Company.
'C' Company.	Right Front Company.
'D' Company.	Support Company.

3.- Advance Parties will be detailed as follows:-
1 Officer per Company and 1 N.C.O. per Platoon.

Lieut.A.S.F. PERCIVAL will proceed to H.Q. 26th Royal Fusiliers and will take over all documents etc.

Advance Parties will report at H.Q. 26th Royal Fusiliers at N 4 central at 6.00 p.m.

They will proceed to Companies and will take over all Trench Stores, Defence Scheme, Progress of Work reports, Patrol Reports etc.

Special care will be taken with regard to Petrol Tins.

Receipts will be taken in duplicate and a copy sent to H.Q. when reporting relief complete.

4.- Guides from 26th Royal Fusiliers will meet Companies at N 6 a 5.8 at 9.15 p.m.
At this point (N 6 a 5.8.) Companies will each leave 1 N.C.O. per Platoon to guide Platoons of 26th Royal Fusiliers back to their positions in the area now occupied by this unit.

5.- Rations and Water will be dumped to-night by limbers at N 10 b 6.6. Ration Parties will collect these as soon as possible after relief.

6.- Companies will move as follows:-

'A' Company 8.30 p.m.	'B' Company 9.15 p.m.
'C' Company 9.40 p.m.	'D' Company 10 p.m.

All movement will be by platoons at 100 yds interval.

7.- Relief complete will be notified to B.H.Q. at N 4 central by runner or by wiring name of Os.C. Companies.

8.- Acknowledge.

(sd) Trevor E.Tatham
Lieut.A/Adjt.
10th Bn.Royal West Kent Rgt

Issued to:-

No. 1 C.O.
2 Adjt.
3 War Diary.
4 O.C. A Coy.
5 O.C. B Coy.
6 O.C. C Coy.
7 O.C. D Coy.
8 26th R.Fusiliers.
9 123rd Inf. Bde.
10 T.O. & Q.M.
11 M.O.
12 File.

S E C R E T. Copy No. 11

10th Bn. ROYAL WEST KENT REGT.

****

OPERATION ORDER NO.36.

****

Ref. Sheet 28. 5/9/18.

1.- The Battalion will move forward to the DICKEBUSCH LAKE Area to-night.

2.- Dispositions. B.H.Q. H 28 d 5.2.

'B' Company immediately W. of VIERSTRAAT - ELZENWALLE Road.
'A' Coy. in rear of 'B' Coy. towards DICKEBUSCH LAKE.
'C' Company between ~~xxix~~ RIDGE WOOD and main VIERSTRAAT - HALLEBAST Road and N.W. of VIERSTRAAT - ELZENWALLE Road.
'D' Company between RIDGE WOOD and VIERSTRAAT - HALLEBAST Road and N.W. of CHEAPSIDE.

3.- Advance Parties of 1 Officer per Company, and 1 N.C.O. per Platoon, and 1 Officer and 1 N.C.O. from B.H.Q. will proceed to the new area at 4 p.m. to-day as already detailed.
They will take over all documents, ammunition and trench stores, special attention being paid to Water Tins.
The latter must be carefully checked.
They will meet their Companies at H 29 c 3.0. at 10 p.m. and guide them to their positions.

4.- Rations will be brought to these H.Q. as usual.
All water bottles will be filled before the Battalion moves as none will be brought up to-night in tins.

5.- Companies will move off as follows:-

'C' 'D' 'B' 'A'

'C' Company will start at 9 p.m. or as soon as rations are issued. Companies will not move off before 9 p.m.

6.- Lewis Guns and ammunition will be carried on the man.

7.- All surplus kit will be returned by ration limbers.
Officers trench bundles will be dumped at these H.Q. by 8.30 p.m.

8.- Relief complete will be notified to H.Q. by runner together with a rough sketch of Dispositions, if possible.

9.- Acknowledge.

(sd) Trevor E. Tatham'
Lieut. A/Adjt.
10th Bn. Royal West Kent Regt.

Issued to:-

Copy No. 1 C.O.
No. 2 Adjt.
No. 3 War Diary.
No. 4 O.C. A Coy.
No. 5 O.C. B Coy.
No. 6 O.C. C Coy.
No. 7 O.C. D Coy.
No. 8 T.O. & Q.M.
No. 9 123rd I.B.
No.10 M.O.
No.11 File.

SECRET   Copy No. 3

10th Bn. ROYAL WEST KENT REGT.

OPERATION ORDER No.37.

Ref. Map Sheet 28.   7th September 1916.

1.- A re-adjustment of the Dispositions of Companies will be carried out to-night 7th/8th inst. as follows:-

2.- 'C' Company will move into the area of ELZENWALLE CHATEAU.
'B' Company will side-step to the right to make room for them.
'A' Company will return to their original positions.
'D' Company will bring back two platoons to the H 35 a area at present occupied by two platoons of 'A' Company.
The remaining two platoons of 'D' Company will remain in the H 35 d area central area.
Map showing these new dispositions is attached.
O.C. Companies will choose the location of their Headquarters as suits them best. Pin-Points of new H.Q. will be sent to this H.Q. as soon as this has been done.
If desired 'B' and 'C' Company H.Q. can remain in ELZENWALLE CHATEAU.

3.- All rations and water will be dumped at B.H.Q. tonight, whence they will be carried to Companies by ration parties.

4.- Completion of these moves will be notified to these H.Q. by using name of O.C. Company.

5.- Acknowledge.

NOTE. These re-adjustments do not effect the orders for reconnoitring the Front Line. This reconnaissance should be carried out as arranged.

(sd) Trevor L.Tatham.
Lieut.A/Adjt.
10th Bn. Royal West Kent Regt.

Issued to:-
Copy No. 1 C.O.
No. 2 Adjt.
No. 3 War Diary.
No. 4 O.C. A Coy.
No. 5 O.C. B Coy.
No. 6 O.C. C Coy.
No. 7 O.C. D Coy.

SECRET

Copy No. 11

10thBn. ROYAL WEST KENT REGT.

OPERATION ORDER No. 40

Ref. Map Sheet 28 and 28 S.W.2

11/9/18

1.- The Battalion will berelieved tomorrow night 12th/13th inst. by 23rd Middlesex Regt. and will proceed tothe Right Support area at present occupied by the latter.

2.- Companies will take over from their opposite numbers and will be disposed asfollows.-

Battalion H.Q. N10 a 3.3.

'A' Company in area N 10 a 6.3.

'B' Company in area N 10 b 9.9.- N 4 d 2.2.

'C' Company in area N4 d 5.6.

'D' Company will remain in their present positions as re-adjusted tonight.

3.- Advance Parties consisting of 1 Officer per Company, 1 N.C.O. per Coy.H.Q. and 1 N.C.O.per Platoon will be detailed by Companies. They will leave the line tonight and will report to H.Q. 23 Middlesex Regt. at 12 noon 12thinst., whence they will proceed to their Companies and take over as usual.

Similar advance parties from the 23rd Middlesex Regt. will report to Companies tonight.

All hot-food containers and other trench stores will be handed over.

4.- Guides/-

4.- Guides. The Advance party from each Battalion will act as guides.

The Advance Party of 23rd Middlesex Regt. accompanied by the rear party 10th Royal West Kent Regt. will be at the BRASSERIE (N 6 a 1.1.) at 8.30 p.m. 12th inst. where they will meet their platoons and guide them to their positions.

The Advance Party 10th R.W.Kent Regt. will be at the BRASSERIE (N 6 a 1.1.) at 10 p.m. 12th inst. where they will similarly meet their platoons and guide them to their new positions.

5.- Rear Party of 1 Officer per Company and 1 N.C.O. per Platoon will be left with the relieving unit for 24 hours.

6.- Rations and Water will be dumped at cross tracks at N 10 b 1.9.) whence they will be fetched byration parties after relief is complete. All empty petroltins will be brought out by Companies and none will be handed over.

7.- Relief complete will be notified to new H.Q. either by runner orby wiring name of O.C. Coy.

8.- Acknowledge.

(sd) Trevor E. Tatham
Lieut.A/Ajt.
10th Royal West Kent Rgt.

Copy No. 1 C.O.
No. 2 Ajt.
No. 3 ACoy.
No. 4 BCoy.
No. 7 123rd I.B.
No. 8 23rd Midd'x Rgt.
No. 9 T.O. & Q.M.
No. 10M.O.

SECRET

Copy No. 8

10th Bn. ROYAL WEST KENT REGT.

OPERATION ORDER No. 59

****

Ref. Map Sheet 28. 11th September 191[illegible]

1.- The following adjustment of Companies will take place tonight Sept. 11th/12th, so that the front line may be held two Companies only.

2.- 'A' Coy. A' Coy. will extend to their right and take over part of the front occupied by 'B' Coy. as far as the spot where the stream crosses the road at about O 7 a 3 .55

'B' Coy. B' Coy. will extend to the right Battalion Boundary and hold the front from O 7 a 3 .95 to the Battalion Boundary at about N 12 d 5 .7 having 4 platoons in the line. Company H.Q. will remain as at present at O 7 a 1 .8

'C' Coy. (a) The Platoon along the B gauge railway will remain.

(b) Two platoons when relieved by 'B' Coy. will take over from two platoons of 'D' Coy. in Reserve Trench in N 12 a

(c) The Platoon in the Forward Post will take over the Trench next 'B' Coy. H.Q. at about N 1[illegible] b 9.3.

These Platoons will come under the command of O.C. 'B' Coy.

Company H.Q. will remain at N 1[illegible] a 6.[illegible].

'D' Coy. The Two platoons in New Reserve Trench which are being relieved by two platoons of 'C' Coy. will move into the Trench behind from N11 b8.5. to N 1[illegible] a 9.6

A Party of 23rd Middlesex Regt. will work on this line in making accommodation tonight from 9 p.m. to 12 midnight and elephant shelters will be delivered and carried to the trench by this company.

(b) The two platoons in BOIS CARRE TRENCH will remain as at present.

3.- The Commanding Officer will meet Company Commanders of 'B' and 'C' Companies at N 6 d 35.35 at 9.1[illegible] p.m. to reconnoitre the new posts to be taken up by 'B' Coy.

4.- 'C' and 'D' Companies will each mount two Lewis Guns for A.A. defence in their areas.

5.- Completion of this exchange to be notified by the code word "FOOT POWDER"

(sd) Trevor E. Tatham Lieut. A/Adjt.
10th Royal West Kent Regt.

Issued to.-

Copy No. 1 C.O.

No. 2 Adjt.

No. 3 A Coy.

No. 4 B Coy.

No. 5 [illegible]

No. 6 D Coy.

No. 7 123rd I.B.

No. 8 spare.

S E C R E T

10th Bn. ROYAL WEST KENT REGT. Copy No. 1

OPERATION ORDER No. 41

Ref. Sheets 28 and 28 S.W.2. 13th September 1918

1.- The Battalion will be relieved by 15th Bn. Hampshire Regt. on the night of 14th/15th inst. and will proceed to the Support Area Left Sub-Sector relieving the 10th Bn. Queen's there.

2.- The four Companies of 15th Hampshire Regt. consisting of two platoons each will take over as follows:-

'A' Coy. Hants takes over from 3 Platoons 'A' Coy. Kents.
'B' " " " " " 1 Platoon 'A' and 2 Platoons 'C'.
'C' " " " " " 2 Platoons 'C' and 1 Platoon 'B'
'D' " " " " " 3 Left Platoons of 'B' Coy. Kents.

10th R.W.Kent Regt. will take over from 10th Queen's as follows
'A' Coy. Kents will relieve 'A' Coy. Queen's in Left Front Support with H.Q. at ELZENWALLE CHATEAU.
'C' Coy. Kents will relieve 'D' Coy. Queen's in Right Front Support.
'D' Coy. Kents willrelieve 'C' Coy. Queen's in the BUND on N.E. side of DICKEBUSCH LAKE.
'B' Coy. Kents will relieve 'B' Coy. Queen's in the BUND on N.W. side of DICKEBUSCH LAKE.

3.- Advance Parties will be detailed as follows:-
'B' and 'D' Companies 1 Officer per Company and 1 N.C.O. per Platoon.
'A' and 'C' Companies 1 Officer and 1 Runner each.
This party will report at H.Q. 10th Queen's at 2.30 p.m. 14th inst. and will arrange accommodation and take over all documents trench stores etc. as usual.
Advance Party from 15th Hants. will arrive at these H.Q. at 8.45 p.m. tonight and will consist of:-
1 Officer and 1 Runner per Company, 1 N.C.O. per Platoon, 1 N.C.O. and2 runners for H.Q.

4.- Guides will be detailed as follows:-
3 Guides for each Company of 15th Hampshire Regt.
'A' Coy. will supply 1 of these for Coy.H.Q. 'A' Coy. Hants.
'B' " " " 1 " " " " " 'B' Coy. Hants.
'C' " " " 2 " " " " " 'C' & 'D' "

In addition to the above
'A' Coy. will supply 2 Guides for the 2 Platoons of 'A' Hants.
'B' Coy. will supply 2 guides for the 2 Platoons of 'B' Hants.
'C' Coy. will supply 4 guides for the 4 platoons of 'C' & 'D' "
H.Q. will supply 1 guide for 15th Hampshire Regt. H.Q.
This party will be at BRANDENBURG (N 4 c 05.55) at 8.45 p.m. 14th inst. and will conduct 15th Hampshire Regt. to their positions. Men detailed for this duty must reconnoitre routes etc during the morning of 14th inst.
10th Queen's will supply guides (5 per Company) to conduct 'A' and 'C' Companies to their new positions.
These guides will be at N 5 c 9.8. on CHEAPSIDE-RIDGE WOOD ROAD by 9.15 p.m. 14th inst.
'B' and 'D' Companies will proceed without guides to the BUND via HALLEBAST CORNER where their advance party will meet them and conduct them to the BUND.

5.- Rations and Water will be dumped as follows:-
H.Q., 'B' and 'D' Companies at H.Q. DICKEBUSCH LAKE at 11 p.m.
'A' and 'C' Companies at Company H.Q. RIDGE WOOD ROAD at 10 p.m.
Os.C. 'A' and 'C' Companies will each detail 1 guide (who should accompany their advance party) to meet this limber at the R.A.P. Main VIERSTRAAT - HALLEBAST ROAD at 9.30 p.m. 14th.

6.- Special care will be taken in handing over and kaking over. Receipts will be taken in duplicate and a copy sent to H.Q. not later than 12 noon 15thinst.

Contd/-

7.- Relief complete will be notified to new H.Q. by wiring name of O.C. Company.

8.- Acknowledge.

(sd) Trevor E. Tatham
Lieut.A/Ajt.
10th Royal West Kent Regt.

Issued to:-

Copy No. 1 C.O.
No. 2 Ajt.
No. 3 War Diary.
No. 4 ACoy.
No. 5 B Coy.
No. 6 C Coy.
No. 7 D Coy.
No. 8 10th Queen's
No. 9 15th Hants.
No.10 123rd I.B.
No.11 T.O. & Q.M.
No.12 M.O.
No.13 File.
No.14 Int.Sgt.

120

S E C R E T.

Copy No. 3

10th Bn. ROYAL WEST KENT REGT.

OPERATION ORDER No. 42.
****

Reference Sheet 28. 18th September 1918.

1.- The Battalion will vacate the present area to-morrow, 19th inst. and will proceed to the LAPPE AREA.
New Headquarters will be at DALLINGTON CAMP L 29 c 8.2.

2.- The Battalion will entrain at HALLEBAST SIDING at 5 a.m. and detrain at REMY NORTH.
Trucks will accommodate 30 men each.
Entraining Strengths will be rendered to B.H.Q. on arrival at the Siding.

3.- Companies will each detail 1 Guide per Platoon to reconnoitre HALLEBAST SIDING. These Guides will report to H.Q. at 11 p.m. to-night and will meet their Companies at these H.Q. at 3.30 a.m. to-morrow.

4.- 'A' Company will move at 2.30 a.m. followed by 'C' Company at 3 a.m. and will proceed to these H.Q. where they will dump their Lewis Guns and Magazines, and Officers' Trench Bundles.
'B' Company will be ready to move at 3.45 a.m. and will be followed by 'D' Company.
All movement will be by Platoons at 100 yards interval.

5.- Lewis Gun Limbers will be at H.Q. at 2.30 a.m. and will be loaded under the supervision of Company Lewis Gun N.C.Os.

6.- Dumps of all Trench Stores of every kind, including Petrol Tins will be formed at each Company H.Q., and a list showing what each dump contains, together with the pin-point of same will be handed in to these H.Q. as each Company passes on its way out.

7.- An Officer from each Company will report "Area vacated and cleaned" to these H.Q.

8.- Breakfasts will be provided on arrival at Billets.

9.- Acknowledge.

(sd) Trevor E. Tatham
Lieut. A/Adjt.
10th Bn.Royal West Kent Regt.

Issued to.-

Copy No. 1 C.O.
No. 2 Adjt.
No. 3 War Diary.
No. 4 O.C. A Coy.
No. 5 O.C. B Coy.
No. 6 O.C. C Coy.
No. 7 O.C. D Coy.
No. 8 123rd I.B.
No. 9 T.O. & Q.M.
No.10 M.O.
No.11 File.

S E C R E T.   Copy No.

1 th Bn. ROYAL WEST KENT REGIMENT.

OPERATION ORDER No. 46.

****

Ref. Map Sheet 2 Edition 3.   27th September 1918

1.- The Battalion will move from the present area to-day and will proceed to the DOMINION CAMP area G 17 a - G 11 c.

2.- Starting Point.   CONDIMENT CROSS ROADS.
Time.   7.2 p.m.

3.- Order of March.   The order will be H.Q., A, B, C, D, Transport.
Companies will proceed to the Starting Point independently and should arrange to reach this point in time to take up their allotted positions in the line of March without a long halt on the road.
An interval of 1   yards will be maintained between Companies.

4.- Dress. Full Marching Order with blankets.

5.- Lewis Guns will be carried on the limbers.   Guns will be brought to B.H.Q. and packed at 3 p.m. under the supervision of the Company Lewis Gun N.C.Os.

6.- Advance Parties will be detailed by Companies as follows:-
H.Q.   2 N.C.Os.
Each Company.   1 Officer and 2 N.C.Os.
Transport.   2 N.C.Os.
This party will be under the command of Lieut. F.E.E. NORRIS and will parade at B.H.Q. at 4.3 p.m. to-day 27th inst.
The party will proceed to G 11 a 6.5. and will report to the Area Commandant BRANDHOEK.   They will arrange accommodation for the Battalion in the LINDE GOOD FARM, ERIE FARM, area G 17 c 8. and G 11 c 5 1
1st Line Transport will find temporary accommodation in G 14 c and d and G 2 a and b.
Application for bivouacs must ~~reach~~ be made to the Staff Captain at DOMINION CAMP between 5 p.m. and 7 p.m.

7.- Rations for 28th inst. will be carried on the Field Kitchens.
Water Bottles will be filled.

8.- All Officers not detailed for duty in the line will proceed to Divisional Reception Camp to-night.

9.- ACKNOWLEDGE.

(sd) Trever E. Tatham
Captain & Adjt.
10th Bn. Royal West Kent Regt.

Issued to:-
Copy No. 1 C.O.
2 War Diary.
3 Adjt.
4 O.C. 'A' Coy.
5 O.C. 'B' Coy.
6 O.C. 'C' Coy.
7 O.C. 'D' Coy.
8 123rd Inf. Bde.
9 T.O. & Q.M.
1 S.O.
11 File.
12 R.S.M.
13 M.O.

26 10th Battn. Royal West Kent Regt. October 1918. Army Form C. 2118.

WAR DIARY
or
INTELLIGENCE SUMMARY.
(Erase heading not required.)

Instructions regarding War Diaries and Intelligence Summaries are contained in F. S. Regs., Part II. and the Staff Manual respectively. Title pages will be prepared in manuscript.

Vol 30

Place	Date	Hour	Summary of Events and Information	Remarks and references to Appendices
HOUTHEM	1st		Ref. Sheet 28. 1/40000. Battalion left HOUTHEM at 9.10 AM. and got to the Camp off the Cross Roads at P15.d 5.3 at 11.30 AM. Remained here till 4 pm and were heavily shelled during this period.	
			The whole Brigade then marched to AMERICA CABt. through TENBRIELEN and were in full view of the Boche who was only 1500 yds away in COMINES. Heavy barrage of 5.9" + 4.2s etc. put down by enemy, which caused a certain amount of casualties.	
			Battalion rested at AMERICA CABt. for the night.	
	2nd		"B" + "C" Coy at noon ordered up to fill gap between 123 and 122 Bde, S. of GHELUWE. "B" Coy in the line + "C" in Support. at 17.00 touch established with 23rd Middlesex on right, and at 17.45 with 15th Hampshires on left.	
			Boche counter attacked at 18.00 on left and the left Battalion fell back, touch however was established by left platoon of "B" Coy. with the E. Surreys, who were in support to the left Battn.	
			Enemy came forward in large numbers but were mown down by our Combined Rifle, Lewis Gun and Machine Gun fire.	
			Boche fell back in disorder after this and both "B" + "C" Coys were relieved by 2/7 CHESHIRES at 03.45 next morning + rejoined Battn at AMERICA CABt.	

D. D. & L., London, E.C.
(A10266) Wt W5300/P713 750,000 2/18 Sch. 52 Forms/C2118/16.

PAGE II

October 1918. Army Form C. 2118.

WAR DIARY
or
INTELLIGENCE SUMMARY.
(Erase heading not required.)

Continued –

Instructions regarding War Diaries and Intelligence Summaries are contained in F. S. Regs., Part II. and the Staff Manual respectively. Title pages will be prepared in manuscript.

Place	Date	Hour	Summary of Events and Information	Remarks and references to Appendices
	3rd		Battalion proceeded to J35. B area for rest.	
			Strength of Battn. Officers 37. Other Ranks 673.	
	4th, 5th, 6th		Battalion resting in J35. B. area.	
	7th		Battalion relieved 26th Royal Fusiliers in area. K.27. relief successful	0046.
	7th, 8th, 9th, 10th		Situation unchanged. Enemy fairly quiet by day except for periods of shelling both at dawn & sunset.	
			By night our patrols were very active especially in vicinity of COOMBE FORK, where Hostile M.G. teams were bombed out on two successive nights by our Patrols.	
			Enemy wire was also cut in several places, by our patrols during tour in line.	
			Battalion relieved by 11th Queens on night of 10th/11th. Battn then proceeded to J35. B+C areas. Sheet 28.	0047
			Strength of Battalion :- Officers 37. Other Ranks 666.	
	11th		Battalion resting at J35 B+C areas	
	12th		Battalion moved to P.5 a. area. 18th K.R.R relieving Battn at J.35. B+C. areas	
	13th		Battalion Bathed, and Situation unchanged.	

D. D. & L., London, E.C.
(A10266) Wt W5300/P713 750,000 2/18 Sch. 52 Forms/C2118/16.

Page III
October 1918.
– Continued –

Army Form C. 2118.

Instructions regarding War Diaries and Intelligence Summaries are contained in F. S. Regs., Part II. and the Staff Manual respectively. Title pages will be prepared in manuscript.

WAR DIARY
or
INTELLIGENCE SUMMARY.
(Erase heading not required.)

Place	Date	Hour	Summary of Events and Information	Remarks and references to Appendices
	14th		II Army attacked at dawn after a very heavy barrage. Battalion moved from P5. at 7.30 A.M. across MENIN ROAD in artillery formation to open country NORTH of same. Slight gas shelling encountered. Got to SWAINE HOUSE in K29.d 2.7 at noon without a casualty and remained there. 123 Brigade in Divisional Reserve in this area.	
	15th		Battalion resting at K29 d. 2.7. Sheet 28.	
	16th		Battalion proceeded to MOORSEELE, and after resting 5 hours, went on to HEVLE via GULLEGHEM, where they remained in Brigade Reserve, who were holding the line of the LYS opposite COUTRAI.	

Continued PAGE IV.

D. D. & L., London, E.C.
(A10366) Wt W5300/P713 750,000 2/18 Sch. 52 Forms/C2118/16.

Page IV

October 1918.

Continued.

Army Form C. 2118.

Instructions regarding War Diaries and Intelligence Summaries are contained in F. S. Regs., Part II. and the Staff Manual respectively. Title pages will be prepared in manuscript.

WAR DIARY
or
INTELLIGENCE SUMMARY.
(Erase heading not required.)

Place	Date	Hour	Summary of Events and Information	Remarks and references to Appendices
NORTH OF GULLEGHEM.	~~16th~~		~~Battn proceeded to MOORSEELE and rested 5 Hours, then proceeded to G.16 d. (HEULE) area Sheet 29 N.W.~~	
	17th 18th 19th		Battn resting at G.16 d. (HEULE) area. Strength of Battn. Officers 46, O.Rs 672. Hostile Shelling very frequent. Enemy aircraft active during night, many bombs being dropped.	
	20th		Battn proceeded to COURTRAI, and billetted for the night.	
	21st	05.45	Battn left COURTRAI + proceeded to N4. d. 8.1, rested 4 hours, then proceeded to O7. c. 40.00	
	22nd		Battn rested at O.7 C. 40.00. and at dusk Battn went into Front Line to attack. Battn HQ at O17. a. 70.40.	
			Details of attack:- Ref Map. Sheet 29. 1/40,000.	
	23rd		Battn took up position on the road running from O.17.a. 2.4 to O12. C.0.2. order of Battle:- D. Coy on left. A Coy Centre, B on right and C in reserve. The final objective of the Battalion was the AVECGHEM — WAFFELSTRAAT ROAD. The Battn had to pass through and relieve on the way the 122nd Inf Bde who were holding a line, O.17. C. 5.1 to O17. a. 1.9. and make good the first objective which was the high ground 400 yards N. of HOOGMOLEN — VIERKEERHOEK ROAD. The left Coy was responsible for the clearing of the houses on the EAST side of the KATTESTRAAT — VIERKEERHOEK ROAD and 100 yds to the WEST of it.	

D. D. & L., London, E.C.
(A10266) Wt W5300/P713 750,000 2/18 Sch. 52 Forms/C2118/16.

PAGE V

October 1918 Continued —

Army Form C. 2118.

Instructions regarding War Diaries and Intelligence Summaries are contained in F. S. Regs., Part II. and the Staff Manual respectively. Title pages will be prepared in manuscript.

WAR DIARY
or
INTELLIGENCE SUMMARY.
(Erase heading not required.)

Place	Date	Hour	Summary of Events and Information	Remarks and references to Appendices
	23rd		Details of attack Contd:-	

The Centre Coy was responsible for 300 Yds of the Front; and the right Coy was responsible for 300 yds of the Front to within 100 yds of the EAST of KWAADESTRAAT — HOOGMOLEN ROAD.

The Battn moved forward at 23.45 in a heavy fog, in sectional blobs preceeded by Scouts, and from the outset came under long range Machine Gun fire, but got to the line held by the 122 Inf Bde, with no losses whatever. Here a pause of 3/4 hour was made to re-organise, and the advance was then resumed. The Battalion at once came under very heavy Machine Gun fire, from the Mill at HOOGMOLEN, the crest of the Hill, and the Chapel EAST of KWAADESTRAAT. O.18.L.8.0., in spite of this however, the Companies made good progress.

Both the Left and Centre were able to advance 400 yds, and 'B' Coy got on to the crest of HILL 66.

The Companies unfortunately could get no further, owing to Machine Gun fire poured into them from three different directions.

The Brigade on the Left of the Battn made no progress, with the result that a nest of Machine Guns were pouring fire into the backs of our men from the direction of the Chapel EAST of KWAADESTRAAT. Other nests of 3 to 5 Machine Guns were firing down on us from the roof of the farm, just behind the ridge on the crest of H66.

D. D. & L., London, E.C.
(A10266) Wt W5300/P713 750,000 2/18 Sch. 52 Forms/C2118/16.

PAGE VI

October 1918

Continued –

Army Form C. 2118.

Instructions regarding War Diaries and Intelligence Summaries are contained in F. S. Regs., Part II. and the Staff Manual respectively. Title pages will be prepared in manuscript.

WAR DIARY
or
INTELLIGENCE SUMMARY.
(Erase heading not required.)

Place	Date	Hour	Summary of Events and Information	Remarks and references to Appendices
	23rd		Details of attack Contd.: A nest situated just behind the ridge, (Which was later discovered to consist of 20 Guns), was sweeping the crest of Hill 66, and a nest of 3 or more Guns sweeping the whole front from HOOGMOLEN Mill. The Battn however tenaciously held on to this position until dawn, but as the left flank was exposed, and there was no cover whatever for the men, it was decided to withdraw to the original line held by the 122nd Inf Brigade. This was done, just as dawn was breaking, with little or no loss whatever.	
	24th		Details of attack:- Ref MAP Sheet 29. 1/40,000. The attack was a continuation of the previous nights attack and the final objective was the same. The frontage of the Battn was slightly different from the previous attack. The frontage in this case being from the WEST Side of the KWAADESTRAAT - HOOGMOLEN ROAD The jumping of position was the track running from WEST to EAST, 200yds N of Hill 66 from KWAADESTRAAF to KATTESTRAAT. "A" Coy who previously held the Centre, was replaced by "C" Coy, and the former came back in support. The main attack commenced at 02.20 from the jumping off position but at 01.00 "D" Coy who was still on left of the Battalion front had to push forward their patrols 300yds to get into touch with the other two companies. This was done after some sharp fighting with enemy posts, and at 01.30 "D" Coy reported that they had reached the jumping off position "C" + "B" Companies reached the jumping off position with no loss whatever at 01.25.	

D. D. & L., London, E.C.
(A10266) Wt W5300/P713 750,000 2/18 Sch. 52 Forms/C2118/16.

Instructions regarding War Diaries and Intelligence Summaries are contained in F. S. Regs., Part II. and the Staff Manual respectively. Title pages will be prepared in manuscript.

WAR DIARY
or
INTELLIGENCE SUMMARY.
(Erase heading not required.)

PAGE VII.
October 1918
Continued –

Army Form C. 2118.

Place	Date	Hour	Summary of Events and Information	Remarks and references to Appendices
	24th		Details of attack continued:-	
			The Brigade on our left was responsible for the clearing of the M.G. nests in the houses and chapel in KATTESTRAAT.	
			"B" Coy, on the right, advanced 100 yds from the jumping off ground & were then held up by very heavy M.G. fire from the crest of Hill 66, and also enfiladed by M.G's from the farm on the EAST side of the crest; and long distance M.G. fire from the Chapel in KATTESTRAAT.	
			"C" Coy in the centre, advanced 250 yds from the jumping off position, and in spite of very heavy M.G. fire succeeded in capturing the farm, and 2 hostile M.G's on the E side of Hill 66.	
			They held on to this position for 2 hours, but were forced to withdraw, as they were being shot in their backs by very heavy M.G. fire from the Chapel in KATTESTRAAT, and enfiladed from the Mill at HOOGMOLEN, and M.G. nests on crest of Hill 66.	
			"D" Coy on the left advanced 300 yds from their jumping off place, but as the Brigade on the left were unable to push forward, they were left with an exposed flank, and were consequently shot in their backs by M.G's from KATTESTRAAT.	
			Finding they were unsupported they were forced to withdraw to the position held by them previous to the attack, and this they did in good order, keeping touch with the centre company.	
			The Enemy re-occupied the farm on the EAST side of the crest after it was vacated by "C" Coy, and still continued to pour a heavy fire on the men from the roofs of the various buildings composing it.	

D. D. & L., London, E.C.
(A10266) Wt W5300/P713 750,000 2/18 Sch. 52 Forms/C2118/16.

PAGE VIII.

Army Form C. 2118.

Instructions regarding War Diaries and Intelligence Summaries are contained in F. S. Regs., Part II. and the Staff Manual respectively. Title pages will be prepared in manuscript.

WAR DIARY
or
INTELLIGENCE SUMMARY.

(Erase heading not required.)

October 1918. Continued –

Place	Date	Hour	Summary of Events and Information	Remarks and references to Appendices
	24th		Details of attack Continued:–	
			The Battalion on the whole made a general advance of 300yds, but owing to its left flank being exposed it could not possibly hold on to this advanced position, and was reluctantly compelled to withdraw to the position held previous to the commencement of the attack.	
	25th		Sheet 29. 1/40.000.	
			The Battalion less "A" + "D" Companies were in Brigade reserve for the attack on 25-10-18. "A" Coy was attached to the 11th Queens for the purpose of "Mopping up" and "D" Coy to the 23rd Middlesex Regt. for a similar purpose. Battn HQ was situated at the farm in O.17 a 0.8 and the other 2 Companies were billetted in the adjoining farms.	
			The Barrage came down at 09.04 and at 11.15 the Battalion less the 2 Coys moved forward in artillery formation, i.e. Sectional blobs, preceded by Scouts – "C" Coy leading – Battn HQ in centre – and "B" Coy bringing up the rear.	
			The route followed was the open Country WEST of the KWAADESTRAAT – KELBERGMOLEN ROAD. Nothing Eventful occurred on the march and at 12.30 a halt was made in the open fields on the western outskirts of KEIBERG. Battn HQ was then established in the group of houses situated just midway between KELBERGMOLEN and HOSKE + remained here until 22.30 that night.	
			"A" Coy who was attached to the 11th Queens, formed up on the KWAADESTRAAT – KATTESTRAAT ROAD, 300yds NORTH of Hill 66 at 0800.	

D. D. & L., London, E.C.
(A10266) Wt W5300/P713 750,000 2/18 Sch. 52 Forms/C2118/16.

PAGE IX

Army Form C. 2118.

WAR DIARY
or
INTELLIGENCE SUMMARY.
(*Erase heading not required.*)

October 1918.
Continued

Instructions regarding War Diaries and Intelligence Summaries are contained in F. S. Regs., Part II. and the Staff Manual respectively. Title pages will be prepared in manuscript.

Place	Date	Hour	Summary of Events and Information	Remarks and references to Appendices
	25th		Details continued:-	
			After the Barrage had moved forward at 0904, they proceeded with "Mopping up" the houses on the KATTESTRAAT – HEESTERT ROAD. There was a good deal of fighting in and about these houses and farms, but they eventually cleared the Boche from these places, and reached the Northern outskirts of HEESTERT at 13.30.	
			From here 2 Platoons were sent forward to fill a gap between the 11th Queens and the 23rd Middlesex at the junction of the roads in P 31. b.	
			at 18.00 the remainder of the Company pushed forward patrols with the 11th Queens and captured the Hamlets of SPICHTESTRAAT and RAAPTORF and formed an out-post line 400 yds EAST of the latter place, linking up with the 23rd Middlesex on the Right, and remained here for the night.	
			"C" Coy who was attached to the Middlesex formed up in the open, about 500 yds NORTH and parallel to the HOOGESTRAATJE – HOOGEMOLEN ROAD, with their right resting on the BOSSUYT CANAL.	
			After the Barrage moved forward at 0904, they followed "C" & "D" Companies of the Middlesex and proceeded to mop up all the Villages and farms in their area & meeting with little opposition on the way.	
			At 1600 they had reached a line 400 yds North West of OKKERDRIESCH with their flanks resting on the OKKERDRIESCH – MOEN Road and OKKERDRIESCH – HEESTERT Road.	

D. D. & L., London, E.C.
(A10266) Wt W5300/P713 750,000 2/18 Sch. 52 Forms/C2118/16.

Instructions regarding War Diaries and Intelligence Summaries are contained in F. S. Regs., Part II. and the Staff Manual respectively. Title pages will be prepared in manuscript.

WAR DIARY
or
INTELLIGENCE SUMMARY.
(Erase heading not required.)

PAGE X

October 1918

Continued –

Army Form C. 2118.

Place	Date	Hour	Summary of Events and Information	Remarks and references to Appendices
	25th		Details continued:–	
			At 1700 they proceeded to clear the village of OKKERDRIESCH, which they did with the loss of one man, and then pushed forward to link up with the 11th Queens who were holding an outpost line 400yds E of RAAPTORF, this was done at 18.30.	
			At 20.45 "C" Company was relieved by a Company of the Middlesex and stayed the night in the village of RAAPTORF.	
			At 22.30 Battn HQ proceeded to BLANCHEAT Farm in O.36 b, accompanied by "B" Company, and were billetted here for the night.	
			"C" Company proceeded to the MOATED FARM in P.31.d about the same hour and remained here for the night. Strength of Battn:- Officers 46. Other Ranks 660.	
	26th		"A" Company pushed forward patrols with the 11th Queens and occupied AVELCHEM at 13.30. At 1600 patrols pushed further afield and established themselves on the banks of the RIVER ESCAUT. 300yds S.E. of AVELCHEM.	
			At 20.00 "A" Company was relieved and rejoined the Battalion at COUTRAI that night. On relief by the 35th Division at 18.00, Battn HQ "B" "C" & "D" Companies marched back to COUTRAI and reached the town at 23.30.	
			Casualties during operations:-	
			Capt. A.K. HARDING. } Killed. Capt. G. GORDON SMITH } 2/Lt. A.J. Stubbs. } " S.W. Cross. } 2Lt. S.C. HARRIS. Wounded. Other Ranks Killed 27. Wounded 64 Missing 3	Contd

D. D. & L., London, E.C.
(A10266) Wt W5300/P713 750,000 2/18 Sch. 52 Forms/C2118/16.

PAGE XI

October 1918 Army Form C. 2118.

Continued –

Instructions regarding War Diaries and Intelligence Summaries are contained in F. S. Regs., Part II. and the Staff Manual respectively. Title pages will be prepared in manuscript.

WAR DIARY
or
INTELLIGENCE SUMMARY.

(Erase heading not required.)

Place	Date	Hour	Summary of Events and Information	Remarks and references to Appendices
COURTRAI.	27th		Battalion at rest in COURTRAI.	
	28th		Battalion bathed, Medical inspection held, & 96 Reinforcements arrived	
	29th		Battalion resting. Enemy aircraft very active during night, many bombs dropped.	
	30		Battalion resting " " " " " " " "	
	31		Battalion resting	

[signature]
Major
Comdg 10th Bn Royal West Kent Regt.

D. D. & L., London, E.C.
(A10266) Wt W5300/P713 750,000 2/18 Sch. 52 Forms/C2118/16.

10 R W Kent Regt

Army Form C. 2118.

WAR DIARY
or
INTELLIGENCE SUMMARY.
(Erase heading not required.)

Instructions regarding War Diaries and Intelligence Summaries are contained in F. S. Regs., Part II. and the Staff Manual respectively. Title pages will be prepared in manuscript.

NOVEMBER 1918

VR 31

Place	Date	Hour	Summary of Events and Information	Remarks and references to Appendices
COURTRAI. (Sheet 29. – 1/40,000)	1st		Battalion marched out from COURTRAI at 13·30 and proceeded to billets in KNOKKE; arriving at latter place at 16·30. Strength of Battalion:- OFFICERS 43. OTHER RANKS 670.	0.0 51
KNOKKE.	2nd		Battalion rested - no work possible owing to bad weather.	
	3rd.		Companies practised an attack in open formation in direction of KREUPE.	
LANGESTRAAT	4th		Battalion left KNOKKE 14·00 hrs and arrived at LANGESTRAAT (1 Kilometre S.E. of ANSEGHEM) at 20·30 hrs. after an uneventful march, and were billeted, being in Brigade Reserve.	0.0. 52
	5th		Situation unchanged - slight shelling in vicinity with 5·9s and 4·2s	
	6th		Situation unchanged - Shelling increased slightly - Battalion Headquarters receiving most attention, owing to close proximity of 60 pdr. Battery.	
	7th		Situation unchanged except for increased shelling. B.H.Q. again shelled with 5·9s, 4·2s (Gas). Casualties - 1 Other Rank Killed.	
	8th	23·30	Battalion received orders to move at once to CASTER and billet there to support 11th Bn. The "Queens" Regt. who had crossed the River SCHELDT. Strength of Battn. OFFICERS 42. OTHER RANKS 631.	
MEERCHE.	9th	04·30	"C" Coy crossed the R. SCHELDT at ELUWHOEK in close support to the 11th "Queens" Regt and took up billets at MEERCHE. Remainder of Battalion crossed the R. SCHELDT between the hours of 11·30 and 12·00. The Battalion formed up at 14·00 hours on a line running approx Q 18.c.0.0 – Q 23.c.0.0. and moved forward in a due easterly direction	

(A10266) Wt W5300/P713 750,000 2/18 D. D. & L., London, E.C. Sch. 52 Forms/C2118/16.

Instructions regarding War Diaries and Intelligence Summaries are contained in F. S. Regs., Part II. and the Staff Manual respectively. Title pages will be prepared in manuscript.

WAR DIARY
or
INTELLIGENCE SUMMARY.
(Erase heading not required.)

November 1918

Sheet 2

Army Form C. 2118.

Place	Date	Hour	Summary of Events and Information	Remarks and references to Appendices
	9th contd.		direction, with C Coy on left with B Coy in support to it, and A Coy on right with D Coy in Support. Reached the NUKERKE-RENAIX ROAD, a distance of 4000 yards without any opposition at 18.30 hours. The dispositions of Companies were slightly altered here, B Coy taking over the left and A Coy coming back in support. At nightfall the Battalion held the road from R.15 central to R 21 Central, with B Coy on the left and C Coy on the right. A Coy were in close support & D in Reserve with Battn H.Q. in Farm & Mill in R.19b.	
	10th		The Battalion resumed advance at 09.00 hours in a due Easterly direction, with the 23rd Middlesex on the left, and the H.L.I. (35th Division) on the right. Disposition of Coys same as previous night. The Battalion gained 1st Objective (AUDENARDE-RENAIX RLY LINE) - 2nd Objective (Line just E of KERKHEM). - 3rd Objective (Line just E. of SCHOORISSE) without meeting any opposition, but on approaching the final objective were held up 10 minutes by Machine Gun Fire from direction of KANAKENDRIES. The 18 pdr attached to the Battalion was thereupon rushed forward to deal with the obstacle. This it did most effectively after firing 8 rounds over open sights at distance of 800 yards. The final objective was then secured and at 16.30 hours the line of Outposts ran approximately 300 yards N & E of KANAKENDRIES to 400 yards E & S of ROOVORST.	O.O. 53

D. D. & L., London, E.C.
(A10266) Wt W5300/P713 750,000 2/18 Sch. 52 Forms/C2118/16.

Instructions regarding War Diaries and Intelligence Summaries are contained in F. S. Regs., Part II. and the Staff Manual respectively. Title pages will be prepared in manuscript.

WAR DIARY
or
INTELLIGENCE SUMMARY.
(Erase heading not required.)

November 1918.

Sheet 3

Army Form C. 2118.

Place	Date	Hour	Summary of Events and Information	Remarks and references to Appendices
SEGELSEM	10/11		The night of 10/11th passed quietly.	
	11th		On the morning of 11th the 134th Inf Bde. passed through our Outpost Line.	
		11.00	Hostilities ceased. All ranks received the message with great enthusiasm.	
	12th		The Commanding Officer inspected the Battalion and complimented the men on their good work.	
	13th		Battalion left SEGELSEM and marched to SARLARDINGE.	O.O. 54
SARLARDINGE	14th		Battalion carried out training.	
	15th 16th 17th		Training, and preparing for further move forward.	
			Strength of Battalion :- Officers 43 Other Ranks 702.	
VOLLEZEEL	18th		Left SARLARDINGE & proceeded by march Route to VOLLEZEEL	O.O. 55
			On arrival Two Companies took over Outposts on the line GRACHT - SPIERINGEN - LEENSTRAET - LE CLOITIE.	O.O. 56
	19th		Battalion resting	
	20th	08.30	Left VOLLEZEEL and proceeded by march Route to LES DEUX ACREN.	O.O. 57
LES DEUX ACREN	21 22		Cleaning up etc. Training under boy arrangement.	
			Strength of Battalion Officers 42 Other Ranks 733.	

D. D. & L., London, E.C.
(A10266) Wt W5300/P713 750,000 2/18 Sch. 52 Forms/C2118/16.

Instructions regarding War Diaries and Intelligence Summaries are contained in F. S. Regs., Part II. and the Staff Manual respectively. Title pages will be prepared in manuscript.

WAR DIARY
or
INTELLIGENCE SUMMARY.
(Erase heading not required.)

Army Form C. 2118.

November 1918
Sheet 4

Place	Date	Hour	Summary of Events and Information	Remarks and references to Appendices
LES DEUX ACREN	23rd		Battalion inspected by Commanding Officer.	
	24th		Presentation of Medal Ribbon by Divisional Commander. "B" Coy represented the Battalion at the ceremony.	
	25th 26th 27th 28th 29th 30th		Battalion carried out short programme of Training daily, the afternoons being devoted to Football and other Sports. An Amusement Committee was formed under [illegible], and Concerts, Dances etc were held. The Divisional Concert Party "The Crumps" visited LES DEUX ACREN and [illegible] ten performances. Strength of Battalion Officers 46 Other Ranks 727.	

[signature] Major
for Lt Col
Comdg 10th Bn R West Kent Regt

D. D. & L., London, E.C.
(A10266) Wt W5300/P713 750,000 2/18 Sch. 52 Forms/C2118/16.

Scheme for practice attack 3.4.18

Reference Map. Sheet 29

Information Enemy are holding line GHELUWE – DOTTIGNIES with outposts in Squares O 13 O 19 N 30
Our troops hold the line of the road O 14 b 7 – O 27 a 2 1

Intention The advance will be continued on the 5th inst: to seize the high ground in N 24

Instructions A + B Companies will attack A Coy on the left. B Coy on the right C Coy in support D Coy in reserve
Boundary between Companies. Grid line N 24 a 0 0 to O 24 c 0 0
Right boundary B Coy N 18 d 4 1 – O 21 c 0 7
Left boundary A Coy N 30 b 1 9 – O 24 a 0 3
Companies will assemble in rear of the front line and pass through Reserve line at Zero

General direction of Advance 270° True

Barrage Barrage will come down on the approximate line O 14 d 5 0 O 20 d 5 0 and move at the rate of 75 yds per minute
There will be a pause of 10 minutes from Zero + 15' to Zero + 25'

Objective Road N 30 a 2 9 to O 13 b 0 6 between boundaries given
Battle patrols to be sent out forward of this line

Zero 11 30

Equipment S A A will not be carried
Lewis Guns to be taken less panniers
N° 27 bombs to be carried

Skeleton Enemy Observers section will illustrate Enemy N° [illegible]
Blue flag indicates nest of 2 or more guns
White flag a single gun

SECRET OPERATION ORDER NO: 52 4th Nov: 1918

WAR DIARY.

SHEET 29 S.E.

1. The battalion will relieve the 10th Rn Queens in the line tonight 4th – 5th inst:

2. Dispositions. Bn H.Q P 18 c. 2.3. "A" Echelon O 17 d 5.9.
The line to be taken over extends from BERCHEM (exclusive) to P 30 central.
Companies will take over from their opposite numbers.
The attached Stokes Gun section will accompany B.H.Q.

3. No advance parties will be sent forward.
One guide per company from the 10th Queens will meet the battalion at P 9 d. 1.3.

4. Order of march. H.Q. Band. A. B. C. D. "A" Echelon
The normal intervals will be maintained on the march.
No movement will take place E of a line drawn through P 3 central P 14 central before 17.00 hours. After this hour all movement will be by platoons at 50x interval.

5. Route. BANHOUT BOSCH – CROSS ROADS O 6 b 3.2 – OOTEGHEM – KLEIN RONNSE – RUIFFELEINDE

Head of column will pass present B.H.Q at 14.00.
The battalion will bivouac for tea at P.C.

6. Rations for the 5th inst will be issued before the battalion moves off if possible, if not they will be issued at P.C.
Water bottles will be filled.

7. Lewis Guns and panniers will be carried on the limbers.

8. All blankets will be dumped in bundles of ten at Qr. Mr. Stores by 12.00 to-day.
All officers valises and O.R boxes will be dumped at H.Q. Mess by 12.00.
Mess boxes will be dumped outside messes by 13.30.
All tools will be dumped at the Transport Lines by 10.00.

9 Dress. Fighting Order. Packs will be carried in place of haversacks.
The latter will be dumped by companies at Qr. Mr. Stores by 12.00.
Greatcoats will be rolled by sections, labelled and dumped at Qr. Mr. Stores by 12.00.

10. Relief complete will be notified to B.H.Q either by runner or by wiring name of O.C. Company.

11. Acknowledge.

Trevor. E. Tatham
Capt & Adjt

File

Operation Order No. 5[illegible]

Sheet [illegible] 28 & 30. 10th Nov 1918

1. The advance will be resumed today at 09.00 hours.

2. B Coy will be on the left. C on the right. A in support. D in reserve.

Attached troops. 2 Vickers Guns will be attached to the 1st [illegible] as [illegible]. The remaining 2 will be attached to the support Coy. 3" [illegible] with each company [illegible]

3. Advance will be made in conjunction with 2nd [illegible] and French on the left & 35th Bn on the right.

4. **Boundaries and Direction**

Inter battalion boundary [illegible]
[illegible]
Boundary [illegible]
Direction of attack due EAST.

5. [illegible]

[illegible]

- 2 -

3. [illegible] will be [illegible] for a protective [illegible] [illegible] [illegible] to [illegible] [illegible] awaiting [illegible] [illegible]. [illegible] machine [illegible] may be available for [illegible] also.

4. [illegible] will [illegible] to [illegible] and await orders. All [illegible] [illegible] [illegible].

Note:- The following features will be [illegible] as far as possible.

Railway [illegible] – [illegible]

N & S line through KERKENNEH [illegible] [illegible]

[illegible] and [illegible]

N & S Road through [illegible] [illegible]

[illegible] NB. C 5. 2

Sgd. [illegible]

[illegible]

SECRET . OPERATION ORDER NO: 54. T.K3

SHEET 30 12th Nov: 1918

1. The battalion will move into reserve to the outpost line tomorrow 13th inst:

2. An advance party consisting of 1 N.C.O per company, 1 N.C.O from Bn H.Q and 1 N.C.O from the transport section will parade at Bn H.Q at 8.45 A.M tomorrow 13th inst:
They will be provided with bicycles and will proceed to SARADINGE (U 10 central) under the command of 2nd LT Edwards.
They will report to the Staff Captain at 11 A.M at U 10 b. 3.3.

3. The battalion will proceed by march route to SARADINGE.

4. Route. N13 d 8.4. N19 b 8.8. N22 a 15.70 N21 d 75.50. N17 c.7.2 thence to PARICKE in O26 O32 b 70.20. O32 b 40.20 to SARADINGE.

5. Starting Point. The head of the column will pass N17 C.7.2 at 10.20.
Bn H.Q will move off at 9 A.M. Companies will take up their position on the line of march as the column passes.

6. Order of March. H.Q. Band. A. B. C. D T. K 3
Companies. "A" Echelon. "B" Echelon.

7. Lewis Guns and panniers will be packed on the L.G limbers under the supervision of company L.G N.C.Os at 8 A.M. Officers' valises, Mess boxes etc will be dumped outside company H.Q ready for collection at 8·30 A.M.

8. Dress. Fighting order with packs in place of haversacks. Steel helmets and S.B.R will be carried.

9. Rations will be carried under company arrangements.

10. Acknowledge.

Trevor. E. Tatham
Capt & Adjt

War Diary TRK

SECRET. – **Operation Order. No 55.**

Ref: Sheet 5. TOURNAI. 17 November 1918.

1. No further information regarding the enemy is available.
2. The 41st Division will commence its march to the German frontier tomorrow 18th inst.
3. The Battalion will act as advance guard to the Brigade.
4. Disposal of Troops VANGUARD.

   1 Section "B" Coy, 1/1st Yorks Cyclists.
   "A" Company. 10th Battn. R.W. Kent Regt.
   1 Section 233rd Coy. R.E.

   O.C. "A" Company will be in command of the vanguard.

   MAINGUARD.

   1 Section "D" Coy. 41st Battn. M.G.C.
   10th Battn. R.W. Kent Regt. less 1 Company in the following order:- H.Q. Band. "B" "C" "D" Company.
   1 Section 190th Bde. R.F.A.
   Transport in order of Units viz: Cyclists. R.E. 10th R.W.K. R.A.

   Advance guard Commander Lieut Col. The Hon. E. R. Thesiger.

5. BOUNDARIES and ROUTE.

   Northern Boundary. VRYHEID — SOUTHERN outskirts of NINOVE.

   Southern Boundary. KILOMETRE 40 on LESSINES — GHISLENGHIEN ROAD to 1. MILE N of ENGHIEN.

   INTER. Bde. Boundary. GRAMMONT — KILOMETRE. 9. on ENGHIEN — NINOVE ROAD.

   123rd Infantry Brigade will march to the GAMMERAGES — EJSBROEK area via PLANKEN — LES DEUX ACREN — VIANE.

6. The head of the main body will pass the road junction 100 yards S. of KILOMETRE. 41 on GRAMMONT — LESSINES ROAD at 09.00 hours. The main guard will be at a point 1. MILE S. of the starting point on the GRAMMONT — LESSINES ROAD at 09.00, with the vanguard 500 yards further in advance, and will move off at 09.00 precisely. The Infantry advance guard will therefore move off from the cross roads opposite the R.W. Kents Transport Lines at 08.00 hours followed by the main guard at 08.07.
7. DRESS. — Fighting order as laid down.
8. Mens packs and blankets, mess boxes and Officers valises will be dumped by Companies at Qr. Mr. Stores by 7.15 am. Each Company will detail a loading party of 1. N.C.O. and 4 men to report to Qr. Mr at 7.15 am.
9. WATER BOTTLES will be filled and the unexpired portion of the days rations will be carried.
10. In future Officers will invariable carry revolvers when they leave their billets.
11. Acknowledge.

(Sgd) Trevor. E. Tatham
Capt. & Adjutant
10th Bn. Royal West Kent Regt.

Secret

Operation Order No 56

Ref. Sheet Brussels. · 18th Nov. 1918 –

1. The Outpost Line for night 18th/19th inst. will be Established by 1500 hours on the Line GRACHT - SPIERINGEN - LEENSTRAET LE CLOTTIE - Rd Junction 400 yards E of S in NATTENDRIES FARM just N of N in GALCENDRIES.

2. The Battalion will be responsible for the NORTHERN SECTOR extending from the Northern Bde Boundary at GRACHT to the road junction at LEENSTRAET. Touch will be gained with 124th Bde on the Left and 11th Bn Queens on the Right.

3. TROOPS. "B" Company will hold the Line from GRACHT on the Left to and including the road immediately N of the S in SPIERINGEN on the Right.
"C" Company will hold the Line from the Right of "B" Company to and including the cross roads immediately W of the L in LEENSTRAET.

4. Outpost Commander. Lt Col The Hon. E.R. Thesiger

Contd/-

- 2.

5. Report Centre. At Cross Roads immediately W of VOLLEZEEL.

6. Line of Resistance In case of attack the picquet line as laid down in para 1 will be held.

7. Group and picquet commanders must be thoroughly acquainted with their duties.

8 Acknowledge.

(Sd) Trevor E. Tatham
Capt + Adjt
10th Royal West Kent Regt.

SECRET.

Operation Order no 57

Ref. Sheets 30. 1/40,000
Tournai 1/100,000

Nov. 20th 1918

1. The Battalion will return to the LES DEUX ACREN -GHOY AREA today, 20th inst.

2. Route. VIANE – LES DEUX ACREN

3. STARTING POINT V.23.d.8.6.

4. TIME. 10·41 hours

5. Companies, Hd Qrs. & Transport will each detail 1 N.C.O to report to HdQrs at 07·00 hours today for billetting purposes. They will proceed under Command of 2/LT SIMPSON to VIANE CHURCH and report to the STAFF CAPTAIN there at 08·00.
Bicycles will be provided.

6. Order of march. – H.Q., Band, A. D. C. B. Transport.
H.Q. will move off at 08·15 followed by remainder.

7. B & C Coy must have their ~~packs~~, blankets, Officers Valises & Mess Boxes ready for collection at 06·30
The Transport Officer & Quartermaster will arrange to collect these ✗, Lorries have been asked for.
"A" & "D" Coy will dump their ~~packs~~ blankets at Quartermaster Stores by 07·30.
Officers Valises & Mess Boxes outside H.Q Mess at 07·30.
These times will be strictly observed.
Packs will be carried on the man.

8. Acknowledge.

(Sgd) TREVOR E TATHAM.
CAPT & ADJT
10TH R. WEST KENT REGT.

✗ By horse Transport and dump at Q.M. Stores, ready for lorries to pick up.

Army Form C. 2118.

Vol 32

Instructions regarding War Diaries and Intelligence Summaries are contained in F. S. Regs., Part II. and the Staff Manual respectively. Title pages will be prepared in manuscript.

WAR DIARY or INTELLIGENCE SUMMARY.

(Erase heading not required.)

Place	Date	Hour	10th Royal West Kent Regt. Summary of Events and Information	Remarks and references to Appendices
	December			
LES DEUX-ACREN	1-10		Training carried out under Company arrangements. Battalion Route Marches etc. Sports held in the afternoons, Concerts and Dances in the evening.	
	11th		The Battalion especially chosen for their clean turnout and smartness on Parade, marched to GRAMMONT in Drill Order, for Inspection by G.O.C. 41st Division and presentation of Medals.	
			During the afternoon a Football Match was played between "A" Coy 10th Bn R W Kent Regt and "B" Coy 23rd Middlesex Regt. The latter winning by 3 goals to 1. This Match was the semi final of the Brigade Competition	
ST PIERRE-CAPELLE	12th		Battalion left LES DEUX-ACREN and marched to ST PIERRE CAPELLE. The March was uneventful.	
LEMBECQ	13th		The Battalion left ST PIERRE CAPELLE and marched to LEMBECQ.	
BRAINE L'ALLEUD	14th		The Battalion left LEMBECQ and marched to BRAINE L'ALLEUD a distance of 9½ miles.	
	15th		Battalion rested. Passes were granted to men wishing to visit BRUSSELS. Others visited the Battlefield of WATERLOO	
	16th		The March was resumed. The Battalion marching to BAISYTHY.	

(A9175) Wt W2358/P360 600,000 12/17 D. D. & L. Sch. 52a. Forms/C2118/15.

Instructions regarding War Diaries and Intelligence Summaries are contained in F. S. Regs., Part II. and the Staff Manual respectively. Title pages will be prepared in manuscript.

WAR DIARY
or
INTELLIGENCE SUMMARY.
(Erase heading not required.)

Army Form C. 2118.

Place	Date	Hour	Summary of Events and Information	Remarks and references to Appendices
BAISYTHY	16th		March past General Sir H S Rawlinson, Bart, G.C.V.O. K.C.B, K.C.M.G. Commanding Fourth Army.	
SOMBREFFE	17th		Battalion left BAISYTHY and marched to SOMBREFFE.	
ISNES	18th		Battalion left SOMBREFFE and marched to ISNES and LES MARAYES.	
LONGCHAMPS	19th		Battalion left ISNES and LES MARAYES and marched to LONGCHAMPS	
VILLE-EN-HESBAYE	20th		Battalion left LONGCHAMPS and marched to VILLE-EN-HESBAYE. Battalion Strength 47 Officers 844 Other Ranks.	
	21-29		Battalion resting and cleaning up in Billets.	
	30-31		Training and Education. Battalion Strength 46 Officers 808 Other Ranks.	

1/1/19.

[signature] Major
Comdg. 10th Royal West Kent Regt.

(A9175) Wt W2352/P360 600,000 12/17 D. D. & L. Sch. 52a. Forms/C2118/15.

Secret.

10th Bn. Royal West Kent Regt.

8th Dec. 1918

Operation Order No 58

Ref. Sheets 5 TOURNAI and 6 BRUSSELS

(1) The battalion will move to the NAMUR AREA in accordance with the attached MARCH TABLES.

(2) "A" DAY will probably be Dec. 11th 1918. March Tables for "H", "I", "J" and "K" days will be issued later.

(3) Advance Party will consist of 1 N.C.O from each Company, 1 N.C.O. from Transport Section and 1 N.C.O and 1 Runner from H.Q. under the command of 2/Lieut D. SIMPSON. They will be supplied with bicycles and will report to the Staff Captain and D.A.A.G. 41st Division as follows:—

"B" Day .... VIANE CHURCH 07.30

"C" Day .... RAILWAY CROSSING 1/4 mile N of second E in PETIT ENGHIEN 07.30

"D" Day .... CROSS ROADS 1/4 mile N of first E in BRAINE LE CHATEAU 07.30

"F" Day .... BRAINE L'ALLEUD Station 07.30

"G" Day .... QUATRE BRAS 07.30

"H" Day .... SOMBREFFE CHURCH 07.30

The party detailed will be permanent throughout the march and will take their orders as to times of departure from billets etc. from 2/Lt Simpson daily. As soon as the party arrives at their next village the Runner will at once be sent to report to Capt T. T. GUEST M.C. at Brigade H.Q. to guide supply wagons to Battn H.Q.

(4) DRESS —— Marching Order with packs. Monkey jackets issued to Nos. 1 of Lewis Gun Teams will be packed on Company Lewis Gun limbers under the supervision of L.G. N.C.Os at 12.00 hrs 9th inst.

(5) BLANKETS will be tightly rolled in bundles of ten, securely labelled by Companies and dumped at Q.M.S Stores by 07.15 hrs. on "B" Day. Officers valises will be dumped outside Coy. H.Q. ready for collection at 07.45 hrs.

Mess boxes will be dumped outside Coy H.Q ready for collection at 08.00

(6) LOADING PARTY consisting of one man per Coy. and one from H.Q. under a N.C.O. to be detailed by O.C. A Coy. will report to the Qr. Mr. at 07.00 on "B" Day and will remain attached to the Qr. Mr. Establishment throughout the march.

(7) Additional Transport. Two motor lorries will be available throughout the march. Cpl. Clifton (H.Q.) will be N.C.O i/c of these, and will take his orders from Lieut NORRIS Bde. H.Q.

The Intelligence Officer will supply Cpl. Clifton with all necessary maps

(8) Throughout the march the 1st Line Transport will accompany the battalion.

(9) Companies will ensure that billets are left perfectly clean and tidy.

(10) On the march the intervals laid down in "Notes on March Discipline" will be maintained.

(Sgd) Trevor E. Tatham Capt. & Adjt.
10th Royal West Kent Regt.

(11) ACKNOWLEDGE.

Issued to

No 1 File	No 8 T.O.	No 15 Sgt. [illegible]
" 2 War Diary	" 9 Quartermaster.	" 16 Cpl. Clifton
" 3 123rd Bde.	" 10 M.O.	
" 4 O.C. A Coy.	" 11 C.O.	
" 5 O.C. B "	" 12 Adjt.	
" 6 O.C. C "	" 13 I.O.	
" 7 O.C. D "	" 14 R.S.M.	

MARCH TABLE TO ACCOMPANY OPERATION ORDER No 58

Day	FROM	TO	Starting Point	Time	Route
"B"	Les Deux Acren	St Pierre Cappelle Area	Rd. Junc: ¼ mile S of ǂ in Les Deux Acren	09.06	BIÉVÈNE
"C"	St Pierre Cappelle Area	LEMBECQ Area	Level Crossing ¼ mile E of 2nd ǂ in ENGHIEN	10.44	ENGHIEN - HAL ROAD
"D"	LEMBECQ. Area	Braine-L'ALLEUD AREA	Cross roads on HAL-Braine-Le Chateau Road 1¼ miles N of Braine Le Chateau	10.11	BRAINE LE CHATEAU X ROADS at MONT St PONT
"F"	Braine L'ALLEUD AREA.	HOUTAIN-BAISYTHY AREA	Rd. Junc. ¼ mile S of R.in. PLANCENOIT.	10.12	VIA GENAPPE
"G"	HOUTAIN-BAISYTHY AREA	SOMBREFFE AREA	QUATRE BRAS.	09.38	NIVELLES - SOMBREFFE ROAD

Order of March "B" Day will be as follows:

H.Q. Band A. B. C. D. Transport

H.Q. will move from the Church Les Deux Acren at 08.30 hours.

War Diary

Operation Order No 59
by Lt Col the Hon E R Thesiger
Comdg 10th R West Kent Regt
12-12-18

1 Reference OO 58 the march will be resumed tomorrow and the Battalion will move to the LEMBECQ area

2 Order of march –
H.Q., Band D. C. B. A Coy.
Transport
H.Q will move off at 9.10 a.m.
D Coy and C Coy will move off in time to take up their position on the line of march in rear of H.Q.
B. A Coys and Transport will take up their positions as the column passes them.

3 Blankets will be dumped in bundles of ten at the nearest point on the main Road to Coy H.Q, ready for collection by lorries at 7.30 am. Officers Valises will also be collected by the lorries. Mess Boxes will be ready for collection at the same point by 8.15 am.

4 Acknowledge.

(sgd) T.E. TATHAM
Capt & Adjt
10th R West Kent Regt

File

To:- All Recipients
of O.O. 58. d/ 9.12.18.

Ref. para 2. "A" DAY. will be December 11th. 1918.

Amendment.

Ref. para. 5. Officers Valises will be dumped outside Coy Headquarters ready for collection by 07-15 instead of 07.45 as stated therein.

10-12-18

(sgd) T. E. TATHAM. CAPT & ADJT.
10TH BN. R WEST KENT RGT.

War Diary

To:- All Recipients
of O.O. 58. d/ 9.12.18

Ref. para 2. "A" DAY. will be December 11th. 1918.

Amendment.
Ref. para. 5. Officers Valises will be dumped outside Coy Headquarters ready for collection by 07-15 instead of 07.45 as stated therein.

10-12-18

(sgd) T. E. TATHAM. CAPT & ADJ.
10TH BN. R. WEST KENT RGT

SECRET

W. Diary

Operation Order No 60
by Lieut Col the Hon E R Thesiger
Comdg 10th R W Kent Regt
13-12-18

1 Ref OO 58 the march will be resumed tomorrow 14th inst and the Battn will proceed to the BRAINE L'ALLEUD AREA

2 Order of march – HQ, Band, B, D, A, C Transport.

3 Starting Point – LEMBECQ CHURCH 9 am
Route – BRAINE LE CHATEAU, E to Cross Roads at MONT ST PONT, – S to cross roads immediately S of KM 16 on BRAINE L'ALLEUD – BRUSSELS ROAD – thence E to MENIL.

4 Blankets will be dumped at Coy HQ at 7.30 am ready for collection by lorries which will collect Officers Valises at the same time.
Mess boxes will be outside Coy HQ ready for collection at 8 30 am

(sgd) T E TATHAM
Capt & Adjt
10th Bn R West Kent

To:- All recipients of O.O. 58.

O.O. No. 61.

Reference O.O. 58 the March will be resumed tomorrow 16th inst. and the Battalion will move to the HOUTAIN-BAISYTHY area.

Order of March – HQ Band C.A.B.D Transport

Starting Point – Level crossing BRAINE L'ALLEUD station 09.03.

HQ 'C' & 'A' Companies move off from BHQ at 08.30

'B' 'D' & Transport will take up their positions on the line of March at BRAINE L'ALLEUD station

ROUTE BRUSSELS-GENAPPE road

Distance 9½ Miles.

Blankets B & D Companies will dump their Blankets at the nearest point on the main road to their respective HQ ready for collection by lorry at 07.15

HQ A & C Companies will dump their Blankets on the road outside their HQ at 07.00 ready for collection by G.S. Wagon & limbers. Officers' valises will be collected at the same time. The Transport Officer will arrange to collect from HQ A & C boxes and deliver to Qr Mr. Mess Boxes will be ready for collection as follows 'B' & 'D' 07.30 HQ A & C at 08.00

(Sd) TREVOR E. TATHAM

Capt. & Adjutant

15/12/18

10th R. W. Kent Regt.

10TH BN R. WEST KENT REGT
Operation Order No 62
16-12-18

1 Reference O.O. No 58. The march will be resumed tomorrow 17th inst, and the Battn will proceed to the SOMBREFFE area

2 Order of March - H.Q, Band, A. B. C. D. Transport.

3 Starting Point - Cross Roads immediately W of P of PATAND 9.10 am. H.Q. will move off at 9.00 am followed by A. B & C Coys. "D" Coy will take up their position on the line of march at the starting point. Transport will take up their position in rear of D Coy at this point.

4 Route - QUATRE BRAS - SOMBREFFE.

5 BLANKETS will be ready for collection outside Coy H.Q. at 7.45 am. Officers Valises will be collected at the same time.
Mess Boxes will be ready for collection at 8.30 am

6 Advance Party will meet 2/LT. SIMPSON at the CAFE near D Coys H.Q. on the main road at 7.30 am

7 Acknowledge

(sgd) T.E. TATHAM CAPT
10th R WEST KEN

War Diary

10th Bn. Royal West Kent Regt.

Operation Order No. 63

1 Reference O.O. No. 58 the march will be resumed tomorrow 18 [illegible] and the battalion will move to 15 [illegible]

2 Order of March — H.Q. [illegible] B C D A [illegible]

3 Starting Point — Cross roads [illegible] mile E of [illegible] on SOMBREFFE — NAMUR Road at 8.15 am.
H.Q will move off at 8.8 a.m. The remaining companies will take up their positions as the column passes them.

4 Route — SOMBREFFE — NAMUR ROAD

5 Lorries — Lorries will report at the above Starting Point at 8.30 am

6. Blankets — Blankets will be ready for collection by lorries outside Coy. H.Q at 6.45 am. Officers Valises will be collected at the same time.
Mess Boxes will be collected as follows —
H.Q, B, C and D Coys at 7.15 am — A Coy at 7.45 am

7 Advance Party will report to 2 Lieut Jemison at the Cross roads crossing at 7.0 a.m.

7-12-18

(Sgd) [illegible] E. [illegible]
Capt & Adjt
10th Bn. Royal West Kent Regt

May '16
Dec '18

War Diary

10th Bn Royal West Kent Regt.

Operation Order No 64

1 — Reference OO No 58 the battalion will resume the march tomorrow 19th inst, and will proceed to LONGCHAMPS.

2 Order of March — H.Q. Band, [illegible] Transport

3 Starting Point – Cross Roads S.W. of [illegible] on the CHATELET – LONGCHAMPS Road. H.Q. will move off at 11.20. Companies will take up their positions as the column passes.

4 Distance — 9¾ miles

5 [illegible] will meet [illegible] at the starting point at 07.00.

6 Blankets [illegible] will be collected [illegible] at [illegible]. [illegible] will be collected at 0.30 a.m.
[illegible] will arrive in billets about 5.30. [illegible] will make [illegible] arrangements as regards dinners.

(Sgd.) [illegible] E. [illegible]
Capt & Adjt.
10th Bn Royal West Kent Regt.

5th Dec 18

War Diary!

Operation Order No. 65.

10th Bn. Royal West Kent Regt. 19.12.1918

1. The march will be resumed tomorrow and the Battalion will proceed to the final area. (VILLE-EN-HESBAYE)

2. Starting Point. The Battn will move off from the Church. LONGCHAMP. at 08.05 hours in the following order :- Headqrs, Band, C. A. B & D Coys Transport.

3 Route. LA VALLE - WASSEIGES - AVIN - GIPLET.

4 Blankets and Officers Valises will be dumped at the Transport Lines at 07.30. The loading party will take charge of these until the arrival of the lorries.

Mess Boxes will be collected at 07.30.

5 Lorries will rendezvous at the Cross Roads at K.M. 2 on EGHEZEE - BIERWAERT ROAD at 10.00.

6 ADVANCE PARTY will meet 2ND LT. SIMPSON at the Church at ~~[illegible]~~ 05.45

(Sgd) T. E. TATHAM. CAPT & ADJT.
10TH BN. R. WEST KENT REGT.

LONDON DIVISION

(LATE 41ST DIVISION)

123RD INFY BDE

10TH BN ROY.WEST KENTS

JAN - FEB 1919

Army Form C. 2118.

Instructions regarding War Diaries and Intelligence Summaries are contained in F. S. Regs., Part II, and the Staff Manual respectively. Title pages will be prepared in manuscript.

WAR DIARY
or
INTELLIGENCE SUMMARY.
(Erase heading not required.)

VR 33

Place January 1919	Date	Hour	10th Bn. Royal West Kent Regt. Summary of Events and Information	Remarks and references to Appendices
VILLE-EN-HESBAYE	1-8		Battalion in Billets. Training carried out Daily from 9am to 1pm, or	
			Educational Classes held during this period in lieu of Training	
			Afternoons were devoted to Sports, etc.	
			Dances, and Concerts by the Battalion Concert Party "The Live Rounds",	
			were held in the evenings.	
			Lorries were allotted the Battalion for Joy Rides, and about 100 men	
			visited LIEGE.	
			Strength of Battalion Officers 47. Other Ranks 800.	
LOHMAR	9th		Battalion proceeded by Route March to HUY and entrained for	O.O. No 1
			COLOGNE AREA.	
	10th		Battalion detrained at HOFFNUNGSTHAL at 10am, and proceeded by	
			route March to LOHMAR.	
			Relieved 1st Battalion Canadian Regt. at LOHMAR.	Jan-Feb
			Strength of Battalion Officers 47 Other Ranks 803	
LOHMAR	11-22		Battalion carried out Training daily from 9am to 1pm.	
			Companies Training for Drill Competition organised by 41st Division.	

(A9175) Wt W2358/P360 600,000 12/17 D. D. & L. Sch. 52a. Forms/C2118/15

Army Form C. 2118.

Instructions regarding War Diaries and Intelligence Summaries are contained in F. S. Regs., Part II. and the Staff Manual respectively. Title pages will be prepared in manuscript.

WAR DIARY
or
INTELLIGENCE SUMMARY.
(*Erase heading not required.*)

Place	Date	Hour	Summary of Events and Information — 10th Bn Royal West Kent Regt.	Remarks and references to Appendices
January 1919				
			"C" Company (Capt. W.A. WATERMAN in Command) were adjudged Winners to represent the Battalion in Divisional Competition.	
			A Rifle Range (200 yards) was built by the Battalion, and firing competitions held.	
			Afternoons were devoted to Football, etc.	
			Concerts and Whist Drives being held in the evenings.	
			Passes were freely granted to BONN and COLOGNE.	
LOHMAR	23rd		Consecration of Colours. – The ceremony of Consecration of Colours was performed by Capt. R.F. BURNETT. C.F.	
			Strength of Battalion. Officers 47 Other Ranks 798.	
SEELSCHIED	24th		Battalion proceeded to SEELSCHIED by March Route and relieved 11th "Queens" in the Outpost Line.	O.O. No 2
	25-29		"A" "B" and "D" Companies on Outpost Duties	
			"C" Company Training for Divisional Drill Competition.	
LIND	30		Battalion relieved in the Outpost Line by 1/1st Bn. Hereford Regt. (34th Division). Battalion proceeded by Lorries to LIND.	

Army Form C. 2118.

Instructions regarding War Diaries and Intelligence Summaries are contained in F. S. Regs., Part II. and the Staff Manual respectively. Title pages will be prepared in manuscript.

WAR DIARY
or
INTELLIGENCE SUMMARY.

(Erase heading not required.)

Place	Date	Hour	Summary of Events and Information	Remarks and references to Appendices
	January	1919	10th Royal West Kent Regt.	
CÖLN-KALK	31st		Battalion proceeded by March Route to CÖLN-KALK	
			Strength of Battalion. Officers 47. Other Ranks 752	
			Numbers despatched to Dispersal Stations for Demobilization etc from 11/11/18 to 31/1/19. Officers NIL Other Ranks. 78	
			4/2/19. [signature] Major Comdg. 10th Bn Royal West Kent Regt.	

(A9175) Wt W2358/P360 600,000 12/17 D. D. & L. Sch. 52a. Forms/C2118/15

SECRET.

10th Bn. Royal West Kent Regt.

Operation Order No. 1

1. Reference 123 Infantry Brigade Administrative Instructions, the battalion will proceed to HUY via BRUIVES by march route on 9th inst. Head of the column will pass the church Ville-en-Hesbaye at 08.00 hrs. Companies will take up their positions on line of march in the following order:—
   H.Q. Band, B, D, A, C.
2. Transport will proceed to HUY leaving at 07.00 hrs under the arrangements of the Transport Officer.
3. H.Q. and Coys. will select not more than 15 men who are unable to march owing to bad boots, to report to Q.M. Stores at 06.45 hrs, where they will be conveyed by lorries to HUY.
4. Lieut E.S. Wheel M.C. will be battalion Entraining Officer and will proceed on lorry leaving Q.M. Stores at 06.30 hrs., and report to Brigade Entraining Officer at 10.30 hrs.
5. O.C. A Coy will detail 2 Officers and 50 O.R.s to detrain vehicles on arrival at destination
6. Officers valises and Mess Boxes will be collected at 3 p.m. on 8th inst. One small package of Mess Kit can be retained, which must be at Q.M. Stores by 07.30 on 9th inst.
7. Blankets will be stacked at Q.M. Stores by 07.00 hrs on 9th inst. "B" Coy will stack their blankets at the dining hall at CIPLET, to be collected by a lorry.
   One blanket per man will be issued at the entraining station for use on the journey.
8. Rations — The unexpended portion of the days rations, plus rations for 10th will be carried on the man.
   Water carts will be filled before entraining.
   Dinners will be cooked in the cookers and issued at entraining point at 13.00 hrs. Cooks will accompany the transport to prepare dinners.
9. Officers will carry revolvers and six rounds of ammunition. Revolver ammunition can be obtained from the Q.M. Stores
10. Dress — Marching Order
11. Acknowledge.

(Sgd) [illegible] E. Tatham
[illegible] & Adjt.
10th Bn. Royal West Kent Regt.

8th Jan. 1919

Secret

10th Bn. Royal West Kent Regt

Operation Order No 2.

Ref. Sheet 2.L. Germany 1:100,000.

1 —— The Battalion will relieve the 11th Battn Queens' Regt in the outpost line on 24th inst.

2 —— Companies will take over as follows:–

"A" Coy. R.W.K. from "A" Queens
"B" " " " "B" "
"C" " " " "D" "
"D" " " " "C" "

"B" & "D" Coys will be in the line. "A" & "C" Coys will be in support.
Bn. H.Q. will be at SEELSCHIED.

3 —— Advance parties will be detailed and will proceed as follows:– "B" & "D" Coys 1 Officer and 8 O.R. This party will proceed to the line under the command of the Senior Officer on Thursday 23rd inst. They will leave B.H.Q. at 10.00 hrs and will report to H.Q. 11th Queens at SEELSCHIED on arrival.
The Transport Officer will arrange to collect the kits of this party as follows:– "B" Coy at 09.15, "D" Coy at 09.35. The limber detailed will accompany the party to Seelscheid and return to these H.Q.
The party will remain with the Queens and will take over all defence schemes, maps, duties of outpost companies, and copies of "Instructions for Outposts" in the line of control.
Billets will also be taken over.
"C" and "A" Coys 1 Officer and 5 O.R. H.Q. 1 Officer and 2 O.R.
This party will proceed from B.H.Q. under the command of Lt. B.T. Cousins at 08.30 hrs and will take over as above on 24th inst.

4 —— Guides from the advance party will meet the Battn at the "Queens" H.Q. at SEELSCHIED at 12.30 with the exception of A Coy which will be at WINKEL.

5 —— The Battn will march off from these H.Q. at 10.00 hrs. Order of march will be:– H.Q. Band B. D. C. A. Transport.
D Coy will join the column at the T. roads at the N.E. end of the village.
Route:– via WINKEL. Dress:– Marching Order with packs

6 —— Officers valises and all blankets will be dumped at Company H.Q. ready for collection as follows:– "D" Company at 08.00, H.Q. A, B, & C. Companies at 08.30 hours.
Further orders as to the collection of these will be issued.
Mess Boxes will be collected as follows:– H.Q. A. B. & C. Coys at 09.15 hours. D Company at 09.40.

7 —— Lewis Gun limbers will accompany their Companies to the line.

8 —— Relief complete will be notified to H.Q. by wire.

9 —— ACKNOWLEDGE

21st Jan. 1919

(Sgd). Victor E. Tatham
Capt and Adjt
10th Battn Royal West Kent Regt

Secret

10th Bttn. Royal West Kent Regt.

Operation Order No 3

Ref Map Germany 2 L 1/100,000

1 —— The Battalion will be relieved by the 1/1st Herefords on 31st inst, and will proceed to the KÖLN - KALK area, staying for the night Jan 31st – Feb 1st at LIND.

2 —— Advance parties as already detailed will proceed to the Köln - Kalk area by returning supply lorries on 29th under the command of Lieut. A.S.F. Percival.

Another advance party consisting of 1 N.C.O. per Company, B.H.Q. and Transport will proceed under the command of Lt Annetts to LIND by the first Stores lorries on Jan 31st. This party will arrange billets for the battalion at LIND for the night Jan 31st – Feb 1st.

This party will parade at Q.Mr Stores at 09.00 Jan 31st.

3 —— H.Q., A, and C Coys and Transport will proceed to LIND by march route under the command of Capt W.A. Waterman.

H.Q. and C Coy will parade at B.H.Q. ready to move off at 11.30. A Coy and Transport will take up their positions on the line of march as the column passes them.

Route via SIEGBURG Order of March H.Q., C, A, Transport

4 —— Blankets, Packs, Officers Valises and Mess Boxes of H.Q., A and C Coys will be ready for collection by lorries at 09.00 outside their respective H.Q.. Lewis Gun limbers of these Companies will be packed under the supervision of Company L.G. N.C.O's, and will accompany the Transport together with Field Kitchens as usual.

5 —— "B" and "D" Companies will proceed to SIEGBURG by motor lorry, thence to LIND by march route. Platoons and posts of these Companies will report to their respective H.Q. independently as soon as possible after they are relieved.

B Coy lorries will report to their Company H.Q. where the Company will board them. "D" Company will march to Bttn H.Q. as soon as relief is complete and will board their lorries there.

Blankets, Lewis Guns, Company Stores, Officers Valises and Mess Boxes will be collected and concentrated at Coy H.Q. by Company limbers. The latter will then be packed with the Lewis Guns and will proceed, together with Field Kitchens, in time to join the Transport on the line of march as above.

The Transport Officer will arrange to collect "D" Coy's Stores etc. and dump them at B.H.Q. where they will be loaded on to the Stores lorries.

"B" Coy's Stores will be collected from their H.Q. direct by lorries. A guard of 1 man will be left until this lorry arrives.

6 —— All guards and posts together with defence schemes, maps, orders for the line of control, and all administrative duties, and will be handed over and explained to the relieving unit.

7 —— Completion of relief will be reported verbally to these H.Q. by O.C. "B" and "D" Companies. H.Q. & C Coy will move off immediately the relieving Companies arrive.

8 —— All billets and latrines will be handed over in a thoroughly clean condition.

9 —— Acknowledge.

(Sgd.) Trevor E. Tatham
Capt & Adjt
10th Bttn Royal West Kent Regt

29th Jan. 1919.

SECRET.

10th Bn. R.W. Kent Rgt

O. Order No 4

(1) The Battn will resume the march to COLN-KALK tomorrow 1.2.1919.

The Bttn will parade on the road outside the barracks and will be ready to move off at 09.30 hrs in the following order:– H.Q.-Band.- A-B-C & D- Transpt.

(2) Blankets and Packs will be stacked at Q.M. Stores by 08.00 hrs.

Officers Valises will be ready for collection at 08.30 hrs. Mess Boxes at 09.00 hrs.

2nd Lt. Edwards will be in charge of Colour Escort. O.C. D Coy will detail 3 Sgts for this duty.

31/1/1919

(Sgd) T. E. TATHAM.

Capt and Adjt

10th Bn. R.W.K. Regt

10 R W Kents

Vol 34

Army Form C. 2118.

Instructions regarding War Diaries and Intelligence Summaries are contained in F. S. Regs., Part II, and the Staff Manual respectively. Title pages will be prepared in manuscript.

WAR DIARY
or
INTELLIGENCE SUMMARY.
(Erase heading not required.)

Place	Date	Hour	Summary of Events and Information	Remarks and references to Appendices
February	1919.			
COLN-KALK	1&2nd		Battalion billeted in HUMBOLDT'S WORKS. These quarters were condemned to	M.O.
	3rd		H.Q.'s & Companies moved to new quarters. A & B. Coys billeted in WIPPERFURTH	Schools.
			H.Q. C & D Coys billeted in KANT Str.	Schools.
	4th-10th		Training carried out daily from 9 am to 1 pm. Educational Classes held instead of	Some part of
			training. Afternoons devoted to sports viz: Football, swimming, boxing etc:	
	7th		Strength of Battn. Officers 45. O.R. 699.	
	11th		Consecration & Presentation of Colours by Army Commander.	
			Rifle Competition held at BRÜCK. B Coy were adjudged the winning Company.	
	12th		Presentation of Belgian Croix de Guerre by Brigade Commander.	
	13th		Capt T. E TATHAM (Adjutant) proceeded to England for demobilisation.	
	14th		Capt W. A. WATERMAN assumed duty as Adjutant.	
			Strength of Battn. Officers 46. O.R. 644.	
	15-18.		Training carried on as usual.	
	18th-25		Battn. on Guard Duty for Brigade	
	21st		Strength of Battn. Officers 43 O.R. 593.	

(A9175) Wt W2358/P561 600,000 12/17 D. D. & L. Sch. 52a. Forms/C2118/15

Instructions regarding War Diaries and Intelligence Summaries are contained in F. S. Regs., Part II, and the Staff Manual respectively. Title pages will be prepared in manuscript.

WAR DIARY
or
INTELLIGENCE SUMMARY.
(Erase heading not required.)

Army Form C. 2118.

Place	Date	Hour	Summary of Events and Information	Remarks and references to Appendices
February				
COLN-KALK				
	26-28th		Battn carried out Training daily from 9 am to 1 pm.	
			Inter-Company Competition arranged at Football.	
			Swimming under Company arrangements carried out in the afternoons.	
			Concerts were held by the Battn Concert Party "The Live Rounds" in the evenings, also	
			Whist Drives were arranged.	
	28th		Strength of Battn Officers 41. O.R. 555.	
			Demobilised during month. Officers 4. O.R. 180.	

[illegible] Major

(A9175) Wt W2358/P360 600,000 12/17 D. D. & L. Sch. 52a. Forms/C2118/15

www.ingramcontent.com/pod-product-compliance
Lightning Source LLC
Chambersburg PA
CBHW080808010526
44113CB00013B/2344
9781474520393